AGENTS AND STRUCTURES IN CROSS-BORDER GOVERNANCE

Agents and Structures in Cross-Border Governance

North American and European Perspectives

EDITED BY BRUNO DUPEYRON,
ANDREA NOFERINI, AND TONY PAYAN

UNIVERSITY OF TORONTO PRESS
Toronto Buffalo London

Toronto Buffalo London
utorontopress.com

ISBN 978-1-4875-0288-1 (cloth) ISBN 978-1-4875-1623-9 (EPUB)
ISBN 978-1-4875-1622-2 (PDF)

Library and Archives Canada Cataloguing in Publication

Title: Agents and structures in cross-border governance : North American and European perspectives / edited by Bruno Dupeyron, Andrea Noferini, and Tony Payan.
Names: Dupeyron, Bruno, editor. | Noferini, Andrea (Lecturer in political science), editor. | Payan, Tony, 1967– editor.
Description: Includes bibliographical references and index.
Identifiers: Canadiana (print) 20230505643 | Canadiana (ebook) 20230505694 | ISBN 9781487502881 (cloth) | ISBN 9781487516222 (PDF) | ISBN 9781487516239 (EPUB)
Subjects: LCSH: Borderlands – Case studies. | LCSH: Mexican–American Border Region – Case studies. | LCSH: Canadian-American Border Region – Case studies. | LCSH: Borderlands – European Union countries – Case studies. | LCSH: European cooperation – Case studies. | LCGFT: Case studies.
Classification: LCC JC323 .A34 2023 | DDC 320.1/2 – dc23

Cover design: Heng Wee Tan

We wish to acknowledge the land on which the University of Toronto Press operates. This land is the traditional territory of the Wendat, the Anishnaabeg, the Haudenosaunee, the Métis, and the Mississaugas of the Credit First Nation.

University of Toronto Press acknowledges the financial support of the Government of Canada, the Canada Council for the Arts, and the Ontario Arts Council, an agency of the Government of Ontario, for its publishing activities.

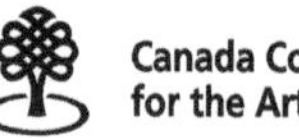

Conseil des Arts du Canada

Funded by the Government of Canada | Financé par le gouvernement du Canada

This volume is dedicated to Francesc Morata i Terra (1949–2014), one of the main architects of this research project.

Francesc was an alumnus of the European University Institute, where he completed his PhD in Law in 1986. He became a professor of political science at the Universitat Autònoma de Barcelona (UAB) in 1998, where he led several research initiatives and academic groups. In 2005, he obtained a Jean Monnet Chair in recognition of his extensive and outstanding contribution to the field of study of European integration and politics.

Borders in general – and cross-border cooperation in particular – was one of his major research interests. And his passion for border studies is what motivated Francesc to become a colleague, mentor, and friend to many of us who shared similar research interests.

Francesc was generous with his bright and candid conversations. He was a multilingual scholar and a cosmopolitan who loved to travel. It is therefore not a surprise that, with the involvement of graduate students and young colleagues in this project, he proposed to build an exchange program exclusively for them. We are glad that this volume contains their work – an enduring testimony to Francesc's kindness.

Contents

Foreword

We live in an era of hypernationalism and anti-immigrant politics. It is easy to assume that these politics have played out in similar ways within and across countries. The purpose of this book is to get on the ground in different places to observe how borders are actually managed. The surprising finding is that there is heterogeneity even within countries as to how borders are managed. The chapters in this book set out to explore what is happening and, more importantly, why border projects are so disparate even within the same country. To this end, this book brings together a unique set of comparative papers that document how actors with varying power and resources have worked to produce border relations as well as the skill with which they negotiate different outcomes in tune with their disparate agendas.

It is rare that an edited volume hangs together empirically as well as the chapters in this volume do. It is even rarer for such a volume to unite the contributors around a similar theoretical or conceptual framework that uses the chapters as a means to advance both our understanding of a particular social phenomenon and the framework itself. The goals of this volume are two: to interrogate the disparate ways in which modern democratic governments are organizing their borders in this era of anti-immigrant and nationalist sentiment; and to gain insights into how strategic action field theory enables us to do so. We are pleased that the contributors to this volume have found inspiration in our "theory of fields" framework and that they have used it with so much skill and to such a profitable end.

This volume starts by making a set of well-reasoned methodological choices to help us begin to make sense of various border projects in the twenty-first century. First, the contributors have chosen to study Europe and the US. They have done so in order to examine the relative power of various national governments to control their borders. The US has a centralized federal state when it comes to borders, whereas in Europe, sovereignty is shared between the national governments and the European Union. This has led to variations among border projects: some are more hierarchical, others more cooperative. The contributors argue that by explaining these cases, they can suggest how the framework might be applied to studies around the world, including in Latin America, Africa, the Middle East, and Asia. Second, the authors have chosen multiple research sites within each larger unit. This has allowed them to determine whether there is variation in forms of organization within countries or isomorphism owing to the presence in a larger political entity. Finally, the use of field theory has pushed all of the case studies to view the structuring of these border "fields" through a similar conceptual framework.

What does field theory do? As the contributors have deployed it, field theory works incredibly well both to structure each case study and to allow comparisons across them. Focusing on each border project as a field allows one to see how the governance of locations around political borders, even within the same country, varies from place to place. In each place, one finds representatives of central governments, but also local governments, city governments, NGOs, and representatives of business. As the key actors negotiate with one another and form coalitions, they generate novel arrangements that reflect their different agendas. There is clear variation in what they are doing and how it works.

As we flatten these fields and bring them into view, readers will begin to sense that they are seeing for the first time how local variations in the power and skills of these groups powerfully shape what the border *means*. These groups organize themselves in various ways from place to place. So, for example, in the US we see the power of the federal government to set a hierarchically organized security agenda, whereas in Europe, where there is more power-sharing between levels of government, we see more cooperative governance spaces with more variation in terms of who has power and influence over how border crossings develop.

Field theory posits that the relative powers and skills of actors in a field are a function of who makes the rules and what kinds of rules they make. Where only one actor, or a handful of actors, have power, their agenda will swamp whatever anyone else wants to do. Where power is more diffuse, the possibility exists for challengers to exert some influence in defining what is and is not going on across borders. This variation in the relative power of actors will be seen to have a profound effect on how border sites are organized. The variations readers encounter in the case studies will revolve around whether there is a single dominant actor or multiple players that have a say, thus producing more cooperation. This is not just about the broader US–European comparison; it will also help us understand what is going on *within* the US and *within* Europe.

So, for example, in the US case, we see some variation between the case studies on the US–Mexican border and the case studies on the US–Canada border. The US has a long history with both countries, but those histories are far from equal. US relations with Mexico have been characterized largely by the former's efforts to dominate Mexico politically and economically. It is not surprising that in the wake of 9/11, given the historically large amount of migration from Mexico to the US, the US viewed Mexico as the most likely place to put up hard barriers to immigration. Some of the case studies in this volume clearly show that the US federal government has militarized the Mexican border and how other groups have been unable to mitigate these efforts. The economic interests of the Mexican and US business communities and the interests of the Mexican government are clearly subordinate to the central goal of the US, which is to police the border. Contrast this with the cases related to the US–Canadian border, where there is a long history of economic and political cooperation between state and provincial governments, with the result that federal efforts to militarize the border have been met with strong blowback, including from the business community. Various actors have been able to keep the borders less militarized and more open to exports and tourism. This is because the structure of these fields reflects the historically significant more equal partnership between US and Canadian business interests and local and state governments.

The European case studies reflect the more open, collaborative political and economic arrangements of EU governments. Since the 1980s, the EU member-states have pushed collectively to remove not only the regulatory barriers between countries but also the physical barriers. National governments have viewed the opening of borders as a means to increase trade, create economic growth, and provide citizens with both jobs and the opportunity to travel and appreciate other cultures. In these places – and especially along the Portuguese–Spanish and Spanish–French borders – the level of cooperation among governments, NGOs, and the business sector is high. Yet one still observes the relative power of nation-states to define their borders. The Sicily–Malta comparison, for example, shows member-state governments clearly in control of their own borders, albeit for joint benefit.

The surprising empirical conclusion of this volume is that even in these times of rising nationalism and anti-immigrant sentiment, there is substantial variation in how borders are constructed and policed in democratic societies. These differences can be explained largely in terms of the history of these borders – a history that revolves mainly around the relative power of governments, businesses, and NGOs and the very different social skills and entrepreneurial capabilities of actors. Field theory offers a way to explain the heterogeneity of both organizations and outcomes. The challenge now will be to apply the framework outside of the well-studied democratic West to see whether it is equally useful in accounting for variation in the dynamics and outcomes of border projects in countries that are less democratic and culturally very different and that typically enjoy much less state capacity than the US and Europe. The editors of this volume are to be commended for setting such a compelling comparative scholarly agenda.

Neil Fligstein and Doug McAdam

Acknowledgments

This edited volume is a collective effort that materialized with the contributions of numerous actors and institutions. We are first indebted to the research assistants who conducted key interviews in North America and Europe. Their work built essential foundations for this transatlantic research project. Colleagues at conferences and workshops, as well as students in class, provided invaluable feedback to help us think more pertinently and critically about our findings. We would also like to thank the administrative and financial services of four universities, El Colegio de la Frontera Norte, the Universidad Autónoma de Ciudad Juárez, the Universitat Autònoma de Barcelona, and the University of Regina, for their support during the duration of this project. This project would not have been feasible without a partnership development grant from the Social Sciences and Humanities Research Council of Canada. Finally, thanks to the University of Toronto Press who came on board early on.

Introduction

1 Comparing Cross-Border Governance in North America and Europe

BRUNO DUPEYRON, ANDREA NOFERINI,
AND TONY PAYAN

Borders are perceived today as more central to and pervasive in people's daily lives than in any previous era in recent memory.[1] This is reflected clearly when it comes to immigration. In the United States, there is great anxiety over immigrants, be they legal immigrants or "Dreamers" or undocumented workers. Similarly, in Europe, there is strong concern over nationalist and xenophobic discourses against migrants and asylum-seekers. This is no coincidence. All of these groups are closely identified with daily bordering processes. In fact, the controversy around them does much to explain how borders are being reinforced between, across, and beyond national boundaries, for the purpose of limiting human mobility across national boundaries. To cope with border-related anxieties, governments are earmarking substantial resources to fortify the "edges" of modern nation-states. Indeed, border reinforcement budgets are increasing rapidly everywhere. Fences are appearing all over the world.[2] Even in "borderless" Europe, one of the cornerstones of the integration process, the Schengen Treaty, has had to resist unprecedented challenges. In 2016, in response to the European migrant crisis, border controls were temporarily reintroduced in seven Schengen countries (Austria, Denmark, France, Germany, Norway, Poland, and Sweden). Several years later, the COVID-19 pandemic of 2020 and 2021 led central governments to issue exceptional, albeit temporary, restrictions to the free circulation of people by closing domestic borders within Europe and limiting access for foreign visitors. Technology is helping central governments step up border surveillance and control, further heightening the impact of borders on people's lives.

Scholars today acknowledge that borders are complex phenomena, and not merely the functional outer edges of modern nation-states, and can be selectively and remotely "triggered."[3] Thus, in addition to being territorialized[4] or "fixed," they can behave like "waves," in the sense that their functions can be relocated away from traditional boundary lines and even away from the borderlands entirely. Crossing a border is not what it used to be – simply stepping over a line. Walking the security line of an airport well within a nation-state is now akin to crossing a border. It is not surprising that research on borders has also shifted to sites where no boundary lines seem to exist but where borders are operated in the form of airports, transport corridors, detention camps, road checkpoints, computer systems, personal identities, and so on. Today, more than ever, it is fair to argue that "borders are everywhere."[5] Yet paradoxically, "borders are not for everyone."[6] For privileged groups, such as cosmopolitan citizens of certain countries, as well as the wealthy – borders mean nothing and can be easily crossed. Thus, borders can be and are selectively enforced and are stronger for some individuals than for others.

As it stands today, borders are legally and administratively defined and redefined; they are deployed by specific state and non-state actors at specific but varying sites; and they target specific individuals or groups of individuals, who interact with them by circumventing or opposing them. Viewed this way, borders are complex fields of domination and resistance for various actors – in effect, they are strategic fields. So it is essential to examine how various aspects of modern borders, some traditional and others more recent, are understood, governed, and regulated; how these aspects affect, jointly or alternatively, people's everyday lives; and how they expand surveillance and control by a nation-state over its citizens and, especially, non-citizens. To these ends, borders must be reconceived as interactive spaces where multiple actors intermingle as they seek to impose their own interests and their own visions of the space. This interaction of actors and interests makes borders dynamic – they are, in many ways, strategic action spaces. And as they intermingle with other broad forces, such as globalization, regionalization, and decentralization, they increase in complexity, which complicates their management. Of course, borders can also overcome traditional nation-states' boundaries and become supra-nationalized, as in the case of EU internal borders. But this may not necessarily do away with pre-established borders; it may simply add new layers to them, rendering them not only horizontally but also vertically more dynamic.

In this book, we set out to capture some of these complex dynamics of borders in the twenty-first century. To accomplish this, we focus on case studies that examine these multiple layers of borders and the different actors that inhabit them and their interests; this encompasses, of course, policy cooperation among governments to manage these spaces. Applying a theory of strategic action, we examine in this volume various regions in North America and Europe that despite straddling a borderline can be viewed as forming a territorial unit, a cross-border space, a cross-border area, a borderland, or a cross-border region. The book ultimately focuses on understanding how governance takes place within regions and across borders through a strategic lens. To be sure, we realize that all borders around the world today share this dynamic character; here, though, we focus on the borders of North America and Southern Europe, not only because they are some of the most complex regions but also because they are some of the most advanced fields when it comes to mechanisms of surveillance and control as well as cooperation frameworks. Thus, they constitute ideal cases for the study of complex governance structures. We also believe that the focus on Southern European cases is doubly justified: first, some border issues like the ones we see today also arose during the European Community's expansion into Southern Europe in the 1980s. At that time, there was a perception that the countries of Southern Europe were isolated in terms of infrastructures and market access at the margins of the continent; within these peripheral countries, border spaces were seen as even more remote. Yet once the integration process was finished, they emerged as more complex and sophisticated than they had been initially. Second, under the framework of Cohesion Policy, the EC developed common multi-level policy responses to resolve these border dynamics in Southern Europe – for example, the Interreg programs that were implemented in European cross-border regions. Thus, in Europe, the case studies are the territory between Spain and northern Portugal (Galicia–North of Portugal Euroregion); the entire Franco-Spanish border from the Atlantic to the Mediterranean (with twelve cases of formalized cross-border agreements, among which this book includes the new Aquitaine–Basque Country Euroregion, the Pyrenees–Mediterranean Euroregion, and the border territory of the Cerdanya); the maritime border area between Sicily and Malta; and the Grande Région between Luxembourg and bordering areas of Belgium, France, and Germany.

This, however, does not mean that the North American cases are less interesting. They have their own complexities, albeit they have followed different historical paths. These case studies are the Cali–Baja Region, comprising California and Baja California; the Paso del Norte region; Cascadia, comprising Washington, Oregon, and British Columbia; and the Quebec–US Northeast region. All these regions display incredible intricacy. Additionally, the book examines various aspects of these borders, including infrastructure development and management, resource-sharing, and political, economic, security, human rights, social, environmental, cultural and community issues. It is hardly possible to cover all aspects of each border in each chapter, but the cases are illustrative overall as to how border regions today are both managed and governed in all their multi-level complexity (See Map 1.1).

Focusing on governance issues in such complex border spaces allows us to address numerous policy issues: how essential infrastructures across borders are built and managed, including roads, bridges, and dams; how water and air contamination is tackled from within cross-border regions; how educational and cultural cross-border initiatives are created and implemented; how the coordination of emergency services takes place across borders; and how cross-border flows are managed. The cases chosen by the authors all demonstrate that border spaces are dynamic, strategic areas, with a multiplicity of actors, interests, issues,

Map 1.1. Case studies analysed in this volume

Source: Author's rendering with cartographic resources obtained from FNSP, Sciences Po Atelier de cartographie, 1554-Planisphère (projection Gall-Bertin), 2018.

visions, and management systems. This in turn helps us see how cross-border public policies need to be coordinated and how sub-national and local governments can build better institutional scaffoldings for cross-border governance, so that structures and agents can interact on a multiplicity of issues – usually, with asymmetric power and information. Overall, our cross-border cases touch on the challenges inherent in governing collective action in border spaces. As Bevir suggests, these challenges focus on markets and networks, even as the hierarchies imposed by states continue to coexist.[7] In addition, these challenges are themselves evolving. They are in flux, and representations of the space may contribute to changes in governing practices, thus generating new governance challenges, which in turn make these representations evolve. This generates a never-ending cycle of dynamic interaction as actors seek to restructure the border space according to their representations and their interests. In brief, our analysis of cross-border governance seeks to capture varieties of social, institutional, and political change in North American and European cross-border spaces.

Cross-Border Governance in a Context of Border Securitization

To view borders in all their complexity is to understand what representations and interests prevail in them as well. Here, territory and sovereignty remain central. Thus, a central issue facing governments in managing border spaces has been how territorial sovereignty is viewed and implemented at borders below the surface of all the other issues at play. For example, nation-states have long framed border areas in political and military terms, but these are now insufficient to address contemporary challenges such as sustainability, migrations, mobility, and social cohesion. Clearly, today, not all border problems can be securitized and dealt with on a political and military basis. The search for economic prosperity makes its own demands, and these are often in conflict with tightly controlled border spaces. Second, in the current environment, especially since 2001, governments are overlooking the socio-economic and cultural aspects of development policies, and some have even attempted to keep cross-border spaces free of most flows, often to the detriment of their own development. Consequently, while cross-border flows are complicated – especially when they are unregulated or illegal – they are also vital to the prosperity of any territory. In this era of supra-territoriality, isolation and autarchy are simply untenable.[8] Third, the perception that cross-border spaces are at the margins of nation-states has been reinforced by sociocultural and ethnic conformities, sometimes accentuated by separatist movements, even though hybridity appears to be the norm in cross-border spaces. Lastly, the coronavirus pandemic that surged between the spring of 2020 and the summer of 2021 triggered national responses that deeply affected border areas. The impact on immigration and human mobility of the pandemic measures that were instrumentalized at borders in 2020–21 is concerning. Those measures are also more evidence that cross-border spaces evolve – that they produce cross-border governance schemes that often resemble struggles between the assertions of a central actor (a federal or national government) and the resistance of other actors in that space.

The authors of this volume are certain that these complexities, while they are visible throughout the world, can be sorted out by examining North America and Europe. Two major global phenomena have contributed to making the North Transatlantic region a fertile place to study border governance today. First, the end of the Cold War contributed to the reconsideration of numerous border zones, not as potential battlefields – which was how the Rhine River was perceived, with only a handful of bridges, located far from one another for military reasons – but as cross-border regions that could rearticulate socio-economic, cultural, and political ties across national boundaries.[9] This reconceptualization of borders in Europe would cement a new, long-lasting era of peace on the continent; it would also encourage the growth of the continent's market economies, redounding in a much richer Europe. In border areas that were not affected by war or its possibility, such as the Canada–US and US–Mexico borders, ideas, practices, and policies flourished, acquiring characteristics much more gradually but also less deliberately than those in Europe. These cross-border governance mechanisms remain to this day more of a patchwork, one that is at times sufficient and at times utterly inadequate for good governance. At some level, border development in North America reflects the lack of urgency in the aftermath of the Second World War in Europe. Second, in a neoliberal context of regionalization and economic integration that encouraged sub-national units to supplement (when not challenging) existing state relations with more autonomous policy initiatives, cross-border governance structures and networks became instrumental in every cross-border region/territory – again, with greater force in Europe thanks to the activism of the European Commission, and with less force in North America, given the asymmetries among Mexico, the US, and Canada. In other words, the expansion of governance mechanisms and networks in cross-border spaces facilitated economic integration processes, for example, the North American Free Trade Agreement (NAFTA) after 1994 and the European single market after 1992, but each within its own historical path and reflecting its own specific needs. The increase in flows of goods and people fostered a variety of cross-border governance mechanisms involving multi-jurisdictional actors in the public, private and not-for-profit sectors – not all of these mechanisms, however, were in sync, and sometimes they actively resisted one another. As mentioned, the EC through its Interreg programs had been actively supporting cross-border governance initiatives since the early 1990s, leading to the establishment of more than 200 cross-border governance structures (Euroregions) and hundreds of cooperation projects across Europe in diverse sectors – for example, infrastructure, environment, culture, education, job market, mobility, and health. All of this generated dynamics among multiple actors that would otherwise have lacked a field on which to interact with one another to pursue their own objectives. North America clearly lags behind in this – mostly by design, given that its cross-border institutional governance development was more heavily influenced by the security fixations of the US.[10] But even so, on both sides of the Atlantic, border spaces have indeed become much more complex. In North America, for example, the Pacific Northwest Economic Region (PNWER) is a cross-border governance entity created in 1991 that includes five US northwestern states and five Western provinces and territories in Canada. PNWER works with public and private sector stakeholders in twenty policy domains to share information, foster policy cooperation, and design and implement policies across national and provincial/state boundaries.[11] Organizational structures like PNWER do reshape the field and allow new opportunities for interaction, most of which would be weak or non-existent under a purely centralized scheme of border control.

Time is a factor in governance evolution. After the collapse of the Soviet Union and the end of communism, the 1990s were years of great optimism, which would last exactly one decade. In 2001, the 9/11 terrorist attacks on the United States challenged, temporarily, the sustainability of globalization, for they triggered a sea change in cross-border governance. Security was suddenly the overriding concern, and "prosperity" would only slowly be brought back into the calculation. Even so, the concept of prosperity to this day remains subordinate to security. Yet issues demand governance, and the central questions have not vanished, key among them being how to sustain the mobility of people and the flow of goods despite external and internal security measures. The answer to this question remains elusive.[12] Within this frame, human mobility is the more controversial aspect of cross-border governance. The increased focus on individuals' mobility has intensified surveillance and control activities; it has also led to the revamping of national security apparatuses and international border security agreements, as well as to questionable individual risk assessments. Worse, due process and privacy rights have been sacrificed to a narrow definition of border security. More recently, the new border environments have been accompanied by, and legitimized by, rhetoric decrying undocumented migration, "cheap foreign labour," and organized crime. Things like these are blamed for many of the ills confronting wealthy countries. And these discourses have contributed in turn to the prioritizing of border security risk assessments over trade flows, market deregulation, and environmental issues as well as human rights. It is certainly paradoxical, indeed ironic, that when border securitization in cross-border areas is intensified, it merely underscores states' impotence as well as their refusal to normalize and regulate other policy issues that are also important.

To make matters worse, bureaucratic vested interests have powerful incentives to maintain the status quo. Loïc Wacquant weighs in on this debate about the role of states, which are hyperactive in certain policy areas and negligent in others. He argues that the parallel implementation by modern states of "workfare"[13] and "prisonfare" policies[14] is not contradictory.[15] Such policies allow for the punitive management of low-skilled labour and simultaneously criminalize those who have been excluded from the job market. Wacquant's metaphor of the "Centaur-state" makes sense of this policy, which is authoritarian and brutal toward lower social categories yet liberal and deferent toward upper segments of the society. The middle classes, especially in high- and medium-income countries, are the losers in globalization,[16] for they are caught between these two poles, able to enjoy some of the rewards of globalization and neoliberal reforms, but also always reminded that the sword of Damocles can easily bring an end to the benefits of their in-between socio-economic status. Some of the populist responses in North America and Europe cannot be understood outside this new dynamic – much of which is clearly manifested at borders. In cross-border spaces, that dynamic is fine-tuned by cross-border governance organizations and actors and their vested interests, thus taking a very different shape with each context at hand. Border policy in the US, for example, has become the focus of rhetoric by populist politicians, who contend that prosperity can be reinstated based on the nation-state as the container of all policy and that all globalization processes can be walled off. Such promises, however hollow, serve as palliatives for the pain caused by borders that can no longer contain the processes of governance.

The rise of populist-nationalist political parties since the 2010s in Europe – the National Front in France, the Cinque Stelle Movement and the Lega in Italy, Alternative for Germany, UKIP (and Brexit) in Britain, Fidesz in Hungary, Vox and Podemos Unidas in Spain, to cite some examples – and also in North America with the election of Donald J. Trump in the US, have had paradoxically little effect on cross-border ties. Populist-nationalist parties see themselves as a pan-European movement that can expand through cross-border cooperation at levels below that of the nation-state. Moreover, these parties – which range from more radical Euro-critical to milder Eurosceptical positions – have usually embraced similar rhetorics against the EU, which is often viewed as a supra-national entity that contributes to reducing national sovereignty, notwithstanding that cross-border projects and policies have been significantly built on EU funds. Thus, the sustained support for already existing cross-border governance structures and networks has notably mitigated the impact of reterritorialization efforts driven by nationalist and populist forces in cross-border areas. This is particularly true for those cross-border initiatives that, over time, have been able to frame the border as a joint resource, employing it to leverage mobility and propel economic growth.

Europe's internal borders are one thing; its external borders are a completely different one. The flow of migrants and asylum-seekers from Syria in 2015 and from other countries before and after that has created a political crisis in the EU. Embracing classical intergovernmental dynamics, EU members have not been able to agree on how to coordinate migration policy, or protect Europe's borders; nor is there any alignment on how many migrants Europe can accept. Some countries promptly re-established border checks at internal borders and erected fences. In 2016, propelled in part by the issue of migration, the British voted yes in a referendum on whether to leave the EU, and this made the entire European project stumble. The US presidential election of the same year brought a nationalist-populist, Donald Trump, to power, and this too was motivated by fears of migration, though some authors have argued that there is no such a thing as a migration crisis at US borders.[17] The evident overreaction to migration in the US compelled border scholars to scrutinize socioeconomic and cultural changes intensely, and it remains for them a puzzle how a diminishing problem could have had the political impact it did. Undeniably, cross-border spaces are the battlefields, where all these actors capture the public imagination, try new policies, experiment with policy innovation, crystallize their vested interests, implement their policies, and resist or negotiate governance arrangements. In the Northern Ireland–Ireland and US–Mexico and US-Canada borderlands, we have seen many of the same anxieties, with many people asking why, at such highly developed and peaceful borders, nationalist-populist movements are so politically necessary. Harsher border and immigration policies in the US have affected cross-border regions, particularly on the southern border and in parts of the Canada–US border, but how have these policies concretely affected peoples' lives and identities in cross-border regions? How have cross-border governance agents and structures responded to these federal policies? Have there been, at the sub-national and cross-border levels, attempts to counter, minimize, or support the effects of the US government's policies?

Considering this multi-layered context, with its multitude of issues, actors, divergent and convergent interests, and overlapping governance systems, and given the privileged treatment accorded to border security, this volume examines cross-border governance in depth and from a comparative perspective. In North America and Europe, cross-border governance schemes have provided formal and informal frameworks to support cross-border cooperation. Analysing how these frameworks have emerged and have been institutionalized is a fundamental task. Those frameworks are increasingly being challenged by the processes of border securitization, thus limiting or jeopardizing decades of cross-border governance along liberal lines as well as public policies that have long favoured coordination and (in some cases) integration over exclusion and enclosed spaces. Understanding how cross-border governance schemes have sought to mitigate some of the negative consequences of border security policies at the cross-border level allows us to discern how concrete national and supra-national power struggles between federal/national and sub-national governments unfold in border areas. In general, we treat border spaces as contested spaces, places of conflict and conflict resolutions, of competition and negotiation, and, ultimately, as places where powerful forces emanating from well beyond the borders – including nationalism, populism, globalization, and fear –collide and are resolved, sometimes for good and sometimes for ill.

The Governance of Cross-Border Spaces

The chapters focus on North America and Europe, although the theoretical framework is applicable to all borders around the world. The authors considered two main challenges in preparing this volume. The first, given the multidisciplinary nature of border studies, was how to avoid juxtaposing case studies around the theme of cross-border governance without mentioning the entire range of cross-border governance issues. The second was how to provide a balanced analysis between structural determinism and agency so as to capture both the great forces that shape borders and the key actors that navigate cross-border governance systems.[18] To these ends, the editors asked each author to consider structure and agency as mutually constitutive and to preserve the nuances of their research in such a way that their analysis could be generalized to all the cases considered here and beyond.

Cross-Border Governance and the Theory of Fields

For the project that gave rise to this volume, the key questions were these: How can the complexities of cross-border governance be captured today? Is there a theoretical framework that can help us understand the whole of cross-border governance but also its parts? The authors of this volume selected the theoretical framework proposed by Neil Fligstein and Doug McAdam in their book *A Theory of Fields*. That framework's main objective is to "[explain] how stability and change are achieved by social actors in circumscribed social arenas."[19] It offers a basis for lending theoretical, empirical, and thematic coherence to the chapters in this volume, for it allows a balancing of structural determinism and agency in discrete but highly complex spaces such as borders. Finally, contributors were asked to explain how the analysis of cross-border governance in North America and Europe can help us understand which border-related public policies might be more effective and how their findings might generate analytical tools that can be applied in border spaces.

Fligstein and McAdam's theoretical framework is multidisciplinary, built on various theoretical layers, including the theory of practice,[20] the theory of structuration,[21] institutional theory,[22] network analysis,[23] and social movement theory.[24] The theory is complex precisely because reality is complex. The contributors to this volume thus surmised that such theories can best help explain cross-border governance. They recognize that the foundations of the theory of fields resonate with their own approaches. Each chapter will employ central components of that theory,[25] thus allowing some theoretical coherence to the chapters in the volume, albeit without precluding the use of additional concepts, theories, and analytical frameworks, such as those used in the studies of European integration (Europeanization, multi-level governance, and territorial cooperation, to mention only some). Moreover, authors were encouraged to add other theoretical layers pertinent to examine their cases, given that Europe and North America are following different paths in cross-border governance.

Additionally, the theory of fields offers a balanced framework for analysing the dynamics between structures and agents and among the agents themselves as they vie for a dominant position on the field of action, since this rests precisely on the articulation between "macrofoundations" (structures) and "microfoundations" (agents). So it is possible for the contributors to this volume to examine the social and spatial dynamics of cross-border governance through the *structures* that determine any given field of cross-border governance and how it evolved over time – as the theory considers change in the field, and through the *agents* that interact within the field – vis-à-vis the structures and each other, and the social dynamics among them as they seek to position themselves as dominant actors in governance structures. At the same time, the theory of fields allows the authors of this volume to use it critically when analysing specific case studies of cross-border governance, and, when necessary, to present its limitations and/or complement it with more pertinent theoretical lenses. Below, we present in more detail Fligstein and McAdam's theoretical framework, which provides stimulating connections between structures and agents in cross-border governance fields.

Fligstein and McAdam's theory allows us "to understand how new meso-level social orders are produced, sustained, and come unraveled."[26] To that end, they rely on seven core elements. The first is the *strategic action field* (SAF, or field). They define the SAF as "a constructed meso-level social order in which actors (who can be individual or collective) are attuned to and interact with one another on the basis of a shared (which is not to say consensual) understanding about the purposes of the field, relationships to others in the field (including who has power and why), and the rules governing legitimate action in the field."[27] Thus, it is possible to identify cross-border governance fields in which cross-border action takes place. The main question here is whether the field being scrutinized is stable or not. A field is considered stable if "the main actors are able to reproduce themselves and the field over a fairly long period of time."[28] By contrast, a field is *not* stable if it is forming or if it has fallen in crisis. One of the main challenges for researchers is to determine where to draw the limits of a field, since a field is connected to, or partly overlapped with, neighbouring fields in many ways. For instance, cross-border governance fields are populated by actors who come from other related fields or who are playing a momentary role in the field of study – for example, law enforcement, international trade, natural resources administration, or environmental management. Observing the nature and limits of the SAF allows us to reflect on the dynamics of change and stability in fields, which leads us to appreciate the composition of other fields and the relationship of the field in question to other dynamics beyond its limits.

Second, fields are composed of two main categories of actors – *incumbents* and *challengers*. Incumbents "are those who wield disproportionate influence within a field and whose interests and views tend to be heavily reflected in the dominant organization of the [field]."[29] They hold, ostensibly, most of the influence within the field and set most of the terms of governance within the field. Hence, their interests and representations structure the field, and this in turn legitimizes them and provides them with resources. Conversely, challengers "occupy less privileged niches within the field and ordinarily wield little or less influence over its processes and operations. While they recognize the nature of the field and the dominant logic of incumbent actors, they can usually articulate an alternative vision of the field and their position in it."[30] This means that challengers generally comply, albeit reluctantly, with the field structure, while readying themselves to transform the field structure at the first opportunity or, over time, to undermine its legitimacy so as to create opportunities to become the dominant actor later on. In this regard it is important to look at the *internal governance units* (IGUs). These complement and reinforce the composition of the SAF, as they are "charged with overseeing compliance with field rules and, in general, [facilitate] the overall smooth functioning and reproduction of the system."[31] IGUs are not external structures that hold jurisdiction over all or part of the field. Interestingly, IGUs can function as actors but also as rule-enforcing and policing bodies that efficiently manage the burden of the incumbents and ensure that the internal structure of the system remains intact. IGUs, however, can also refer to the processes and procedures to which all field actors must subject themselves. That is, they are internal bodies/organizations that defend the incumbents' interests and their dominant representation. Their presence serves to legitimize and naturalize the logic and rules of the field. They collect and provide information about a given field for both incumbents and challengers. Cross-border governance fields can have several types of IGUs, both formal and informal, ranging from information- and experience-sharing networks to institutionalized associations of border regions – such as some Euroregions in the EU. These organizations, which include actors, rules, and procedures, when they legitimize and sanction other actors, are in effect defending the status quo and are generally a conservative force during periods of conflict.[32]

Third, Fligstein and McAdam propose the concept of *social skill*, which "highlights the way in which individuals or collective actors possess a highly developed cognitive capacity for reading people and environments, framing lines of action, and mobilizing people in the service of broader conceptions of the world and of themselves."[33] This notion of social skill is closely related to the idea of strategic action, defined as "the attempt by social actors to create and sustain social worlds by securing the cooperation of others."[34] In fact, an actor's strategic action implies the mobilization of a set of social skills to secure cooperation from other actors. Clearly, however, such social skills are also useful both to mobilize people to challenge the system when an opportunity presents itself (in the case of the challengers) or to defend the status quo (in the case of the incumbents). Often the result is partly a function of the skills of the actors vying to control the field.

Fourth, Fligstein and McAdam suggest, with the idea of the *broader field environment*, that a specific field is "embedded in complex webs of other fields."[35] How are we to conceptually organize this veil of complexity? Three distinctions can be made: *distant* and *proximate* fields, *dependent* and *interdependent* fields, and *state* and *non-state* fields.[36] In this way, it is possible to break down connections between fields and achieve a better understanding of how a specific field fits within its broader environment. In the case of border fields, law enforcement, trade, and environmental and resource management fields are closely related. The political environment in the national capitals is not proximate but can have a profound impact on the border field, as can public opinion and perceptions of the border in places far from it. Other fields can be conceived as dependent, such as cross-border infrastructure and security management. Finally, non-state actors matter quite a lot; for example, organized crime can use the border as a resource, but so also can bureaucrats and their agencies, which are state actors that heavily influence the functioning of the field. The general point here is that other fields must be considered, for no one field is completely isolated from the broader context in which it is situated.

Fifth, the theory of fields contends that *exogenous shocks* from other fields may lead to the *mobilization* of challengers, which may in turn produce the conditions for the *onset of contention*. Such shocks can of course create a reaction among the incumbents as they mobilize to defend their dominance in the field. In cross-border governance fields, exogenous shocks have been limited but intense. As we outlined earlier, fear tactics combining terrorism, immigration, and organized crime have shaken the structures and logic in North American border fields since 2001, especially along the southern border. Similarly, in Europe, terrorism, immigration, scaremongering rhetoric, and growing social anxiety about the future of the continent and about globalization in general have helped harden internal and external borders, thus weakening the work of cross-border governance fields. Interestingly, in both instances, challengers have been arising in state fields, in the political arena and the security bureaucracy, but also among non-state actors, including NGOs and other critical actors, who may want to see a more open or a more closed border environment.

Sixth, *episodes of contention* follow the definition proposed by McAdam. Such episodes "can be defined as a period of emergent, sustained contentious interaction between … [field] actors utilizing new and innovative forms of action vis-à-vis one another."[37] Contentious episodes produce uncertainty and crises within the field, which in turn provoke "perceptions of threat and opportunity."[38] This leads each actor to struggle in the conflict affecting the field – some to preserve their prerogatives and others to change the field in their favour. Going back to the exogenous shocks that have been limited but intense in North America and Europe, the contributors to this volume were discussing whether so-called border security crises represented a series of episodes of contention in a stable border field or were only aspects – momentary but with lasting effects – of the formation of border fields. In any case, the struggle over control of the field can be analysed through framing analysis[39] in the sense that the symbolic de/re-construction of the field by incumbents and challengers is not just instrumental or tactical but echoes the fundamental legitimizing principles on which the field is built for each group of actors.[40]

Finally, *settlement* of a field occurs when "the field is no longer in crisis," specifically, "when a generalized sense of order and certainty returns and there is once again consensus about the relative positions of incumbents and challengers."[41] Once more, is this era of border securitization a form of settlement of border fields in North America and Europe, a sort of "new normal" for cross-border regions? Or should border securitization be viewed as an ongoing crisis of border fields in which state and non-state actors vie for two different structures and logics of the field? This is a key question as we examine border fields. Today, border securitization and the actors behind it prevail over all other sectors, with minor adjustments, such as to enable free trade and people's mobility, but such concessions are always trumped by security priorities. Alternatively, border securitization may find itself subordinated to free trade logic and to other sectors that do not impede flows of goods and people – culture, the environment, and so on – although clearly, this is hardly the case today (see Table 1.1).

Four Main Puzzles of Cross-Border Governance

Theories are hardly useful if they are not applied. In this volume, the authors contend that border fields today are extremely complex and require powerful meso-level theories to explain their dynamics. Four key puzzles have emerged in border studies today that can help structure the empirical orientation of this volume; all four will be subjected here to the theoretical analysis proposed by Fligstein and McAdam. First, border scholars have been debating whether

Table 1.1. Brief Glossary of the Theory of Fields

Theory of Fields	"An integrated theory that explains how stability and change are achieved by social actors in circumscribed social arenas."[42]
Strategic Action Field (SAF)	"A constructed meso-level social order in which actors (who can be individual or collective) are attuned to and interact with one another on the basis of a shared (which is not to say consensual) understanding about the purposes of the field, relationships to others in the field (including who has power and why), and the rules governing legitimate action in the field."[43]
Incumbents	"Those who wield disproportionate influence within a field and whose interests and views tend to be heavily reflected in the dominant organization of the [field]."[44]
Challengers	"[They] occupy less privileged niches within the field and ordinarily wield little or less influence over its processes and operations. While they recognize the nature of the field and the dominant logic of incumbent actors, they can usually articulate an alternative vision of the field and their position in it."[45]
Internal Governance Units (IGUs)	"[They are] charged with overseeing compliance with field rules and, in general, [facilitate] the overall smooth functioning and reproduction of the system."[46]
Social Skill	"[The concept of social skill] highlights the way in which individuals or collective actors possess a highly developed cognitive capacity for reading people and environments, framing lines of action, and mobilizing people in the service of broader conceptions of the world and of themselves."[47]
Strategic Action	"The attempt by social actors to create and sustain social worlds by securing the cooperation of others."[48]
Broader Field Environment	A specific field is "embedded in complex webs of other fields." This broader field environment can be divided into three main categories, *distant* and *proximate* fields, *dependent* and *interdependent* fields, and *state* and *non-state* fields.[49]
Episodes of Contention	"[They] can be defined as a period of emergent, sustained contentious interaction between … [field] actors utilizing new and innovative forms of action vis-à-vis one another."[50]
Settlement of the Field	"[Occurs when] the field is no longer in crisis (…), when a generalized sense of order and certainty returns and there is once again consensus about the relative positions of incumbents and challengers."[51]

Source: Author's rendering with data from Neil Fligstein and Doug McAdam, *A Theory of Fields* (New York: Oxford University Press, 2012), 42–51. http://doi.org/10.1007/s11186-014-9237-0.

cross-border governance follows a series of unique stages of growth, à la Rostow, or whether they must be analysed through other lenses. Popescu proposes that border regions go through three main stages that contribute toward the deepening of their governance structures.[52] On one level, nation-states need to conclude binational or multilateral treaties if they hope to influence the sub-national actors that prompt cross-border collaborations, for instance, in the field of cross-border urban planning in Mexico–US[53] and in the fields of health and higher education along the Franco-Spanish border (see Berzi, in this volume). This may involve creating country-specific cross-border instruments (bilateral international agreements) as well as supranational legal instruments (for example, the European Grouping of Territorial Cooperation [EGTC] Regulation; the North American Free Trade Agreement [NAFTA], now named the US–Mexico–Canada Agreement [USMCA]; and the International Boundary and Water Commission [IBWC] in North America). On another level, sub-national authorities need to decide what kinds of cross-border policy issues they must prioritize as well as what cross-border governance structure will accompany each policy cycle. Most actors at any given time interact within these pre-established channels. Still another level relates to the management of the border region after it has been created; this one calls for mundane multi-level governance work among public, private, and not-for-profit actors across the border, to implement and monitor cross-border policies and programs. In a similar vein, Durà and colleagues suggest that "three main stages of spreading and diffusion of Euroregions"[54] can be distinguished in a historical and European context. Prior to the 1990s, cross-border governance structures did exist, but they were institutionally and financially weak. In the 1990s, several Euroregions were created with the support of the Council of Europe's Madrid Convention and EU Interreg programs. In the 2000s, additional Euroregions were established, and these have benefited since 2007 from the formal inclusion of European territorial cooperation as an official objective of cohesion policy, that objective being to "to reduce the negative effects of borders as administrative, legal and physical barriers, tackle common problems and exploit untapped potential."[55] Granted, a historical and regional perspective certainly accounts for the general development of several cross-border regions; however, the chapters in this volume present case studies of cross-border agents and structures as they have developed more recently. North America has followed a different, more haphazard path, one in which central governments have provided very few channels for sub-national actors to create and reproduce their own interactions and sub-national actors have shown enormous weakness in their attempts to negotiate field prerogatives for themselves. In most of the case studies in North America, readers will find that institutional and financial support mechanisms are limited and unevenly distributed. The theory of fields will allow us to compare the two regions; it will also help us map each field within its respective broader field environment, enabling us to compare the stability of and changes in border governance fields with their broader field environments in North America and Europe.

Second, cross-border governance schemes often entail multi-level frameworks and networks that intensify internal complexities. This empirical reality merits a similarly complex theoretical approach that can capture and help explain change and continuity in governance in such complex fields. This is particularly true given that multi-level governance[56] can be observed in numerous border regions.[57] Moreover, initial typologies, developed with the number of governments involved, their corresponding levels (local, provincial, regional, national, supra-national), and so on, are clearly insufficient to explain change in governance or accurately capture the behaviour of field actors. A more theoretical multi-level approach is especially useful in North America, where border regions are loosely pieced together, with a mix of formal and informal connections and without any supra-national or national framework;[58] where multiple issues and interests are at stake; and where other field environments envelop border regions. A major difference between North American and European cases is that in the latter, the EC maintains a presence and a role in cross-border regulation, though the Europeanization of cross-border policy should not be exaggerated, nor should its success.[59] Indeed, cross-border cooperation in Europe displays singularity, diversity, and complexity.[60] Still, each cross-border region in Europe has, in practice, ample room to elaborate specific governance architectures that match its multi-level characteristics. In this regard, the conceptual toolbox of the theory of fields is especially valuable since it is possible to analyse how multi-level border governance structures evolve over time and how actors participate in changing the field. Fligstein and McAdam offer several hypotheses that can be transposed onto the subject matter of this volume. First, initial resource allocations may affect whether border governance fields become organized hierarchically or cooperatively. This points clearly to a difference between North America and Europe as well, given that the EU has created specific programs and regulation for territorial cooperation on its four dimensions – cross-border, inter-regional, trans-national and, more recently, macro-regional, incentivizing cooperation – whereas North America's resource assignment is more hierarchical and even perverse. Also, a border governance field that is well-connected to other fields is likely to be more stable. In that regard, Europe seems to have been more successful, for it has developed institutional umbrellas that have helped democratize border fields by providing local actors with channels and incentives that allow them to participate more fully in defining the units of governance. Finally, the role of states may be predominant during episodes of contention.[61]

Third, solving specific cross-cultural politico-administrative equations often requires cross-border governance innovations; it is not enough to rely on sluggish policy and governance transfers that cannot be transposed onto different cross-cultural contexts. The theory of fields emphasizes the importance of *innovative action*, which often takes shape during episodes of contention.[62] If, for example, we consider that "three US–Mexico border wars" – drugs, immigration, and homeland security/terrorism – have combined to create a state of exception along the southern US border,[63] we may conceive that border as fertile ground for contention, and we can then ask what forms of innovative action are being put forward by challengers such as human rights organizations, migrant and refugee advocacy groups, and environmental NGOs. Or should we instead ask this question: Can border actors who disagree with the militarized border security agenda on the US–Mexico border maintain their efforts of innovative action in such a hostile environment, an environment that slowly shifts to the US–Canada border?[64] But innovative action in border governance fields should not be limited to possible onsets of contention or major episodes of contention. The contributors to this volume contend that border governance first and foremost seeks to address everyday policy, legal, and administrative obstacles caused mainly by state actors, as well as non-state actors. In this sense, border governance is a rather mundane activity, albeit one that requires sustained innovative action, exemplified by the mobilization of activists and NGOs in response to the violence against women in Ciudad Juárez[65] and in the work of the Border Policy Research Institute in the border region of Cascadia.[66] Similarly, in Europe, innovative cross-border projects may be presented as innovative border actions to solve specific cross-border problems as well as to transfer best practices,[67] for instance regarding the cross-border hospital of Cerdanya on the Spanish–French border[68] and the trans-boundary Prespa Park in the tense Southeast European border region.[69]

Finally, cross-border cooperation and partnerships between the public, private, and not-for-profit sectors and civil society impose additional governance complexity. From the perspective of the theory of fields, the dichotomy of state/non-state actors is a useful starting point for making sense of this final layer of the border governance puzzle. The state is a system of fields that claims to define and protect territorial sovereignty. State fields have over time developed rules, procedures, and techniques to regulate how state and non-state fields interact with one another and how each field is internally managed. These authoritative norms are exercised toward state and non-state actors.[70] These same norms materialize through the peaceful or violent administration of a territory, the growth of urban areas, and the increased mobility of people. The impact of state fields on non-state fields (e.g., the economic and social fields) may be significant and create dependencies or interdependencies.[71] For instance, without the ongoing support of the EC's Interreg programs (supra-national state field), European cross-border regions (which can be either multi-level sub-national state fields or a mix of multi-level sub-national state and non-state fields) would be unlikely to survive. Conversely, states and state fields can be dependent on non-state fields.[72] In North America after 9/11, key economic fields required state actors to take specific measures to counterbalance the effects of increased border security for dominant economic actors. Examples of this were the Nexus card (US–Canada border) and the Sentri Card (US–Mexico border).[73]

While the theory of fields provides "instructions" for solving these four puzzles, the chapters in this volume also rely on additional tools when recommending the most pertinent solutions for scholars and practitioners. These solutions will be determined in part by the comparative analysis of cross-border governance in the North American and European case studies.

Comparing Cross-Border Governance in North America and Europe

How are we to compare different cross-border governance structures and agents in North America and Europe? The contributors to this volume all resort to Fligstein and McAdam's comprehensive theoretical framework on the supposition that it lends itself to an interdisciplinary perspective. With this theoretical toolbox as a guide, it will be possible to use similar conceptual tools to compare various case studies, even when the authors come from different disciplinary perspectives (political science, geography, public policy, economics). This common theoretical approach, coupled with a systematic comparative analysis, is an innovative added value in an edited volume of border studies.

The two main parts of this volume offer a first comparative insight between North American and European forms of cross-border governance. While cross-border governance in North America shifted from a multi-polar to a monocentric form of governance, mainly due to US federal border securitization policies, cross-border governance in Europe has remained multi-level, though recent border strains must be scrutinized and monitored. In the conclusion to this volume, the case studies in both parts will lead us to emphasize three issues. First, which border governance issues may be relevant to a comparative analysis of North American case studies? Which elements are relevant to the European cases? Second, which comparative methods (e.g., most similar systems design, process tracing) and analytical concepts (mainly borrowed from the theory of fields) can be used to compare these salient border governance issues in each region? Third and finally, what can we learn from each regional comparative analysis in terms of new hypotheses, as well as theory testing and theory building? A paired comparison will be used[74] to compare the comprehensive findings from each of the two main parts, allowing us to discern the main differences and similarities between cross-border governance in North America and Europe. This nested comparison will offer two complementary comparative layers of analysis: a rich and detailed comparison of case studies in each region, followed by a more theory-oriented comparative analysis of border governance.

In sum, this volume contributes to filling a knowledge gap by providing a comprehensive, interdisciplinary, and comparative evaluation of cross-border governance in North America and Europe and by exploring practical, policy, social, legal, and theoretical issues related to the main theme outlined above.

The Rest of the Volume

The first part of this volume focuses on North American border governance. The second part examines European border governance. The third and final part will distil the volume's key theoretical and empirical lessons.

Part One: Cross-Border Governance in North America

North America has long been paradigmatic for the study of borders. It is a unique area with divergent histories, disparate levels of economic development, and clashing legal, political, and cultural systems. Despite intense integration and strong human and capital flows, its history is one of continual conflict, from territorial disputes to disagreements over security and resource management. Thus, the authors view it as fertile ground for examining complex borders and governance from the perspective of a multitude of actors, interests, flows, and subsystems.

The chapters on North America suggest that 9/11 had a ripple effect with varied effects: each cross-border governance field encountered a crisis, and the crisis in each field generated distinct field resettlements in the US–Mexico and the US–Canada borderlands. In chapter 2, Kathleen Staudt and Pamela Cruz study the Paso del Norte metropolitan region in the central US–Mexico borderlands. They argue that the field of border governance in Paso del Norte is dominated by US border security policies. Challengers of the field on both sides of the border – business NGOs and government officials – seem unable, for all their resources and social skills, to influence proximate fields at higher scales and convince them that all US states have a huge stake in trade with Mexico. At the Texas and US federal levels, borderlands are often framed negatively; it simply is not grasped that the US–Mexico border is one of the main gateways to inter-American trade.

In chapter 3, which also focuses on the Paso del Norte border area, Tony Payan analyses the complex cross-border governance field that involves incumbents and challengers, emphasizing its institutional deficiencies. He draws attention to three groups of actors that do not fit easily within the framework of field theory, (a) those that navigate between incumbents and challengers, (b) those that are left out of the benefits the system generates, and (c) those that operate within the field but outside the legal system of governance – such as criminal organizations that use the borderlands as staging areas for their operations. He concludes his chapter with a series of governance and policy recommendations to tackle these issues.

In chapter 4, Eduardo Mendoza Cota examines another segment of the US–Mexico border, the San Diego–Tijuana border area, where increased border crossings have expanded economic relations but also exacerbated social problems as a result of the asymmetrical cross-border integration in this area. Mendoza-Cota's original approach to cross-border governance views the border security apparatus as a proximate field. Business and governmental organizations use the asymmetries of the border area to their benefit, as is visible on the US side in particular. Meanwhile, though, social externalities are mostly discarded on the Mexican side of the border, where NGOs act with limited support from incumbents. This has resulted in a border landscape of spatial segregation and socio-economic inequalities that closely follows the boundary line, reinforced by the neighbouring border security field that deports undocumented migrants to Tijuana.

In chapter 5, Guadalupe Correa Cabrera takes up the SAF theory to explain the creation of a new and emerging field – the newly internationalized energy field around the Gulf of Mexico – where various actors are vying for control of the governance units. In the past, this field had been relatively settled by the closed, state-led energy regime that prevailed in Mexico. But after the constitutional and legal reforms passed by Mexico in 2013–14, the newly liberalized energy sector immediately intersected with a much older field of governance – organized crime. Correa Cabrera argues that the presence of organized crime, the militarization of security along the border, and Mexico's recent energy reforms have all merged to form a new field of contention, centred strongly around the hydrocarbons industry. This is generating a major struggle for control of energy corridors and flows, that is, the field's governance units. In effect, Mexico's constitutional and legal changes have brought about an external shock in this field, so that a struggle has ensued over control of the governance of the cross-border energy field. That struggle is just beginning.

Victor Konrad in chapter 6 focuses on the Canada–US Pacific Northwest border region, which is characterized by a multi-scalar governance arrangement of agents and structures. Konrad shows how this border governance field gradually emerged as a result of globalization, achieved stability, entered a period of crisis after 9/11, and has recently resettled. He focuses on two governance entities that cooperate at different scales: the International Mobility and Trade Corridor, which has a specific regional focus in the Pacific Northwest, and the Pacific Northwest Economic Region, which has a broad trans-regional purpose. The resettlement of the field is tangible in the 2011 Beyond the Border Accord, which seeks to articulate at the cross-border level the interests of incumbents and challengers.

Regarding the eastern end of the Canada–US border, in chapter 7 Bruno Dupeyron examines the Quebec–US border, examining the notion of "paradiplomacy" (a term coined in the early 1990s) to describe instances of "parallel diplomacy" by non-central state actors. Cross-border governance between Quebec and the contiguous US states is multi-faceted and multi-level, and implies the management of shared border policy issues such as trade, the environment, security, and human mobility. It also involves resolving tensions between the international priorities of the Canadian federal government and Quebec's paradiplomatic objectives. Dupeyron focuses on the dynamics between incumbents, challengers, and internal governance units of interconnected fields, and shows that Canada's multiple diplomatic agendas have been used to stabilize the Quebec–US cross-border governance field.

Part Two: Cross-Border Governance in Europe: Europeanization, Institutionalization, Regionalism

Economic integration has advanced among the EU member-states. The contributors to this section show how European cross-border governance largely stabilized with the institutional and financial support of EU institutions, mainly the EC. The first Euroregions date back to the early 1960s; the 1990s then saw an explosion of cross-border cooperation agreements as the integration process deepened and a common market took shape. Though historical, legal, and policy asymmetries have profoundly structured each cross-border field, the reform of cohesion policies and the introduction of the INTERREG initiative in the early 1990s strongly contributed to the creation and stabilization of a common framework for cross-border policies at the European level.

In chapter 8, Andrea Noferini analyses the Pyrenees–Mediterranean Euroregion's emergence and deepening institutionalization in the early 2000s. The focus is on the eastern side of the Franco-Spanish border, a territory that presents a dense set of institutional, cultural, and economic cross-border linkages but that has been historically separated by an administrative and political frontier. In his study of the PMER – which is home to more than 14 million Europeans – the author applies elements of the theory of fields, in particular the notion of the SAF, combining it with the multi-level governance approach usually applied in European integration studies.

In chapter 9, Francesco Camonita examines the Interreg cross-border cooperation program between two Mediterranean territories: Sicily, a sub-national entity of the Italian state, and Malta, a sovereign state. The mapping of the multi-level field shows the predominance of established political and administrative incumbents, limited and isolated challengers, and the existence of several internal governance units that tend to work together. Camonita adds to his analysis a new category of actors, "field participants," who work closely with incumbents and internal governance units to design and implement Interreg cross-border projects. It is the field participants who ultimately legitimize the cross-border governance field.

In chapter 10, Matteo Berzi analyses the dynamics between several fields that tend to fragment cross-border governance along the Pyrenees, the Spain–France border, into a dozen or so cross-border governance arrangements. Berzi demonstrates that there is an asymmetry between French and Spanish institutional actors: the local and regional French actors are less competent than the Spanish. As a consequence, cross-border governance schemes are limited to local and regional actors, with minimal common denominators, and such schemes as there are involve very modest institutional, financial, and technical resources. The lack of a transversal cross-border governance approach in the Pyrenees (except for the Working Community of the Pyrenees) reveals a form of exceptionalism at work in Europe.

In chapter 11, Thomas Perrin focuses on a sub-strategic action field: Euroregional cultural policy. He examines the dynamics of this sectoral issue in two case studies – again, the Pyrenees–Mediterranean Euroregion, and also the Grande Région, consisting of Luxembourg and bordering regions of Belgium, France, and Germany. Perrin shows how cultural policy in borderlands can be ambivalent: identity dimensions in border areas can either weaken or foster the sub-field. That is, cross-border cultural projects can enlarge and strengthen incumbents' partnerships, but at the same time, various factors can hinder their implementation. Perrin points to the vulnerability of cultural actors' positions in the sub-field: they can be subject to ascending or descending mobility, alternating between the positions of incumbent and challenger.

In chapter 12, Celso Cancela Outeda studies the governance of the border region between Galicia and northern Portugal. Actors on the Spanish–Portuguese border, influenced by their central governments, have been able to establish a cross-border governance framework that includes a political body, the Galicia–Norte Portugal Working Community, and an executive entity, the Galicia–Norte Portugal European Grouping for Territorial Cooperation (EGCT). Cancela Outeda notes that the Galicia–Norte Portugal EGCT is not the only cross-border governance field in the area: by the early 1990s, local authorities had already formed the Atlantic Axis, which plays several roles at different scales – it is a cross-border governance actor, think tank, and lobby. Several "Eurocities" complement this mosaic of cross-border governance: the Eurocities Chaves–Verín, Tui–Valença, and Monção–Salvaterra de Minho.

In chapter 13, Xavier Oliveras examines the Pirineus–Cerdanya EGCT, in the eastern Pyrenees close to Andorra. After analysing the historical emergence of cross-border relations in the area and the recent stability brought about by the creation of the EGCT in 2012, Oliveras turns to the relationship between this cross-border governance field and two sectoral neighbouring fields:

trans-boundary waters, and the construction sector/cross-border real estate market. He shows how these two issues came to be contentious for incumbents and challengers in cross-border governance when they induced two successive exogenous shocks: the drought of 2006–8 and the economic crisis of 2008–15, which led to their "nationalization" by local actors. In the end, those contentious issues only strengthened cross-border governance institutions.

In chapter 14, Antoni Dura focuses on the western Pyrenees, where cross-border governance between the Basque Country and the Aquitaine Region is now emerging, though the border area is one of the most dynamic in the Pyrenees. Cross-border cooperation is multilevel and noticeable in several policy areas, such as transport and mobility, health care, culture, and education. The lack of stability in the field is due to the corresponding lack of mechanisms required to articulate the different levels of cross-border governance.

Part 3: Comparing Cross-Border Governance in North America and Europe: Conclusions

The final section of this volume addresses the theory – SAF, a great achievement of Fligstein and McAdam – used to examine the case studies. It analyses its value for understanding border governance today, pointing out its potential weaknesses, not to subtract from its value but to improve it. The SAF has never been applied to border contexts, and, like every valuable theory, it may need improvements as it is applied to areas not anticipated by the original authors. Finally, we turn to the case studies themselves and draw from them lessons about the governance of these difficult spaces known as borderlands, where nation-states both clash and cooperate, integrate, and separate, and inevitably build systems of governance that differ from those they build to govern the homeland. The contributors to this volume are confident that important conclusions can be drawn for the benefit of our theorizing on borders – conclusions that, at the end of the day, will contribute solidly to our understanding of these human constructs that continue to puzzle us: borders.

NOTES

1 Alexander Diener and Hagen Joshua, *Borders: A Very Short Introduction* (New York: Oxford University Press, 2012).

2 Elisabeth Vallet, ed., *Borders, Fences, and Walls: State of Insecurity?* (New York and London: Routledge, 2016), https://www.researchgate.net/publication/308013130_Elisabeth_Vallet_ed_Borders_Fences_and_Walls_State_of_Insecurity; Edina Lilla Mészáros, "Barbed Wire, Border Walls, and the 'Art' of Fencing out Migrants and

Refugees: An Assessment of the EU and American Bordering Practices," *Research and Science Today* 2, no. 18 (2019): 75–89.

3 Reece Jones and Corey Johnson, *Placing the Border in Everyday Life* (New York and London: Routledge, 2016).

4 R. Haesbaert, *O mito da desterritorialização: do "fim dos territórios" à multiterritorialidade* (Rio de Janeiro: Bertrand, 2004).

5 Étienne Balibar and Erin M. Williams, "World Borders, Political Borders," *PMLA* 117, no. 1 (2002): 71–8, http://www.jstor.org/stable/823250; Chris Rumford, "Theorizing Borders," *European Journal of Social Theory* 9, no. 2 (May 2006): 155–69, https://doi.org/10.1177/1368431006063330.

6 A.-L. Amilhat-Szary and F. Giraut, eds., *Borderities and the Politics of Contemporary Mobile Borders* (New York: Palgrave Macmillan, 2015); Thomas Nail, *Theory of the Border* (Oxford and New York: Oxford University Press, 2016), https://www.redalyc.org/journal/530/53052145008/53052145008.pdf.

7 M. Bevir, "Governance as Theory, Practice, and Dilemma," in *The SAGE Handbook of Governance*, ed. Bevir (Thousand Oaks: Sage, 2011): 1–16; M. Bevir and R.A.W. Rhodes, eds., *Rethinking Governance: Ruling, Rationalities, and Resistance* (New York and London: Routledge, 2016).

8 J.A. Scholte, *Globalization: A Critical Introduction* (New York: Palgrave Macmillan, 2002).

9 M. Perkmann and N.-L. Sum, eds., *Globalization, Regionalization, and Cross-border Regions* (New York: Palgrave Macmillan, 2002).

10 Tony Payan and Pamela Cruz, *Binational Commons: Institutional Development and Governance on the U.S.–Mexico Border* (Tucson: University of Arizona Press, 2020).

11 PNWER, "About Us" (2016), http://www.pnwer.org/about-us.html.

12 M.B. Longo, *The Politics of Borders: Sovereignty, Security, and the Citizen after 9/11* (Cambridge: Cambridge University Press, 2018).

13 J. Peck, *Workfare States* (New York: Guilford Press, 2001).

14 L. Wacquant, "The Wedding of Workfare and Prisonfare in the 21st Century," *Journal of Poverty* 16, no. 3 (2012): 236–49.

15 L. Wacquant, "Revisiting Territories of Relegation: Class, Ethnicity, and State in the Making of Advanced Marginality," *Urban Studies* 53, no. 6 (2016): 1077–88.

16 B. Milanovic, *Global Inequality: A New Approach for the Age of Globalization* (Cambridge, MA: Harvard University Press, 2016).

17 W. Gruben and T. Payan, *"Illegal" Immigration on the U.S.–Mexico Border: Is It Really a Crisis?* (Houston: Rice University, Baker Institute for Public Policy, 2014), https://www.bakerinstitute.org/media/files/files/4d562970/MC-Immig-Gruben_Payan-101714.pdf.

18 F. Dépelteau, "Relational Thinking: A Critique of Co-Deterministic Theories of Structure and Agency,",*Sociological Theory* 26, no. 1 (2008): 51–73.

19 Neil Fligstein and Doug McAdam, *A Theory of Fields* (New York: Oxford University Press, 2012), 3, http://doi.org/10.1007/s11186-014-9237-0.

20 Pierre Bourdieu, *Distinction: A Social Critique of the Judgement of Taste* (Cambridge, MA: Harvard University Press, 1984), https://www.mit.edu/~allanmc/bourdieu1.pdf; Pierre Bourdieu and Loïc J.D. Wacquant, *An Invitation to Reflexive Sociology* (Chicago: University of Chicago Press, 1992).
21 Anthony Giddens, "Beyond the Sociology of Conflict," *Sociology* 13, no. 2 (May 1979): 340, https://doi.org/10.1177/003803857901300224; Giddens, *The Constitution of Society: Outline of the Theory of Structuration* (Berkeley: University of California Press, 1984).
22 Paul J. DiMaggio and Walter W. Powell, "The Iron Cage Revisited: Institutional Isomorphism and Collective Rationality in Organizational Fields," *American Sociological Review* 48, no. 2 (1983): 147–60, https://doi.org/10.2307/2095101; John W. Meyer and Brian Rowan, "Institutionalized Organizations: Formal Structure as Myth and Ceremony," *American Journal of Sociology* 83, no. 2 (1977): 340–63, http://www.jstor.org/stable/2778293; W. Richard Scott, "The Adolescence of Institutional Theory," *Administrative Science Quarterly* 32, no. 4 (1987): 493–511, https://doi.org/10.2307/2392880.
23 Ronald S. Burt, "The Network Structure of Social Capital," *Research in Organizational Behavior* 22 (1992): 345–423; Mark S. Granovetter, "The Strength of Weak Ties," *American Journal of Sociology* 78, no. 6 (1973): 1360–80, http://www.jstor.org/stable/2776392; Florence Passy, *Social Networks Matter. But How?* (Lausanne: University of Lausanne, 2003).
24 Douglas McAdam and Hilary Boudet, *Putting Social Movements in Their Place: Explaining Opposition to Energy Projects in the United States, 2000–2005* (New York: Cambridge University Press, 2012).
25 Fligstein and McAdam, *A Theory of Fields*, 8–13.
26 Fligstein and McAdam, *A Theory of Fields*, 31.
27 Fligstein and McAdam, *A Theory of Fields*, 9.
28 Fligstein and McAdam, *A Theory of Fields*.
29 Fligstein and McAdam, *A Theory of Fields*, 13.
30 Fligstein and McAdam, *A Theory of Fields*.
31 Fligstein and McAdam, *A Theory of Fields*, 13–14.
32 Fligstein and McAdam, *A Theory of Fields*, 14.
33 Fligstein and McAdam, *A Theory of Fields*, 17.
34 Fligstein and McAdam, *A Theory of Fields*.
35 Fligstein and McAdam, *A Theory of Fields*, 18.
36 Fligstein and McAdam, *A Theory of Fields*, 18–19.
37 Douglas McAdam, Sidney Tarrow, and Charles Tilly, *The Dynamics of Contention* (Cambridge University Press, 2001), 253.
38 Fligstein and McAdam, *A Theory of Fields*, 21.
39 E. Goffman, *Frame Analysis: An Essay on the Organization of Experience* (Cambridge, MA: Harvard University Press, 1974).
40 Fligstein and McAdam, *A Theory of Fields*, 22.

41 Fligstein and McAdam, *A Theory of Fields*, 22–3.
42 Fligstein and McAdam, *A Theory of Fields*, 3.
43 Fligstein and McAdam, *A Theory of Fields*, 9.
44 Fligstein and McAdam, *A Theory of Fields*, 13.
45 Fligstein and McAdam, *A Theory of Fields*.
46 Fligstein and McAdam, *A Theory of Fields*, 13–14.
47 Fligstein and McAdam, *A Theory of Fields*, 17.
48 Fligstein and McAdam, *A Theory of Fields*.
49 Fligstein and McAdam, *A Theory of Fields*, 18–19.
50 McAdam, Tarrow, and Tilly, *The Dynamics of Contention*, 253.
51 Fligstein and McAdam, *A Theory of Fields*, 22–3.
52 Fligstein and McAdam, *A Theory of Fields*; Fligstein and McAdam, "Toward a General Theory of Strategic Action Fields," *Sociological Theory* 29, no. 1 (2011): 1–26.
53 S. Peña, "Cross-Border Planning at the U.S.-Mexico Border: An Institutional Approach," *Journal of Borderlands Studies* 22, no. 1 (2007): 1–18; M.T. Vázquez, "Mexico–US Bilateral Planning: Institutions, Planners, and Communities," *European Planning Studies* 9, no. 5 (2001): 649–62.
54 A. Durà, F. Camonita, M. Berzi, and A. Noferini, *Euroregions: Excellence and Innovation across EU borders. A Catalogue of Good Practices* (Barcelona: UAB, 2018), 45.
55 European Commission, *Cooperation across Borders 2007–2013* (Brussels: EU, 2013), http://ec.europa.eu/regional_policy/en/policy/cooperation/european-territorial/cross-border/2007-2013.
56 S. Piattoni, *The Theory of Multi-Level Governance: Conceptual, Empirical, and Normative Challenges* (Oxford: Oxford University Press, 2010).
57 J. Anderson, L. O'Dowd, and T.M. Wilson, eds., *New Borders for a Changing Europe: Cross-Border Cooperation and Governance* (London and Portland: F. Cass, 2003); M. Perkmann, "Policy Entrepreneurship and Multilevel Governance: A Comparative Study of European Cross-border Regions," *Environment and Planning C: Government and Policy* 25, no. 6 (2007): 861–79; T. Chilla, E. Evrard, and C. Schulz, "On the Territoriality of Cross-Border Cooperation: 'Institutional Mapping' in a Multi-Level Context," *European Planning Studies* 20, no. 6 (2012): 961–80.
58 Joachim Blatter, "From 'Spaces of Place' to 'Spaces of Flows?' Territorial and Functional Governance in Cross-Border Regions in Europe and North America," *International Journal of Urban and Regional Research* 28, no. 3 (September 2004): 530–48, https://www.unilu.ch/fileadmin/fakultaeten/ksf/institute/polsem/Dok/Volltexten_zu_Publikationen/from_spaces_of_place_to_spaces_of_flow.pdf; V.A. Konrad and H.N. Nicol, *Beyond Walls: Reinventing the Canada–United States Borderlands* (Aldershot: Ashgate, 2008).
59 B. Dupeyron, *L'Europe au défi de ses régions transfrontalières. Expériences rhénane et pyrénéenne* (Bern: Peter Lang, 2008).

60 B. Wassenberg, B. Reitel, J. Peyrony, and J. Rubió, *Territorial Cooperation in Europe: A Historical Perspective* (Brussels: Publications Office of the European Union, 2015).
61 Fligstein and McAdam, *A Theory of Fields*, 189.
62 Fligstein and McAdam, *A Theory of Fields*, 21.
63 Tony Payan, *The Three U.S.–Mexico Border Wars: Drugs, Immigration, and Homeland Security* (Santa Barbara: Praeger Security International, 2016).
64 Anderson et al., *New Borders for a Changing Europe*, 2005.
65 K.A. Staudt, *Violence and Activism at the Border: Gender, Fear, and Everyday Life in Ciudad Juárez* (Austin: University of Texas Press, 2008).
66 Border Policy Research Institute (BPRI), "Cannabis in Cascadia: Impacts of Legalization in the Region," *Border Policy Brief* (Western Washington University, 2018), https://cedar.wwu.edu/bpri_publications/110.
67 D. Stead, "Best Practices and Policy Transfer in Spatial Planning," *Planning Practice and Research* 27, no. 1 (2012): 103–16.
68 R. Séchet and R. Keerle, "The Cross-Border Hospital Project of Puigcerda: The Difficulties of Cross-Border Health Cooperation Even in a Favorable Context," *Annales de géographie* 675, no. 5 (2010): 536–59.
69 I. Christopoulou and V. Roumeliotou, "Uniting People through Nature in Southeast Europe: The Role (and Limits) of Nongovernmental Organizations in the Transboundary Prespa Park," *Southeast European and Black Sea Studies* 6, no. 3 (2006): 335–54.
70 Fligstein and McAdam, *A Theory of Fields*, 68–70.
71 Fligstein and McAdam, *A Theory of Fields*, 71–3.
72 Fligstein and McAdam, *A Theory of Fields*, 74–7.
73 M.B. Sparke, "A Neoliberal Nexus: Economy, Security, and the Biopolitics of Citizenship on the Border," *Political Geography* 25, no. 2 (2006): 151–80.
74 S. Tarrow, "The Strategy of Paired Comparison: Toward a Theory of Practice," *Comparative Political Studies* 43, no. 2 (2010): 230–59.

PART ONE

Cross-Border Governance in North America: From Multipolar to Monocentric Governance

2 "Getting It": Business NGOs and Political Actors Talk about the US–Mexico Border Region

KATHLEEN STAUDT AND PAMELA L. CRUZ

We don't want to destroy the border in order to save it.

Michael Chertoff, US Secretary of Homeland Security, 2007

In this chapter, we analyse business voices and their organized power on the central US–Mexico border, the Paso del Norte metropolitan region of El Paso and Ciudad Juárez. The region has long been viewed as an interdependent economic region,[1] albeit one with five- to ten-fold inequalities between the two sides.[2] Indeed, Iñigi Moré, in his data-driven analysis, declares it to be the seventeenth most unequal border in the world.[3] More than 2 million people live in the El Paso–Ciudad Juárez metropolitan region. That region is the largest global manufacturing site along the 2,000-mile international border. Fourteen million people live on the two sides of the border, 82 million in the ten border states.[4] In 2020, Ciudad Juárez was home to more than 300 manufacturing plants that employed 375,000 workers. International borders are ideal sites for examining business voices. At borders, two or more sovereign governments existm each with historic nationalist agendas to control the movement of people and goods over the border and to generate revenue from there. Major shifts occurred with the move toward export-processing manufacturing (in this region, in the 1960s), the General Agreement on Tariffs and Trade, and various regional free trade regimes such as NAFTA (North American Free Trade Agreement) and its recent iteration signed in 2020 by three governments, the US, Mexico, and Canada Agreement (USMCA). In the blossoming field of border studies over the past two decades, scholars have articulated the continuum of relative closed to open movement in our still-bordered world, analysing the simultaneous debordering and rebordering that occurs.[5] Policy-makers in Washington, DC, in particular have pursued rebordering, given the US national security agenda and nationalist (bordering on racist) "othering" narratives about immigrants from Mexico. Those policies, aimed at interdicting threats, immigrants, and drugs, are being enforced by a multitude of federal agencies. And they have been reinforced by border walls/fences extending 800 miles along the near 2,000-mile border. It is important to learn how business people deal with walls, fences, and the national security apparatus and how they are adapting to an increasingly militarized border.

Despite the rebordering, the US–Mexico borderlands economy continues to be interdependent. Yet it struggles with rules and regulations that stifle or deter movement and delay traffic at international ports of entry. Over and over, we heard business and government interviewees in El Paso claim that they "get it" and that they long for others, especially the US government, to "get it" too. By "getting it," our interviewees were referring to an understanding of the opportunity the border presents for inter-American trade across borders.

How do the voices of private business fare in these circumstances? We posit, as a preliminary argument, that despite the presence of strong and influential business NGOs in the Paso del Norte region, which partner with US local governments and political representatives of the border region who together "get it," business voices cannot overcome the overwhelming obstacles of the national security agenda and its multiple enforcement arms imposed at the US federal and state levels. Nor do mainstream policy-makers "get" the huge stakes that all US states have in trade with Mexico. Meanwhile, the COVID-19 health pandemic has revealed the extent to which US national security increasingly confronts the need to maintain the cross-border "supply chains" of partly processed manufacturing products in order to sustain the US economy. Yet timely and courteous traffic flows continue to be inhibited by a militarized security agenda and the US border guard apparatus.

This chapter has three sections. First, we draw on the sociological theoretical perspectives that frame this study and generate its questions and methodologies (see also chapter 1). Then we provide a brief economic history of the region in light of those theoretical perspectives. Finally, we analyse common themes in the Paso del Norte borderlands as revealed by interviews with business and government actors. We weave theoretical insights into our findings.

Theoretical Perspectives and Methodologies That Flow Therefrom

Theoretical Framework

In a brilliant synthesis of structure and collective strategic action, Neil Fligstein and Doug McAdam developed a general theory of what they refer to as strategic action fields (SAFs). As they define SAFs, collective actors vie "for strategic advantage in and through interaction with other groups in what can be seen as meso-level social orders."[6] We find meso-level theorizing ideal for the study of cross-border relations in borderlands. This theoretical approach pays attention to context, which is crucial for any study of borderlands, where "space matters."

Fligstein and McAdam identify seven key components of their theory. First, SAFs are the units of analysis wherein actors interact under common understandings. In our study, the field is the Paso del Norte organized business community and local government officials. Second, we unpack the incumbents, challengers, and governance units, including changing elected representatives and contrasting forms of local government in two sovereign states – Mexico and the US. The third element consists of social skills, which we assess in our analysis of the interviewees (including their narratives as they have made their way into local media). The fourth element is the broader field environment, which for our analysis consists of other allies and opponents and especially the federal governments in Washington, DC, and Mexico City respectively that craft the border policies. The fifth and sixth elements consist of what Fligstein and McAdam call "exogenous shocks, field ruptures, and the onset of contention"[7] and the episodes of contention. The final element focuses on the resolution of such tensions, which in the model are always dynamic and temporary.

Methodology

Our sources were twenty-three semi-structured tape-recorded face-to-face interviews conducted in mid-2013 that lasted thirty to ninety minutes each, with stakeholders on both sides of the border;[8] fifteen in-depth media interviews with other stakeholders; seven observed public speeches by prominent actors; website analysis; and close monitoring of local media. Moreover, both authors have lived and worked in the borderlands for decades: Staudt has been an adopted *fronteriza* since 1977 and has written many books on the border political economy, and Cruz is a native-born *fronteriza*.

Business and Government: Wherefore the Borderlands?

For more than a half century, social scientists have analysed the close, influential relationship that business organizations enjoy with governments. As delineated by theorists,[9] both elite and pluralist, who acknowledge the inequality of plural organizations as they vie for influence in government policy-making (scholarship that began with Dahl in 1961), organizations that represent business have strong stakes in government decisions about taxes, subsidies, and regulations. In the US, they are organized into generalist chambers of commerce at the local, state, and national levels as well as into specialized, sector-specific organizations that represent manufacturing, chemical production, food, transportation, and security, among others. In countries where money influences politics, epitomized by the US, these organizations wield power through political campaign contributions, Political Action Committees ("PACs"), the dissemination of model legislation to states through groups such as ALEC (American Legislative Exchange Council) in the US, and service as political appointees to boards, commissions, and agencies. The "revolving door" phenomenon is also relevant: officials on leaving government may move to the private business sector as high-end consultants, and vice versa. More recently, some of these actors have brought a "binational" US–Mexico perspective to their work. We differentiate here between those who, in the words of our interviewees, "get it," and those who emphasize national security, surveillance, and border controls. Among the former, we count revolving-door business/government players such as former Ambassadors Tony Garza and John Negroponte; among the latter, we count former DHS Secretary Michael Chertoff, who was quoted in the epigraph, and his successors.

In Mexico, business groups are organized into specialized, sectoral, and regional associations, as well as chambers of commerce, following both corporatist and pluralist models. Business affiliation was once mandatory; since a 1992 Supreme Court decision, it has been voluntary. Relations in Mexico between government and business have been little studied. In a comparative analysis of big-business voluntary associations in Mexico, Schneider analysed their sometimes close, sometimes tense relations with the executive branch and the latter's long-held tendency to exclude the business sector from politics and top-level appointments.[10] As Roderic Camp noted[11] in his seminal, albeit dated, book about business and politics in Mexico, only 15 per cent of "top entrepreneurs held national political office, while only 10% of all cabinet members had management level experience in the private sector."[12] Schneider analysed four independent and influential big-business associations: the Mexican Business Council (Consejo Mexicano de Negocios, CMN), formerly known as the Consejo Mexicano de Hombres de Negocios (CMHN); the Business Coordinating Council (Consejo Coordinador Empresarial, CCE); the Coordinator for Foreign Trade Business Organizations (Coordinadora de Organismos Empresariales de Comercio Exterior, COECE) [in NAFTA negotiations]; and the Employers' Confederation of the Mexican Republic (Confederación Patronal de la República Mexicana, Coparmex), which began as an organization of Monterrey industrialists. Voluntary associations often adopt a low profile, with small staffs, and exercise quiet, crucial, and less-than transparent influence; as one CMHN founding member told Schneider, "no es secreto, pero es discreto"(it is not a secret but it is discreet).[13] In another revealing insight, Schneider wrote that while business was excluded from the NAFTA bargaining table, "they were figuratively and sometimes literally in the "cuarto de junto" (room next door)."[14] Regarding the relationship between independent businesses and the Mexican government, Thacker analysed how influence shifted from domestic industries to large, exporting firms in the ascendant neoliberal global economic context of the 1980s and thereafter.[15]

At the central US–Mexico border more than two decades ago, Staudt and Coronado (2002) analysed cross-border networks in several sectors as they impacted business, labour, the environment, and human rights.[16] They found binational business networks to be the most solid, given the shared material interests in profit and the assistance that local and state governments provided to create and nurture businesses. However, their analysis did not cover the post-9/11 era, which led to a strengthened security apparatus; nor did it cover the tenfold increase in murders in Ciudad Juárez between 2008 and 2011. In 2015, Staudt and Méndez documented that the *maquiladora*/export-processing industry saw an increase in investment and job growth after 2009, despite the 2008 economic recession in the US, during which the local auto industry experienced cutbacks and sub-contract cancellations.[17] In his comparison of metropolitan governments in Mexico, Ward specifically analysed how the municipality of Ciudad Juárez "offers a greater opportunity for economic elites to exercise direct influence, especially when there is a considerable degree of consensus and common vision among the elite."[18] Ciudad Juárez and the State of Chihuahua – which rotated between the two largest political parties in 1980s–90s Mexico (i.e., between PRI and PAN [Partido Acción Nacional]) – returned to PRI governance in the 2000s, and after it did, the city's murder rates between 2008 and 2012 created some fissures among the elite.[19] After Enrique Peña Nieto was elected president, he framed a new narrative that offered a positive vision of Mexico's future. For American readers, Shannon O'Neill in *Two Nations Indivisible* (2012) projected a similar vision of a growing Mexican middle class; in the preface, though, she acknowledged that her work was partly funded by our earlier-mentioned CMHN, which Camp calls "the single most important organization of the private sector."[20]

There is a large body of literature on business at borderlands, yet few if any studies have analysed what we focus on in this chapter, that is, precisely how business NGOs connect with their allies within and outside government (which is what SAFs examine). The late Robert Pastor called for a North American Community and broadened free trade in the Americas, but he stopped well short of advocating an EU-type model with supra-national institutions.[21] At the US–Mexico border, local actors are unable to capitalize on cross-border governance institutions, although Emmanuel Brunet-Jailly contends that with regard to security-versus-economy tensions at the US–Canada border, "economic interdependence frames the post 9/11 Canadian-American border security regime."[22]

Historical Lens: The Border as a Rarely Stable Field

Our attention to history, necessarily brief, is examined through the theoretical lens provided by Fligstein and McAdam and their account of shocks in the

SAF environment. The Paso del Norte borderlands have rarely been stable. The entire area was once part of Mexico, which lost half its territory to the United States after 1848, after which borderlines were drawn by the Treaty of Guadalupe Hidalgo in 1848, the Gadsden Purchase of 1853, and the Chamizal Agreement in the early 1960s. Once the threat of war dissipated, a trade agenda seemed to take hold. The El Paso Greater Chamber of Commerce was founded in 1899, "during the time of a porous/open border," chamber CEO Richard Dayoub told us in an interview (he is now a lobbyist). Ciudad Juárez has been an economic powerhouse since the turn of the previous century.[23] In the 1960s, the Border Industrialization Program led to reduced US tariffs, and this paved the way for export-processing industries (i.e., *maquiladoras*). A regional economy eventually was firmly established by the 1994 North American Free Trade Agreement (NAFTA), followed six years later by the US–Mexico–Canada Agreement. In the years since NAFTA, the debate about that treaty's costs and benefits has continued. Pastor writes that NAFTA was supposed to work the "magic of a free market" but that it had no answers to market failures, such as pollution, crime, uneven welfare,[24] and national governance institutions, which were limited to dispute-settling mechanisms.[25]

Border narratives have often been used to advance political ambitions. Talk of trade associated with NAFTA predominated in the early 1990s, but there later arose a competing narrative revolving around rising immigration, drug wars, and anti-terrorism. Silvestre Reyes, at one time the Border Patrol Director for the El Paso Sector and the progenitor of a Border Blockade in September 1993, ran successfully for the US Congress in 1996 and over seven terms helped craft a "Border Security Industrial Complex."[26] This complex of government, security businesses, and security agencies conducted "wars" on terror, on immigration, and on drugs, especially after the 9/11 attacks on New York City and Washington, DC.

The increasing brutality of the drug trade – the Paso del Norte region is one of its gateways – slowed border crossings, given the Americans' ineffective drug interdiction strategy.[27] Security machinery and personnel delayed northbound cross-border trade traffic for hours at a time despite Mexico being Texas's top trading partner. This raised shipping costs and reduced economic opportunities in the borderlands. After 9/11, DHS personnel delayed traffic even more by establishing southbound checks, generating long lines in both directions. The people of the border frequently cross it to shop, entertain themselves, and visit relatives and friends, and long lines impede this. In 2008, the government began requiring US citizens to use passports for re-entry where verbal declarations or driver licences had once been sufficient. Finally, violence and murders rose in Ciudad Juárez, peaking in 2010; between 2008 and 2011, that city saw around 10,000 murders.[28] Binational industry promoters described Juárez as a "thriving industrial community" but also as "a city of competing realities" and "cartel-related violence,"[29] where "casualties" were "hits, not random shootings."[30] Niño and colleagues have documented how "homicides reduce commercial activity in statistically significant manners."[31] The 9/11 attacks dramatically and singularly shifted US priorities toward "securing the nation's borders." Mexico transposed its economic and social interests from the bilateral agenda to support US security priorities, strengthening the cooperation between the two countries.[32] Trade gave way to security on both countries' agendas,[33] and many cross-border communities and businesses quickly encountered a new security regime, which included longer lines and additional inspections. Benítez and Rodríguez[34] describe how San Diego declared a state of economic emergency due to the decrease in business after 9/11; however, it was only temporary, as border trade underwent a rapid "adaptation." Businesses perhaps were the quickest to adjust, as their primary concern, besides profits, is to provide consumers with the products they demand. Castillo[35] explains how Mexico's high degree of centralization pertains to border regions: national interests prevail over local ones, rendering border residents voiceless in decisions affecting their interests.

Payan and Vásquez[36] analysed the costs of homeland security and found that even though there was a decrease in cross-border business in the weeks after 9/11, businesses soon returned to normal as they "complied with the new rules and absorbed the new costs, which in turn has helped a large number to take their merchandise across more efficiently under a new inspections regime." While some of our interviewees still mention 9/11 as a factor in the security challenges and obstacles they have encountered, another crisis soon followed, this one related to drug-related violence in Mexico. The soaring violence in Ciudad Juárez affected daily life and business. Mexico now prioritized a security agenda to fight another kind of war, this one on drugs ("la guerra contra el narcotráfico"), launched in 2006 by the then Mexican president, Felipe Calderón. Reflecting the shared responsibility implicitly set out in the security-oriented Mérida Initiative of 2008, the US partnered with Mexico in its fight against narco-trafficking. Ramos (2011) has examined the background to the Mérida Initiative and the challenges it posed, noting that on both sides of the border, the private sector harboured reservations about collaborating with the government, partly because of the economic crisis, but primarily due to the security policy emphasis, which affected trade and economic activity.[37] Mexico's National Institute of Statistics and Geography (Instituto Nacional de Estadística y Geografía [INEGI]) calculated that around 11,000 businesses closed as a result of the violence.[38] Thousands of businesses were impacted, and business owners who refused to pay or could not pay extortion fees (known as *cuotas*) were at risk of robbery, arson, kidnapping, or murder. Criminal activity rose, and people took advantage of the resulting fear, corruption, and lack of police and governmental authority and control. Niño and colleagues (2013) examined organized crime homicides in Ciudad Juárez and economic conditions in El Paso. They found that as violence escalated in Juárez, El Paso firms working in cross-border and trade-related services were negatively impacted by "supply-chain disruptions and business closures south of the border"; moreover, border city shoppers would frequent El Paso shopping areas more than retail outlets in Mexico (16).[39]

Findings: Interviews Through Theoretical Lenses

In academic literature, businesses and their NGOs are often viewed as core holders of power – as "incumbents," in Fligstein and McAdam's model – within fields of governance such as cities, states, or nations. However, within the SAF of the Paso del Norte community, we identified most of the local actors we interviewed as challengers within the overarching US federal security agenda. Furthermore, that same agenda had been adopted by the Texas political establishment and in Mexico after 9/11 and the 2008–12 drug war, as well as after 2014, as more and more immigrants began seeking refuge and asylum in the US. It often happens that challengers conform to the order while awaiting "new opportunities to challenge the structure and logic of the system."[40] In our analyses of their voices in this chapter, we found that business people and their NGOs sought opportunities to challenge the security order in gentle ways, from the edges, by strengthening alliances within the business community and articulating a common vision of the region as a whole, rather than as separate cities in two nations. In this binational vision, business people and their NGO representatives seek out best practices to work more fruitfully with the challenges and obstacles posed by the US security agenda. They work hand in hand with the El Paso local government but less so with Juárez municipal government, given the structural and budgetary weaknesses of municipalities (*municipios*) in Mexico.

We identify the incumbents as the security policy actors located at the centre of both countries, in Washington, DC, and Mexico City, where national policies are made, sometimes with little or no consultation with border communities. Meanwhile, at the Texas state level, political opportunists exploit fears over security, especially around election time. The formal governance units in this region's SAF are the vertically structured government agencies whose task it is to implement the security agenda; these range from cabinet-level political appointees in the executive branch and national-level politicians in Congress to local enforcement arms of the DHS, the DEA (a branch of the Department of Justice), and the Department of Defense. These governance units are themselves influenced by the incumbents and by "the logics that are used to justify that dominance."[41]

In our interviews with the "challengers" (for incumbents, see Payan's chapter in this volume), we found that many had crossed employment and institutional borders in the US: they had worked in business, then in government, be it in elected or appointed positions, or both, then in business again. We share the insights of interviewees from both sides of the border regarding the complicated and sometimes conflictual nature of cross-border business on the El Paso–Ciudad Juarez border, categorizing them into four key themes:

1) solidarity with the broader region of Ciudad Juárez, El Paso, and southern New Mexico;
2) frustrations over security machinery, long waits in cross-border lines, and business impediments;
3) celebrations of (mostly local) policy collaborations among officials, businesses, and NGO representatives; and
4) hopes and visions that decision-makers in national and state capitals will understand the border and allow space for border voices to be heard in policy-making as it relates to a "seamless" border taking us "back to the future," which we interpret to mean the free trade agenda of the post–Second World War era,[42] the growth of export-processing industrialization through *maquiladoras* beginning in the 1960s, and the economic regionalism associated with NAFTA and now, the USMCA (sometimes called NAFTA 2.0).

Solidarity with People and the Region

Our interviewees, whether born on the US side or the Mexican side of the border or elsewhere in both countries, expressed their fondness for the region and its multicultural, multilingual characteristics. For them, a key to the success of their region was its capacity to bring together businesses, organizations, and people that "get it." The solidarity that border residents have is unique and is a consequence of their geographic position, the fusion of cultures, and the crises and opportunities that affect both sides of the border. A Mexican businessman, explaining his ties to the border area, told us that "a *fronterizo (borderlander)* speaks to you in English and Spanish, they handle both currencies by memory, they eat American and Mexican cuisine, they celebrate Cinco de Mayo but also Thanksgiving … It is that mix that only we *fronterizos* have" (quotes from Spanish, Cruz translations). (We offer a reminder from footnote 1 that we do not link the interviewees to quotes, but we list those interviewed in an appendix). Many of our interviewees were proud to be Juarenses and *fronterizos* and acknowledged the unique opportunities and advantages that border life had offered them; as one put it, "I would have never made it to where I am in another city in Mexico … The border opened a sea of opportunities." The same sentiment was echoed by a businessman on the US side: the "border was key to my success."

The interviewees longed for a better balance between security and efficient cross-border traffic. Two former mayors persistently underscored the "need to work regionally" and "to speak with one voice," as did others. One former mayor resorted to a famous Paul Newman movie, *Cool Hand Luke*, to quip "what we have here is a failure to communicate."

On the US side, both local public officials (former and current) and business people emphasized "shared key values": "people here have an honest and acute understanding of the border." Some Mexican business people acknowledged that "we really have more overlap with the American side than sometimes with what we have with other cities in our own country." Some used terms such as "sister-city environment" and "connected cities." They believed that the current (at the time of the interviews) elected US congressional representatives Beto O'Rourke (TX–16) and Pete Gallego (TX–23) "got it." Business people and their NGO representatives cited different figures regarding the number of jobs in El Paso that were connected to job creation in Ciudad Juárez: one said 1 in 5, and another 1 in 11, though in the past the oft-quoted figure was 1 in 20 (in other words, guesstimates rule).

Many interviewees recited the same mantra, "We work as a region." For them, the challenge was to communicate border assets and challenges to policy-makers in the capitals; they saw a "need to educate Austin and Santa Fe." The Republican Party – aligned with security discourse and militarism – has dominated Texas executive and legislative branch politics since 2002. Both Texas Governor Rick Perry and his successor Greg Abbott have called for more troops on the border to address security threats. On both sides of the border, interviewees said that neither Washington nor Mexico City understood or "got" border dynamics. A Juarense who works in economic development told us that "Ciudad Juárez is much more related to El Paso, Texas, than [to] many other parts of the Mexican republic, and sometimes Mexico City and Washington, DC, can't see that." Some emphasized their desire for both nations' capitals to see and acknowledge them as one region and to craft policies that would be sound for both countries.

Frustrations with Border Bashing and Security Machinery

Almost uniformly, interviewees cited negative experiences with national border policies and procedures that were producing considerable delays (hours in many cases). Crossers who live, work, shop, conduct business, and study on either side of the El Paso–Ciudad Juárez border recounted rude behaviour from US and Mexican customs agents. One Juarense shared his worst experiences while crossing the border: "Long waiting times … and inspections, on both sides. I've had experiences with people who shouldn't even be there [referring to US and Mexican customs agents]. They should put people there who are kind, professional, informed, and who try to facilitate things, not make them worse." Businesses and their NGOs expect better from the federal government, noting waits of "two hours due to archaic procedures." When questioned about the obstacles to cross-border cooperation, one interviewee said, "Why do they treat us like they do on the bridges? Is that COOPERATION? [in a sarcastic voice]. The bridge wait times are sometimes super slow."

Interviewees recognized the importance of security: "9/11 changed things." Even so, security was being used as an "excuse to avoid dealing with issues that bring competitiveness in the region." When politicians demanded more security, said one businessman and former elected official, they were "cutting off noses to spite their faces" and "hurting our economy." Some were so "myopic" that they had no clue about the stakes in play with the export trade to Mexico. "The more you wait, the costlier it is." A businessman on the Mexican side said, "We must have a relationship such as the European countries, with no borders. If we don't hurry up and do something, our region will be a failure … The United States will stop being the power it has been until now."

The frustrations, obstacles, and challenges shared by Mexican business voices were multiple, and many wondered whether a sustainable way to overcome the dominant security orientation was even possible. A dejected Mexican businessman said that "things in the border region are different … They don't take both sides into account. Why? Well, it's because they don't live here, they don't know it … Washington and Mexico City have forgotten and neglected us." Mexican interviewees noted that neither capital city understood the border; some mentioned specific difficulties with the Mexican government. Some alluded to Mexico's centralized institutions, which resulted in policies being made far from the border. Some also alluded to local authorities' lack of decision-making powers, right up to the mayor (*presidente municipal*). Others commented on the dearth of federal resources, on administrative turnover (i.e., the constitution's no-succession principle, at all levels, selectively changed since 2014), and on policy changes that were making it difficult for border businesses to thrive. They also said that the Mexican government did not understand the challenges that border businesses faced when trying to compete with US firms. "We have to support and encourage economic activity in our city," said one interviewee, "not deter, make it difficult, or prohibit it."

Interviewees criticized national policies and how they were being implemented at the border. "All the laws work against us," said one public leader, and many laws were being "made in Washington, DC, and Mexico City without consultation with border cities." She described the mainstream perceptions as reflecting "incredible hysteria about the border and a little racist." She wished "everyone would leave us alone. We'd get a lot done." Another declared: "They get in the way – both governments." The border had become a hostage to forces that were preventing reasonable policy reforms. "Why aren't they expediting lines with technology and gadgets? They are taking things to an extreme." While there "used to be long lines only going north, now they're south and north … [people] even wait to go south."

Respondents criticized calls by some national-level politicians for "more militarization of the border" in exchange for immigration reform. Some business people excoriated the tradeoffs that were being made between security and trade, viewing this not as a partisan issue (i.e., Democratic or Republican) but as an economic one. According to an El Paso businessman and former mayor, "security is the obstacle … The "drug war" is an abject failure. As long as there is demand, it [drugs] will come. We're pouring money down the drain." Claiming that he had many friends in law enforcement, he added that "we should *prevent* [his emphasis] drug use and addiction. We only catch the stupid ones or those who snitched on others." Yet few business people were willing to criticize the US war on drugs publicly.

In a clear example of the tradeoff between security and business interests, in 2010 the El Paso Convention and Visitors Bureau changed maps that had been in use since 1978 that showed the entire, two-city metropolitan region of El Paso and Ciudad Juárez (see map 2.1).[43] The new map failed to include Ciudad Juárez (at the time being torn by violence), instead showing the space south of the borderline as an empty desert, as if it did not exist.[44] Chihuahua's tourism director in Juárez said they were looking for a way to "establish more formal relationships, between Mexican government officials, American government officials, and the chambers of commerce … Why? Because they realize that if things go wrong in Juárez, El Paso will automatically suffer too, but what they do want is the economic flow that they get from us." Examples like this, including the way the border is visually packaged, illustrate underlying tensions in cooperation.

The CEO of the El Paso Central Business Association, whose members depend on pedestrian crossers, expressed horror at US border guards' treatment of crossers. He said that the CBA was taking steps to welcome pedestrian shoppers, such as handing out water. "We gave away 7,000 bottles. Why? Customers were waiting two hours on the bridge." He wanted CBP officials to "greet crossers with a smile." The CBA board president estimated that 14,000 pedestrians were coming downtown every week to shop – more than were going to outlet malls.[45] Besides outlet malls, El Paso has two large regular malls, as well as an upscale mall designed to attract wealthy Mexicans. The then-El Paso Director of Economic Development, now Deputy City Manager, said that we need to "quantify the Mexican shoppers." Some national chain stores show outlier sales here due to retail shoppers from Mexico.[46]

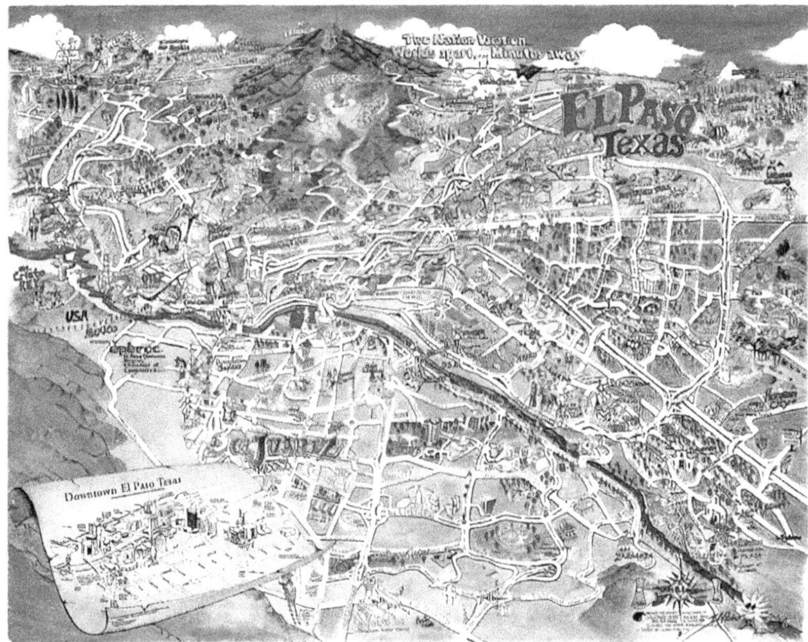

Map 2.1. El Paso Tourism Map

Source: Adam Martin, "A Hopeful Juárez Is Finally Back on the Map," *The Atlantic* (24 May 2012), https://www.theatlantic.com/international/archive/2012/05/hopeful-juarez-finally-back-map/327690.

US practices were discouraging crossers, most of whom were customers, rather than encouraging them. We heard no one who thought a border wall would be anything but a waste of money; they all viewed it as a costly symbol, "not a good use of money." "They're building walls, but should be tearing them down." Through resolutions, El Paso City Council representatives sometimes criticized federal policies on immigration, the border wall, and the drug trade,[47] publicly challenging those policies in ways most business people do not in interviews.

Government employees' transit across the border had been hampered by US State Department advisories. The director of an office in charge of Juárez promotion and marketing commented on those cross-border obstacles: "We still have limitations due to the alerts … and lack of trust of our neighbours to come to the city. This demonstrates that there is a lack of an adequate media plan that can make us see that things in Ciudad Juárez have improved." The City of El Paso had developed a special policy regarding US State Department advisories: federal professionals "needed country clearance" to cross. University administrators, who draw substantial numbers of Mexican students and business people for various MBA programs, expressed frustration with travel prohibitions that were hampering recruitment.[48] In the late 1980s, the Texas state legislature authorized that northern Mexican students who qualified (to which most applicants qualify) could pay in-state tuition rates. Educators would like to encourage more student enrolment from Mexico – not just students from along the northern border, but those from the rest of Mexico, given the ties between Texas, the US, and Mexico.

Celebrations of Small Wins

Stakeholders celebrated the achievement of several goals, all incremental improvements around the edges of a still-dominant border security paradigm that gets full play in every political election season and every attempt at immigration reform. This includes calls for massive increases in the DHS budget and staff to "secure" the border before immigration reform is even contemplated. Texas benefits from $80+ billion in exports to Mexico, which generates hundreds of thousands of jobs, yet the dominant incumbent rhetoric continues to revolve around securing the border against Mexico and Mexicans.

The president of a foundation to promote the quality of life in Juárez commented that through workshops and events dedicated to border issues, "we have succeeded in a little more awareness of the importance that Mexico has to the United States and that the United States has to Mexico. I think it brings us a step closer, although it might not seem that way – with the walls that are being built. But there is a greater awareness by both countries."

On the El Paso side, interviewees claimed several concrete victories on the margins, though these did not touch the core of the border security regime. These small changes opened the door for local governments, local businesses, or individuals to pay for new procedures and staff that would reduce wait times at the border – wait times that were burdening the entire country. Thus, businesses were in fact legitimizing the security agenda. We include some examples of these small victories:

- The CEO of Greater El Paso's Chamber of Commerce said that the "Trusted Traveler" ideas and procedures, including the design of the Dedicated Commuter Lane idea came from the private sector fourteen years ago. Frequent travellers can pay both governments (over $300 annually) for background checks to use shorter lanes at the bridge.
- El Paso's (former) city manager noted improvements on the pedestrian bridges, which were now shaded and provided restrooms. She also

celebrated the cultural and art exchanges involving collaboration between museums on both sides of the border.

- A former El Paso mayor and co-chair of the Border Mayors Association (with co-chair, the Tijuana Municipal President) noted the achievements of businesses that had developed technologies and thus had a material stake in system adoption.[49]
- The Cross-border Trade and Enhancement Act awarded El Paso as a pilot city to use local revenue, amounting to $1.5 million annually, to pay overtime and hire new officers to reduce wait times at the bridge. In effect, El Pasoans are now helping pay for federal government responsibilities that benefit all fifty states.

Local business associations and representatives stressed the positive dialogue they enjoyed with locally assigned border security enforcers, who understood the border region but whose hands had long been tied by policies made in Washington, DC. Various interviewees said they "work well with them," "they are great to work with," and "they try to do best, within policy, to help." Those same stakeholders also worked at the margins to challenge the methodologies and indicators used, for example, to calculate bridge wait times – usually broadcast and posted on websites in ways that underestimate the *real* wait times (a forty-minute announced wait time can turn into hours). Even a report from the highly respected US Government Accountability Office (GAO) criticized the procedures and the reliability of wait time data.[50] In Ciudad Juárez, private radio stations seem to produce more accurate estimates of wait times. Drivers call in their experiences to the station, and announcers share that information over the waves. Social media like Facebook enable border crossers to join groups of frequent cross-border users, who post pictures, videos, and real-time information on the bridges and wait times.[51]

Some US federal policies have speeded up long-term visas for business investors and job creators. A local El Paso economic development official, commenting on the EB5 investment visa program,[52] said his city may well attract Mexican investors who meet the minimum investment amounts to be eligible for a green card (which allows lawful permanent residence in the US). Moreover, El Paso benefited from new businesses and job creation when extortion and violence in Juárez prompted restaurants to close there and reopen on the US side of the border.

Losses also occur, mourned by businesses and their media. Juarense businesses suffered a major loss when in early 2014 Mexico's federal government equalized VAT rates across the country, thus removing a privilege for border Mexicans in the form of a lower VAT. However, in 2018, Mexican President Andrés Manuel López Obrador decreed a tax cut for the northern region of

Mexico; this included lowering the VAT from 16 per cent to 8 per cent for more than 40 municipalities on the US border.[53]

Finally, a major "win" for the region involved the election of a new US congressman, Beto O'Rourke, to represent the El Paso region. He articulated a trade and border security agenda that departed sharply from that of his predecessor, Silvestre Reyes. Several interviewees praised his challenger-like advocacy for the region in Washington and their access to him and his office for dealing with obstacles and problems. When he decided to run for the US Senate (he lost), his successor was Verónica Escobar, a progressive when it comes to immigration reform. Moreover, the tide seems to be turning on the harsh discourse of the "war on drugs," given its failures, and given that around half of US states have legalized marijuana for medical and/or leisure, regulating its production and sale for adults.[54]

Hopes and Visions with and for Border Voices

An enlightening part of our interview guide included questions about hopes and visions for the future of the border. Mexican interviewees shared their visions of a "borderless" border, of collaborating as one region, and their hope that one day Mexico and the US would synchronize their laws. One said about his vision "that we can live like one region, in which legislative issues are not an obstacle for commercial exchange ... and that only is achieved with the participation on both sides of the border, from the community, organizations and governments." Interviewees believed that through communication, feedback, sharing best practices, and creating programs and policies aligned with the best interests of businesses and both countries, it would be possible to make advances in cross-border governance and forge strong network ties within the region.

On the US side of the border, a businessman and former mayor hoped that we could "return the border to normalcy so that people on both sides can enjoy rich traditions and cultures. This is a very special place to live. I hope that security and commerce can balance out." Another public leader went further about the border as a model for the mainstream: "We could be the model for what the rest of the country looks like in the future." Other border communities were exhibiting forward thinking; as an example, this woman cited the International Bank of Commerce (IBC) in Laredo, which "gets the culture" of the border. Yet the business community's continuing adaptation to and compliance with the security agenda belies their commitment to playing a leadership role in the return to normalcy.

Some US interviewees offered concrete suggestions for achieving the vision. One former local and state government official, now a consultant for small business, said that businesses "need to understand the other side: how to do business there" (e.g., cash more than credit in Mexico). He calls for mutual "financial literacy" and a focus on details like "signs in kilometers *and* miles." But his ultimate vision was of "a seamless border … not unlike our northern border." He contended that realistically, all vehicles could be scanned for contraband: technology could lead the way, as an alternative to building more walls. Others offered creative ideas, such as a shared entertainment district along both sides of the river. The city manager hoped that tourists would return and spend more time on both sides of the border. Interviewees in the US praised the private sector's ability to develop solutions: "Commerce leads the way." Yet US business people also longed for the kind of influence in Washington, DC, that they perceived Mexican businesses enjoyed in their own capital city: "Mexican [border] business has huge input in D.F., more than ours, due to security." As one said, former border czar Alan Bersin "is a plus" and former US President George W. Bush "got it."

Given US states' role in export trade and job creation, and the benefits they garner from both, US interviewees saw the need for state-level cooperation. We expected to hear about the border states' legislative and governors' associations, but only one stakeholder mentioned them. He noted that New Mexico had created a Border Authority within the executive branch of state government. As that office's website touts,[55] the Santa Teresa crossing wait times are far shorter than those in El Paso. New Mexico Governor Susana Martinez (2011–19) often reached out to Governor César Duarte, her counterpart in the State of Chihuahua, and as the newly built (for $400 million) Union Pacific rail/truck facility illustrates, New Mexico has made major strides. El Paso's City Economic Development Director said that Governor Martinez had been "able to write a check which we couldn't write."[56] Texas state leaders do not publicly acknowledge or support high-value trade and job creation in Mexico. We often heard the mantra of regional cooperation, yet we also saw evidence of competition: among business NGOs, all competing for membership dues and large sponsorships (donations); between New Mexico and Texas, with the latter taking trade with Mexico for granted even as its politicians demonized the border; and among non-security businesses, security businesses that enhance trade (such as Secure Origins), and militarized security businesses, all tied to contracts with the federal government within the Border Security Industrial Complex.

Some Mexican interviewees longed for a free trade zone (*zona libre).* When asked about ways to facilitate cross-border interaction, one interviewee answered: "A zone where there would be certain types of controls we understand are important like security and health, but that don't virtually limit our conviviality … closing the doors for us to interact, to relate, and to do business together." Along the same lines, another interviewee commented on the possibility of a *zona libre*, which seemed like a dream, though they had been created in Europe: "We now have the degree of maturity to create a zone that can compete with Europe in the same way they compete with us." Without cross-border governance institutions, such hopes may indeed be only dreams.

The SAF today consists of fragmented incumbents that share core beliefs about security threats, run a complicated apparatus of security machinery fighting multiple wars against drugs and terrorism, and control the flow of asylum-seekers and migrants. Refugee controls strengthened after 2014, especially during the Trump administration, and a "zero tolerance" immigration policy resulted in a multitude of family separations and ongoing inhumane treatment in public and private-for-profit detention centres, as well as the strongly criticized 2019 Migrant Protection Protocols (MPP) program, aka "Remain in Mexico."[57] Incumbents' concessions to challengers' concerns have opened opportunities to privatize costly privileges for the select few who can pay to cross the border efficiently (SENTRI, DCL), for businesses, which absorb the costs of surveillance technology, and for local governments and their taxpayers, who fund federal government responsibilities to staff and open more lanes to reduce congestion at the ports of entry, even though that trade benefits the entire nation, not just El Paso. Border congressional representatives today straddle the incumbency and challenger roles, and city council representatives sometimes pass resolutions that challenge the security status quo. But local challengers are weak in the context of the dominant security agenda emanating from Washington, DC, which funds security agendas in and with Mexico through the Mérida Initiative and drug wars.

The City of El Paso has one of the lowest per capita incomes among large US cities. Its people could benefit from the border gateway if they were not presently burdened by the congestion of that gateway. One representative wondered how more trade and job creation might remain in the region rather than continue on to Michigan and all the other states that benefit from trade with Mexico. UTEP's (former) Business Dean Nachtmann, who serves on the board of one of twelve Federal Reserve Bank offices (the El Paso office, which educates business on policy changes in Mexico), said that "we have this great international product flow across the border, but where is most of it going? It's not staying here. Even though that flow is worth billions every year, the city will tell you there is not much they get out of that. The city's not exactly able to tax that flow."[58] We wonder who "gets" this issue.

As we noted earlier in this chapter, along with the "vertical hierarchy" that Fligstein and McAdam mention, we see some differences between businesses and their NGOs on the Mexican and US sides of the border. On the US side, businesses and their NGOs work closely with local government, especially in city government. Even those organizations that claim they need no government support – like the Borderplex Alliance, a regional not-for-profit dedicated to economic development and prosperity in the Ciudad Juárez, El Paso, and southern New Mexico region[59] – methodically list on their websites all the government subsidies in the form of tax incentives available to businesses that locate in the region.[60] Presumably for the sake of creating jobs, property tax abatement for new businesses shifts the revenue-generating burden onto the residents and existing local businesses. Yet the Borderplex Alliance's first big "win" in 2013 was to negotiate a call centre operation in El Paso, with jobs that paid near the minimum wage. This was not unlike the call centres established in the 1990s after El Paso's garment factories closed, which hardly transformed El Paso's economy – a questionable win that drew extensive critical media coverage. Meanwhile, revolving doors exist between business and government: businessmen become mayors, and vice versa. A former Borderplex Alliance vice-president for business development, Retired Army Colonel Cary Westin, was named director of El Paso's Economic and International Development Department and, subsequently, Deputy City Manager.

Local business people and officials long for the influence they perceive Mexican businesses as having with their own government. While some Juarense business people and NGOs wield great influence with the federal government, there is less to obtain from municipal governments. Also, municipal government in Mexico is relatively ineffectual in matters related to economic development. Mexico has a federal system in which municipalities lack a strong financial base – something that many US local governments do have. The latter are able to tap considerable property tax revenue as well as support from the state government.[61] Mexican local chambers of commerce provide little opportunity for leadership, consultation, and voice.

Questions might also be asked about businesses' perceived influence over federal and national government incumbents, given that northern Mexican businesses and their NGOs were unable to retain the special privileges they had once been granted in the form of a lower VAT along the border. When *maquiladoras* were first established, they enjoyed tax breaks, but as of 1 January 2014, the 11 per cent special rate was increased to 16 per cent, putting an end to special zone status, and this probably pushed more pedestrian shoppers north of the border, where they spend $4.5 billion annually in Texas border cities.[62] An industry media outlet, *Juarez–El Paso Now*, ran a series of articles about this change under the header "Tax Reform *wounds* maquiladoras" (our emphasis) in November 2014. The following month, it published an editorial about the "big blow" to the economy, next to a Photoshopped picture of mid-nineteenth-century President Benito Juárez with a raised eyebrow. That editorial declared: "The old pledge to the business community south of the border to make Juarez a free-trade zone to be able to better compete with El Paso is now a futile exercise."[63] Mexico's most recent president instituted some changes early in his administration.

The challengers adapt, finding ways to work within the system. Many of them have signed up for and pay to use the SENTRI dedicated commuter lanes, which make for shorter waiting times when crossing the border. Some businesses pay for additional inspections of their cargo. One of our interviewees commented on these additional inspections, saying that his firm has a special department to check its own shipments before they leave Mexico. Every day, businesses risk being contaminated by drugs, arms, or suspected terrorism, so they have strengthened their own surveillance practices, in addition to complying with the security agendas of both countries. Moreover, some businesses have opted to participate in the Customs-Trade Partnership Against Terrorism (C-TPAT), run by US Customs and Border Protection (CBP). This is a voluntary public–private sector partnership that offers trade-related businesses an opportunity to "play an active role in the war against terrorism," thereby ensuring a rapid and more secure supply chain for the company, suppliers, and customers.[64]

These security-enhancing trade practices are a sign that governance units and challengers are working within an overarching system – that they acknowledge the importance of safe and efficient trade as well as the need to safeguard their own interests. This is a small attempt at coordination between the business sector and the security regime. The obstacles and challenges resulting from the security apparatus have compelled business/trade/commerce entities to work with governance units as well as with other challengers who share the same vision and acknowledge the interdependence between the two communities.

In this era of neoliberal globalization, as manifested in the binational trade context of the Paso del Norte region, limited government and market economies reign supreme. A key factor in this region is the unequal wage structure along this highly unequal border. We cannot help but remark on what we did *not* hear in our interviews: support for higher wages in *maquiladoras*, where assembly line workers are stuck earning the legal minimum wage ($25 to $50 per week). However, we must note that when Andrés Manuel López Obrador (AMLO) was elected to Mexico's presidency in late 2018, one of his first acts was to double the legal minimum wage at the northern border and to lower the tax rate there. Juarense workers continue to earn a weekly wage that is less than the daily wage in El Paso, part of "getting it" about the business opportunities in the region. We note just three exceptions to this "screaming silence" about the importance of strengthening workers' wages to magnify the multiplier effects of capital investment, retail sales, and consumer demand in the region. Two such voices were those of educators, who were interested in the long-term benefits of human capital investment that higher education provides. According to UTEP's Dean of Business, "it does no good to bring business into a region if they're not going to grow the salary base … We've got to be able to figure out that it is not our mission to market the cost of labour; it is our mission to market the productivity of labour … What I want to market is that we have an educated, productive workforce. Companies are looking for talent, not cheap talent, that is productive."[65] One education leader said that "global competitiveness can't depend on low-wage workers. We export graduates." And one Juarense business person told us that "Juárez cannot simply continue to be a provider of cheap labor, with no added value … We need to make the jump … so that the benefits of this exchange that occurs naturally by being a border leaves [the city and workers] with that added value … that there be better wages, better businesses, to build better infrastructure [and] … have a fairer city to be able to compete." These remarks are among those rare statements that question the *maquiladora* model of development, one that may need to be transformed if the entire region is to advance and become more prosperous for the many. Yet Fligstein and McAdam's theoretical model offers no category for unorganized, subaltern, and muted voices.

Conclusions: Reflections on Voice, Challenge, and Security Incumbents

In this chapter, we have explored the links between business and local government in a neoliberal global economy situated in the trans-national Paso del Norte metropolitan region of El Paso, Ciudad Juárez, and southern New Mexico. In this SAF, many business people, their NGO representatives, and local government officials lay out a common vision of "getting" the opportunities offered by a border region with cross-border alliances and describe the benefits of limited-regulation trade and wage governance regimes – benefits that are being undercut by the overwhelming and vertically imposed security regime, which is largely an outgrowth of US federal policies to combat drugs, terror, and immigrants.

We have analysed the challenger voices of businesses, their representatives, and local officials, focusing on interviews conducted in mid-2013, in-depth printed interviews, and close coverage of the local media. We have alluded to subsequent changes between 2014 and 2020 regarding migration. The COVID-19 pandemic has generated much uncertainty as to the future of cross-border mobility and the interactions of incumbent and challenger actors in the Paso del Norte. This chapter has focused on interviewees' expressions of solidarity across the region, their frustrations with security policies in the top-down incumbency regime, their celebrations of small victories, and their visions for the future. On deeper examination, the small victories have placed a burden on local taxpayers, who contribute funds to speed up cross-border business flows though that should be a federal responsibility, given that it benefits the entire US and that job creation throughout the US depends on export trade to Mexico. Moreover, underneath the expressions of solidarity, there is competition between El Paso and Juárez, and Texas and New Mexico, and within the business community over security and non-security (or security-enhancing contractors).

Elite theorists presume that business is all-powerful. Yet we have seen in this chapter some of the weaknesses of businesses and their NGOs. More specifically, when it comes to trans-national trade issues, even in the borderlands, local businesses and their NGOs have little voice in government except at the local level. In local government, especially on the US side of the border, they exercise more influence than is warranted by the public interest. Besides interacting regularly with city officials, they enjoy the benefits of musical chairs/revolving doors as influential people move from business to government and back again. In earlier decades, Juarense businesses and their NGOs were ascendant in business/national government relations as a result of the growth of the *maquiladora* system at Mexico's northern border; but they seem to have lost influence. Businesses on both sides of the border express solidarity in their gentle challenges to, but also acquiescence to, the incumbents who operate the heavy security regime, which has added costs to and imposed time delays on cross-border trade. The organizations formed to connect border legislators and the ten border governors (six in Mexico, four in the US) have never developed into vehicles for challenging the security regime. The Border Mayors/Municipal Presidents' Association is history: it no longer operates along the near 2,000-mile border.

Cross-border governance models focus more strongly on government and the privileged, organized constituencies that influence political decision-makers. The models say little about those left out of governance, including working people, though profits are being made on their backs as a result of wage regulations. Moreover, it is local property taxpayers who shoulder the responsibility for international bridge traffic and infrastructure though the entire US benefits from the gateway these provide. We hope that later researchers and policy-makers will take these missing voices into account and include democratic accountability in their analyses so that change may come. With or without an EU-type North American union, historic inequalities must diminish.

We challenge those who apply Fligstein and McAdam to expand their models to include voices for democratic governance, whether those voices are organized and funded or not. In one of the greatest crises to impact the borderlands since 9/11, the COVID pandemic, there has been little to no cross-border cooperation with regard to testing and vaccinations. Instead, the land border has been closed to non-essential travel except for the liberally defined "essential" work in supply-chain manufacturing and the northbound transport of goods therefrom. The US, with its ironically labelled Migrant Protection Protocols – also known as the Remain in Mexico program – continues to return legitimate asylum-seekers to northern Mexican cities, resorting to health rationales from the decades-old Article 42. It is not clear how long Mexico will tolerate the US southbound transfer of migrants and asylum-seekers.

NOTES

1 Oscar Martínez, *Border People* (Tucson: University of Arizona Press, 1994).
2 Kathleen Staudt, *Border Politics in a Global Era: Comparative Perspectives* (Lanham: Rowman and Littlefield, 2017).
3 Iñigi Moré, *Borders of Inequality* (Tucson: University of Arizona Press, 2011).
4 Kathleen Staudt and Irasema Coronado, *Fronteras No Más: Toward Social Justice at the US–Mexico Border* (New York: Palgrave USA, 2002), ch. 1.
5 David Spener and Kathleen Staudt, *The US–Mexico Border: Transcending Divisions, Contesting Identities* (Boulder: Lynne Rienner Press, 1998).
6 Neil Fligstein and Doug McAdam, "Toward a General Theory of Strategic Action Fields," *Sociological Theory* 29, no. 1 (2011): 2.
7 Fligstein and McAdam, "Toward a General Theory."
8 This study was granted Institutional Review Board (IRB) approval from the University of Texas at El Paso on 1 May 2013 (IRB reference # 431390–1). We would like to thank our colleagues from the Universidad Autónoma de Ciudad Juárez (UACJ), Alejandra Payán and Héctor Gómez, who provided research assistance in collecting the Juárez interviews. The interviewees' names are not used for quotations, but records are on file with Staudt and Cruz. This work was supported by the Social Sciences and Humanities Research Council of Canada (SSHRC), under the Partnership Development Grant titled "The Transformations of Cross-Border Governance: North America and Europe in Comparative Perspectives" (2012–17).
9 William Dumhoff, *Who Rules America? Power, Politics, and Social Change* (New York: McGraw-Hill, 2006); C. Wright Mills, *The Power Elite* (New York: Oxford University Press, 1956).
10 Ben Ross Schneider, "Why Is Mexican Business So Organized?," *Latin American Research Review* 37, no. 1 (2002): 77–118.
11 Roderick Camp, *Entrepreneurs and Politics in Twentieth-Century Mexico* (New York: Oxford University Press, 1989), 12, 82.
12 Cited in Schneider, *Why Is Mexican Business So Organized?*, 2.
13 Schneider, *Why Is Mexican Business So Organized?*, 8.
14 Schneider, *Why Is Mexican Business So Organized?*, 14.
15 Strom C. Thacker, "Private Sector Trade Politics in Mexico," *Business and Politics* 2, no. 2 (2000): 161–87.
16 Staudt and Coronado, *Fronteras No Más*.
17 Kathleen Staudt and Zulma Méndez, *Courage, Resistance, and Women in Ciudad Juárez: Challenges to Militarization* (Austin: University of Texas Press, 2015), ch 2.
18 Peter Ward, "Metropolitan Governance in Mexico: Mission Impossible?," in *Metropolitan Governance in the Federalist Americas: Strategies for Equitable and Integrated Development*, no. l, ed. Peter K. Spink, Peter M. Ward, and Robert H. Wilson (Notre Dame: University of Notre Dame Press, 2012), 165.

19 Staudt and Méndez, *Courage, Resistance, and Women*, ch. 2.
20 Shannon O'Neill, *Two Nations, Indivisible* (New York: Oxford University Press, 2013), 83.
21 Robert A. Pastor, *Toward a North American Community: Lessons from the Old World for the New* (Washington, DC: Institute for International Economics, 2001), ch. 2.
22 Emmanuel Brunet-Jailley, "NAFTA, Economic Integration, and the Canadian–American Security Regime in the Post-September 11, 2001 Era: Multi-Level Governance and Transparent Border?," *Journal of Borderlands Studies* 19, no. 1 (2004), 123–42.
23 Oscar Martínez, *Border Boom Town* (Austin: University of Texas Press, 1978).
24 Pastor, *Toward a North American Community*, 186.
25 Pastor, *Toward a North American Community*, 28.
26 Kathleen Staudt, Tony Payan, and Timothy Dunn, "Closing Reflections: Bordering Human Rights, Democracy, and Broad-based Security," in *Human Rights along the US-Mexico Border*, ed. Kathleen Staudt, Tony Payan, and Z. Anthony Kruszewski (Tucson: University of Arizona Press, 2009), 185–202.
27 Selections in Tony Payan, Kathleen Staudt, and Z. Anthony Kruszewski, eds., *A War That Can't Be Won: Binational Perspectives on the War on Drugs* (Tucson: University of Arizona Press, 2013).
28 Staudt and Méndez, *Courage, Resistance, and Women*, 2015.
29 Interview with Bob Cook, president of REDCO, 15 May 2011 (Listed below).
30 Interview with Alan Russell, president and CEO of TECMA, 6 February 2011 (Listed below).
31 Pedro Jr. Niño, Roberto A. Coronado, Thomas M. Fullerton, and Adam G. Walke, "Cross-Border Homicide Impacts on Economic Activity in El Paso," (2013): 6 (unpublished manuscript).
32 Rafael Velázquez Flores and Jorge A. Schiavon, "El 11 de Septiembre y la Relación México-Estados Unidos: ¿Hacia la Securitización de la Agenda?," *Revista Enfoques* 6, no. 8 (2008): 68, http://www.redalyc.org/articulo.oa?id=96060805.
33 Raúl Benítez Manaut, "México-Estados Unidos: paradigmas de una inevitable y conflictiva relación," *Nueva Sociedad* 206 (2006), http://www.nuso.org/upload/articulos/3400_1.pdf.
34 Raúl Benítez Manaut and Carlos Rodríguez Ulloa, "Seguridad y Fronteras en Norteamérica del TLCAN a la ASPAN," *Frontera Norte* 18, no. 35 (2006): 17, http://132.248.9.34/hevila/Fronteranorte/2006/vol18/no35/1.pdf.
35 Manuel Angel Castillo, "Fronteras, migración y seguridad en México," *Alteridades* 15, no. 30 (2005): 55, https://www.redalyc.org/pdf/747/74703005.pdf.
36 Tony Payan and Vásquez, "The Costs of Homeland Security," in *Border Security in North America and Europe*, ed. Emmanuel Brunet-Jailly (Ottawa: University of Ottawa Press, 2007).
37 José María Ramos, "Gestión de la seguridad en la frontera norte e Iniciativa Mérida: antecedentes y desafíos," in *Migración y seguridad: Nuevo desafío en*

México, ed. Natalia Armijo (México City: CASEDE, 2011): 73–90, http://www.seguridadcondemocracia.org/mys/cap4.pdf.
38 Cited in Tony Payan, "Ciudad Juárez: la Tormenta Perfecta," in *Migración y Seguridad*, ed. Armijo, 128, http://www.seguridadcondemocracia.org/mys/cap7.pdf.
39 Niño et al., "Cross-Border Homicide Impacts," 2013.
40 Neil Fligstein and Doug McAdam, "Toward a General Theory of Strategic Action Fields," *Sociological Theory* 29, no.1 (2011): 6.
41 Fligstein and McAdam, "Toward a General Theory."
42 Pastor, *Toward a North American Community*, 19.
43 Adam Martin, "A Hopeful Juarez Is Finally Back on the Map", *The Atlantic*, 24 May 2012, https://www.theatlantic.com/international/archive/2012/05/hopeful-juarez-finally-back-map/327690.
44 Martin, "A Hopeful Juarez."
45 Interview with George Salom, Jr, president, Central Business Association, 14–20 July 2013 (listed below).
46 Speech by Cary Westin, El Paso Economic Development Director, District no. 8, City Council Weekly Talk, 31 March 2014 (listed below).
47 Kathleen Staudt and Beto O'Rourke, "Challenging Foreign Policy from the Border: The Forty-Year War on Drugs," in Payan, Staudt, and Kruszewski, eds., *A War That Can't Be Won*, 217–38.
48 Interview with Bob Nachtmann, dean, UTEP College of Business Administration, 22 January 2012 (listed below).
49 Readers can check Project 21 at https://ftp.dot.state.tx.us/pub/txdot-info/freight/meetings/secure-origins.pdf.
50 US Government Accountability Office, "Report to the Ranking Member, Subcommittee on Immigration, Refugees and Border Security, Committee on the Judiciary, U.S. Senate," July 2013, http://www.gao.gov/assets/660/656140/pdf.
51 See Pamela Cruz and Manuel Gutiérrez, "Cross-border community organizing on the US–Mexico border," *Houston Chronicle Baker Institute Blog*, 22 September 2016, https://blog.chron.com/bakerblog/2016/09/cross-border-community-organizing-on-the-u-s-mexico-border.
52 See US Citizenship and Immigration Services (USCIS), "EB-5 Immigrant Investor Program" (n.d.), https://www.uscis.gov/eb-5.
53 See Baker McKenzie, "Decree of tax benefits for the Northern Border Region," 16 January 2019, https://www.bakermckenzie.com/en/insight/publications/2019/01/decree-of-tax-benefits.
54 See selections in Payan Staudt, and Kruszewski, eds., *A War That Can't Be Won*.
55 See New Mexico Border Authority website, www.nmborder.com.
56 Speech by Westin, 2014 (listed below).
57 See American Immigration Council, 2020; US Commission on Civil Rights, 2019; Congressional Research Service, 2019.
58 Interview with Nachtmann, 2012 (listed below).

59 Speech by Rolando Pablos, CEO, Borderplex Alliance, El Paso, Federal Reserve Bank, 21 October 2013 (listed below).
60 See Borderplex Alliance website, https://www.borderplexalliance.org.
61 David Spener and Kathleen Staudt, *The US–Mexico Border: Transcending Divisions, Contesting Identities* (Boulder: Lynne Rienner, 1998).
62 Elliot Spagat, "Mexican sales tax hike seen as boon for Texas border towns," *Austin American-Statesman*, 1 January 2014, https://www.statesman.com/story/news/2014/01/01/mexican-sales-tax-hike-seen-as-boon-for-texas-border-towns/9898348007.
63 Editorial, "The Borderplex Alliance is bullish for 2014," *Juarez El Paso Now*, February 2014, 34–6.
64 US Customs and Border Protection (CBP), *CustomsTrade Partnership against Terrorism (C-TPAT): Meeting the Supply Chain Security Challenges of a 21st Century Economy* (2014), http://www.cbp.gov/linkhandler/cgov/trade/cargo_security/ctpat/ctpat_program_information/ctpat_brochure.ctt/ctpat_brochure.pdf.
65 Interview with Nachtmann, 2012 (listed below).

Interviews – Ciudad Juárez: Economic/Business

- Lic. Juan Carlos Talavera Noriega (Desarrollo Económico)
- Manuel Sotelo (Fletes Sotelo)
- Fernando Ávila Ortega (FECHAC)
- Sergio Nevárez (Reparto S.A.)
- Francisco Moreno (Centro de Convenciones)
- Armando Prado (CANACO)
- Viridiana Vázquez (CANACINTRA)
- Demetrio Sotomayor (Turismo de la zona norte)
- Cristina Cunningham (CANIRAC)
- Jesús Otero (Century 21)

Interviews – El Paso

- Robert Andrade, business consultant
- Javier Araujo, REDCO/Borderplex Alliance
- John Cook, Co-Chair, Border Mayors Association
- Byrd, Susie, Ex-City Councilperson
- Richard Dayoub, El Paso Greater Chamber of Commerce
- Dennis Melones, Central Business Association
- Lydia Nesbitt-Arronte, Borderplex Alliance
- Diana Natalicio, President, UTEP
- Beto O'Rourke, U.S. Congressman
- Jorge Ramos, Borderplex Alliance
- Uribarri, Laura, UTEP MBA program, downtown El Paso
- Wardy, Joe, businessman/former Mayor
- Wilson, Joyce, City Manager

Speeches

- Rolando Pablos, CEO, Borderplex Alliance, El Paso, Federal Reserve Bank, 21 October 2013)
- Roberto Coronado, Federal Reserve Bank, El Paso Office, 11 April 2014
- Global Competitive Conference, with Woody Hunt, Edward Fesser, and others, 19 April 2014
- Governor Susana Martínez, Union Pacific Inauguration, 28 May 2014
- Jerry Pacheco, Union Pacific Inauguration 28 May 2014
- Cary Westin, El Paso Economic Development Director, District no. 8 City Council Weekly Talk, 31 October 2014

El Paso Inc. Q&A (in-depth interviews) – Reprinted in the 2012 and 2013 Book of Lists

- Bob Cook, President REDCO, 15 May 2011
- Alejandra de la Vega Foster, businessperson, philanthropist, sports team owner
- Myrna Deckert, CEO, Paso del Norte Health Foundation, 8 July 2012
- Paul Foster, MountainStar Sports Group, 5 August 2012
- Miguel Gómez, Chairman, La Red, 26 February 2012
- Chuck Harre, Chair, Greater El Paso Chamber of Commerce, 5 February 2012
- Manny Mora, VP, C4 Systems, General Dynamics, 21 October 2012
- Bob Nachtmann, Dean, UTEP College of Business Administration, 22 January 2012
- Rolando Pablos, CEO, Borderplex Alliance, 3 March 2013
- J. Antonio Rico, Chair, El Paso Hispanic Chamber of Commerce, 15 January 2012
- Alan Russell, President/CEO, TECMA, 6 February 2011
- George Salom, Jr. President, Central Business Association, 14–20 July 2013
- Cathy Swain, Executive Director, Hub of Human Innovation, 17 June 2012

Juarez-El Paso NOW (in-depth interviews)

- Annaelisa Holguin, Esp. International Affairs and Trade Development Manager, City of El Paso.
- Jaime Bermúdez (reprinted from 2003). Note: JB was also interviewed in El Paso Inc in 1995, reprinted 2 September 2011.

3 The Structure of Cross-Border Governance on the US–Mexico Border

TONY PAYAN

Governance is a process whereby a set of actors in a territory or a policy space establish and enforce principles, norms, and rules by which everyone must abide. These can be democratically made and fairly enforced, or not, but they provide a degree of certainty in expectations of behaviour for all dwellers or participants within that territory or policy space. Broadly speaking, governance can be generated in three sometimes complementary ways. First, it can be produced by a centralized and hierarchical state, which generates these principles, norms, and rules (in the form of laws and ordinances) and enforces them through relatively well-organized and competent bureaucracies. Second, it can be accomplished through networks of individual and collective actors following broadly held tenets, such as cultural and social norms or codified and uncodified market rules. Third, it can be carried out by assemblages of individuals or myriad informal groups, which compete to exert influence over the substantive content of prevailing principles, norms, and rules and to enforce them on a day-to-day basis. They may rely on non-institutionalized and even *ad hoc* interactions.[1] The result, however, is the same: a system of governance in which dwellers and participants within a territory or policy space learn to behave and interact according to relatively well-understood principles, norms, and rules regarding what is and what is not allowed – and banishment or punishment is generally the consequence of not adhering to them. Thus, governance is a complicated phenomenon involving structures (principles, norms, and rules) and agents interacting within a field of action in a mutually constitutive dynamic.[2]

In a border region, governance is even more complex because it involves not only, at one level, the interactions of structures and agents *within* a territory or policy space but also, at another level, the interactions of two sets of agents and structures *across* distinct territories or policy spaces that are mutually exclusive by the fact of state sovereignty. In effect, "state sovereignty … resonates both with 'internal' socio-political order and with 'external' socio-political order

... Borders define the spatial scope of the exertion of legal authority ... The *bordered territory* has become the prevalent social form through which sovereignty is performed."[3] Thus, in nationally *bordered spaces*, be they territorial or policy realms, agents travel across boundary lines carrying interests, identities, and rights acquired and exercised within their own system of governance and interact with other agents and structures operating within the opposite space with their own interests, identities, and rights. In effect, when agents cross an international border, expectations of behaviour can sometimes change drastically because the operative principles, norms, and rules in that field are quite different from those in their own field. Interestingly, in nearly all border areas of the world, borderlanders by necessity develop unique skills and competencies in handling two very distinct governance systems. Many also learn to take advantage of grey areas produced by gaps in law enforcement practices embedded in mutually exclusive governance systems – such as criminal agents – or to take advantage of cross-border market differentials – such as investors and shoppers.

Similarly, border dwellers are not all the same, and they may exhibit solidarity or complicity with other agents across the border. Thus, border governance systems are populated by *border guards*, those charged with controlling border flows, and *border users*, those who view the border as a resource and use it as such. Both of these groups, however, interact within and across fields in an environment of ongoing contestation, whether highly conflictive, as in territorial disputes,[4] or less so as border guards and border users interact daily to exert control over spaces and flows or to resist it.[5] This has led some to argue that border governance is better explained by network rather than hierarchical governance or by a combination of the two.[6] A hierarchical versus network governance approach to borders, however, still leaves open questions about the role that other less visible agents – such as cross-border civil society (especially the disorganized) and even criminal organizations – play in cross-border governance. After all, border spaces are themselves broken down into many singular subsystems within and across the broader governance environment – and while they may be subject, hierarchically, to state control on their home side, they also weave networks across the international border and produce additional structures of governance in very specific policy spaces. Other actors never cross the border at all and seldom engage in binational activities. All of this points to the simultaneous existence of hierarchical, state-centric as well as network-based governance and even informal and much less institutionalized forms of governance. Moreover, relying on one system of governance or the other de-emphasizes other key issues, such as power dynamics, conflict, resistance, and change.

Given the complex, fragmented, and multilayered nature of border spaces, a *system of systems*, or better yet, a *field of fields* approach, with space for all types of actors and different forms of governance, is more useful. In the end, borders are not like other national territorial and policy spaces, and therefore border governance requires an approach that can consider the multifaceted and dynamic *and* trans-national nature of border regions,[7] as well as their multisystemic character. This is relevant even today because central governments are increasingly invested in strong control of fringe territories and borders[8] and desire to govern all policy spaces with a stronger command. Yet their authority to produce governance must still be negotiated with myriad other agents within and across borders and is contested by nonconformist actors and interests that reinforce or challenge the system of governance.

Border governance is further muddled by the fact that border spaces suffer from a serious democratic deficit[9] as the nation-states of the twenty-first century have progressively sought to assert their sovereignty and strengthen their authority at their edges. To that end, they have deployed additional instruments to control flows,[10] often leading to subtle but powerful conflicts between border guards and border users. Any observer of border areas can see, for example, that, at the same time that the modern nation-state seeks to exert its authority over its borderlands, *border users* employ different modes of resistance to hardened borders and strive to soften the boundaries to extract the benefits of more liquid borders (e.g., smoother legitimate trade and travel).[11] Indeed, for border users, the differentials produced by varying levels of development between one side of the border and the other are a valuable resource,[12] and they often resist further control. This is true for trans-national corporations, just as it is for organized criminals and all actors in between. In this sense, border governance is the result of contestation and competition among multiple agents to produce and reproduce and to challenge and break down the principles, norms, and rules of the field. Thus, border governance often appears to evolve through what Lindblom called "muddling through."[13] Even in Europe, where sovereignty is pooled and joint governance is relatively advanced, the issue remains tricky.[14]

Thus, a field of fields[15] approach is ideal for capturing the emergence, evolution, and changes in the structural configuration of border governance and for understanding how several types of governance can be necessitated by and coexist within spaces such as border regions. A field of fields approach can account for horizontal governance subsystems – agents operating their political, bureaucratic, social, cultural, and economic interests, identities, and rights within their specific subsystem, within their local and national fields, and up against the governance subsystems on the other side of the border; and for vertical subsystems, with actors operating at the national, state, and local levels and beyond (e.g., legitimate corporations and criminal syndicates). In that sense, understanding border governance necessitates a dissection of the entire field into subfields, often with their own systems of governance. And those subfieldsh interact in complex ways even while ultimately structuring governance for all agents within and across fields.

Keeping this in mind, this chapter focuses on the emergence, structuration, and change of governance in spaces of mutually exclusive sovereign authority – borders. The focus is not on the difference between governance and good governance,[16] but on the development and functioning of governance in divided spaces and how actors construct and navigate governance[17] in border contexts. It focuses on the subfields and their governance dynamics in the broader border field and on how these subfields and governance systems interact with one another within and across national territories. And at an empirical level, as a crucial case study,[18] it focuses on the US–Mexico border's governance system in the twenty-first century, examining its evolution over the past two to two and a half decades, under the assumption that several key events have influenced its current state: the end of the Cold War, the advent of the North American Free Trade Agreement (NAFTA), the catastrophic events of 11 September 2001, and the rise of populism in 2016. It analyses how multiple actors seek an open border even as others seek to exert an opposite vision, and how central governments and their powerful bureaucracies deal with cross-border flows as well as how border users negotiate their daily lives and carry out their activities through the structures that bind and constrain them.

This chapter relies on the theory of fields proposed by Neil Fligstein and Doug McAdam,[19] which allows for an understanding of systems within a system or fields within a field and permits an understanding of interactions and changes over time. The chapter complements this central theoretical framework with a typology of governance – hierarchical, network, and non-institutionalized governance[20] – arguing that all three types of governance have come to exist side by side on the US–Mexico border and that different subsystems rely on different forms of governance. Together these concepts help us understand how diverse actors stack up in the field of action, the US–Mexico border.

A Theory of Fields

Fligstein and McAdam's theory of fields is ideal for examining border governance. It proposes the existence of constructed social fields, populated by agents or actors who interact with one another on the basis of shared understandings about the field. Borders qualify as constructed social fields with these characteristics.[21] The theory of fields also posits that different agents in a social field compete to craft and enforce principles, norms, and rules within that field, as well as to resist them. In effect, the theory assumes that no field is value- or interest-neutral. Instead, agents continuously engage in a struggle to seize the governance units so as to implement their vision of the field and incorporate their interests into the governance structure, especially when dramatic changes in the environment occur. Such changes provide incumbent agents (those whose principles, norms, and rules prevail) with the opportunity to reassert and advance their dominance of the field, even while the governed (those who disagree with the prevailing principles, norms, and rules) challenge the status quo. That is also true of border environments, as border guards and border users continuously struggle to control and to resist control. Indeed, scholars agree that borders are by nature spaces of contestation.[22] Moreover, the theory posits that agents within a specific subfield – bureaucratic, social, economic, cultural, and so on – often interact with agents in other subfields in the broader field environment. A border can also be viewed as a collection of fields bumping against one another in the broader field environment – as much within the national environment as across the border. Finally, the theory considers the native capacity of field agents/actors to exploit external shocks or crises within the field to enact their interests and incorporate them into the units of governance. In this regard, borders are spaces where agents often take advantage of external shocks – terrorist attacks, migration surges, new binational accords, and the like – to try to assert their interests and incorporate them into the field's governance units. These building blocks of the theory of fields capture the dynamism of the US–Mexico border. All of this provides an opportunity to visualize the borderlands as a field of fields that at the same time can accommodate different types of governance – hierarchical, network, or non-institutionalized – in different subfields.

The theory of fields incorporates change as well. It helps the student of the US–Mexico border to consider the punctuated events and gradual developments by which the field changes over time – both of which are evident in the US–Mexico binational borderlands. Indeed, because the theory posits that change in a field can occur through external shocks – for example, the emergence of new institutions (principles, norms, and rules) that originate in events such as geostrategic changes, free trade agreements, migration surges, or terrorist attacks – it can help explain periods of rapid transformation in border governance. In effect, at certain moments, destabilizing changes in the environment can prompt the incumbent agents (e.g., dominant economic organizations, social groups, or bureaucracies) that govern the field to interpret change as a challenge to their status from revisionist agents. Other actors, the *governed*, can see such shocks or changes in the environment as opportunities to revise the field (challengers) and capture the units of governance for their own purposes. Thus, periods of contention are normal in any field environment and will inevitably emerge. The US–Mexico border has seen such periods of rapid change, including the end of the Cold War (1990), the advent of NAFTA (1994), the 9/11 terrorist attacks (2001), caravan migration (after 2014), and the rise of populism (2016). The theory considers that at the end of these periods of contention, a field eventually settles again under the same and strengthened governance units favouring the incumbent agents, who oversee compliance with the system – that is, the incumbents have reinforced their dominance, or the challengers have established a new governance structure that favours their interests. A key question raised by the theory, then, is whether these key historical events brought about periods of contestation at the US–Mexico border and who emerged "victorious." The theory allows observers of the US–Mexico border to consider two other essential elements as well. One is the abilities, skills, and resources of the incumbent actors in the field to face challenges to their authority and overcome them; the other relates to the abilities, skills and resources of the challengers to mount challenges against the incumbents and pursue dominance of the field through a new set of governance units. Here, it is hypothesized that the border security industrial complex seems to have had the ability, skills, and material and organizational resources to assert its dominance of the field in each crisis.

Finally, the theory considers the role that the broader field environment (e.g., ideology, discourse, popular narrative, the political environment) may play to the advantage of one or the other set of agents or actors in their struggle to maintain dominance in the field or to challenge it. After all, the Trump administration, with its emphasis on the border as a threat, did not originate at the border. It arose as part of a speech act originating in a national political campaign and in the apprehensions of the American public regarding the border. Thus, here too it will be important to examine which actors were able to weave into the general field environment the kind of rhetoric that best suited them in order to achieve their dominance goals. Finally, when fields are largely unsettled because of prolonged contestation, actors generally have an incentive to negotiate to restore order to the field, given that disorder is generally undesirable to *every* player in the field – it becomes ungovernable. In such circumstances, the governance units will generally entail a compromise, until a new opportunity presents itself to mount a battle for dominance. Under settlement, the governed seek to negotiate and carve out specific privileged spaces, fully sanctioned by the incumbents, so as to be able to pursue their interests to the best of their ability. That too has been the case at the US–Mexico border, as we will see below.

Some Key Definitions from the Theory of Fields

In general, the theory of fields, as posited by Fligstein and McAdam, builds on seven crucial concepts. All these concepts are essential building blocks to generate a plausible picture of cross-border governance at the US–Mexico border.

1. Strategic action fields – the fundamental strategic areas where collective action by field players takes place.

2. Incumbents, challengers, and governance units – incumbents enjoy disproportionate advantage and adapt the field to suit their interests; challengers occupy less privileged niches and wield relatively little influence over its operation; governance units are the basic units charged with overseeing compliance with field rules.
3. Social skills and the existential functions of the social – the cognitive capacities of all actors to understand the field, interpret the environment, identify opportunities, outline the lines of action, and mobilize to increase their dominance of the field or to challenge it.
4. The broader field environment – the context in which the field is located and how it relates to other social fields, including the ability to draw in resources, legitimacy, and allies, among other assets.
5. Exogenous shocks, mobilization, and the onset of contention – where exogenous shocks refer to the social turbulence that arises periodically and is seen as a threat by the incumbents and as an opportunity by the field challengers; the period during which both sides mobilize their resources to fend off the challenge and reassert their dominance or to mount a challenge to the status quo and dominant players; and the time when the struggle among the actors in the field to revise the structure of governance begins.
6. Episodes of contention – the period of time during which the two sides mobilize to mount a challenge and fend it off.
7. Settlement – the new period of stability during which the incumbents have either reasserted their dominance or been forced to share the field under new governance and the challengers have achieved their goal or renounced their struggle.[23]

Types of Governance Systems

Clearly, when examining border contexts, it is often not enough to appeal to a single theory. Single-theory approaches tend to explain only certain aspects of a problem. Given that periods of "governance stability" in a territory or policy space can last for years and even decades, zooming in on the structure of governance at any given moment or at any given layer of the overall structure is as useful as it is in periods of turmoil or conflict. Doing so can help discern how governance in practice varies from one sub-field to another and within the broader field. In this understanding, as mentioned before, this text complements Fligstein and McAdam's theory of fields with a typology of governance. Layering these two theoretical approaches can aid in understanding the complexity of border governance *in toto*. And combining approaches – a field of fields theory and a typology of governance – can help us grasp how various forms of governance coexist and how they change over time, permeating a field, such as the border. Moreover, this dual approach enables a more comprehensive understanding of the type of governance structure that prevails in a given sub-field in a given period and allows us to examine the micro-challenges in the day-to-day practices of border users and how border guards exert their power in the field.

Indeed, to the observer of the US–Mexico border strategic action field (SAF), it is evident that it is not possible to speak of a single *type of governance* in the field. Instead, several types of governance are simultaneously present along and across the sovereign line that divides the two countries. After all, borders are fields made up of multiple sub-fields, which makes it possible for different types of governance to coexist side by side, each with its own characteristics, not unlike scenarios such as civil wars.[24] At one level, for example, the state (especially on the US side) has achieved the administrative capability to assert itself strongly at its periphery through its powerful and well-entrenched border bureaucracies. It has deployed human and material resources capable of carrying out the mandates emanating from the national capital and matching the general national discourse regarding the border. Indeed, the presence of state agents along the borderlands is evident – multiple bureaucracies with prominent visibility, with considerable budgets, myriad high-tech gadgets, thousands of personnel, and numerous physical barriers. All of these segment the border space and wield relatively effective control of the border. Studying border bureaucracies can lead to conclude that hierarchical or vertical governance is dominant in the borderlands – the first type of governance, which we described earlier in the chapter. The exertion of the state at the borderlands, however, does not suffice to understand border SAF governance. The growing presence and assertiveness of the state may in fact be a sign that other actors are challenging, explicitly or implicitly, its control of the border. Some argue that even though the state has managed to assert itself at the border quite authoritatively, other economic, social, and even criminal actors continue to challenge its authority.[25] Borders are nearly always in contention.[26]

Lowering our vision level to take another close look at the US–Mexico border SAF reveals the existence of network-based governance sub-systems in certain other borderland sub-fields. Along and across the borderline, for example, there are clusters of businesses, organizations, social groups, churches, and individuals among whom exchanges of capital, goods, services, and information happen. Often extensive coordination among them occurs through cultural understandings, mutual expectations, contractual obligations, collective and individual reputations, and shared interests.[27] The links among these actors are more horizontal and equal. None can impose its will over others, but they benefit from cooperating. And these actors are important because they often control the local economy (as in business-oriented organizations) or articulate social relations (as in extended families or clubs) and also because they tend to be tightly knit networks outside the state apparatus, even while interacting intensely with it as they move back and forth. Thus, they must negotiate spaces of autonomous action and even privilege to pursue their group and individual interests across the borderline. These actors are largely conservative, however, in that they fully acknowledge the authority of the state and generally abide by the conditions of the governance units imposed by border guards.

Interestingly, down one more echelon, the border SAF is also a place where our third type of governance is also present – a less institutionalized type of governance, that is, assemblages of individuals who navigate their interests along and sometimes against the established governance units. Put another way, the border SAF is populated by actors that, along with more organized groups that rely heavily on networks to influence the governance units, very much inhabit the field and use the border, often daily, even while remaining largely unorganized. They are the working poor, activists, citizens, and even shoppers and clandestine workers (such as maids and day labourers), most of whom could be considered "the governed" but who organize around specific issues and moments of crisis. An example is the cross-border activism around the Juárez femicides in the 1990s.[28] The kind of governance these actors practise is considerably looser but sporadically flares in the form of protest or pushback. It is often restructured in terms of what the incumbent governance units (e.g., the security bureaucracy) allow, but it also often exhibits signs of dissent. These actors are a fundamental part of the field, for they provide many of the economic, political, and social inputs of the border governance ecosystem.

Finally, populating the border SAF is yet another group, an integral part of the broader field but constituting a sub-field unto itself – a group that is often overlooked by governance studies: organized crime. Organized criminal groups are structured as a network around a black market and have essentially a pure profit motive. In materializing their profits, however, they are not interested in abiding by the governance units (evidently), nor are they interested in fundamentally changing them. They are more interested in subverting them in a kind of surreptitious yet frontal challenge to them and, especially, to the authority of state agents – or in simply and preferably operating out of sight. These actors are not anarchic *per se*, as they do have rules, understand market forces, and pursue specific interests. This kind of governance exists against the state but also influences the behaviour of other actors and the health of the principles, norms, and rules that prevail in the field environment, if only because these actors have little or no regard for formal authority. They would prefer the absence or weakening of the state and the general principles, norms, rules, and (lax) processes under which legalized cross-border interaction occurs. These actors are just as strategic in that they interact with other actors in the field and understand its institutions, which actively seek to undermine their interests and have the potential to do so.

When examining the border as a field of fields, layer by layer and policy space by policy space, we must acknowledge that all three types of governance coexist and that much depends on the sub-field we are examining and on the interests of the actors inhabiting it. Borders, after all, are complex spaces that separate at one level and join at another – places where institutional development and governance systems differ from one side to the other, where market forces change as borders are crossed, and where actors view border differentials as profit opportunities.

Methodology

To grasp the configuration of the governance structure of the US–Mexico border today, this chapter relied on the content of seventy-one interviews with actors on both sides of the border. The interviews were conducted by a team of researchers within a much larger project. That team included two of the contributors to this volume – Dr Kathleen Staudt and Dr Tony Payan – as well as Pamela L. Cruz, Alejandra Payan, and Héctor Gómez, these last three being students at the time at the University of Texas at El Paso and the Universidad Autónoma de Ciudad Juárez. These seventy-one semi-structured interviews generated almost 100 hours of audio. The interviews were designed to assess how various agents view their field of action, how they interact with one another, and what kind of border they think they live in or would like to live in. Each interviewee was asked about their personal life on the border, their organization and the work they did with it, and their thoughts on life on the border. These interviews were conducted in person, and all of them were recorded and made available for the research team to write a series of papers on various aspects of the border, including the environment, health, security, immigration, infrastructure, and trade. The interviewees were from all walks of life, and most of them had a binational life – in business, politics, law enforcement, activism, and education. All of them were borderlanders and expressed deep concern about the direction the border had taken over the past two to two and a half decades. Most of them were open to speaking about their own experiences and those of their organizations. Very few law enforcement agents on the US side agreed to interviews – something that has a meaning of its own, as will be explained later.

The theoretical frameworks chosen for this study – a theory of fields and a typology of governance systems – can help generate important hypotheses on border governance. First, border environments can be viewed as fields of action where actors compete for influence over the principles, norms, and rules that govern behaviour. If that is the case, we should be able to determine who these actors are and how they mobilize to maximize their influence to pursue their own vision of the border – one that favours their interests. A corollary to this is that actors whose interests are not favoured by the principles, norms, and rules – and the governance units that underpin them – should exhibit strategies of resistance against them. Second, when opportunities for change arise, we should be able to see actors jockeying to position themselves to change the governance system, with some of them defending the status quo (the incumbents) and others challenging the established norms (the challengers). A corollary to this is that agents will seek to capture the narrative within the field in order to prepare the ground for change – something challengers would do – or, alternatively, double down on the prevailing narrative – something the incumbents would do. A third hypothesis is that we should be able to see actors in the field of action take advantage of their skills and resources to advance their dominance – something incumbents would do; or to negotiate flexibility within the governance rules – something challengers would do; or to seek to skirt with no consequences the principles, norms, and rules – something illegalized actors (criminal) would do. A fourth hypothesis has to do with the presence of more powerful and less powerful actors on a scale that determines the instruments at each actor's disposal to influence governance rules or to resist them. Dividing actors into incumbents and challengers is not enough. There are important divisions among them as well, and sometimes they carve out privileges even against other incumbents or challengers.

In general, conceiving the border as a field of action, in combination with the coexistence of several types of governance levels, can help us understand the structure of governance in the borderlands, appreciate how the field itself has evolved and changed, and ultimately answer the central questions of this chapter: Who governs? What do they do to govern the field? And how do they govern it?

The US–Mexico Border a Strategic Action Field – a Field of Fields

Fligstein and McAdam do not consider border environments in their work. Their case studies focus on race relations and the mortgage securitization field. As already mentioned, to use Fligstein and McAdam's strategic action field (SAF) theory in border contexts, it is necessary to consider an additional tier, a border that divides all structures and agents in the broader field into two large fields governed by mutually exclusive sovereigns. Border SAFs are thus more complex than Fligstein and McAdam's theory would suggest because they comprise two adjacent *national* fields, each of which has various sub-fields. Some sub-fields are contained purely on one side of the border; others straddle the border. That is, the larger cross-border field, divided by a boundary, contains sub-fields that interact in complex ways not only with one another *within* the nation but often also *across* boundaries. Border spaces and processes are thus stacked within the national boundary and layered across borders. To reiterate, border SAFs are spaces where agents interact with one another within their national and local structures as they pursue their goals, and often also interact with a second set of agents in the adjacent national and local structures where these other agents pursue their own goals. Moreover, sometimes agents on one side of the border cannot achieve their goals without the cooperation of certain agents on the other side of the border – law enforcement and manufacturing corporations are two examples. That is, actors on one side of the border plan and execute many of their actions not only vis-à-vis other sub-fields on their own side but also with a second set of action fields on the other side of the border in mind. Indeed, many cannot achieve their goals without considering both sets of fields. At the border, nearly all actors must consider the complex interactions between what the players on their side of the line are doing and what the *other side*'s players are doing that can affect all players in the broader trans-boundary space.

A few detailed examples of this are provided next. Elevated levels of crime and violence on the Mexican side of the border can affect the calculations of those who would treat the border as a resource – for example, US citizens who plan to access medical services on the other side of the border. Similarly, limiting the fight against drug trafficking to the border would probably be a less than effective strategy. US law enforcement must seek a territorial presence well into Mexico if they hope to anticipate what organized criminal groups will do. Cooperation on environmental and natural resource issues also requires that government agencies and civil society organizations treat the environment as a single space, sometimes conceptually erasing the border and sometimes considering how two different institutional approaches to dealing with it can fit into a cooperative whole. In that sense, trans-boundary spaces are now akin to what Putnam has called a "two-level game."[29] As Putnam put it, "two-level games seem a ubiquitous feature of social life" (460), and the border is no exception – indeed, almost all of life is at least a two-level game.

So Fligstein and McAdam's theory does not capture the entire nature and character of the *border* as a strategic action field (of fields). The nature of borders, and certainly the nature of the US–Mexico border, is such that we need to adjust the theory of action fields to consider an even more complex set of interactions among players inhabiting various action sub-fields – sometimes more than one at the same time – as well as complex interactions among the several sub-fields, where different types of governance prevail. Doing this will help us discern where in the field actors are located and how they interact with one another as they seek to use the border and profit from it as a resource.[30]

The Players

Players can be classified not only as incumbents and challengers, according to Fligstein and McAdam. Incumbents have succeeded in capturing the governance units; challengers are always looking for an opportunity to do so. On the border, it is more complicated than this, for sovereignty silences the rights of certain players. At the border, there are players, particularly those who do not carry certain political rights, who are voiceless. Thus, the cross-border SAF also divides players into those who have a voice and those who are voiceless. Classifying all actors in an action field as simply incumbents or challengers would not suffice. One set, the incumbents, consists generally of players who govern; the other set comprises actors who are governed. Then there is a third tier who would not even dream of challenging the status quo – for example, undocumented residents on the "other" side, or very poor factory workers who are structurally oppressed, not just "governed." Moreover, there are also those who would not adhere to any rules but seek to skirt or even undermine them – for example, criminal enterprises trafficking in drugs or persons. When faced with increasingly oppressive governing structures, challengers at the border may split, with some mobilizing to negotiate spaces of privilege for themselves and their networks. They join resources, reputations, and influence to speak in one voice and push back against the incumbents. Within the business and entrepreneurial community, for example, the Designated Commuter Lane (DCL), also known as the Secure Electronic Network for Travelers Rapid Inspection (SENTRI) lane, and the Customs-Trade Partnership Against Terrorism (C-TPAT) program on the US–Mexico border are two cases where the incumbents – generally understood to be the border security agencies – have carved out a space to satisfy the demands of specific types of challengers – the business and corporate communities – for expedited legitimate trade and travel. Such privilege is hardly open to those who cannot pay for it. Clearly, the poor cannot easily access those venues and must remain "in line" and under the stern scrutiny of security agencies. Criminals, for their part, seek neither to negotiate around the units of governance nor to exert any kind of influence over the field. They simply undermine it. In that sense, Fligstein and McAdam's division of incumbents and challengers is useful but not complete. While the business and corporate communities remain challengers – for they would prefer an open border – they have nonetheless used their skills to carve out certain freedoms for themselves. Civil society can hardly negotiate such spaces of freedom, though they may have more success in their national context. And criminals simply play their own game. This implies that not all challengers are equal. The next two sections break down the players according to Fligstein and McAdam's framework, as well as make distinctions among them as demanded by the border context.

The Incumbents

Fligstein and McAdam's incumbents/challengers classification is useful. The incumbents on the US–Mexico border are clearly identified as the border security agencies, specifically Customs and Border Protection (CBP) and the Border Patrol (BP), but there are also other agencies with specific mandates, such as the Drug Enforcement Administration (DEA) and some thirty other federal agencies that together provide tactical, operational, and intelligence support to border control. Immigration and Customs Enforcement (ICE) too has become an aggressive agency, reinforcing the idea that borders are dangerous places. These actors rely on hierarchical governance – legal and political mandates that originate in Washington, DC, and often the state capitals. They have vast resources and high-tech gadgets to gain full operational control of the border. Security agencies have seized the position of gatekeepers and established the narrative that the border is a "dangerous place" – one that only they can secure. Even so, the border has never been under greater operational control; illegal border crossings are at a historic low;[31] and border agents face less danger than regular police in American cities.[32] Law enforcement agencies see chaos and disorder everywhere and portray the borderlands in that light, even though the statistics do not bear that depiction.[33]

A principal tactic of control involves the wait lines at the ports of entry along the border. CBP keeps those lines long not only for *security* reasons but also for *symbolic* reasons. In holding up those lines, they are sending a clear message: the border space is governed not by networks but by a clear hierarchy, atop which is CBP itself. CBP's manipulation of wait times at ports of entry was widely viewed by interviewees as a tactic of control, as was its treatment of border users in general. "CBP officers are not too courteous" was a common complaint. Some interviewees for this study also complained that CBP defines risk as *zero* risk, an unrealistic and often unjustified mindset. Draconian measures at the border are often implemented not because they are necessary but because they are a means to assert the dominance of specific actors. Many of the interviewees expressed dismay at the behaviour of agents at the border, citing their use of discretionary powers to punish border users. They control the border in part by instilling uncertainty. Some businessmen interviewed complained that CBP costs them thousands or even millions of dollars a year by holding back their cargo trucks for no reason except to exert their authority. The national political environment dictates that the incumbents have the upper hand. President Donald Trump was clear about his zero tolerance policy toward migrants at the border. The nation-state, especially through the policies its bureaucrats craft in Washington, DC, emanates authority that reaches into the "front line" at the border.

Yet not all federal agencies can be considered incumbents. There are many other agencies that provide governance on issues ranging from cross-border health to environmental issues. But they possess neither the resources nor the grip on the border narrative that law enforcement agencies enjoy. These agencies include the US–Mexico Border Health Commission, the International Boundary and Water Commission (IBWC), the Commission for Environmental Cooperation (CEC), and the North American Development Bank (NADBANK). These agencies are a vital component of border governance and clearly are part of the hierarchical state-centric governance system, but they do not dominate the narrative around the border, nor do they possess the ability, skills, or resources to impose their mandate over the border up and against the security-industrial complex. In fact, the Department of Homeland Security (DHS) has the authority to waive a full range of environmental laws and regulations to build additional border barriers, including Trump's pet project, a border wall. That is a clear sign that their weight in the governance system is less than optimal. Even so, they are formal agents, part of a national hierarchical structure, and can cross the border. In other words, for them, the border is relatively thin, for they can cross back and forth and try to do their work as best as they can.

We conclude, then, that even though these government agencies operate within a hierarchical understanding of border governance, given that they were created by government fiat and operate within strict laws and regulations of a national and binational character, they are not all equal. Some, like the security-oriented agencies, enjoy much greater discretionary powers, increased resources, and wide political support in Washington, DC, and state capitals, and control the narrative that envelops the border. In that sense, we can refine the theory of fields by breaking out the different agencies that may dwell in a space but cannot be considered incumbents in the full sense of the theory.

The Challengers

Fligstein and McAdam offer a second category of actors in each action field – challengers. But this simple category presents some of the same problems as the incumbent category, and perhaps more. Over the course of seventy-one interviews, it became clear that the business community fits the profile of the challenger in the theoretical framework. They were dissatisfied with the governance landscape at the US–Mexico border. They wanted to see a more open border, and many of them waxed nostalgic about the more fluid border of the past. Some praised the North American Free Trade Agreement (NAFTA) and all the benefits it had brought for business on the border. They often referred to themselves as a binational, bilingual, bicultural "community." Even so, they set themselves apart from the security agencies, whom they accused of not really understanding the need to create a truly binational metropolitan area in the El Paso–Ciudad Juárez (Paso del Norte) region. In this regard, they conceived of themselves as challengers.

The business community along the US–Mexico border – many of its members hold two passports and even own homes on both sides of the border – sees itself as a network. They have created a parallel structure of governance, one based on network governance. They have not organized themselves hierarchically.

Instead, they have formed business and industry associations, economic alliances and think tanks, chambers of commerce, visitors' bureaux, and investment and management partnerships, and are generally linked by their participation in binational markets, including the mammoth *maquiladora* industry that dots the landscape from Tijuana to Matamoros. They tend to be bilingual, and their children enjoy full cross-border mobility. A great many organizations represent their interests, which they cross-link effectively. There is no single mode of interaction among them, nor is there a single point of contact and negotiation with the incumbents. Instead, there often emerge key leaders and spokespersons who establish contact with the incumbents and seek to negotiate expedited processes to promote their interests. The Borderplex Alliance in El Paso, Texas, is one important example of how the business and entrepreneurial class articulates its interests and wields its resources to move local agendas in their own favour. While they often work with the security community, they cannot override it – their resources and skills only take them so far.

A prominent concern for the local business and entrepreneurial community was how hard they found it to defend their own commercial interests, which involved persuading governments to ease tight security policies, which in turn meant having to navigate the US and Mexican political and policy environments. Some of the interviewees said they understood the need to maintain a safe border, but they also pointed out that security was often prioritized over prosperity. The two, in their view, should enjoy equal priority.

Recent conditions on the Mexican side, however, especially the spike in crime and violence, have divided this community in another way. Most of the interviewees in El Paso's business community said they preferred not to visit Ciudad Juárez or that they no longer did so. Many of them in fact said they tried to avoid going to "the most dangerous city in the world." Yet at the same time they wanted to promote the region as a global manufacturing centre. An interviewee put it this way: "I no longer go to Ciudad Juárez because of the violence … and time consumption, north and now south too … but we go to other parts of the world to attract business and tell them 'We know what you have heard about Juárez, but it is still a good place to do business and it is getting better.'"

One solution that has been advocated by the challengers vis-à-vis the border is to find a way to profit from it while reducing their own risks in using the border as a resource. The *maquiladora* business community, with its many manufacturing plants in Ciudad Juárez, wants to eliminate any need to cross the border. One interviewee proposed an automated system whereby all merchandise would use a *universal freight shuttle service*;[34] that is, an automated system would move pre-inspected cargo containers across the border. This radical shift in the flow of goods would acknowledge human beings as the threat.

Almost all the challengers portrayed the capital cities as obstacles. They "try to educate Washington and Mexico City," several of them said. Clearly, they are largely unhappy with the status quo, which has marked them as challengers. But they are only one kind of challengers, and they do not represent the voices of all the other residents of the strategic field of action. In that sense, just as with the incumbents, not all challengers are the same.

The Voiceless

It would be a mistake to think that the business community and other formally constituted groups with defined interests are the only challengers. They are not the only actors dissatisfied with the dominance of the security-focused agencies at the US–Mexico border. Fifteen million people live along the border, 2.2 million in the Paso del Norte region alone. Most of these borderlanders are middle class or working poor, and many of them cross the border clandestinely and without authorization to work as maids, babysitters, day labourers, and so on. They too could benefit from greater access to the border, but they do not have it and they certainly do not possess the ability, skills, or resources – or the organization – to even think of mounting a challenge to the security apparatus or to negotiate spaces of privilege for themselves. They almost always cross in fear, surveilled and controlled and often humiliated by border agents. And increasingly, they are not crossing the border at all, as the ports of entry have become quite oppressive spaces. Worse, many workers in Mexico do not even have access to a visa to enter the US. This does not mean they are happy with the situation – they are simply much less powerful and often voiceless when it comes to the shape of governance at the border. Of course, they are never consulted and may even be viewed as a threat to the prosperity and security of the US.

These silent challengers are scattered throughout many different communities and have few opportunities for organizing to lobby for their own interests – although some try to organize around issues such violence against women or for political rights. The latter include those who are protesting the destruction of Segundo Barrio (the Second Neighborhood/Ward), the oldest and most iconic neighbourhood in El Paso. But these are not well-organized, sustained efforts. They go as easy as they come. Thus, the paradox of the US–Mexico border region is that the most vital part of a community's governance – civil society – is increasingly being silenced on both sides of the border. The trans-border space that involves civil society, including factory workers, is rather unorganized. There are important voices on human and immigration rights – including migrant shelters and refugee homes – but they focus largely on responding to the needs of those whom the governance system seeks to punish, expel, or control. The civil society links between the two sides of the border are relatively weak and have been further weakened by deliberate policies to erode attempts to organize across the border.

So one could hardly call civil society – especially cross-border civil society – a challenger. Yet its place in the governance structure cannot simply be dismissed by labelling these people as "the governed." They too are actors, and they aspire to a border that would serve their interests; they too seek to negotiate the governance structure in a way that enables them to benefit from border differentials. Mexican shoppers who crowd US shopping malls and stores are one example of citizens using the border to stretch their family budgets. Also, Mexican doctors' offices and pharmacies serve tens of thousands of uninsured or underinsured Americans. And many poor families complement their income by sneaking into the US to work as maids, gardeners, and caretakers. All these groups, however, prefer not to engage with US border agents, and when they do, they comply carefully with all those agents' rules and instructions. To protest could bring about harassment or, in the case of Mexicans, the loss of their visa. Generally speaking, most borderlanders detest the security apparatus, which they perceive as excessive, but dare not protest. One survey respondent, for example, marked the choice "bueno" (good) when referring to the treatment meted out by border agents, but verbally went on to complain about their handling of people at the waiting line. She simply did not want to leave a record that she had ever complained about what CBP calls "customer service."

Organized Crime

This chapter proposes the inclusion of yet another important challenger at the border – organized criminal groups. They may seem fringe actors, but they influence the dynamics of the border by allowing the security apparatus to legitimize its dominance of the border action field. Organized crime consists of a black market network of actors who do not negotiate with the authorities – say, the way the business and entrepreneurial community does. But neither does that network passively accept the terms of governance imposed by the incumbents. Instead, organized criminal groups are prepared to undermine the governance units in order to carry out their illegal activities. Their mode of resistance is considerably different from that of the other "challenger" groups. They bribe, threaten, corrupt, and use force on others, and they generally succeed in using the border to smuggle drugs as well as humans. They are a dynamic group, much like the business community. Their smuggling methods are incredibly creative and include drugs hidden in vehicle compartments, produce, furniture, and so on. They exploit every soft spot along the border, including ports of entry, specific routes between ports of entry, and even tunnels. Lately, they have adopted advanced technologies to accomplish their goals, including drones.[35]

Interestingly, they provide the elements for the narrative that federal security agencies use to legitimize the construction and reinforcement of the border SAF's units of governance. Organized crime is as strategic an actor as the business community, but it is not interested in carving out spaces of privilege for themselves – they could not do it in any event, except by corrupting US agents, which does happen.

Exogenous Shocks, Mobilization, and Contention at the Border

The interviewees cited several contradictory events as crucial in the evolution of the border environment. Since the Fligstein and McAdam theory of fields relies on "external shocks" to understand how periods of contention begin, it is important to examine such events. The first was the end of the Cold War (1990). Many expected the end of communism to begin a process of rebordering, particularly because many saw it as the dawning of a new era of globalization, political cooperation, and economic integration. Yet that did not happen. Although many scholars were optimistic about "the end of history"[36] and the literature on borders championed concepts such as "debordering,"[37] the period did not last long; instead, nation-states sought to assert and reassert their dominance at their peripheries. Some states, like Yugoslavia, even sought to remake the nation-state along ethnic lines. Others were predicting as early as the mid-1990s that the coming conflict would be civilizational.[38] In the end, by the mid-1990s, the US was reasserting its control of the US–Mexico border and rapidly expanding its security agencies to control the border.[39] Thus, the Cold War's end resulted in a reassertion of security agencies, which were ideally positioned to assuage the new fears that emerged in the 1990s – illegal immigration, drug smuggling, and other "non-conventional" threats. Most other border actors could not come close to achieving a place within the governance structure of the US–Mexico border.

The second external shock – as well as an opportunity to remake cross-border governance – was NAFTA. That trade agreement was negotiated and signed as one among a wave of important cross-border initiatives in Europe and North America in the 1990s. The end of the Cold War had accelerated the globalization process, which reached the US–Mexico border, where it provided an additional framework for cooperation in the form of a trade accord. NAFTA would reshape the US–Mexico border by providing new opportunities for the business and entrepreneurial communities to assert their influence over governance units. They did not necessarily have carte blanche, however – the same year the agreement took effect, security agencies stepped up their efforts to control the border. In fact, in 1994, even while NAFTA was inaugurating a new era on the border, Silvestre Reyes, then chief of the CBP, began a major operation to "seal" the border between ports of entry – an operation later named "Operation Hold the Line." The simultaneous appearance of NAFTA and Operation Hold the Line, which would be replicated along the entire US–Mexico border under a different name, can be seen today as marking the onset of contention.

US security agencies may have viewed NAFTA as a threat to their ability to control the border, especially because it came accompanied by the "Idea of North America."[40]

The rest of the 1990s were a period of simultaneous opening and closing of the border. The forces of law and order and the business and entrepreneurial communities crafted a discourse that sought to balance "prosperity and security." The conjunction "and" signals an attempt to reconcile two values that often appear contradictory. In the end, security would prevail over economic interests, but the business community at the border was able to negotiate with the security incumbents, even at the expense of social solidarity with the rest of the borderlands. Many interviewees in fact had little to say about the larger mass of border residents. Those in the business and political communities appeared to have an idyllic image of the border and largely ignored the systematic exclusion of so many borderlanders from any of the privileges that they themselves were able to slice out of the security apparatus.

The third breaking point, the 9/11 terrorist attacks, was an opportunity for the border security complex to reassert its interests over those of all other actors. Once the Department of Homeland Security was created and border agencies were reorganized, border security bureaucrats became the undisputed incumbents. Other actors were left to adjust to the priority placed on security by both the principals (political forces) and the agents (bureaucrats). Even the highly organized business and entrepreneurial community had to adjust to the new environment. It would be years before they were able to negotiate certain prerogatives for expedited processing for trade and travel. Slowly, border security agencies weaved a complex network vertically to their political allies, and horizontally to the industry that provided them instruments of control, in a kind of border industrial complex; only then did they allow the business and entrepreneurial community to negotiate certain freedoms to use the border in pursuit of their interests more efficiently, even as they subjected borderlanders to increasing surveillance, monitoring, inspection, and even punitive measures.

A fourth crucial point that border security agencies used to reinforce their dominance, backed by powerful rhetoric at every turn – one that enabled them to take advantage of every border crisis – was the spike in undocumented immigration through 2007 and especially the spike in unaccompanied minors in 2014, which has been followed every summer since by caravans of migrants from Central America and beyond. These caravans have enabled the security agencies, especially the DHS, to continue to present themselves as the solution to this "invasion." These waves of migrants arriving at the border in search of asylum seem to sow fear in the minds of regular Americans. Moreover, those migrants have been handled so ineptly by the US federal bureaucracies, perhaps on purpose, that the sense of crisis at the border has been heightened, as have public perceptions of the bureaucracies' importance. This has added weight to their appeal for additional resources, which, so far, they have been receiving.

Finally, all these fears – of terrorism, of globalization and economic decline, and of migration – have been wielded adeptly to create a sense of crisis and urgency in the broader field environment – especially in US politics – so that other actors have been able to capitalize on the moment to advance not only a specific rhetoric but also their political careers and their own policy agendas. One of these actors has been Donald Trump, who ran for the presidency in 2016, largely by appealing to the worst fears embedded in the American national psyche and redirecting them toward the border, which he successfully depicted as a fundamental threat to American safety and security. Throughout the Trump administration in Washington, DC, border security agencies were among his closest allies on the ground. And throughout his four years in office, they gained enormous power and resources – much of which went to fund a border wall – and even enjoyed enormous impunity in their abuse of migrants and other border users.

The security bureaucracies at the US–Mexico border have proven to be extremely skilful at using major events and even smaller crises to assert their dominance over the border environment, as well as reinforce the perception that border agents are all that stands between order and chaos. Hardly any politician who visits the US–Mexico border, for example, dares call out loud for a more open border – that would be the kiss of death for any political career. On almost all scores, the border security community has managed to outmanoeuvre all other actors in the border action field to secure its dominance over the units of governance. Most border uses are negotiated around the premise that security is fundamental and that all cross-border flows must undergo scrutiny under the conditions set by the security bureaucracies themselves. Most activity at the border presents no threat to national security or public safety, yet the border agencies have managed to depict the region as an extremely dangerous place – a site of lawlessness, chaos, violence, and grave threats to national security. Even actors who would otherwise be able to negotiate special privileges for themselves, such as the business community, have had to silence themselves simply to preserve their prerogatives. In today's national climate of poisonous rhetoric around the border, border security bureaucracies are now able to act with total impunity.

The following figure shows the entire border strategic action field, which is divided into four types of actors. There are the state actors, whose governance most resembles traditional, hierarchical, state-centric governance. For them, the border is relatively thin, as they largely control it and extract acquiescence from nearly all other actors. Then there are the economic actors, whose organization in the field most closely resembles network governance and who have managed to negotiate special spaces for themselves and their interests, though

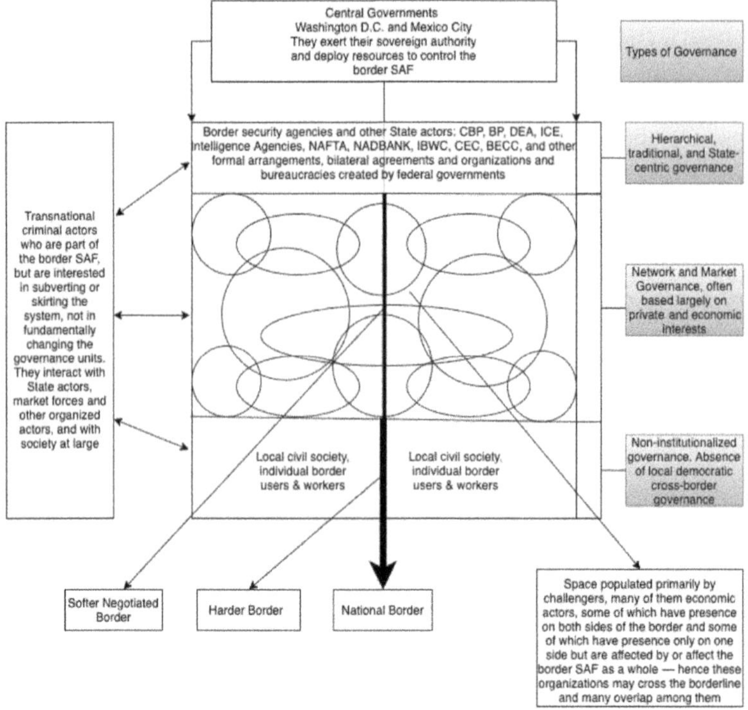

Figure 3.1. The border strategic action field, complemented by a scheme showing the primary three types of governance that coexist on the border.

Source: Author elaboration.

always in terms of what the border security industrial complex permits. Then there is local civil society and workers, who could be defined as "the governed" and very often as the "powerless" and the "voiceless" – an indication that not all potential challengers are united or have the ability to present a united front. Finally, to the left, there are the organized criminals, who operate as a network and interact with all other actors, legal and legitimate, but play by their own rules, seeking to subvert the system though not necessarily to overturn its governance structure. They, however, also influence the shape of governance on the border and provide an important building block for security agencies' efforts to further legitimize their dominance. The graph also shows how the border becomes "thicker" the farther down one goes in both power grade and governance type.

Stability at the US–Mexico Border

Over the past twenty-five years or so, the US–Mexico border has gone through three key periods of change (i.e., opportunities for governance change). The major struggle has been between the two most powerful groups – the security industrial complex and the internationalized business and entrepreneurial community. At every turn, the former seems to have prevailed. Perhaps that is why the border has experienced a period of stability, with a dominant narrative and clear boundaries between those who govern and those who are governed. But not all is quiet at the border. Organized crime continues to have considerable success in pursuing its goals of penetrating the border and extracting enormous profits from illegal drug trafficking, human smuggling, gun running, and other illicit activities. Criminals, however, are not entirely useless for the preservation of the status quo. They do provide the boogie man the security industrial complex needs in order to keep depicting the border as a lawless and chaotic place and to extract increasing amounts of funding and technology to "control" it. It is also true that the economic elites have accepted the status quo and found ways to negotiate and maintain spaces of privilege for themselves – albeit in increasingly precarious conditions, as evidenced by the restrictions to all non-essential travel at the border during the COVID-19 pandemic in 2020. Many Mexican passport holders, for example, were not allowed to cross the border at all, even those who enjoyed privileges such as access to the Designated Commuter Lane. It is perhaps in civil society, and especially among the working poor, that the most effective control instruments are honed over time. These people are denied visas, or their visas are snatched away for minimal infractions of the rules, and they are constantly intimidated by being questioned and scolded, or worse. The ports of entry have become spaces of fear and trembling.

The Coexistence of Governance Systems

The theory of fields is extremely useful to explain three key periods of potential contention at the US–Mexico border – the end of the Cold War, NAFTA, and the 9/11 terrorist attacks. With each of these, there was always the possibility that some actors would advocate strongly for a more open border. They failed in their efforts when confronted by the security concerns present in the broader field environment and the political skills of the border security industrial complex. However, the theory of fields falls apart when it posits the existence of two groups in each field – incumbents and challengers. Clearly, there are several types of incumbents, some of whom fit well within the traditional, hierarchical type of governance, but whose vision of the border is largely constrained by the security apparatus. Not all challengers are the same, either. Some, despite their status as challengers, can carve out for themselves certain privileges – dual citizenship, fast lanes across the border, and so on – but others remain largely voiceless and ignored. Still others play within the field, but outside and against its rules, norms, and principles as they seek to undermine these for illegal profits.

Thus, when one zooms in on the structure of governance at a single point in the past three decades, the US–Mexico border is a complex space where several types of governance coexist within and across national boundaries. Diverse groups use the border as a resource, pursuing whatever structure of governance is best suited for their purposes, although clearly some have considerably less power and capacity to maximize their interests within the field of action.

Conclusion

Understanding governance in border contexts is a complex endeavour. It requires solid theories that consider not only the structure and the agents that interact with it and among themselves but also theories that examine each set of agents to figure out how they cope with the structures they interact with, whether they do so as incumbents – with varying degrees of power and skills – or as challengers – also with varying degrees of power and skills to negotiate privileges and comply with the rules, norms, and principles in ways that allow them to pursue their interests. In this regard, Fligstein and McAdam's theory of fields did provide essential building blocks to understand the dynamics of the border field of action; however, a clearer picture of cross-border governance emerged when a typology of governance forms revealed that actors interact not only with the structure and other field actors but also among themselves within each group, thus strengthening or weakening their ability to preserve their dominance or to mount important challenges to transform the field.

This way of understanding governance at the border helped draw a fuller picture of how two sets of structures and actors interact not only within but also across national boundaries and how they respond to changes in the field environment. The sorting of actors into smaller groups further reveals that not all actors are the same and that not all possess the skills and material resources to change the governing narrative and mount a clear challenge so as to enact their own vision of the border. At the same time, this two-theory examination of the US–Mexico border helps us discern why the border security industrial complex has managed to prevail after every recent external shock and has been able to prevent other actors from changing th system.

Finally, this double model of cross-border governance is applicable not just to the US–Mexico border; it can also be applied in other border contexts, for it is possible to find the same kinds of governance units, types of actors, preferences, and relationships at every other border. The double model can account not only for how a field changes over time but also for how the structure itself parcels out actors into smaller groups as they pursue different visions and interests of their field.

NOTES

1 Oliver Treib, Holger Bähr, and Gerda Falkner, "Modes of Governance: Toward a Conceptual Clarification," *Journal of European Public Policy* 14, no. 1 (July 2006): 1–20.
2 There are of course debates about the construction of governance. Institutionalist or positivist approaches may see it as arising from deliberate rule making and enforcing. Others believe that it emerges in more complex ways, through the construction of rules that shape expectations and behaviours but do not fix them. Agents, too, can challenge these expectations and behaviour. Here, we assume that governance is constructed. See Mark Bevir, "The Construction of Governance," in *Governance, Consumers, and Citizens: Consumption and Public Life*, ed. Bevir and Frank Trentmann (London: Palgrave Macmillan, 2007).
3 Kristine Beurskens and Judith Miggelbrink, "Special Section Introduction – Sovereignty Contested: Theory and Practice in Borderlands," *Geopolitics* 22, no. 4 (2017): 749–56.
4 Alexander C. Diener and Joshua Hagen, eds., *Borderlines and Borderlands: Political Oddities at the Edge of the Nation State* (Lanham: Rowman and Littlefield, 2010).
5 Reece Jones and Corey Johnson, eds., *Placing the Border in Everyday Life* (Burlington: Ashgate, 2014).
6 Joachim Blatter, "Beyond Hierarchies and Networks: Institutional Logics and Change in Transboundary Spaces," *Governance* 16, no. 4 (2003): 503–26.
7 Enrico Gualini, "Crossborder Governance: Inventing Regions in a Trans-national Multi-Level Polity," *Planning Review* 39, no. 152 (2003): 43–54.
8 This may be the result of a fundamental insecurity lodged in the nation-state today. One result has been a considerable increase in border control, including walls and barriers. See Elisabeth Vallet, *Borders, Fences, and Walls: State of Insecurity?* (New York: Routledge, 2016).
9 Tony Payan, "Crossborder Governance in a Tristate, Binational Region," in *Cities and Citizenship at the US–Mexico Border: The Paso del Norte Metropolitan Region*, ed. Kathleen Staudt, Julia Monárrez, and César M. Fuentes (New York: Palgrave Macmillan, 2010).
10 Mathias Albert, David Jacobson, and Yosef Lapid, eds., *Identities, Borders, Orders: Rethinking International Relations Theory* (Minneapolis: University of Minnesota Press, 2001).
11 For a fuller explanation of the term "liquid" in the post-9/11 context, see Zygmund Bauman and David Lyon, *Liquid Surveillance: A Conversation* (Cambridge: Polity Press, 2013).

12 Christophe Sohn, "The Border as a Resource in the Global Urban Space: A Contribution to the Cross-Border Metropolis Hypothesis," *International Journal of Urban and Regional Research* 38, no. 5 (September 2014): 1697–711.
13 Charles E. Lindblom, "The Science of 'Muddling Through,'" *Public Administration Review* 19, no. 2 (Spring 1959): 79–88.
14 Markus Perkman, "Building Governance Institutions across European Borders," *Regional Studies* 33, no. 7 (October 1999): 657–67.
15 Note that in this chapter, system and field are used interchangeably, as the Strategic Action Field (SAF) allows for just such synonymizing of terms. See Neil Fligstein and Doug McAdam, *A Theory of Fields* (New York: Oxford University Press, 2012), http://doi.org/10.1007/s11186-014-9237-0.
16 Yu Keping, "Governance and Good Governance: A New Framework for Political Analysis," *Fudan Journal of the Humanities and Social Sciences* 11, no. 1 (March,2018): 1–8.
17 Robert L. Glicksman, "Dynamic Governance in Theory and Application," *GW Law Faculty Publications and Other Works*, Public Law Research Paper no. 791 (February 2016), https://scholarship.law.gwu.edu/cgi/viewcontent.cgi?article=2456&context=faculty_publication.
18 John Gerring, "Is There a (Viable) Crucial-Case Method?," *Comparative Political Studies* 40, no. 3 (March 2007): 231–53.
19 Fligstein and McAdam, *A Theory of Fields*, 2012.
20 Mark Bevir, ed., *The Sage Handbook of Governance* (Thousand Oaks: Sage, 2013).
21 Bevir, ed., *The Sage Handbook of Governance*.
22 James Anderson and Liam O'Dowd, "Contested Borders: Globalization and Ethnonational Conflict in Ireland," *Regional Studies* 33, no. 7 (August 2010): 681–96.
23 Fligstein and McAdam, *A Theory of Fields*, 3–24.
24 Nelson Kasfir, Georg Frerks, and Niels Terpstra, "Introduction: Armed Groups and Multi-layered Governance," *Journal Civil Wars* 19, no. 3 (January 2018): 257–78.
25 Carolyn J. Hill and Laurence E. Lynn Jr., "Is Hierarchical Governance in Decline? Evidence from Empirical Research" (unpublished paper), (April 2004), http://faculty.georgetown.edu/cjh34/hilllynnjpart.pdf.
26 Maestri Gaja Maestri and Sarah M. Hughes, "Contested Spaces of Citizenship: Camps, Borders, and Urban Encounters," *Citizenship Studies* 21, no. 6 (2017): 625–39; Pierre Monforte, "The Border as a Space of Contention: The Spatial Strategies of Protest against Border Controls in Europe," *Citizenship Studies* 20, nos. 3–4 (2016): 411–26.
27 Candace Jones, William S. Hesterly, and Stephen P. Borgatti, "A General Theory of Network Governance: Exchange Conditions and Social Mechanisms," *Academy of Management Review* 22, no. 4 (October 1997): 911–45.
28 Kathleen Staudt, *Violence and Activism at the Border: Gender, Fear, and Everyday Life in Ciudad Juárez* (Austin: The University of Texas Press, 2008).

29 Robert D. Putnam, "Diplomacy and Domestic Politics: The Logic of Two-Level Games," *International Organization* 42, no. 3 (Summer 1988): 427–60.
30 Christophe Sohn, "Modelling Cross-Border Integration: The Role of Border as a Resource," *Geopolitics* 19, no. 3 (August 2014): 587–608.
31 Customs and Border Protection, "Total Illegal Alien Apprehensions by Months 2000–2017" (2017). See https://www.cbp.gov/sites/default/files/assets/documents/2017-Dec/BP%20Total%20Monthly%20Apps%20by%20Sector%20and%20Area%2C%20FY2000-FY2017.pdf.
32 Bob Ortega, "Is Border Patrol Work Dangerous? Not Compared to Being a Cop," *CNN Investigates* (1 May 2018), https://www.cnn.com/2018/05/01/us/border-patrol-agent-less-dangerous-than-being-police-officer-invs/index.html.
33 Paul Mutsaers, "Introduction to the Anthropology of Police: Law and Disorder Everywhere?" (2016), https://www.law.ox.ac.uk/research-subject-groups/centre-criminology/centreborder-criminologies/blog/2016/03/introduction.
34 Steve Roop, "Futuristic Shuttle May Transform Freight Transportation," *Texas Transportation Researcher* 43, no. 4 (2007): 14.
35 Gina Harkins, "Illicit Drone Flights Surge along US–Mexico Border as Smugglers Hunt for Soft Spots," *Washington Post*, 24 June 2018, https://www.washingtonpost.com/world/national-security/illicit-drone-flights-surge-along-us-mexico-border-as-smugglers-hunt-for-soft-spots/2018/06/24/ea353d2a-70aa-11e8-bd50-b80389a4e569_story.html?noredirect=on&utm_term=.18f86a9570a6.
36 Francis Fukuyama, *The End of History and the Last Man* (New York: Free Press, 1992).
37 Mathias Alert and Lothar Brock, "Debordering the World of States: New Spaces in International Relations," *New Political Science* 18, no. 1 (December 1996): 61–105.
38 Samuel P. Huntington, *The Clash of Civilizations and the Remaking of World Order* (New York: Simon and Schuster, 1996).
39 Timothy J. Dunn, *Blockading the Border and Human Rights: The El Paso Operations That Remade Border Enforcement* (Austin: University of Texas Press, 2008).
40 Robert A. Pastor, *The Idea of North America: A Vision of a Continental Future* (Oxford: Oxford University Press, 2011).

4 Incumbent and Challenger Stakeholders in the San Diego–Tijuana Border Region: Economics and Migration

JORGE EDUARDO MENDOZA COTA

The border between the US and Mexico has seen important changes as a result of the economic and social interactions generated by contiguity. The new challenges posed by changes in economic relations between the two countries and the stronger enforcement of anti-migration policies have spurred the development of cross-border public, private, and not-for-profit organizations. Challenges have arisen as a result of the expansion of economic relations and the problems generated by the border's impact on migratory flows.

The San Diego–Tijuana border region has seen increased economic interaction as a result of the expansion of *maquiladora* activities. Also, the region's growing population and cross-border economic activities have generated infrastructure and governance challenges that need to be addressed by both governmental and private sector organizations.[1] In addition, the US government's practice of turning over deported migrants to the border cities of Mexico, without providing them with resources that would allow them to return to their regions of origin within Mexico, has created social problems that need to be attended to by the federal government. Since the end of 2018, Central American migrants have been crossing Mexico in caravans in the hope of entering the US as asylum-seekers, and this has led the US to tighten its grip on the border. The flow of deported migrants in the San Diego–Tijuana region has not been fully addressed by local and federal officials, given the lack of sufficient resources. Because of this, private stakeholders have emerged with the objective of helping migrants, both those crossing *to* the US and those being deported *from* the US.

This chapter analyses the growing interdependence among organizations that are contributing to the governance of the region's shared challenges and opportunities, as well as the different perspectives and goals of migrants' rights groups as they attempt to manage the problems arising from migration (i.e., anti-migration) policies at the border – in particular, the growing numbers of deported Mexican migrants. I will discuss those economic stakeholders that represent powerful economic interests in the region and that are seeking business opportunities at the binational level. These stakeholders can be viewed as *incumbents*, given their economic resources. I will also discuss those stakeholders that are dealing with the labour and social problems that deported migrants have imposed on the region. These types of stakeholders can be viewed as *challengers* in the sense that they have fewer financial resources for confronting the interests of incumbent organizations. Finally, I discuss the political struggle of those social and economic organizations that are trying to solve the multitude of problems that flow from transborder interactions. Those interactions take place between incumbent and challenger stakeholders and together define the San Diego–Tijuana border governance scheme. The following research has gathered information and analysed the visions, obstacles, and achievements of both types of stakeholders regarding the management of economic development and the organizations that support deported Mexican migrants.

Economics of the San Diego–Tijuana Border Region

The North American Free Trade Agreement (NAFTA), signed in 1994, reduced tariffs and opened investment opportunities for its member countries. This helped bring about a strong surge in economic relations between the US and Mexico. This economic integration has had strong economic repercussions at the border. As a consequence of the rapid growth of *maquiladoras*, Mexico's northern border has become a magnet for foreign direct investment (FDI).

San Diego and Tijuana have both been deeply affected by the economic integration of the US and Mexico. In 2010, the population of that region reached 4,654,996 (3,095,313 in San Diego and 1,559,683 in Tijuana).[2] San Diego has been attracting people for many years, whereas Baja California, in general, has a much lower population density. However, the state and the city of Tijuana have seen an increase in population since NAFTA came into effect in 1994. Finally, the population on the Mexican side of the border tends to be younger, and some of them cross the border to supplement the labour force in San Diego's service and construction sectors.

San Diego's economy is characterized by high productivity and technological development. Tijuana's is more low-tech, based on in-bond assembly manufacturing plants (*maquiladoras*), services, and tourism, and has a lower-skilled labour force. It is worth noting that San Diego County's GDP is considerably greater than Tijuana's (see appendix 1). Nevertheless, the two economies are closely linked and today comprise an important cross-border business region.

Baja California's per capita income is significantly lower than that of San Diego. Baja California has a strong concentration of *maquiladora* industries; the salaries these pay and the quality of the jobs are significantly lower than in San Diego. Commercial flows between the two are strong. Around 16 per cent

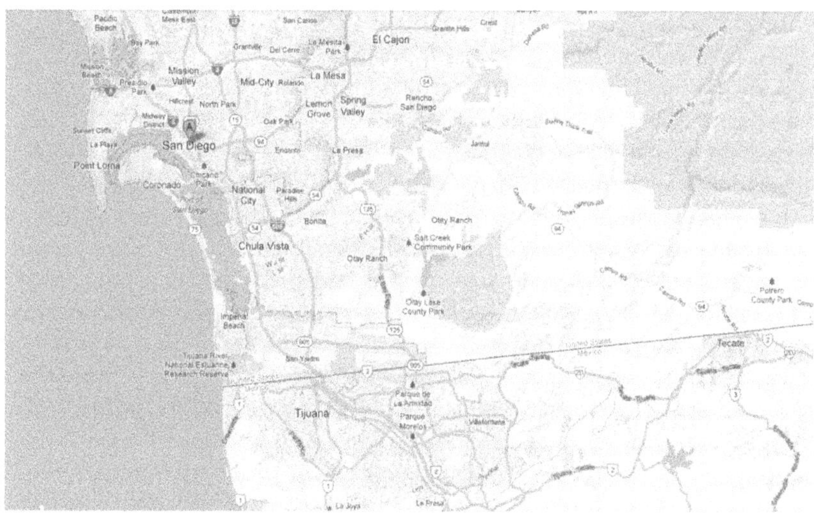

Map 4.1. San Diego–Tijuana Region

of US exports to Mexico come from California, and around 70 per cent of California's exports to Mexico pass through Baja California. This is highly relevant to the present study, for much of that trade crosses the border between San Diego and Tijuana.[3]

The Economic Profiles of San Diego and Tijuana

San Diego's economy is characterized by economic clusters, the most important of these being entertainment and tourism and the high-tech sector (communications, aerospace, biotech, and biomedical products). Large numbers of San Diegans work in business and finance, sales, education, health care, and administration.[4] The city's economy is quite diversified, and there are other significant economic activities besides these, such as publishing and marketing, clean technology, and horticulture.

Defence contracts to San Diego firms have encouraged growth in high-innovation sectors such as aerospace, software, communications, and electronics. Also, the city's universities and research institutes have generated local biotech, biomedical, and pharmaceutical industries. All of these have shaped San Diego's economy and will continue to do so.[5] Other factors that have positively impacted the city's competitiveness are its business-friendly tax structure and its supply of both highly skilled and less skilled labour.[6]

San Diego is an important exporting city; it represented 12.2 per cent of California's total exports in the same year. Its main exports are high-tech goods such as electronic equipment, computers, and transportation equipment.[7] The main importer of San Diego's manufactured goods is Mexico, followed by Canada. Both economies are members of NAFTA.

Tijuana is an important manufacturing centre, as reflected in its GDP. This manufacturing boom is directly related to the expansion of *maquiladora* activities in Baja California: inputs are shipped in bond to the *maquiladoras* from the US, assembled in Mexico, then re-exported back to the US. Clearly, Tijuana has important economic interactions with California and particularly with San Diego.

The rapid growth of the *maquiladoras* has had a strong impact on other economic sectors, for it has generated additional income in the border cities and thereby increased trade and service activities in the border region.[8] The most important manufacturing activities in Tijuana involve electronics, computers, and communication equipment; it is these that provide the most jobs. Other important manufacturing activities – and job generators – are electrical components, power generating equipment, and furniture making. Tijuana also has a well-developed service and wholesale/retail economy.[9] The proximity of California's stronger economy has helped foster Baja California's tourism and service sectors.

Restrictive Migration Policies and Mexican Deported Migrants

Tijuana is a magnet for Mexican migrants, who come there hoping either to cross the border or to stay there and find work in a *maquiladora*. As a result, the city has experienced strong pressures in the labour market and a growing demand for social and public services as well as infrastructural development. Adding to this pressure has been the US policy of deporting undocumented migrants, especially in recent years. This has increased the numbers of unemployed, underemployed, and informally employed.

In response to the massive flow of Mexican migrants, the US government has developed various strategies for containing Mexican migrants and reducing their numbers in the US. Orrenius has identified three phases of that enforcement.[10] Initially, in the late 1970s, it involved increased funding for equipment and technology. A second phase was related to drastic changes in immigration and border enforcement policies, which led to increased funding to expand the Border Patrol as well as to the strengthening of penalties for illegal migrants. The third phase, which started in 1993, aimed to shift migration flows from urban to less populated areas; this strategy led to Operation Hold the Line in El Paso, Operation Gatekeeper in San Diego, and Operation Safeguard in Nogales, Arizona.[11]

During the 2010s, as a response to the increasing flows of Mexican migrants, the Obama and Trump administrations developed a phase-four migration strategy.[12] This one seeks to increase the number of individuals removed from the US on the basis of various criminal offences, both minor and serious. Also, non-citizens arriving in the US, including permanent residents, can be detained if they are considered inadmissible. As a result, between 2005 and 2010 there were fewer apprehensions of Mexican migrants at the border, but there was also a rapid increase in deportations of undocumented Mexican migrants based on criminal violations.[13] Also, today there are many more "voluntary returns" to Mexico of undocumented migrants after they have been apprehended. It is considered a voluntary return when a migrant is returned to Mexico on deportable grounds.[14] As a result of the intensification of border enforcement and deportations, the circularity of Mexican migration has decreased for undocumented migrants.[15]

Deported Migrants at the Tijuana Border

As a result of stringent migration policies, removals and deportations of workers to Mexican border cities have increased. According to the Encuesta sobre Migración en la Frontera (EMIF), in 2009,[16] the number of deported migrants to the most important Mexican border cities was 552,726. After that year a decrease was observed, down to just 214,794 in 2014. The percentage of male deported migrants was was 82 per cent in 2009, increasing to 86.7 per cent in 2014.[17]

Regarding the level of schooling of the deported migrants, in 2014 around 40 per cent only had elementary schooling. Also, between 2009 and 2014 the percentage of migrants with secondary schooling decreased from 37.8 to 31.1 per cent (see appendix 2). Thus, the level of schooling of the deported migrants to the border cities of Mexico is very low and continues to decrease.

The deportation statistics for 2014 of Mexican migrants sent to the border cities of Mexico indicate that in the case of Tijuana, 57.8 per cent indicated that they had been deported without a proper trial (see appendix 3). Clearly, in addition to removals based on criminal and administrative grounds, large numbers of deported migrants were being sent back to Mexico as returnees or inadmissible migrants or considered deportable aliens by the US.

In 2014, 23.8 per cent of deported migrants interviewed in the EMIF indicated that they were not employed in Mexico and would probably be returning to the US (see appendix 4). In Tijuana, 41.7 per cent of deported migrants interviewed considered that they had enough skills to get employment in the city's labour market, while 25 per cent had partial or limited labour skills, which would reduce their chances of finding work.

Clearly, the low levels of schooling and low labour skills of the migrants deported to Tijuana have placed pressure on Mexican institutions and on the absorption capacity of the local labour market. Consequently, Mexican consulates have had to provide assistance to deported migrants, who are given help to communicate with their families in Mexico, as well as legal advice (see appendix 4). Most migrants, though, have not communicated with the Mexican consular authorities in the US and have not received any help. Also, many did not receive any help even when they did communicate with the consulate. And many found that economic assistance to return to their places of origin was very limited.

With respect to the desire of deported Mexican migrants to return to their places of origin, note that a large percentage of the migrants interviewed in the principal Mexican border cities stated that if financial support were available, they would be willing to go back. However, a higher percentage of those in Tijuana declared that they would prefer to stay there (see appendix 5). So the city faces increasing pressure to absorb additional workers into its labour market and to increase the public services demanded by Tijuana's growing population.

As mentioned earlier, the growing number of deportations by the US government has created an inflow of Mexican migrants returning from the US. Those deported migrants have exacerbated the social and economic problems at the border. Because of the increasing difficulties of crossing the border to work in the US, deported Mexican migrants are less likely to want to return there. As a result, labour, social, and health pressures have increased in Mexico's border cities.

More and more deported migrants end up on the streets and can find no support from not-for-profit organizations; many have been staying in the Tijuana River channel, known as "El Bordo." Because they lack financial resources and legal ID, most of the migrants deported to Tijuana are unable to work in the formal sector. So to earn money, they work informally as car washers, bricklayers, hawkers, and so on.[18] We can conclude that deported migrants in Tijuana have expanded the city's informal labour market and also have deepened social problems such as crime and drug addiction.

Since 2018, a new migratory trend has developed: the formation of caravans from Central America crossing Mexico to reach the US. These migrant caravans are made up of people from Guatemala, El Salvador, and Honduras, who are crossing Mexico in order to seek asylum in the US. As a result of this trend, the Trump administration made significant changes in US migration policy, based on the idea that immigration posed a security threat. Under the new migrant protection protocols (MPPs), asylum-seekers arriving at the US border have had to return to Mexico pending asylum proceedings. Also, a metering policy has been established, which applies to migrants who have not yet been inspected and who thus have to remain in Mexico. These new policies have brought new problems to Mexico's northern border cities, for they must somehow cope with growing numbers of Central American migrants on their side of the border.

Power Struggle and Predominance in Stakeholders of the San Diego–Tijuana Border

Actors in the San Diego–Tijuana Border Region

The social and political power struggle within the border region can be analysed by applying the theory of strategic action fields (SAFs) developed by Fligstein and McAdam, which they describe as "an integrated theory that explains how stability and change are achieved by social actors in circumscribed social arenas."[19] Both economic and migration support organizations work within a strategic action field. In the San Diego–Tijuana SAF, economic and social issues are fundamental to cross-border governance. The problems in the border region impose different challenges that determine the ways in which different groups of actors from Mexico and the US try to enforce their objectives and defend their interests.

By applying the theoretical perspective of SAFs, it is possible to describe how different organizations interact in a social environment. Using a typology derived from this theoretical approach, we can analyse the power struggles and regulations faced by the stakeholders.[20] The various organizations at the border include stakeholders, social movements, and government institutions based on mutual interests.

Using this approach, we can divide the stakeholders into two main categories. First, there are the *incumbents*, that is, organizations with significant influence and economic, social, and political power, whose objectives are considered dominant. For the purpose of this study, both government institutions and economic organizations would be considered incumbent, given their strong impact and resources in the region. Second, there are the *challengers*, which have fewer resources and have a smaller impact and less influence. These stakeholders often have alternative views and objectives with respect to the dominant group. In this analysis of the San Diego–Tijuana region, the migrant support organizations are considered *challengers*.

Methodological Aspects

This study aims to understand the social movements that are emerging along the US–Mexico border. Semi-structured interviews were conducted to obtain information for the analysis of the economic factors that are determining the expansion of both economic and migrant support organizations at the border. Their struggles and accomplishments were then compared and contrasted. Using the information from the interviews, a database was constructed to study the economic and migration activities developing at the border. The interviews followed a pattern of questions based on theoretical and empirical findings regarding economic integration and cross-border organizations and the social impact of migration on Tijuana. The interviews consisted of a set of questions structured around the following themes: personal experience, organizational objectives, achievements of the organization, obstacles to managing border governance and cooperation, identification of main actors, proposals to improve cross-border economic cooperation and governance, reflections on the border, and opinions on NAFTA and its impact on the economy of the border region.

Visions and Achievements of the Economic and Migrant Support Stakeholders

Economic Organizations in the San Diego–Tijuana Border Region

To understand how the economic forces of integration in the border region have encouraged and influenced the development of business and economic stakeholders, eleven business and governmental organizations were interviewed. The six business organizations were the Smart Border Coalition, the Mexico Business Center of the San Diego Regional Chamber of Commerce, the Economic Development Council of Tijuana (Consejo de Desarrollo Económico de Tijuana; CDT), the San Ysidro Chamber of Commerce, and Economic and Industrial Development of Tijuana DEITAC-EDC (see appendix 6). In general terms, these are not-for-profit organizations financed by state and municipal governments as well as the private sector. They also do project planning and implementation for urban development to support economic and social growth. Two of the six organizations are based in Tijuana, two in San Diego, and two are binational.

The US stakeholders are networking groups; they also run public awareness campaigns and community promotions that generate opportunities to participate in activities and discussions. These focus on cross-border commerce, international presence, and economic opportunities to support the economic and social growth of their members. On the Mexican side, the stakeholders' activities include planning and implementing urban development and linking actors and economic interests between California and Baja California. In particular, the CDT promotes infrastructure, education, the environment, industry and services, and infrastructure development.

It is important to underscore the importance of the Smart Border Coalition. This binational organization describes itself as a cross-border facilitator and coordinator. Its members come from enterprises such as SIMNSA Health Care, Kiocera, Sempra, RA Capitol Advisors, Calimax supermarkets, Grupo ATISA, and Solar Turbines Caterpillar. It also counts as members public figures such as the mayors of Tijuana and San Diego and the Mexican and US consuls. Its stated objectives are to bring together leading academic, business, and civic communities from both sides of the San Diego–Tijuana international region to develop policy positions, deliver special events and programs, and encourage growth of the cross-border economy.

With respect to governmental organizations that promote economic development, the following three are the most important: the San Diego Association of Governments (SANDAG), Binational Affairs of Baja California State, and Binational Affairs of Tijuana City Hall. They all promote economic development in the border region. On the US side, the organizations that stand out are San Diego's City Hall and the Regional Planning Agency of SANDAG. The latter, on which nineteen city and county governments are represented, has a program to promote economic development along the border. It has a Borders Committee that provides oversight for planning activities that impact the San Diego region on both sides of the border. It coordinates the planning and delivery of transportation projects to move people, goods, and services more efficiently between the US and Mexico.

Other stakeholders interviewed were the San Ysidro Chamber of Commerce and the Mexico Business Center. The former was created to support the economic and social growth of its members through networking, public awareness, and community promotions. On the Tijuana side, one prominent organization is the Office of Binational Affairs of Baja California State, which links actors and interests between California and Baja California with regard to economic, social, political, cultural, and academic issues. Another important organization is the Tijuana Economic Development Corporation (DEITAC), which helps foreign and Mexican companies to plan business ventures in Mexico and to find partners who are willing to do business on the Mexican side. Additionally, Mexican companies can find help promoting their products internationally through a Directory Classified Listing and a Web page.

US–Mexican Business Synchronization and the Emergence of Economic Organizations

After the NAFTA agreement was signed in 1994, cross-border economic synchronization greatly intensified at the regional level. NAFTA boosted FDI and trade, deepening the already existing economic ties between San Diego and Tijuana. That agreement was a strong external shock to the region, one that encouraged the formation of economic organizations along the border.

Some economic development organizations view the border as a "mega-region," in contrast to the national governments of the US and Mexico. The US government's concept of borders is rooted in national security criteria, which increases the obstacles for border crossings, which works against the vision of an economically integrated border region that local actors have encouraged.

For stakeholders who support cross-border business and economic activities, NAFTA has encouraged cross-border trade in the region, especially for companies that have operations on both sides. According to one Mexican business organization, "when NAFTA was signed, the border industries were primarily *maquiladoras*; however, over time, some of them have been transformed into second and third generation manufacturing plants."[21]

However, when it comes to cross-border cooperation related to social, cultural, and environmental issues, parallel agreements and the Committee on the Cooperation of North America that were created to counteract the harmful effects of NAFTA on communities and the environment have not functioned properly. These agreements and commissions lack sufficient resources, and their recommendations have drawn little response from the federal government.

Organizational Capacities

A private organization typically has a board of directors and a council and follows a strategic commerce and business plan. Binational organizations include both US and Mexican senior business members of companies that have plants on both sides of the border. In most cases, there is also a working committee that includes stakeholders and government officials from both sides of the border.

The CDT's general assembly is presided over by the municipal president (i.e., mayor) of Tijuana, and its secretary is that city's Secretary of Economic Development. The government of Tijuana is of great importance to CDT because, even though it is not an official institution, it receives funding from the local government to manage various projects such as the new border crossing for pedestrians and automobiles, "El Chaparral."

A cross-border organization's impact is related to how well it is funded by local governments on both sides of the border. In the Tijuana–San Diego region, these resources are used to promote infrastructure projects such as the Otay 2 port of entry (Mexico Business Center) as well as economic sectors such as medical appliances and aerospace manufacturing (DEITAC). Organizations on both sides of the border are looking to improve the economic infrastructure to allow more trade, investment, and pedestrian flows between the two urban areas. They also encourage economic activities that take advantage of the geographical proximity and low wages provided by the city of Tijuana and the capital and technology provided by the economy of San Diego.

Economic Organizations in the Border Region: Their Achievements

The stakeholders have achieved a great deal in the economic field. With respect to infrastructure projects, El Chaparral, the new port of entry in San Ysidro, has been built, and a second port of entry in Otay is being promoted at the local binational level. Also, various international events have been held, such as Tijuana Innovadora, to promote alliances that would benefit residents of both sides of the border.

A second important example of business cooperation is the Cross Border Xpress (CBX), the international bridge that now connects Tijuana's airport to the US. With support from the Smart Border Coalition, and funding from both sides of the border, the CBX was completed in 2015, in collaboration with the Grupo Aeroportuario del Pacifico, which is the enterprise that manages the Tijuana airport. This project has strengthened economic interaction between San Diego and Tijuana by expanding the number of flights to and from both cities. The facilities include areas for passengers and guests, retail, food, and beverages, and short- and long-term parking, as well as an office of US Customs and Border Patrol.

In terms of legislative achievements, Senate Bill Initiative 12228 was sponsored by local stakeholders with the goal of obtaining funding for border infrastructure to support businesses in the area. Also, various agreements have been signed to encourage collaboration among the region's Chambers of Commerce. Key to cross-border management is binational cooperation to develop infrastructure. US, Mexican, and binational organizations Joint have lobbied jointly in San Diego and Tijuana (CDT) and at the federal level for a railway between San Diego and Tijuana.

Major projects in the border region have served largely to encourage new investment in Tijuana and coordinate infrastructure development so as to take advantage of lower costs derived from proximity to the US market and the relatively low wages paid in Tijuana. Strong efforts have been made especially in the electronics, energy, automotive, and aerospace sectors.

Challenges and Obstacles to Managing Cross-Border Economic Cooperation

To the degree that the US and Mexican economies are synchronized, economic recessions in the US can have a powerful impact on economic activities directly linked to Mexico, such as foreign direct investment, export manufacturing, and trade. The 2008–9 recession in the US was highly destabilizing to the Tijuana–San Diego region, for it sharply reduced economic activity there, which slowed down the consolidation of economic organizations.

In this context, stakeholders pointed out that an additional obstacle for economic organizations has been the lack of monitoring agreements, projects, and programs due to changes in local and federal governments. Negotiations related to the border are conducted in Washington, DC, and Mexico City, and government agencies in those capitals lack knowledge about local border issues and problems. At the same time, local actors lack influence and have no decision-making power, because the border is a federal domain, one that on the US side is closely linked to issues of national security. A particularly fraught issue is that long delays at border crossings increase costs to businesses. As a member of the Economic Development Council of Tijuana noted, "I cross the border every day; some days I stay in Tijuana and other days in San Diego. Because of my business I cross the border almost every day. Therefore, one of the main obstacles for my work is the border. There is a border crossing that creates problems for planning the right time to move between the two cities."

Other obstacles were mentioned by the stakeholders: perceptions that the Mexican side of the border was a violent place; "warnings" for Americans not to travel to Baja California; the different languages; and the lack of knowledge of cultural practices on both sides of the border.

Some stakeholders acknowledged that two cultures and thinking systems both meet and diverge at the border. Also, it is a highly unequal place in economic terms. Finally, the border region shares an ecosystem, and because of the intense economic activity in the *maquiladora* industry, cross-border cooperation is vital in order to address issues arising from industrial pollution. That cooperation can be hard to achieve.

Proposals to Improve Border Cooperation

The US stakeholders averred that it would be very useful to have a representative in Mexico, to support US firms in promoting economic growth on the Mexican side of the border. They considered it important to increase business activity on both sides to improve the region's economy as a whole. Another significant economic and governance issue was finding ways to make border crossings more efficient. One way would be to increase the number of rapid access entry ports, such as SENTRI and Ready Lane. Also, driver's licences with radio frequency chips could be developed, as had been done in Canada.

On the Mexican side, stakeholders posited that Mexican public officials needed to develop a "border mentality"; to that end, Tijuana's mayor should create a Borders Public Office. The two local governments needed to reach agreements that would allow people to cross the border more quickly and easily. Also, a student exchange program would be worthwhile. Mexican universities sometimes send students to attend classes at universities in the US; to a lesser extent, US students attend Mexican schools.

Stakeholders representing economic associations suggested that entrepreneurial cooperation could be fostered by developing more integrated enterprises, an example being CareFusion, a firm with a corporate office in San Diego and a manufacturing plant in Tijuana. Another proposal related to economic development in the border region was for a "migration fund" to support returned migrants. Its financial resources would cover the costs of providing shelter and helping migrants to return to their regions of origin in Mexico. It could be funded by both the local and federal governments.

In summary, proposals for stronger economic cooperation in the region focus on addressing the problem of slow border crossings in order to speed up flows of capital, commodities, and labour. Also, strategic projects should be developed to improve economic conditions so as to encourage business activities. Strong cross-border cooperation is closely associated with the cooperation and synchronization of local and federal public agents and private organizations and businesses.

Cross-Border Governance and Migrant Support Organizations in Tijuana

Regarding migrant issues, interviews were conducted with seven organizations that focus on supporting migrants arriving in Tijuana. Four are Mexican, three are binational. The Mexican organizations are the Consejo Estatal de Atención al Migrante (State council of Migrant Attention), the Consulate General of México in San Diego, Veteranos Deportados (Deported Veterans), and the Mexican Ministry of Foreign Affairs. The binational organizations are Angeles de la Frontera (Border Angels), Coalicion Humanitaria Pro-Migrante (Pro-Migrant Humanitarian Coalition), and the Binational Front of Indigenous Organizations. Five of these organizations are directly related to human rights and migration activities, and two are governmental organizations that give some attention to problems generated by migration in the Tijuana region (see appendix 7).

These organizations focus mainly on programs that return migrants to their place of origin and that provide temporary accommodation for those who choose to remain in the city, with an emphasis on migrants concentrated in the neighbourhood known as El Bordo, on the Tijuana River. They have also established screening programs that channel migrants with criminal and/or health problems such as mental illness and addiction (Consejo Estatal del Migrante). Additionally, organizations like Border Angels focus on preventing the deaths of migrants in the Imperial Valley desert and mountains and areas close to the US–Mexico border.

Some organizations support veterans who have been deported to Mexico, providing them with shelter and food (Veteranos Deportados); some defend the rights of migrants in transit from Central America to Chicago, encouraging communities to address the social causes of immigration and violence.

Finally, one of the organizations interviewed deals with Indigenous migrants from Oaxaca living in California and Baja California.

Achievements and Challenges of Pro-Migrant Organizations

The organizations helping migrants and deported migrants have limited resources and depend on government funding and public donations to run their operations. They have had some important successes. Angeles de la Frontera initially focused on helping migrants living in Tijuana's ravines. After a surge of deaths of undocumented migrants in the desert, it began sending members to the desert to set up "watering stations" for migrants. Presently, its main efforts involve providing water along the border from San Diego to Brownsville and delivering food and clothing. It also offers legal advice and holds conferences about the hardships migrants face. It played an important role in organizing protests against US immigration policy held in March 2006 in Los Angeles, Chicago, and Dallas. It had also raised people's awareness of the plight of deported migrants living in El Bordo.

The Consejo Estatal de Atención al Migrante, founded in the 1990s as an immigrant support group, especially for migrants living in El Bordo. It runs programs to return migrants to their places of origin and provides temporary accommodation for those who are not returning to their places of origin. It has screening programs for migrants with criminal and health problems and helps them find shelter. It has forged links with the secretaries of Public Security, Public Health, State, and Integrated Family Development as well as to the Municipal Councils.

One goal of the council is to convince the federal authorities to craft a special law for Mexican migrants in transit, which could be done without affecting the laws that protect foreigners in the country. Another is to convince them to develop municipal and/or state registers of migrants at Tijuana and Mexicali. Still another is to develop spaces where the demand for workers can be linked to migrants able to work – for example, at call centres, where bilingual skills are very useful. In 2014, such call centres employed around 250 migrants. Finally, the council provides migrants will financial help to return to their places of origin in Mexico.

An important stakeholder in this field is the Coalicion Humanitaria Internacional Pro-Migrante. This is actually a network of organizations, including Casa del Migrante and Angeles de la Frontera, and it has expanded exponentially in the past six years. It provides food and shelter for migrants. It takes in donations in food, and sometimes money, especially from the US. It has developed a portal called Por-capacidades, a tool for fostering civil society organizations around themes such as leadership, fiscal issues, and funding. It is trying to strengthen its contacts with the public and academic sectors in order to make its goals and achievements known. It has implemented training workshops for leaders in the border region; as of 2014, around 7,000 leaders had participated in these. It has provided $150,000 in technical assistance to affiliated organizations in the network in order to improve administration and strategic planning.

Another successful organization is Veteranos Deportados. This one provides shelter to deported veteran migrants who are homeless in Tijuana. Initially, the shelter provided three weeks; later, one week. Deported homeless who are addicts are required to go into treatment so as not to affect others. The organization provides three meals a day and helps deported migrants find work, arrange ID cards, and contact their families by email.

This organization receives important support from veterans in other countries. There are volunteers for legal and health issues, as well as a psychologist who works with deported mothers. It is trying to learn how to better manage fundraising and utilize social media.

Challenges Faced by the Organizations

During the Obama administration, the US deported large numbers of migrants. That trend intensified under the Trump administration. The economic recession in the US between 2008 and 2013 limited employment opportunities for Mexican migrants; however, the recent economic recovery in the US has reduced the pressure to continue boosting deportations. According to some of the organizations interviewed, most businesses are using Mexican migrants solely as cheap labour. Also, from the human rights perspective, Mexican migrants suffer mistreatment both while they are working in the US and when they are deported back to Mexico.

A major challenge faced by organizations on the Tijuana–San Diego border has to do with the region's physical distance from the federal authorities, in both the US and Mexico. The federal governments have not paid enough attention to their border cities and have provided them with insufficient resources to cope with the problems they are facing. As a result, the stakeholders lack the personnel to attend to the problems facing deported migrants. One official with El Consejo Estatal del Migrante, a public organization, clarified the problem of limited resources for supporting the returned migrants: "The Federal Government only provides 200 million pesos for supporting migrants in the whole country. In 2013, Baja California received less than 6 million pesos, which is not nearly enough to cover the aid and assistance to returned migrants."

A lack of resources has made coordination between organizations more difficult. Some of them said they needed to be classified as non-governmental associations; this would increase the financial support they receive and enable them to conduct lobbying. In particular, poor communication between organizations supporting migrants and incumbent organizations has made it harder for the former to garner more financial resources from the private sector. Finally, some organizations pointed to the poisoned environment they have to face, especially the negative attitude of US Border Patrol officers, who were at times very aggressive.

Conclusions

Increasing economic integration between the US and Mexico has affected economic and social relations in the border region. Because of the size of California's economy and its expanding economic interactions with Baja California, the San Diego–Tijuana border is now one of the most important regions with cross-border economic relations.

Synchronization of the two border cities' economies has propelled the creation of business organizations. Economic organizations have emerged in both cities, and some of these were founded specifically as binational groups. Their presence today meets the need for cooperation in economic areas and infrastructure projects that will contribute to development on both sides of the border. The members of these organizations are public officials and entrepreneurs; thus, they are viewed as having more control and political power in the San Diego–Tijuana border region. In that region there are now strong asymmetries at the economic, political, and cultural levels. The border has become a porous place with intense flows of workers, investments, and trade. Increasing business activity has blurred the border from an economic perspective.

The *incumbent* organizations have been organized largely by business executives whose companies have a presence on both sides of the border, in addition to government officials from both sides. The regional impact of these organizations is a function of their members' business management skills. Their main achievements have been in infrastructure development, which has boosted trade and investment and smoothed the flow of people across the border. The US–Mexico–Canada Agreement (USMCA) may create opportunities to increase investment, and stronger global supply chains for the three countries may encourage further integration of the US–Mexico border region.

The main achievements of cross-border economic cooperation have been thanks to local private organizations. The prospects for further local economic development depend greatly on whether the two federal governments increase their involvement in regional organizations and encourage their growth. Local institutions will need to lobby for these things.

The emergence and expansion of migrant support organizations has been a response to the increasing flows of deported Mexican migrants. The Obama and Trump administrations encouraged a migration strategy that entailed sending migrants back to Mexico if they had committed crimes, however minor. On top of that, non-citizens entering the US, even if they were permanent residents there, could be detained almost at the whim of the border authorities. Mexican migrants were generally transported to Mexico's border cities. Those cities have been greatly affected by this flow of deportees as well as by the presence of prospective migrants who hope to cross the border in the other direction. Their sheer numbers have generated labour, health, and crime problems.

Organizations, both public and private, have been founded to protect migrants' human rights and draw attention to problems generated by migration in the Tijuana region. These groups help migrants return to their places of origin, provide temporary accommodation, and screen and channel migrants with criminal and/or health problems. They also work to prevent the deaths of migrants in the rugged terrain of the Imperial Valley.

Among their main achievements has been the fostering of awareness in the Latino population, which provided important support for the Latino demonstrations in Los Angeles, Chicago, and Dallas that protested US immigration policy. Also, these organizations have supported deported migrants living in El Bordo along the Tijuana–San Diego border. Other important achievements have been the provision of temporary accommodation for deported migrants who are not returning to their places of origin, the development of a municipal and/or state register for migrants at the border cities of Tijuana and Mexicali, and the creation of spaces where the demand for workers can be linked to migrants who are able to work (for example, at call centres). Also, some organizations have provided meals and helped deported migrants find work, obtain ID cards, and contact their families.

The cooperation between economic and migrant support organizations is uneven. Economic stakeholders wield political influence; by contrast, migrant support organizations lack resources as well as the ear of the federal authorities in both the US and Mexico. The federal governments and the border cities have not paid enough attention or provided enough resources to the latter groups. Clearly, migrant support organizations are *challengers* in this particular border region.

Central American caravans journeying to the US are another problem. The US and Mexican governments have not coordinated their response to this problem, nor have the authorities in San Diego and Tijuana. Overall, there is a lack of ongoing formal links between NGOs and government institutions, and this has resulted in incoherent governance of migration flows. Organizations supporting migrants need to improve their own coordination if they are to strengthen their impact on the problem of migrants who linger in Tijuana.

The SAF theoretical approach was very useful tool for analysing the power struggles between the various stakeholders in this border region, as well as for examining the role of governmental institutions and their interactions with incumbents and challengers.

Appendix 1: Economic indicators of the region San Diego–Tijuana, 2016

	San Diego	Baja California	Tijuana	San Diego–Tijuana
GDP million $ (2018)	219,361,505	28,797	12,959	219,374,464
Labour force employed (2018)	1,463,420	1,034,332	735,920	2,199,340
Unemployment rate (2019)	2.9%	2.2%		

Source: Bureau of Labor, Databases, Tables and Calculators by Subject, accessed July 22,2020 and National Survey of Occupation and Employment (ENOE), Economic Information Bank, INEGI.

Appendix 2: Level of schooling of deported migrants in Tijuana (%)

Year	2009	2010	2011	2012	2013	2014
No schooling	5.9	2.3	3.2	1.7	2.0	2.6
Primary	37.8	27.0	39.0	36.9	42.1	38.3
Secondary	35.9	48.8	37.7	39.8	34.0	31.1
Preparatory	17.2	17.2	11.9	12.0	12.9	12.3
Primary and technical school	0.2	0.1	0.1	0.0	0.1	
Secondary and technical school	0.5	1.2	0.2	0.1	1.4	0.2
Professional	2.3	1.2	1.7	1.5	2.9	3.4
Elementary		0.1	0.1	0.2	0.0	0.5
High school		1.9	5.0	6.1	4.3	9.5
College		0.2	0.9	1.6	0.2	1.6
Total	156,286	119,233	78,899	59,845	46,873	29,998

Source: Own elaboration with data from EMIF databases for 2099–14. 1. Matamoros, Nuevo Laredo, Piedras Negras, Ciudad Juárez, Nogales Mexicali y Tijuana.

Appendix 3: Migrants with deportation trial (2014)

Region	Live in Mexico or USA[1]	Yes	No	Does not know	No response	Not specified	Total
Matamoros	19,567	4,597	23,079		1,272	–	48,643
Nuevo Laredo	8,766	4,546	17,289	–	89	–	30,690
Piedras Negras	2,977	5,968	18,507	–	3,005	–	30,481
Ciudad Juárez	1,542	2,462	4,476	–	101	–	8,581
Nogales	4,836	1,231	17,031	–	14	–	23,112
Mexicali	5,488	3,178	32,152	–	2,246	–	43,284

Region	Live in Mexico or USA[1]	Yes	No	Does not know	No response	Not specified	Total
Tijuana	16,294	1,807	11,534	41	296	28	30,000
Total	59,470	3,789	124,068	41	7,023	28	214,791

Source: Own elaboration with data from EMIF databases for 2009–2014. 1. Matamoros, Nuevo Laredo, Piedras Negras, Ciudad Juárez, Nogales Mexicali y Tijuana. 1. Living more than one year

Appendix 4: Type of support and help received by deported migrants from the Mexican Consulate

Region	Mata-moros	Nuevo Laredo	Piedras Negras	Ciudad Juárez	Nogales	Mexicali	Tijuana	Total
Migrant did not use his right to communicate with the Mexican Consulate	14,795	5,512	1,994	1,321	4,460	4,713	10,862	43,657
Economic help	486	–	43	–	–	203	33	765
Non-used airplane ticket refund	233	–	–	–	–	–	68	301
Belongings recovery	78	89	–	–	–	29	28	224
Communication with other family members	568	2,977	122	115	289	348	4,240	8,659
Legal consultation	1,355	89	195	107	39	–	331	2,116
None	1,201	98	247	–	49	29	564	2,188
Other	34	–	21	–	–	–	62	117
Does not know	76	–	–	–	–	–	–	76
No response	741	–	356	–	–	167	106	1,370
Total	19,567	8,765	2,978	1,543	4,837	5,489	16,294	59,473

Source: Own elaboration with data from EMIF, database 2014. 1. Matamoros, Nuevo Laredo, Piedras Negras, Ciudad Juárez, Nogales Mexicali y Tijuana.

Appendix 5: Percentage of migrants who are willing to return to their place of origin

	Mata-moros	Nuevo Laredo	Piedras Negras	Ciudad Juárez	Nogales	Mexicali	Tijuana	
Lives in Mexico and stayed at least one year in the USA	59.67	71.44	90.23	82.03	79.08	87.26	45.69	72.27
Yes	29.24	25.11	6.85	12.61	14.56	5.68	23.92	17.74
No	7.87	3.45	1.04	5.36	6.36	6.67	28.84	8.70
Does not know	0.38	0.00	0.11	0.00	0.00	0.00	0.60	0.19
No response	2.84	0.00	1.77	0.00	0.00	0.39	0.95	1.11
	48,515	30,690	30,457	8,581	23,112	43,063	30,001	214,419

Source: Own elaboration with data from EMIF, database 2014. 1. Matamoros, Nuevo Laredo, Piedras Negras, Ciudad Juárez, Nogales Mexicali y Tijuana.

Appendix 6: San Diego–Tijuana border stakeholders interviewed

Stakeholders interviewed	Description	Area	Sector	Origin
1. Smart Border Coalition	Catalyst to bring together leading academic, business and civic communities from both sides of the San Diego / Tijuana International region to develop databases and special events and programs for promoting growth of the cross-border economy.	Business	Private	Binational
2. San Diego Association of Governments, SANDAG	Regional Planning Agency. Association of 18 cities and county governments of the San Diego region.	Government	Public	American
3. Economic Development Council of Tijuana (Consejo de Desarrollo Económico de Tijuana) CDT	Non-profit organization financed by state and municipal governments, and the private sector. Project planning and implementation for city development.	Business	Public & private	Mexican

Stakeholders interviewed	Description	Area	Sector	Origin
4. Economic and Industrial Development of Tijuana DEITAC-EDC	Non-profit organization formed by Mexican and American companies that provide information services for the business sector.	Business	Private	Binational
5. Mexico Business Center of San Diego Regional Chamber of Commerce	Offers businesses activities and discussions that focus on cross-border commerce, international presence, and economic opportunities.	Business	Private	American
6. San Ysidro Chamber of Commerce	Created to support the economic and social growth of its members through networking, public awareness, and community promotions.	Business	Private	American
7. Binational Affairs, City Hall Tijuana	Municipal City Hall of Tijuana	Government	Public	Mexican
8. Consulate General of Mexico in San Diego	The Mexican diplomatic representation or consular post in San Diego	Government	Public	Mexican
9. Binational Affairs, City of San Diego	Municipal City Hall of San Diego	Government	Public	American
10. Mexican Ministry of Foreign Affairs	To broaden and deepen Mexico's political, economic, cultural, and cooperative relationships with all regions	Government	Public	Mexican
11. Binational Affairs, Baja California State	This area belongs to the Baja California state government and links actors and interests between California and Baja California in economic, social, political, cultural, and academic issues.	Government	Public	Mexican

Source: Author elaboration.

Appendix 7: Characteristics of stakeholders

Stakeholders interviewed	Description	Area	Sector	Origin
Consulate General of Mexico in San Diego	The Mexican diplomatic representation or consular post in San Diego.	Government	Public	Mexican
Ángeles de la Frontera	Border Angels is a non-profit organization supporting humanity. The organization consists of volunteers who want to stop unnecessary deaths of individuals travelling through the Imperial Valley desert areas and the mountain areas surrounding San Diego County, as well as the areas located around the United States and Mexican border.	Human rights & migration	Private	Binational
Consejo Estatal de Atención al Migrante	Public organization created to solve and manage issues related to a program to return to their place of origin; program temporary accommodation for those who choose to remain in the state in decent facilities, with emphasis on migrants concentrated in the area known as "El Bordo" on the Tijuana River; Screening program and channelling of migrants with criminal and/or health problems (mental illness and addictions); Strengthen and assist with migrant shelters and Respect and promotion of human rights of migrants.	Human rights & migration	Public	Mexican
Coalición Humanitaria Pro-Migrante	The coalition brings together organizations that seek to defend the rights of migrants in transit from Central America to Chicago in the United States. Encourage all community to address the social causes of immigration and violence.	Human rights & migration	Private	Binational

Stakeholders interviewed	Description	Area	Sector	Origin
Mexican Ministry of Foreign Affairs (Secretaría de Relaciones Exteriores, SER)	To broaden and deepen Mexico's political, economic, cultural, and cooperative relationships with all regions for the benefit of comprehensive development of all Mexicans.	Government	Public	Mexican
Veteranos deportados	Organization supporting veterans who have been deported to Mexico, provides shelter and food for migrants deported.	Human rights & migration	Private	Mexican
Binational Front of Indigenous Organizations	FIOB is a community-based organization and a coalition of Indigenous organizations, communities, and individuals settled in Oaxaca, Baja California, and the State of California in the United States. Founded on 5 October 1991 in Los Angeles, California.	Human rights & migration	Private	Binational

Source: Own elaboration with information from stakeholder interviews.

NOTES

1 Jorge Eduardo Mendoza and Bruno Dupeyron, "Economic Integration, Emerging Fields and Cross-Border Governance: The Case of San Diego–Tijuana," *Journal of Borderlands Studies* 35, no. 2 (2020): 1–20. https://doi.org/10.1080/08865655.2017.1367711.

2 National Institute of Statistics and Geography (INEGI), *Population Census* (2010); US Census Bureau, American Community Survey (2008–12).

3 Own estimations based on data from the US Department of Transportation, Research and Innovative Technology Administration, Bureau of Transportation Statistics, TransBorder Freight Data.

4 Bureau of Labor Statistics, *Occupational Employment and Wages in San Diego–Carlsbad*, Western Information Office (May 2020). https://www.bls.gov/regions/west/news-release/occupationalemploymentandwages_sandiego.htm.

5 San Diego Association of Governments (SANDAG), *Traded Industry Clusters in the San Diego Region* (December 2012), https://www.sandag.org/uploads/publicationid/publicationid_1715_15318.pdf.

6 R.E. Feinberg and G. Schuck, *San Diego, Baja California, and Globalization: Coming from Behind* (Los Angeles: Pacific Council on International Policy, 2001).

7 US Census Bureau, US Trade Home, https://usatrade.census.gov/data/Perspective60/View/dispview.aspxps.
8 J.E. Mendoza, "Integración económica, ingresos y empleo en las ciudades fronterizas de México y los Estados Unidos en la década de los noventa," in *El TLCAN y la Frontera México-Estados Unidos, aspectos Económicos*, coord. J.E. Mendoza (El Colef, Miguel Ángel Porrúa, 2007).
9 National Institute of Statistics and Geography (INEGI), https://www.inegi.org.mx/sistemas/bie.
10 Pia M. Orrenius, "Illegal Immigration and Enforcement along the US-Mexico Border: An Overview," *Economic and Financial Review-Federal Reserve Bank of Dallas*, no. 1 (2001): 2–11.
11 Sarah Bohn and Todd Pugatch, "US Border Enforcement and Mexican Immigrant Location Choice," *Demography* 5, no. 52 (2015): 1543–70.
12 Anil Kalhan, "Rethinking Immigration Detention," *Columbia Law Review Sidebar* 110 (2010): 42–58.
13 Jeffrey S. Passel, D'Vera Cohn, and Ana Gonzalez-Barrera, *Net Migration from Mexico Falls to Zero – and Perhaps Less*, Pew Research Center Report 23 April 2012, https://www.pewresearch.org/hispanic/2012/04/23/net-migration-from-mexico-falls-to-zero-and-perhaps-less.
14 Philip L. Martin, "Trump and US Immigration Policy," *California Agriculture* 71, no. 1 (2017): 15–17, https://calag.ucanr.edu/Archive/?article=ca.2017a0006.
15 Douglas S. Massey, Jorge Durand, and Karen A. Pren, "Border Enforcement and Return Migration by Documented and Undocumented Mexicans," *Journal of Ethnic and Migration Studies* 41, no. 7 (2015): 1015–40.
16 Northern Border Migration Survey (Encuesta sobre Migración en la Frontera, EMIF), El Colegio de la Frontera Norte, https://www.colef.mx/emif.
17 EMIF, Data Bases de Matamoros, Nuevo Laredo, Piedras Negras, Ciudad Juárez, Nogales, Mexicali y Tijuana (2009–14), https://www.colef.mx/emif/informes_publicaciones.html.
18 Laura Velasco and S. Albicker, *Estimación y Caracterización de la Población Residente en « El Bordo » del Canal del Río Tijuana*, Reporte Ejecutivo de Resultados de Investigación (El Colegio de la Frontera Norte, 2013).
19 Neil Fligstein and Doug McAdam, *A Theory of Fields* (New York: Oxford Univeristy Press, 2012), http://doi.org/10.1007/s11186-014-9237-0.
20 Neil Fligstein and Doug McAdam, "Toward a General Theory of Strategic Action Fields," *Sociological Theory* 29, no.1 (2011): 1–26.
21 Jorge Eduardo Mendoza Cota, "Economic Integration and Cross-Border Economic Organizations: The Case of San Diego–Tijuana," *Estudios Fronterizos* 18, no. 35 (Universidad Autónoma de Baja California, 2017), https://www.redalyc.org/journal/530/53051786002/html.

5 Mexico's "Drug War," the Energy Sector, and an Emerging Strategic Action Field*

GUADALUPE CORREA-CABRERA

Introduction: An Emerging Energy Field in Mexico

A Theory of Fields and Mexico's Energy Sector

After more than seven decades of government control of the oil industry that started with the 1938 nationalization of foreign oil companies, Mexico passed a landmark bill that is supposed to change the country's future development and create a new social and economic order involving the cooperation of the public and private sectors (both foreign and national) in energy generation. Mexico's 2013–14 energy reform was passed after a violent armed conflict that some have defined as a war or a civil war.[1] This had specific effects on all actors involved. It changed the configuration of Mexico's political/electoral map, which facilitated the passage of energy reform but also limited social mobilization and attempted to modify land ownership and use. This led to massive displacements of people escaping violence in key areas of the country, particularly in Mexico's Northeast and the border region in general.

These factors – sparked in part by the paramilitarization of organized crime and the Mexican government's response to it, as well as the passage of far-reaching constitutional reforms aimed at transforming the energy sector in Mexico – resulted in a profound social and economic transformation of the country. This transformation can be explained using Neil Fligstein and Doug McAdam's general theory of Strategic Action Fields (SAFs), which unpacks the relationship between social movement theory and the sociology of organizations.[2] SAF

* This is a slightly revised and updated version of the article titled "Transforming Mexico's Energy Field: The Intended Consequences of a Drug War," *Small Wars and Insurgencies* 30, no. 2 (2019): 489–517. Permission was obtained from this journal to reproduce the present material.

theory focuses on "collective strategic action," that is, on those "efforts of collective actors to vie for strategic advantage in and through interaction with other groups in what can be seen as meso-level social orders."[3]

Fligstein and McAdam hold the view that SAFs "are the fundamental units of collective action in society." More specifically, an SAF "is a meso-level social order where actors (who can be an individual or a group) interact with knowledge of one another under a set of common understandings about the purposes of the field, the relationships in the field (including who has power and why), and the field's rules."[4] Fligstein and McAdam view SAFs "as socially constructed arenas within which actors with varying resource endowments vie for advantage."[5] According to them, in most fields, "dominant or incumbent actors will have a frame of reference that encapsulates their view of the field, while dominated or challenger actors will have an oppositional perspective."[6]

Fligstein and McAdam's approach also "tries to define a sociological view of strategic action and link it to the possibilities for change in SAFs at different moments in their evolution."[7] Their theory "provides a way to understand if a meso-level social structure is emerging, stable, or in the process of transformation."[8] Under this scenario, SAFs always seem to be "in some flux as the process of contention is ongoing and the threats to an order always in existence."[9] In the case of Mexico, stable SAFs existed several years after the oil industry was nationalized in 1938 by president Lázaro Cárdenas. In fact, Mexico's nationalism and industrialization after the revolutionary period were rooted in this new socioeconomic model, which was supported by the state's monopoly on energy. Stability allowed for several years of development and economic growth in Mexico.

Soon after the revolution, SAFs underwent a gradual destabilization process that culminated in a genuine crisis, that is, "a more extreme version of 'normal' contention within the field."[10] The end result of this would be, in the words of Fligstein and McAdam, "a genuine transformation of the field or fundamental restructuring of power relationships within the field."[11] The present account describes the transformation of Mexico's post-revolutionary energy field – referred to as the "nationalized energy field" – in the context of a war against militarized drug traffickers, the alleged deterioration of Mexico's energy model, and the final passage of energy reform; it does so by analysing the different components of Fligstein and McAdam's field theory.[12] I contend here that the recent and potential structural field changes in the Mexican case were a response to both a massive security crisis and a crisis in Pemex and Mexico's energy sector. It seems that these conditions have given rise to an emerging field – a "privatized energy field" – that has at its centre energy reform and that is currently transforming Mexico's socioeconomic order. The dynamics described here have to do with the concept of cross-border governance in that they involve policies intended to erase borders to the participation of transnational capital in the quest for North American energy integration.

Field Crisis: Mexico's Drug War and Declining Energy Production

SAFs that emerged after Mexico's revolutionary period experienced major transformations, especially in the 1990s, when the country underwent democratization and economic transformation through the implementation of so-called neoliberal economic reforms. However, the foundations of Mexico's post-revolutionary SAFs were maintained, in that essentially, the oil industry continued to be a state monopoly. Recently, that model has experienced a severe crisis, driven largely by the new configuration of organized crime in Mexico, the government's response to it, and a crisis in the energy sector itself. In the past few years, the security crisis has been so acute and economic reforms so sweeping that the post-revolutionary field or nationalized energy field has been transformed.

It also seems that this transformation has been spearheaded in part by the paramilitarization of organized crime[13] and the Mexican government's responses to that phenomenon. The diversification of organized criminal activities and the involvement of criminal syndicates in the energy sector have also contributed to that transformation. Mexico's security crisis and its economic consequences, combined with a deterioration in Mexico's energy sector, have brought about a field rupture that seems to have radically transformed socio-economic relations in Mexico.

THE NATIONALIZED ENERGY FIELD RUPTURE

An energy crisis – or the perception of it – was supposedly a main concern of those who supported energy reform in Mexico. According to national and international reports, in the years prior to the reform, Mexico's oil and gas production was declining. Pemex, at that time the world's only remaining state-owned oil monopoly, "was reeling under large financial losses while still funding about one third of the government's budget through taxes."[14] Many people raised concerns about Pemex's track record, highlighting financial losses, oil and gas theft, and corruption.[15]

Over the past few years, several reports – especially by foreign analysts – have pointed to the decline in oil and gas production, the precarious situation of the hydrocarbons industry, and the poor prospects for Mexico's energy sector. Many have warned that the country may one day soon become a net energy importer. Mexican domestic crude oil production has been falling steadily for almost a decade – from 3.4 million barrels per day in 2004 to about 2.5 million. According to several analysts, this has been due to insufficient investment in hydrocarbon exploration and production. Analysts Shannon K. O'Neil and

James S. Taylor write that "with limited domestic refining capability and strong demand, the country [became] a net importer of refined petroleum products, such as lighter grade gasoline and diesel. And in natural gas, Mexico's growing consumption needs (for power generation and to meet industry demand) [outstripped] its productive capacity, leaving the country as a net importer of the fuel."[16]

Most analysts agree that the waning of Mexican crude production has been due in large part to the precipitous decline of the Cantarell field in the Gulf of Mexico, where output fell by over 75 percent in a decade. That field provides a very significant share of Mexico's total oil output, and it seems that Mexico's other oilfields are incapable of replacing Cantarell in the short term. Thus, a key objective in Mexico's energy reform has been to reverse the reecent decline in oil and gas production. "[Giving] international oil companies new access to Mexican oil fields was supposed to change this overall trend." By some estimates, through these legal changes and the ensuing technical assistance and potential massive investments in the sector, the country would "increase oil production to as much as 4 million barrels per day by 2025."[17]

Toward an Emerging SAF: Mexico's Energy Field after Energy Reform

In sum, a field crisis in Mexico – that is, a crisis in the Mexican nationalized energy field – at the beginning of the twenty-first century had two main components: a massive security crisis – especially at the border – and a crisis of the energy sector. At first glance, these two phenomena seem unconnected. The administration of Felipe Calderón (2006–12) focused on the security crisis. By the end of his tenure, close attention was being paid to the development of the energy sector (especially in Mexico's Northeast) so as to reverse the decline in oil and gas production. When Enrique Peña Nieto began his administration (*sexenio*) in 2012, he prioritized energy reform. This, however, entailed diverting attention from the fight against organized crime in order to pass structural reforms and thereby transform the nation (*transformar a México*). Energy reform, in particular, seems to have become the foundation of an emerging SAF after a massive security crisis and the deterioration of the post-revolutionary energy project in Mexico. This transformation also changed key aspects of cross-border governance as well as Mexico–US border and energy relations. Andrés Manuel López Obrador of the MORENA Party assumed the Mexican presidency on 1 December 2018. His energy policy is different from that of his recent predecessors. He proposes to reverse some key aspects of energy reform. It is not yet clear whether he will succeed, given the powerful economic interests that have a hand today in this sector.

The opening of Mexico's energy sector to private companies happened slowly, becoming more visible during the administration of Carlos Salinas de

Gortari (1988–94). A reform of Article 3 of the Electric Energy Public Service Act (Ley del Servicio Público de Energía Eléctrica) was introduced on 23 December 1992 to incorporate the so-called independent power producers (IPPs); this allowed the private sector to generate electricity and sell it to the Federal Electricity Commission (CFE). Subsequent attempts to open the energy sector to private capital met little success: changes were limited, and proposals for substantial reform faced stiff opposition. President Vicente Fox of the National Action Party (PAN) (2000–6), for example, tried to pass a multitude of reforms, but they were obstructed by the PRI; even so, he was able to somewhat modify the country's energy legislation through the Energy Sectorial Program (2001–6). Finally, some private contractors were allowed to participate in the energy sector through multiple service contracts (*contratos de servicio múltiple*). Those contracts represented an important advance for private capital in Mexico's hydrocarbon sector. Through these contracts, Pemex accepted the collaboration of transnational companies, such as Schlumberger and ICA Flour Daniel, in order to develop the Chicontepec reserve and generate infrastructure for CFE and Pemex.

Plans to open up Mexico's energy sector have not been developed exclusively by the Mexican government. Media reports indicate that at least since 2004, the US government has been arranging access to the natural gas reserves along the Gulf Coast between Tamaulipas and Tabasco; production there would be guaranteed until at least 2030. The US strategy has been to offer "novel funding schemes and high technology for projects of exploration and exploitation of hydrocarbons in Mexico, as part of the proposed integration of North America."[18] To that end, some meetings have been held between Mexican authorities and their US counterparts as well as representatives of energy companies. The people present during these conversations have included then US President George W. Bush, Felipe Calderón (in his position as Secretary of Energy), and representatives of the National Petroleum Council.[19]

At that time, the US delegation shared with the Mexican authorities a document that detailed investment opportunities in Mexico's energy sector; it included a map of Mexico's natural gas reserves. The proposed projects and activities, according to this document, would increase natural gas reserves by 425 percent by the year 2030. According to that document, exploiting these opportunities would benefit both nations; however, their development was stalled due to the lack of clear rules, adequate legislation, and judicial security.

This study was presented by then US Secretary of Energy, Abraham Spencer, to his counterpart in Mexico, Felipe Calderón, and then to President Bush; it had the backing of the National Petroleum Council and the US Department of State. It also had been approved by the chairmen of prominent trans-national energy companies such as British Petroleum, Chevron, ConocoPhillips, ExxonMobil, Halliburton, Kinder Morgan Energy Partners, Marathon Oil, Royal

Dutch Shell, Schlumberger, and Valero Energy. The same study highlighted the concerns of US government authorities and businesses regarding Mexico's reluctance to open the energy sector, claiming that this would limit productive investment and prevent crucial developments in the natural gas and oil sectors.[20]

On 20 December 2013, after seventy-six years of state monopoly, Mexico's Congress finally passed far-reaching constitutional reforms to open the energy sector to private participation and international investment.[21] Soon after, a series of new laws and amendments were passed to create the legal and regulatory framework within which foreign energy companies would be able to operate in Mexico. These reforms, which would fundamentally reshape Mexico's energy landscape, included twelve amended laws and nine new secondary laws; the changes would govern the upstream, midstream, and downstream hydrocarbon sectors. Enabling or secondary legislation was approved in August 2014.[22]

Since these reforms, domestic and foreign private investors has been allowed "to participate in activities like refining, transportation, storage and distribution of oil, natural gas, fuels and other oil products." Also, the private sector can now participate in the exploration and production of oil and gas in three new ways – through licences and profit- and production-sharing agreements.[23] It can also participate in electricity generation. The reforms include a new regulatory framework that divides oversight of the oil and gas sectors among a group of entities, including the Secretariat of Energy, the National Hydrocarbons Commission (CNH, in Spanish), the Energy Regulatory Commission (CRE), the National Agency of Industrial Safety and Environmental Protection of the Secretariat of Environment and Natural Resources (SEMARNAT), the Secretariat of Finance and Public Credit (SHCP)[24], and two new centres – the National Natural Gas Control Center (CENAGAS) and the National Electricity Control Center (CENACE).[25] What is more, Pemex and the Federal Electricity Commission (CFE) are no longer monopolies; they now operate as state-owned productive enterprises.[26]

Emerging Field: Mexico's Privatized Energy Field

According to Fligstein and McAdam, after a field crisis and during the process of field transformation, "some group or set of individuals must propose to others a new collective frame for the field. If they fail to do so, the SAF may simply collapse and become an unorganized social space."[27] Mexico today is transitioning toward an emerging social field that at this point seems relatively unorganized. Fligstein and McAdam define an "emerging field as a social space" where rules are uncertain but "where actors, by virtue of emerging, dependent interests, are being forced increasingly to take one another into account in their actions." The emerging field in Mexico has been influenced by the passage of energy reforms in the context of a new political configuration and the ongoing security crisis in different parts of the nation.

During a transition toward an emerging field, the state becomes a key actor. Fligstein and McAdam note that "states aid in the creation of new social space as intended and unintended consequences of state actions." Within this framework, states are also "the focus of attention from emerging SAFs."[28] In Mexico's emerging field, the state has emerged as a crucial factor in the militarization of security strategy, the support and passage of energy reform, and protection of business interests – mainly in the energy sector – through a renewed role for law enforcement agencies.

All of this may contribute to the development of Mexico's energy sector and to the strengthening of cross-border cooperation in North America. Developments in this sector may become the focus of an emerging SAF in Mexico. That country is the world's eighth largest oil producer[29] and is believed to have the world's fifth or sixth largest shale gas reserves. Thus, the "sector's liberalization is expected to attract billions of dollars in new investment, increase oil and gas production, lower electricity costs and make Mexico's industry more competitive."[30] The US Energy Information Administration (EIA) has predicted that Mexico's energy reform will bring about a sharp increase in the country's oil production, "raising it by about 75 percent by 2040."[31] The EIA attributes this projected growth essentially to "new contract structures that energy companies will be allowed to use under the reform plan.[32] Similarly, Pemex has estimated that "with adequate investment and technology exploring deep-water reserves could add as much as 27 billion barrels of oil to Mexico's proven reserves."[33]

Applying the Theory of Fields to Mexico's Case

To sum up, SAF change in Mexico involves some key players and strategies and is happening in the context of a drug war, extreme violence in some regions (especially along the border), and a supposed energy crisis, and in a broader field environment of regional energy opportunities. It is worthwhile mentioning that this field transformation is not just impacting Mexico; it also has key implications for trans-border governance and especially for US–Mexico border and energy relations. These impacts may eventually extend to the entire North American region at a moment when energy independence seems to be a key regional priority.

Incumbents, Challengers, and Governance Units

INCUMBENTS

In the present analytical framework, "incumbents are those actors who wield disproportionate influence within a field and whose interests and views tend to be heavily reflected in the dominant organization of the SAF."[34] In Mexico, the incumbents in a post-revolutionary but newly "democratized" order were essentially a *panista* administration (preceded by a president affiliated to the National Action Party, PAN), the state-owned energy companies (PEMEX and CFE), and a considerable number of small private proprietors and social landowners (particularly *ejido*[35] landowners or *ejidatarios*). In Mexico's emerging SAF after the security crisis and energy reform, the composition of the incumbents changed. The PRI came back, winning the 2012 presidential election and consolidating its congressional majority. Energy reform was passed during a PRI administration. Other prominent major incumbents in this new field seem to be (national and foreign) private trans-national energy and energy service companies.

As previously mentioned, Pemex had suffered a visible decline, commonly attributed to insufficient capital and operational capabilities as well as the involvement of trans-national criminal organizations (TCOs) in hydrocarbon theft from Pemex's pipeline network. Under the new framework, foreign and private domestic energy companies will be able to explore, produce, and refine oil, operating under contract with the Mexican government and competing with Pemex.[36] Thus, major international energy corporations (such as Exxon-Mobil, Shell and Chevron), the world's largest oilfield services companies (e.g., Halliburton, Baker Hughes, and Schlumberger), and some smaller (but very productive) private oil and gas businesses will be the new incumbents in Mexico's privatized energy SAF. Recently, they have seemed ready to expand their participation in Mexico's market, and some think that the biggest companies will be drilling offshore in the deep waters of the Gulf of Mexico in the near future.[37] It is worth noting that this environment has changed somewhat in the past several years under the "Fourth Transformation" government of Andrés Manuel López Obrador (AMLO) and with the recent historic collapse of crude oil prices.[38]

In the near future, a number of Mexican energy and energy service companies may join this new group of incumbents. Some of these businesses have already worked for Pemex, and with the passage of energy reform they could evolve into independent operators in the exploration and exploitation sectors. These companies include Alfa and Grupo México, as well as Carlos Slim's Carso Oil & Gas.[39] These companies are viewed as the best-positioned ones in Mexico's oil sector, for they are already operating in mature oilfields and on marine platforms.[40]

CHALLENGERS

Challengers "occupy less privileged niches within the field and ordinarily wield little influence over its operation."[41] Previous challengers to the established order have largely been TCOs or so-called drug cartels (Los Zetas, in particular), transnational energy companies, and the PRI and the Mexican "left." These last two challengers had held important positions in the Congress and Senate, as well as key governorships, until Mexico's presidency came into the hands of the PAN for twelve years (2000–2012), a time of crisis and transition. In the emerging privatized energy field, some of these challengers have become incumbents. The new challengers seem to be the Mexican political left, environmental groups, groups opposing fracking, and *ejidatarios* and small private landowners, who have noted the new legislation's impact on their interests.[42] In fact, there is no consensus in the country regarding the benefits of energy reform; "the Mexican people appear divided" over this issue.[43]

Just after the reform was passed, the political left "tried to organize a referendum to undo the changes, warning that Mexico could obtain less oil money if the reform is badly implemented, or if the terms are too generous to private firms."[44] Actually, it seems that in some regions of Mexico, a number of small entrepreneurs and landowners (including *ejidatarios*) have started to organize to defend their properties.[45] What is more, activists have begun organizing to block the practice of hydraulic fracturing (fracking), arguing that it would contaminate much of the water necessary for agriculture and human consumption and damage the environment in many other ways.[46]

GOVERNANCE UNITS

Governance units have been key in Mexico's recent security and energy field crises and transformations. These formal units "are charged with overseeing compliance with field rules and, in general, facilitating the overall smooth functioning of the system."[47] In recent times, Mexico's government, besides passing energy reforms, has implemented an unconventional strategy to solve its security crisis. At first glance, these two processes have little obvious connection; even so, they both have contributed to the transformation of Mexico's energy field, in the process modifying the roles of incumbents and challengers.

Governance units "are generally there not to serve as neutral arbiters of conflicts between incumbents and challengers, but to reinforce the dominant logic, and safeguard the interests of the incumbents. Ordinarily, then, governance units can be expected to serve as defenders of the status quo and are a generally conservative force during periods of conflict within the SAF."[48] In Mexico, governance units performed a distinct role determined by an important field crisis; the result was an SAF transformation that inverted the roles of some incumbents and challengers. Some thought this might change when AMLO became president in December 2018, and it seems that at first, he did have different goals. However, the SAF transformation has been so profound recently that big economic/energy interests may well come out on top, and it is very possible that the process described here will not be reversed. What is more, the "new" US–Mexico–Canada Agreement (USMCA) – which replaced the North American Free

Trade Agreement (NAFTA) – has established some rules to prevent changes to the new regional energy order.[49]

SOCIAL SKILLS

Mexico's recent SAF transformation also required that some incumbents, key challengers, and governance units develop effective social skills. Fligstein and McAdam define social skills "as how individuals or collective actors possess a highly developed cognitive capacity for reading people and environments, framing lines of action, and mobilizing people in the service of these action frames."[50] In their view, "social skill is the idea that people want to produce collective action by engaging others." They also contend that "in unorganized or unstable SAFs, these skills are at the greatest premium." By applying adequate social skills, predominant actors may "be able to build political coalitions or have enough resources to produce a hierarchical field." This seems to have happened in Mexico in recent years. The Mexican case clearly highlights the cognitive, empathetic, and communicative dimensions of effective social skills.[51]

During a time of extreme violence, a drug war, and an energy crisis, some key corporate actors, working closely with the Mexican government, advanced energy reforms by applying a number of adequate tools, as well as effective social skills. Overall, Mexico's energy field transformation was made possible through the use of specific strategies and social skills, including (a) effective government discourse and control of the national media, (b) the international mainstream media's support, (c) effective communication strategies by corporate interests linked to the energy sector, (d) a fragmented party opposition, (e) deep divisions within the Mexican "left," and (f) a relative absence of advocacy in some regions dominated by organized crime.

The Peña Nieto administration's campaign for energy reform was quite successful. His communication strategy, combined with political deals with key national and international political and economic actors and the configuration of Mexico's political power structures (particularly within the legislative chamber), achieved the desired goals. So he was able to consolidate the efforts of past administrations and multinational corporate interests in a landmark energy bill that would transform Mexico's energy sector as well as its socio-economic structure, especially at the border region. Communication efforts and the related social skills to make this possible had first been intensified during the administration of Felipe Calderón, who was simultaneously fighting a drug war. Around this time, the country's former Secretary of Energy, Jordy Herrera, confirmed the discovery of large shale reserves on the Mexican side of the US–Mexico border. Herrera suggested that the discovery "could change the face of Mexico's energy industry" and that further investment was needed to develop this important sector.[52]

People and groups linked to energy companies now mobilized and made strong efforts to increase public support for energy reform in Mexico. These actors highlighted the potential benefits of energy reform and the problems caused by Pemex's monopoly over the oil industry. People affiliated with the Council of Foreign Relations (CFR) were extremely active promoting the reforms. Prominent leaders in the energy sector have long been closely associated with the CFR. For instance, David Rockefeller, son of John D. Rockefeller, Standard Oil's founder, was president of the CFR from 1970 to 1985. Former Halliburton director Lawrence S. Eagleburger was also a member of this organization. The following comment by two CFR members, Shannon K. O'Neil and James S. Taylor,[53] shows how social skills supporting energy reform are being used in the present context of field transformation:

> Pemex, the world's only remaining state-owned oil monopoly that faced no competition, has for many years lacked the necessary capital, expertise and equipment to operate productively. After falling behind, Mexico is finally taking actions that will allow its energy sector to catch up to global developments, allowing private investment in every segment of the hydrocarbons sector, even while clearly affirming the Mexican State's sole ownership of the minerals in the subsoil.[54]

In 2014, a CFR-sponsored independent task force report titled *North America: Time for a New Focus* was released. It recommended ways to deepen North American integration, focusing on four key areas, one of which was energy. The task force was chaired by David H. Petraeus, retired US army general and chairman of the KKR Global Institute, and Robert B. Zoellick, former president of the World Bank Group and chairman of Goldman Sachs's International Advisors. The project was directed by Shannon O'Neil. Their document recommended in particular that the US government encourage greater energy connections with Canada and Mexico and approve additional pipeline capacity. The task force also called for an end to restrictions on energy exports, including oil and liquefied natural gas (LNG).

Another actor who actively promoted energy reform, thus displaying the social skills utilized by energy companies in Mexico, has been Antonio "Tony" Garza, former US ambassador to Mexico and legal counsel for the law firm White & Case in Mexico City, where he advises US energy companies and others who want to invest in Mexico. He is also chairman of ViaNovo Ventures, the investment arm of the boutique management consultancy firm ViaNovo. ViaNovo Ventures focuses on large energy infrastructure projects, with an emphasis on US–Mexico market entry.[55] Just after the passage of Mexico's energy reform, Garza distributed a press release published by large Texas newspapers, including the *Houston Chronicle* and the *Austin American-Statesman*, in which he claimed that "Mexico took a giant leap toward a new economic future" with the new legislation.[56] It is worth noting that Garza "sits on the board of directors of Basic Energy Services Inc., an oil and gas well services company headquartered in Fort Worth."[57] Through people like him, using similar arguments or "marketing" strategies, energy companies have wielded their social skills to further their interests in Mexico's energy sector.

Another factor that facilitated energy reform and prevented effective mobilization against it is the extreme violence that has inflicted Mexico over the past few years – and that has been especially virulent in the border states (which at one time had been the most peaceful and stable ones). The recent security crisis has affected social mobilization in Mexico. In particular, in zones controlled by criminal organizations – especially those where Los Zetas and similar groups have had a strong presence – and in areas where the confrontation between armed groups and federal forces has resulted in massive violence, disappearances, and displacements, people have less desire to mobilize. So it is plausible that militarization in Mexico – both criminal and "official" – has had the ultimate effect of cracking down on opposition to energy reform.

This phenomenon has indirectly supported the efforts of energy companies and strengthened their position in promoting these historic changes. Overall, the Mexican left and civil society groups opposing the reforms – and alleging a loss of sovereignty derived from recent constitutional changes – have shown very limited capacity. This has been especially evident in key states like Tamaulipas, Veracruz, and Coahuila – all once under the control of Los Zetas or similar groups – where people tend not to mobilize due to fear of organized crime or militarization. People in these areas may fear retribution, given the close links between state and local governments and organized crime.[58] These patterns have been reinforced by the absence of mobilization by the oil workers' union and by the effective social skills of businesses operating with the support of the US and Mexican governments. During AMLO's administration, attempts have been made to address this situation, but the results are still uncertain.

THE BROADER FIELD ENVIRONMENT AND NEIGHBOURING FIELDS

In Fligstein and McAdam's framework, all SAFs are "embedded in complex webs of other fields."[59] These so-called neighbouring fields are in constant interaction, and major developments in key fields can strongly influence a number of related fields. Fligstein and McAdam recognize three sets of binaries that, in their view, characterize these other neighbouring fields and their relationships with a given SAF.[60] These binaries relate to distance, inequality, and state capacity. In the present case, the other (neighbouring) fields have mainly to do with conditions in the world energy markets – especially those in North America – and plausibly, with the US border security-military-industrial complex that engages in arms production and provides security services to transnational companies operating in extremely violent environments.

Such determining (neighbouring) fields are mostly vertical. They also show ample inequalities and are led by corporate interests (transnational energy companies and arms-producers). They also point to the reduced power of Mexico's former oil and electricity monopolies and of small and medium-sized national businesses and landowners. Mexico's field transformation has also been influenced by other state fields in a new context of concentration of political power and social repression in the wake of Mexico's "drug war." Actually, these changes have been designed and implemented by Mexico's government and supported by other foreign governments (especially by the US).

The main neighbouring field that apparently has brought about this new reality has to do with ideas about US/North American energy independence, Mexico's strategic location, and the availability of unexplored energy resources – mainly oil and shale gas reservoirs in Northeastern Mexico and the Gulf Corridor.[61]

Settlement in an Emerging Field: Mexico's Energy Sector after Reform

According to the present analytical framework, the stability of a field is essentially a function of its relations to other fields. One "can say that a field is no longer in crisis when a generalized sense of order and certainty returns." In a stable field, "challengers successfully sustain mobilization and slowly begin to institutionalize new practices and rules."[62] In the case of Mexico, it has been clear that through "sustained oppositional mobilization" – both in the energy sector and in the context of a grave security crisis – and with the participation of governance units, the country's energy field has begun "to gravitate toward a new – or refurbished – institutional settlement."[63]

Energy Reform: Favouring Transnational Energy Companies

In this new context, both state actors and other external parties have been instrumental in restoring field order. "In general, if proximate fields are the source of the destabilizing shocks that set contentious episodes in motion, they often provide the models for the settlements that bring these crises to a close."[64] Mexico's case is a good example of how state actors and external parties that enjoy pre-eminence in the energy sector abroad – essentially trans-national energy companies supported by the governments of their countries – have started to solve the major crises in the energy field with the aim of eventually achieving stability.

With regard to state actors, it is worth noting that from the start of his administration, the former president of Mexico, Enrique Peña Nieto, modified his discourse, distancing himself from his predecessor, Felipe Calderón. That meant his focus was not on security, but on economic development, productivity, and the modernization of Mexico; this last included the passage and successful implementation of key structural reforms (tax reform, education reform, and, especially, energy reform) that would make the others possible. It seemed that in Peña

Nieto's view, the era of insecurity and violence in Mexico had been left behind, and the country needed to focus on its commercial relations with the world, as well as on fuelling competitiveness and implementing the reforms. According to this vision, in the long term, Mexico would eventually become a world power.[65]

The Mexican government's approach to promoting growth and economic development has been supported by the private sector and especially by transnational energy companies. For example, when referring to energy reform, ConocoPhillips CEO Ryan Lance says it "represents an interesting opportunity for the industry." He sees Mexico as "a resource-rich country" that can do and "is doing interesting things today to attract investment." Thus, he is "looking forward to the opportunity to go participate there."[66] There seemed to be a consensus among Mexican government officials and the business community during the Peña Nieto administration – both national and transnational – that energy reform would "eventually boost oil production, increase the country's natural gas supply, and lower the cost of electricity generation."[67] Mexico's energy reform has been reinforced by the recent passage of other structural economic reforms (fiscal reform, labour reform, education reform). Overall, these changes have been designed to improve "the ease with which companies can do business in Mexico, removing legal obstacles and furthering labor flexibility."[68]

Structural reforms in Mexico, particularly energy reform, have opened new areas of opportunity for foreign companies and seem to promote settlement in an emerging field in Mexico. The changes that ended state-owned Pemex's monopoly over the nation's vast energy resources – and that allowed foreign direct investment in Mexico's energy industry for the first time in seventy-six years – have been well-received by the international community and seem to be the beginning of a new era of development and stability in the country after a period of war and energy crisis.

Under this historic constitutional reform, private international energy companies can now develop unexplored oil and gas resources. This has generated at least four areas of opportunity that may eventually promote the stability of an emerging SAF. Those areas of opportunity are related to (1) shale oil and gas resources, (2) the generation of additional pipeline infrastructure and opportunities to invest in midstream infrastructure, (3) partnerships between Pemex and private investors, and (4) private investment in electricity generation.[69] Additionally, under the new energy strategy, which includes three new types of contracts, foreign companies are now allowed to book oil and gas reserves for financial reporting purposes.[70] This "is a particularly attractive incentive for investment in Mexico's energy sector."[71]

Business-Led Cross-Border Governance and New Energy Infrastructure

Despite the violence related to organized crime in Mexico, in recent years there have been significant investments in infrastructure – particularly in the border

Map 5.1. National Program of Infrastructure (2014–2018) Projects

Source: Government of Mexico, Programa Nacional de Infraestructura 2014–2018 (Mexico City, 2014).

region – aimed at promoting cross-border trade and energy development in hydrocarbon-rich areas. The same new infrastructure connects the main national commercial poles with those still in development and with the main markets of Asia, Europe, and, of course, the United States. In recent years, despite extreme violence, commercial and energy infrastructure expanded significantly in Mexico. Such developments were reinforced with further investment projects (highways, roads, bridges, hydroelectric stations, and a variety of energy infrastructure projects) that have connected important poles of development in strategic hydrocarbon-rich areas (see maps 5.1 and 5.2). In Mexico's emerging field, this may contribute to a settlement arising from trans-national private investments in the energy sector.

Another key agreement in an emerging SAF linked to energy development is the Transboundary Hydrocarbons Agreement. A few days after the passage of Mexico's energy reform, the US Congress approved a binational treaty that established a framework for US offshore oil and gas companies and Pemex to jointly develop trans-boundary oil and natural gas reserves along the US–Mexico

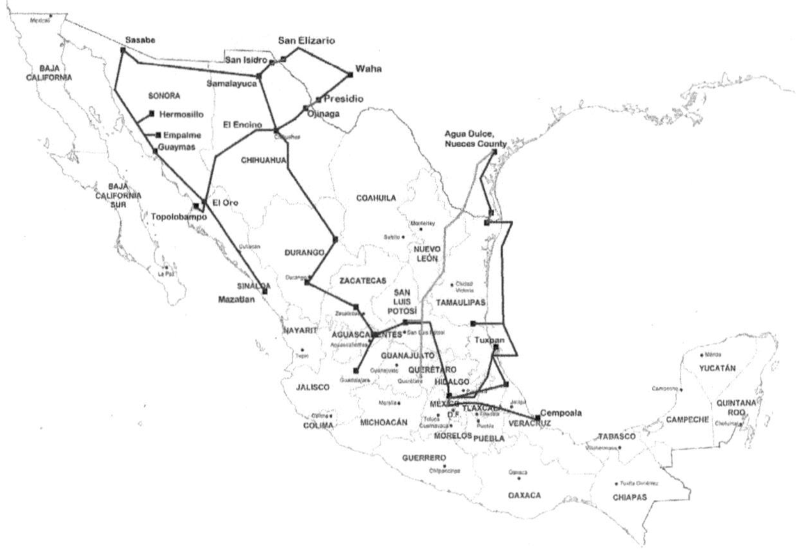

Map 5.2. An extended natural gas pipeline network

Source: CFE.

maritime boundary in the Gulf of Mexico.[72] The agreement provides access to nearly 1.5 million acres of the U.S outer continental shelf and paves the way for the development of common safety and environmental standards.[73]

Agreements of this type, as well as the new energy infrastructure that has been built recently – particularly in the border region – or that has been projected for the coming years, have been strengthening business-led cross-border governance. This is all part of an emerging field centred on the energy sector, one that involves key players in two neighbouring nations and that seems to largely benefit the trans-national business community. This new reality has been also shaped by the passage of further legislation and by proposals to protect economic interests and investments that would promote settlement in an emerging SAF.

NATIONAL PROGRAM OF INFRASTRUCTURE (2014–2018)

Settlement in Mexico's emerging field will be happening in the context of a series of major reforms and initiatives, including the National Infrastructure Program (PNI, in Spanish) of former president Enrique Peña Nieto. The PNI outlined major programs and projects in the areas of energy, water, telecommunications, transportation, urban and rural development, health, and tourism. The Government of Mexico anticipated that under that program, nearly $600 billion in infrastructure investment would take place over a four-year period, tapping a mix of federal, local, and private sources.[74] The plan would develop 743 projects, including highways, hydraulic projects, mines, hospitals, and a variety of urban and rural projects, under the slogan "Mover a México" (To Move Mexico) (see map 5.1).

Many of the projects contained in the PNI were directly linked to hydrocarbon exploration and production. Francisco Cravioto, who researches public policies related to extractive industries at the NGO Fundar, Center for Research and Analysis, and who is also a member of the Mexican Alliance against Fracking (Alianza Mexicana contra el fracking), stated in 2014 that most of the projects that were part of the PNI, including aqueducts, gas pipelines, highways, and cable network construction, would essentially strengthen energy reforms.[75] The plans of the current Mexican president seem completely different, but as already noted, not many things have changed during the first years of his administration.[76] What is more, he seems to be pushing to "slow down clean energy."[77]

EXTENDING THE NATURAL GAS PIPELINE NETWORK

Mexico's energy reforms have carved out space for an emerging field based on the projected significant development of the country's oil sector. Such reforms "are being used to generate new sources of electricity and to add hundreds of miles of new natural gas pipelines and power lines" in Mexico.[78] Billions of dollars have been allocated to build power plants, electrical distribution facilities, and natural gas pipelines in the coming years. US pipeline companies and gas producers, in particular, will benefit from such developments.[79] Mexico's CFE has recently called for a significant number of new energy projects, which were up for bid by the summer of 2015.[80] The bids for the construction of gas pipelines are of special importance (see map 5.2). This has to do with Mexico's attempts to increase its own domestic supplies of natural gas.[81] In this context, a number of US gas export pipeline projects that could support additional natural gas exports to Mexico have been announced. These projects are supposed "to double existing capacity."[82] Notwithstanding the last administration, Mexico's current one is trying to reverse some of these dynamics.

Land Ownership and Use in an Emerging Field

Mexico's new reality, driven by energy reform and potential investments in this strategic sector, required some key changes in legislation related to land ownership and use. These changes were made in anticipation of potential land-related conflicts associated with hydrocarbon exploration and production and with the creation of new, energy-related infrastructure projects. These plausible conflicts "stem from the fact that all of these projects will necessarily require the right of way to access and work on the resources in the subsoil of privately owned as well as on so-called 'socially owned' lands in regions targeted for energy development."[83] Thus, in order to avoid land-related conflicts, new energy legislation was passed. Under this legislation,

> energy development projects are a matter of public and national interest. They take priority over any other use of the land. In order to enforce this priority, the lawmakers address the issue of land ownership and land use in Chapter IV, Articles 100 to 117 of the Petroleum Act as it relates to energy development projects ...These articles establish that all landowners and users, whether of private or social lands, are obligated to sell their property or to negotiate one of several types of agreements with the energy corporation that was granted the contract to carry out energy projects on the property. In other words, landowners and users are to permanently or temporarily cede their property for energy projects.[84]

Hence, through the implementation of energy reform, land owners and users may be affected by specific investment projects targeted to develop this strategic sector, and they will not have the right of refusal. Note that the new legislation does not use the word "expropriation." Mexico's government "has been categorical in saying that outright expropriation of lands is out of the question, but that all landowners and users would be encouraged to negotiate with energy companies." However, the law seems to be somewhat contradictory. "Under the legislation, if landowners and users and energy companies do not achieve a negotiated agreement within 180 days, companies have the ability to ask a federal judge to force the cession of land use or to ask the Ministry of Agriculture to initiate compulsory mediation on how the land will be ceded." More specifically, "the law precludes the landowner's ability to say no and halt operations by denying access to the property."[85]

Public and Private Security: Militarization and a New "Gendarmerie"

New energy legislation was crafted during the Peña Nieto administration to benefit corporate interests as well as to create jobs and economic opportunities. Business-led cross-border governance became a reality under an emerging strategic action field (a privatized energy field) in Mexico. The idea was to promote investment in strategic sectors, which supposedly would lead to economic development and stability. In this new context, the issues of insecurity, violence, and organized crime were still of great concern. Hence, during its first years, to promote investment, Peña Nieto's administration tried to portray Mexico as a secure country. It also designed strategies to ensure the protection of economic interests so as to prevent investment from fleeing the country.

For example, in 2014, Peña Nieto announced the launch of a new police unit specifically intended to protect the production chain and take on other unorthodox assignments: the *gendarmerie*.[86] This unit was initially conceived as "an alternative to the armed forces being active in domestic security activities, and its creation was the first step toward lessening Mexico's reliance on the army and the marines." The *gendarmerie* would "have an explicit focus on protecting strategic regional industries."[87] Besides protecting rural commerce, this unit would guard mines and boost security at tourist beaches.[88] Many saw the creation of this group as largely an effort to promote business and investment. At the inauguration of the *gendarmerie* in August 2014, Monte Alejandro Rubido, then national security commissioner, declared that this group "would be deployed particularly to areas where criminals have caused economic distress or threatened commerce or tourism."[89]

Concluding Remarks: Challenges to Stability in an Emerging Field

Legislative changes and proposed investments in the energy sector, commercial alliances, and related policies to promote energy development during Peña Nieto's administration seemed to bode well for the consolidation of a new SAF in Mexico after a drug war. However, the stability of this emerging field is still subject to a number of challenges and limitations, including a new government in Mexico with a "new" vision in terms of energy policy;[90] a new world energy order and new geopolitics of energy; sagging prices for hydrocarbons; organized crime; corruption and insecurity; environmental concerns (regarding climate change, in particular); water availability constraints; fiscal constraints; and potential land-related conflicts, in addition to other forms of social unrest. No matter how many advances have been registered in the recent past in this sector, the stability of this emerging privatized energy field is still uncertain.

Mexico's previous government, in conjunction with the private sector, planned more than 740 major projects throughout the country, including roads, pipelines, hydroelectric dams, wind farms, and other energy-related projects. These projects were meant to generate strong economic growth and development. However, a number of human rights defenders, environmental groups, and other activists contend that these infrastructure works will displace entire communities, damage the environment in a number of ways, lead to water shortages, exacerbate inequality, and harm small farmers and cattle ranchers.[91]

Security concerns and new government priorities are among the main roadblocks to stability in a new strategic action field in Mexico that centres on the energy sector. While the large trans-national energy companies "have experience dealing with potentially insecure environments, and in some cases have their own security, smaller players want assurances that gang activity in development areas will be controlled."[92] Over the past few years, some hydrocarbon-rich areas have registered a strong presence of armed groups. In fact, some energy companies (mainly Pemex contractors) in these zones (e.g., the Burgos Basin) have been making extortion payments to groups like the Jalisco New Generation Cartel (CJNG, in Spanish), the Sinaloa Cartel, and some cells of what were Los Zetas and the Gulf Cartel, simply to be able to operate.[93]

Some progress has been made against these organizations, but criminal groups that operate in these strategic zones "still threaten, steal, extort, kidnap for ransom, and even terrorize the industry's personnel." The Government of Mexico has not yet established "complete control of regions rich in hydrocarbons in the country." Its "failure to recover vast swaths of territory lost to [criminal paramilitary groups] and bring it into full government control under the rule of law" puts the reform initiative's promises and the stability of the new SAF at risk.[94]

A further key challenge to a stable privatized energy field in Mexico has to do with water availability. The previous Mexican government viewed shale oil and natural gas development as a core part of its strategy to develop the energy sector and thereby create jobs and spur economic growth.[95] But shale energy depends on water, and limited availability of fresh water may hinder the development of shale resources, which require "fracking" techniques.[96] According to a 2014 World Resources Institute (WRI) report titled *Global Shale Gas Development: Water Availability and Business Risks*,[97] Mexico has large quantities of shale gas but limited supplies of fresh water. "Rapid urbanization and increasing demands for food and energy in Mexico have driven national water withdrawals to steadily increase over the past few decades, making water management a challenge in Mexico and imposing a significant cost to the country's economy."[98]

In fact, water scarcity could discourage energy developers from investing in Mexico.[99] The consolidation and stability of a new SAF in Mexico will require that investors in the energy sector be allowed access to this valuable natural resource. Peña Nieto's administration attempted to change the current legislation related to water usage with the aim of advancing the exploitation of shale gas. The previous government, through the National Water Commission (Conagua), had proposed some important legislative changes – additions and reforms to various parts of the National Water Act – to promote the construction of dams, water treatment plants, and other private megaprojects to store and transport water.[100] Under the proposed legislation, some of these projects were going to be "public utilities" that, in the event of conflict, would take precedence over activities in other sectors.

The new legislation on land ownership and use under Mexico's energy reform and the proposed changes to the Natural Water Act could have led to social conflict. The participation of big private trans-national interests in Mexico's hydrocarbon markets may yet generate "challenges ranging from peaceful local protests to potentially violent social unrest associated with the displacement of farmers, ranchers, and other land users, including indigenous peoples." It is plausible that "resistance movements, protests, social unrest, and even individual and communal standoffs against energy projects … arise in the near future."[101]

Veracruz environmental activist Hipólito Rodríguez contends that the aforementioned projects portend a very worrisome scenario for social organizations. In passing energy reforms, the previous Mexican government "legalize[d] a series of processes that break a number of historical agreements reached in the 1930s in the country." Those reforms meant that "very destructive initiatives," such as the development of shale resources through fracking, would be prioritized over all other forms of land use.[102] According to Rodríguez, Mexico's previous government was planning to give "legal permission for the performance of a series of actions that [were] of expropriatory nature." Such actions would "take from the peasant and indigenous organizations the land that they have conquered through agrarian reform."[103]

This comment characterizes an emerging SAF that started to take shape after a period of severe security and energy crises, which led to landmark energy reform legislation that promised to transform Mexico through the massive development of its energy sector. It is premature to declare that this transformation will have the desired positive impact in Mexico's economy. It is also uncertain that this process will continue (or will end) under the AMLO administration. What *is* clear is that this new framework promotes transnational business interests and business-led cross-border governance. Indeed, the dynamics described here are about cross-border governance because they involve policies meant to erase barriers to the participation of trans-national capital in the quest for North American energy integration.

It is worth noting that the main discourse of Mexico's previous government and some concerns of the business community and US citizens have more to do with economic considerations. The current government's priorities regarding this sector seem little different, especially under the new USMCA. In the first two decades of the present century, security issues became a priority. The paramilitarization of organized crime in Mexico and government responses to that phenomenon have apparently helped prepare the ground for an important transformation in the country that will modify socio-economic structures and represent a fundamental change in strategic action, not only in Mexico but beyond its borders as well.

Acknowledgments

The author thanks Bruno Dupeyron for his comments and feedback and Carlos Daniel Gutierrez Mannix for his help drawing the maps presented in this article.

NOTES

1 On the argument of the existence of a war or civil war in Mexico, see Correa-Cabrera, *Los Zetas. Inc.: Criminal Corporations, Energy, and Civil War in Mexico* (Austin: University of Texas Press, 2017), ch. 6. See also Aguilar Camín, "La Guerra Perdida de México," *Milenio*, 6 March 2015, http://www.milenio.com/firmas/hector_aguilar_camin_dia-con-dia/guerra-perdida-Mexico_18_476532362.html.
2 See Neil Fligstein and Doug McAdam, *A Theory of Fields* (New York: Oxford University Press, 2012), http://doi.org/10.1007/s11186-014-9237-0.
3 Fligstein and McAdam, *A Theory of Fields*, 2; Fligstein and McAdam, "Toward a General Theory of Strategic Action Fields," *Sociological Theory* 29, no. 1 (2011): 2. The authors define strategic action as "the attempt by social actors to create and maintain stable social worlds by securing the cooperation of others." According to their view, "strategic action is about control in a given context." Hence, the "creation of identities, political coalitions, and interests serves to promote the control of actors vis-à-vis other actors" (Fligstein and McAdam, "Toward a General Theory," 7).
4 Fligstein and McAdam, "Toward a General Theory," 3.
5 Fligstein and McAdam, "Toward a General Theory," 3.
6 Fligstein and McAdam, "Toward a General Theory," 4.
7 Fligstein and McAdam, "Toward a General Theory," 7.
8 Fligstein and McAdam, "Toward a General Theory," 20.
9 Fligstein and McAdam, "Toward a General Theory," 5.
10 Fligstein and McAdam, "Toward a General Theory," 15.
11 Fligstein and McAdam, "Toward a General Theory," 20.
12 This article contains a significant number of journalistic sources. It is worth noting that most of the available information regarding Mexico's drug-trafficking organizations, drug-related activities, and organized crime in general has been released and analysed by reporters. Academic work on these subjects is still in a very preliminary stage due to the extremely high risks of doing field research in areas controlled by criminal groups. A further difficulty experienced by academics studying these phenomena is the limited access to government intelligence and classified information that would provide them with a more accurate picture of the security situation and the clandestine activities of these groups. The use of secondary sources and media articles is therefore justified.
13 On this phenomenon, see Correa-Cabrera, *Los Zetas. Inc.*
14 Roman Kilisek, "Mexico's Energy Reforms: Can Mexico Emerge as a Prime Global Oil and Gas Industry Expansion Prospect?," *Breaking Energy*, 8 January 2014, para. 8, http://breakingenergy.com/2014/01/08/mexicos-energy-reforms-can-mexico-emerge-as-a-prime-global-oil-gas-industry-expansion-prospect.
15 Elinor Comlay, Mica Rosenberg, and M.B. Pell, "Special Report: Mexico Looks the Other Way as Contractors Fleece Oil Giant Pemex," Reuters, 23 January 2015,

http://mobile.reuters.com/article/idUSKBN0KW1LZ20150123?irpc=932; Clare Ribando Seelke et al., *Mexico's Oil and Gas Sector: Background, Reform Efforts, and Implications for the United States* (Washington, DC: Congressional Research Service, 2014); EIA, "Country Reports: Mexico"; Shannon K. O'Neil and James S. Taylor, "A Primer: Mexico Energy Reforms," *Vianovo*, 16 March 2014, http://vianovo.com/news/a-primer-mexico-energy-reforms.

16 O'Neil and Taylor, "A Primer," para. 3.

17 Kilisek, "Mexico's Energy Reforms," para. 8.

18 Noé Cruz Serrano, "Desde 2004 quiere EU gas natural de México para Garantizar Abasto," *El Universal*, 2 April 2004, para. 2, http://www.quiminet.com/noticias/quiere-eu-gas-natural-de-mexico-para-garantizar-abasto-1656770.htm.

19 Cruz Serrano, "Desde 2004."

20 Cruz Serrano, "Desde 2004."

21 Amendments to Articles 25, 27, and 28 and transitory articles of the constitution.

22 See Government of Mexico, "DECRETO por el que se expide la Ley de Hidrocarburos y se reforman diversas disposiciones de la Ley de Inversión Extranjera; Ley Minera, y Ley de Asociaciones Público Privadas" (Mexico City: Official Gazette of the Federation, 11 August 2014); Government of Mexico, "DECRETO por el que se expiden la Ley de Petróleos Mexicanos y la Ley de la Comisión Federal de Electricidad, y se reforman y derogan diversas disposiciones de la Ley Federal de las Entidades Paraestatales; la Ley de Adquisiciones, Arrendamientos y Servicios del Sector Público y la Ley de Obras Públicas y Servicios Relacionados con las Mismas" (Mexico City: Official Gazette of the Federation, 11 August 2014).

23 The reform will supposedly open up approximately 85 per cent of shale gas and oilfields in Mexico to private investment. Foreign energy companies will have access to "vast untapped oil reserves, including fields in the deep waters of the Gulf of Mexico." The majority of these lie off the coast of Tamaulipas and Veracruz. Kathryn Haahr, "Addressing the Concerns of the Oil Industry: Security Challenges in Northeastern Mexico and Government Responses," Mexico Institute Working Paper (Washington, DC: Wilson Center, January 2015), 6.

24 The SHCP will establish the fiscal terms applicable to each contract type, as well as royalty rates and taxes, and will design the parameters of a new oil sovereign wealth fund, the Mexican Petroleum Fund for Stabilization and Development (FoMePe). This fund will be overseen by the Central Bank. See O'Neil and Taylor, "A Primer."

25 CENAGAS will own and operate the national gas pipeline systems, and CENACE will do the same with the electricity grid.

26 O'Neil and Taylor, "A Primer."

27 Fligstein and McAdam, "Toward a General Theory," 18.

28 Fligstein and McAdam, "Toward a General Theory," 13.

29 According to the *CIA World Factbook*, in 2014 Mexico had an estimated 10.3 billion barrels of proven oil reserves.

30 Juan Montes, "Mexico opens energy sector to private investors," *Wall Street Journal*, 7 August 2014, para. 6, http://online.wsj.com/articles/mexico-opens-energy-sector-to-private-investors-1407392884.

31 Timothy Cama, "EIA predicts 75 percent increase in Mexico's oil output," *The Hill*, 24 August 2014, para. 1, http://thehill.com/policy/energy-environment/215923-eia-predicts-75-increase-in-mexicos-oil-output#.VB1awcUf2ts.facebook. Before the reforms, the predicted trends were different. The EIA said that oil production in Mexico would fall considerably, "bottoming out to 1.8 million barrels a day in 2025, and then it would 'struggle' to stay between 2 million and 2.1 million barrels in 2040" (para. 5).

32 Cama, "EIA predicts," para. 6.

33 Kilisek, "Mexico's Energy Reforms," para. 9.

34 Fligstein and McAdam, "Toward a General Theory," 5.

35 An *ejido* is a unique Mexican form of collective landownership.

36 Montes, "Mexico opens energy sector," 2014.

37 Alison Sider, "The latest oil boom, 36,552 feet below the Gulf of Mexico," *Wall Street Journal*, 18 October 2013, http://blogs.wsj.com/corporate-intelligence/2013/10/18/the-latest-oil-boom-36552-feet-below-the-gulf-of-mexico.

38 David Sheppard et al., "US oil price below zero for first time in history," *Financial Times*, 20 April 2020, https://www.ft.com/content/a5292644-958d-4065-92e8-ace55d766654.

39 Carlos Slim, Mexico's wealthiest man and one of the world's richest people, seems to be one of the best prepared new national actors who will participate in the country's energy business. His investment portfolio in the energy sector includes companies that have been involved for years, directly and indirectly, in other countries, like the United States, Colombia, Argentina, and Mexico. In April 2015, Slim's global conglomerate company, Carso Group, merged his main energy infrastructure and perforation businesses to create Carso Oil & Gas. See Rolando Hinojosa and Alejandro Dabdoub, "Llenos de energía," *Reporte Índigo*, 13 July 2014, http://m.reporteindigo.com/nota.php?id=69325.

40 "Las nuevas petroleras Mexicanas," *CNN Expansión*, 29 January 2014, http://www.cnnexpansion.com/negocios/2014/01/24/quienes-seran-las-nuevas-petroleras. Other smaller Mexican companies that could plausibly participate in the sector successfully are Altos Hornos de México (AHMSA), Cotemar, CP Latina, Demar Instaladora y Constructora, Grupo R, Monclova Pirineos Gas (MPG), Oceanografía, and Oro Negro, among others. All these businesses have accumulated experience in the recent past since they have participated as Pemex contractors or have worked in other countries in energy-related activities. See Salvador Camarena, "Listos para la Fiebre Petrolera?," *SinEmbargo*, 4 February 2014, http://www.sinembargo.mx/opinion/04-02-2014/21345.

41 Fligstein and McAdam, "Toward a General Theory," 6.

42 See Tony Payan and Guadalupe Correa-Cabrera, "Land Ownership and Use under Mexico's Energy Reform," issue brief, Mexico Center, James A. Baker III Institute for Public Policy, Rice University, Houston, 29 October 2014a.

43 Montes, "Mexico Opens Energy Sector," para. 18.

44 Montes, "Mexico Opens Energy Sector," para. 21.

45 Patricia Mayorga, "Narco 'ablandó' zona de Chihuahua rica en gas shale: Morena", *Proceso*, 21 August 2014b, para. 7, http://www.proceso.com.mx/?p=380107.

46 Mayorga, "Narco 'ablandó' zona de Chihuahua." For example, a group calling itself "Chihuahua vs Fracking" mobilized recently and asked the executive and legislative local powers to prioritize the protection of water resources and to place this need ahead of any international (or national) entrepreneurial interest. This was with the aim of guaranteeing the quality and accessibility of water for human consumption, as well as urban, rural and environmental supply for current and future generations.

47 Fligstein and McAdam, "Toward a General Theory," 6.

48 Fligstein and McAdam, "Toward a General Theory," 6.

49 See David A. Ganzt, "The United States–Mexico–Canada Agreement: Energy Production and Policies," Baker Institute for Public Policy, Center for the United States and Mexico, Rice University, Houston, 17 September 2019, https://www.bakerinstitute.org/media/files/files/a7b744b6/bi-report-091719-mex-usmca-5.pdf.

50 Ganzt, "The United States–Mexico–Canada Agreement," 7.

51 Ganzt, "The United States–Mexico–Canada Agreement.

52 Noé Cruz Serrano, "Hallan yacimientos de gas en Tamaulipas," *El Universal*, 25 October 2011, http://www.eluniversal.com.mx/finanzas/90533.html. Herrera guaranteed that the exploitation of the new shale gas deposits would promote the country's annual GDP growth by one percentage point (para. 4).

53 Shannon K. O'Neil is the vice-president, deputy director of studies, and Nelson and David Rockefeller senior fellow for Latin America Studies at the Council on Foreign Relations (https://www.cfr.org/expert/shannon-k-oneil). Taylor is also a member of the CFR and founding partner of Vianovo, a "boutique management consultancy that specializes in high-stakes brand, policy and crisis issues" (see http://vianovo.com).

54 O'Neil and Taylor, "A Primer", para. 3.

55 Shannon Young, "American media misses the story on Mexican oil reform," *Texas Observer*, 10 February 2014), para. 14, https://www.texasobserver.org/american-media-misses-story-mexican-oil-reform.

56 Young, "American media misses the story," para. 15.

57 Young, "American media misses the story," para. 16.

58 Dawn Paley, "Off the Map in Mexico," *The Nation* 292, no. 21 (2011): 22.

59 Fligstein and McAdam, "Toward a General Theory," 8.

60 Fligstein and McAdam, "Toward a General Theory," 8. This particular classification distinguishes between (1) distant and proximate fields; (2) horizontal versus vertical fields; and (3) state versus non-state fields.

61 These trends might change in the future with the renewed roles – and stronger leverage – of countries like China and Russia on the world energy markets.
62 Fligstein and McAdam, "Toward a General Theory," 10.
63 Fligstein and McAdam, "Toward a General Theory," 22.
64 Fligstein and McAdam, "Toward a General Theory," 10.
65 See Shannon K. O'Neil, *Two Nations Indivisible: Mexico, the United States, and the Road Ahead* (New York: Oxford University Press, 2013); and Thomas L. Friedman, "How Mexico Got Back in the Game," *New York Times*, 23 February 2013, http://www.nytimes.com/2013/02/24/opinion/sunday/friedman-how-mexico-got-back-in-the-game.html?_r=0.
66 David McCumber Hearst, "Another Eagle Ford south of the border?," *Laredo Morning Times*, 31 January 2015), para. 31, http://m.lmtonline.com/business/article_9c9a3a5c-a9a2-11e4-aace-076fd54814a3.html?mode=jqm.
67 Haahr, "Addressing the Concerns of the Oil Industry," 6.
68 Dawn Marie Paley, *Drug War Capitalism* (Oakland: AK Press, 2014), 90.
69 O'Neil and Taylor, "A Primer," paras. 19–21. See also Government of Mexico, "DECRETO por el que se expiden la Ley de Petróleos Mexicanos y la Ley de la Comisión Federal de Electricidad," 2014b.
70 Cama, "EIA Predicts 75 Percent Increase."
71 Dolia Estevez, "Booking Oil Reserves Is an 'Attractive Incentive' for Foreign Companies in Mexico, Says US," *Forbes*, 4 September 2014, para. 6, http://www.forbes.com/sites/doliaestevez/2014/09/04/booking-oil-reserves-is-an-attractive-incentive-for-foreign-companies-in-mexico-says-u-s. Even in the United States, some recent changes have reinforced energy relations with Mexico. In August 2015, the US Department of Commerce announced the approval of "licenses for swaps of American light crude oil in exchange for imports of heavy Mexican crude oil." Sergio Chapa, "US Commerce Department approves crude oil swap with Mexico," *San Antonio Business Journal*, 14 August 2015a, http://www.bizjournals.com/houston/news/2015/08/14/u-s-commerce-department-approves-crude-oil-swap.html?ana=e_hstn_nrg&u=mfJGhtX5JSlT/ATWytrhmg0779b38c&t=1440022510.
72 See Seelke et al., *Mexico's Oil and Gas Sector*; and US Department of the Interior, "Secretary Jewell Applauds Passage of U.S.-Mexico Transboundary Hydrocarbons Agreement" (press release), 23 December 2013, http://www.doi.gov/news/pressreleases/secretary-jewell-applauds-passage-of-us-mexico-transboundary-hydrocarbons-agreement.cfm.
73 According to estimates of the Department of Interior's Bureau of Ocean Energy Management (BOEM), this area contains approximately "172 million barrels of oil and 304 billion cubic feet of natural gas." US Department of the Interior, "Secretary Jewell Applauds Passage," para. 3.
74 Government of Mexico, *Programa Nacional de Infraestructura 2014–2018* (Mexico City, 2014).
75 Erika Ramírez, "Programa Nacional de Infraestructura, Despojos por Venir," *Contralínea*, 23 September 2014, para. 21, http://contralinea.info/archivo-revista/index.php/2014/09/23/programa-nacional-de-infraestructura-despojos-por-venir/.

76 Samantha Gross, "AMLO Reverses Positive Trends in Mexico's Energy Industry," Brookings Institution, 20 December 2019), https://www.brookings.edu/blog/order-from-chaos/2019/12/20/amlo-reverses-positive-trends-in-mexicos-energy-industry.

77 Justin Villamil, "Why Mexico is pushing to slow down clean energy," *Washington Post*, 17 July 2020, https://www.washingtonpost.com/business/energy/why-mexico-is-pushing-to-slow-downclean-energy/2020/07/16/fbfcd0f4-c779-11ea-a825-8722004e4150_story.html.

78 Sergio Chapa, "A look at 24 new energy projects up for bid in Mexico," *San Antonio Business Journal*, 23 June 2015b, para. 1, http://www.bizjournals.com/sanantonio/blog/eagle-ford-shale-insight/2015/06/a-look-at-24-new-energy-projects-up-for-bid-in.html?ana=e_hstn_nrg&u=mfJGhtX5JSlT/ATWytrhmg0779b38c&t=1435633918. There are plans to generate an additional 1,442 megawatts of power and to lay down approximately 1,500 miles of natural gas pipeline as well as around 2,000 miles of power lines. This would represent more than $9.8 billion in infrastructure investments (para. 3).

79 Bob Black, "US Natural Gas Exports to Mexico Taking Off," *Financial Times*, 3 August 2015), para. 1, http://www.forbes.com/sites/drillinginfo/2015/08/03/u-s-natural-gas-exports-to-mexico-taking-off.

80 Chapa, "A Look at 24 New Energy Projects," para. 2.

81 EIA, "US Natural Gas Exports to Mexico," para. 6.

82 EIA, "US Natural Gas Exports to Mexico," 1.

83 EIA, "US Natural Gas Exports to Mexico," 1.

84 EIA, "US Natural Gas Exports to Mexico," 2.

85 EIA, "US Natural Gas Exports to Mexico," 3.

86 At the beginning, the *gendarmerie* would "comprise about 5,000 new recruits and function as a division of the 36,000-officer federal police." It was conceived as "an elite civil force, not a military one, drawn from well-educated young recruits with no prior police experience as well as veteran police commanders." Randal C. Archibold, "Elite Mexican police corps targets persistent violence, but many are skeptical," *New York Times*, 22 August 2014), para. 3, http://www.nytimes.com/2014/08/23/world/americas/familiar-flaws-seen-in-mexicos-new-elite-police-force.html?_r=0.

87 Patrick Corcoran, "Mexico's new gendarmerie: Security game changer or window dressing?," *InSight Crime*, 29 July 2014, http://www.insightcrime.org/news-analysis/mexicos-new-gendarmerie-security-game-changer-or-window-dressing.

88 Joshua Partlow and Gabriela Martinez, "Mexico launches new police force to guard commerce," *Washington Post*, 22 August 2014, para. 8, http://www.washingtonpost.com/world/the_americas/mexico-launches-new-police-force-to-guard-commerce/2014/08/22/902d0b04-d5fb-4bfe-bb2e-713198114f4b_story.html. For more on the *gendarmerie*, see Miguel Moguel, *El Debate Entre Políticas de Seguridad, Democracia y Derechos Humanos: El Caso de la Nueva Gendarmería Nacional* (Mexico City: Fundar, Centro de Análisis e Investigación, 2014).

89 Archibold, "Elite Mexican police corps," para. 6.

90 Édgar Sígler, "Los 3 puntos clave del plan energético de AMLO: Producir, procesar, generar," *Expansión*, 10 December 2018), https://expansion.mx/empresas/2018/12/10/puntos-plan-energetico-amlo-producir-procesar-electrizar.

91 See Camarena, "Listos Para la Fiebre Petrolera?," 2014; Luis Hernández Navarro, "La reforma al campo, cuentos Chinos," *La Jornada*, 8 April 2014, http://www.jornada.unam.mx/2014/04/08/opinion/017a1pol; Patricia Mayorga, "La fracturación hidráulica es nociva para la salud: 'Chihuahua vs fracking,'" *Proceso*, 4 September 2014a, http://www.proceso.com.mx/?p=381343; and Tony Payan and Guadalupe Correa-Cabrera, "Seguridad, Estado de Derecho y Reforma Energética en México," in *El Estado de Derecho y la Reforma Energética. Mexico City: Tirant Lo Blanch México*, ed. Tony Payan and Stephen Zamora (Mexico City: Tirant Lo Blanch, 2016): 403–34.

92 McCumber Hearst, "Another Eagle Ford south of the border?," para. 12.

93 See Alfredo Corchado and James Osborne, "The new border: Eyes are on Mexico's untapped potential," *Dallas Morning News*, 13 July 2014, http://res.dallasnews.com/interactives/border_energy; and Payan and Correa-Cabrera, "Land Ownership and Use."

94 Payan and Correa-Cabrera, "Land Ownership and Use," 4.

95 It is worth noting that the current government of Andrés Manuel López Obrador does not seem to support these projects.

96 Paul Reig, Tianyi Luo, and Jonathan N. Proctor, *Global Shale Gas Development: Water Availability and Business Risks*. Washington, DC: World Resources Institute, 2014.

97 This report draws on WRI's Aqueduct Water Risk Atlas and is a global and country-specific resource to help stakeholders evaluate freshwater availability across shale plays worldwide. It has a special focus on eleven countries, including Mexico.

98 Reig, Luo, and Proctor, *Global Shale Gas Development*, 55.

99 Keith Schneider, *Water Scarcity Could Deter Energy Developers from Crossing Border into Northern Mexico* (Traverse City: Circle of Blue and Wilson Center, 2015).

100 Angélica Enciso, "Buscan favorecer explotación de gas shale con cambios a la legislación sobre el Agua," *La Jornada*, 10 March 2014, para. 1. http://www.jornada.unam.mx/2014/03/10/politica/015n1pol.

101 Payan and Correa-Cabrera, "Land Ownership and Use," 4.

102 Jesús Ramírez, "Los políticos Mexicanos que son socios de petroleras extranjeras", *Vanguardia*, 10 December 2013, para. 31, http://www.vanguardia.com.mx/lospoliticosmexicanosquesonsociosdepetrolerasextranjeras-1900041.html.

103 Ramírez, "Los políticos Mexicanos, » para. 32.

6 Reshaping Cross-Border Governance in the Pacific Northwest Borderlands

VICTOR KONRAD

It is late June of 2020. The second seismic shock to border governance in less than twenty years has manifested itself as a closure of the US–Canada border for all but essential crossings. In 2001, the events of 9/11 immediately altered the ways in which the border was imagined by authorities in the US and in Canada,[1] and border governance was reshaped to accommodate and articulate heightened security. The impact of the COVID-19 pandemic also has been extensive, ranging from immediate reductions in cross-border trade and mobility to impacts on social and cultural interactions across the boundary. By the end of 2020, border governance had defaulted to strict rules and restrictions within an uncertain timeline. These restrictions would ease by the middle of 2022.[2]

In the Pacific Northwest borderlands, the Border Policy Research Institute (BPRI) has recorded a substantial reduction of more than 80 per cent in cross-border mobility based on passenger vehicle crossing patterns.[3] The immediate impact on retail shopping near the border in Whatcom County, Washington, has been devastating, and the BPRI anticipates that the border restrictions related to COVID-19 may have a long-term impact on Canadian shopping behaviour in the adjacent US and that this impact will be similar to post-9/11 patterns.[4] The restrictions related to the pandemic can be viewed as a part of, and certainly parallel to, a general narrowing of border governance. In the Pacific Northwest borderlands, cross-border environmental governance remains overly dependent on informal networks, with few "NGO to NGO" partnerships that are jointly planned, funded, and endorsed by governments.[5] The upcoming implementation of the REAL ID Act in the US will require identification that confirms identity and citizenship for all domestic as well as international flights. Yet unlike the Western Hemisphere Travel Initiative (WHTI), which aimed to standardize travel documentation for use across borders, the REAL ID Act may result in the differentiation of travel documents used by Americans and Canadians, as well as increased complexity of documentation used at the border.[6] In the Pacific Northwest borderlands, this may result in border management complications and, paradoxically, in regression in the advanced border governance models and practices originating in this cross-border region.

Governance impacts all aspects of border interaction, yet border governance remains "undertheorized" by border studies specialists and scholars of governance. Some issue areas – environmental governance foremost among these[7] – have seen substantial research and attention, but many border governance issues remain to be explored thoroughly.[8] In 2009 and 2010, a study of the "breaking points" of border interaction in the Cascade Gateway in the Pacific Northwest cross-border region of North America (map 6.1) completed 98 interviews with border stakeholders, primarily in the business, education, enforcement, and government sectors. In all instances, stakeholders were asked questions related to border governance practices and issues. In a parallel survey of 160 border stakeholders, 83 respondents replied to 50 statements on a five-point scale of agreement. Issues of border governance comprised almost one half of statements, with most of these probing views on how the border works and on border management in the BC–Washington border region.[9] Among these issues were concerns about governance outsourcing and the recurrent mantra of overregulation, but most concerns about governance in the new era of security primacy along the US–Canada border related to the apparent lack of governance vision along the newly recalibrated scale of governance application from de-emphasized "port authority" to expanded federal control at all scales.[10] The results of the interviews and the parallel survey, though completed almost a decade ago, continue to resonate and provide a rich source of information for the ongoing discourse of border governance in the region. Stakeholders were asked: "Where is the border vision leading border governance?"; "What laws apply in the ever-thickening bubble zone?"; "Whose job is it to rebuild the border?"; "Top down and bottom up governance are not meeting. Is the IMTC (International Mobility and Trade Corridor) the solution, or just part of the solution?" The anxiety and frustration among border stakeholders regarding shortcomings in effective border governance generated strong opinions and observations: "Silos of border programs are run by different agencies but they do not interact"; "Agreements under the radar of federal agencies are often effective until discovered to be not binding"; "The post 9/11 discourse about the border narrows as the border thickens"; "Rapidly evolving border agencies are subject to 'mission creep' and 'budget seeking'"; "The policy 'wonks' and groups are in Washington and Ottawa not at the regional level where they are needed. Look at the EU models!"; "Usually there is no 'border person' in a government department, and it does not happen until the 'parking lot' is evident."[11] According to many border stakeholders in the Pacific Northwest borderlands, border governance simply did not measure up to expectations from a demanding public that previously had been entitled to cross the border with ease.[12]

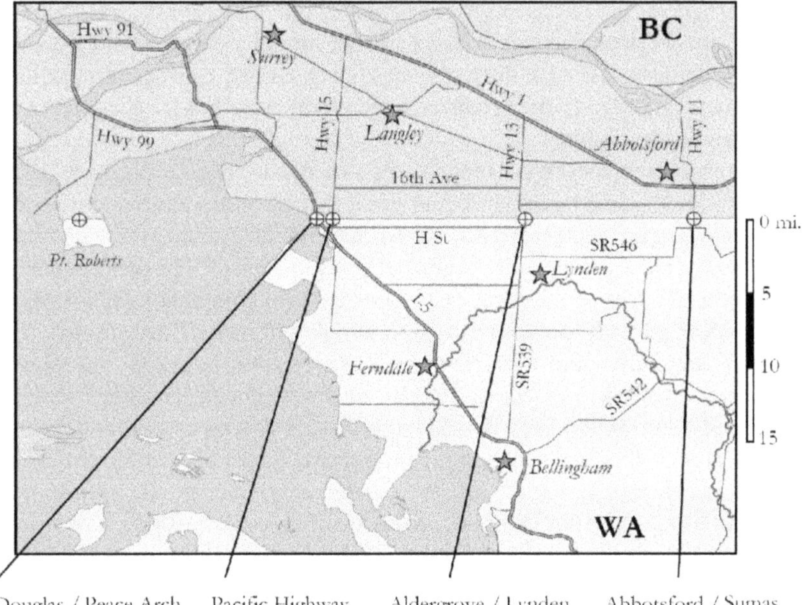

Map 6.1. The Pacific Northwest Border Region

Note that border stakeholders in the Pacific Northwest are generally supportive of evolved border policy but register considerable concern over practice. Alper and Hammond add that "highly centralized border security arrangements are not facilitative of good border governance" and that border governance should "allow for regional input and action, and encourage it."

Clearly, the rules, procedures, processes, and patterns for crossing borders changed in the early twenty-first century.[13] Yet in the Pacific Northwest, governance structures for managing an evolving border changed more slowly, albeit with sudden lurches toward the exercise of centralized authority, back to a modicum of local and regional input, toward militarization and simultaneously toward a dependence on rapid technological enhancements. Meanwhile, research on cross-border governance applied to the region has focused on environmental governance: many researchers are inspired by ecological traditions in the region and transportation policy by the Border Policy Research Institute (BPRI).[14] Research has since gained more breadth and momentum with the BC regional studies of the Borders in Globalization Project.[15] A growing awareness and understanding of cross-border governance has been fostered by efforts to conceptualize the Cascadia region[16] and articulate its "partnerships" in governance.[17] This has received national and international recognition through the work of Canada's Policy Research Initiative,[18] yet the literature on cross-border governance in the region has not expanded significantly, particularly when compared to the extensive research on cross-border governance in European border regions.

European researchers have assembled a rich dossier of case studies focused on cross-border governance, and, moreover, they have strived to define cross-border governance and theorize how it works. Foremost among these theoretical advances are a set of studies evaluated by Mikhailova.[19] The conceptualizations have nuances of meaning that help expand a comprehensive vision of cross-border governance. Scott envisions a milieu in which different national, political, legislative, and administrative cultures come together and enable the actors involved to assess trajectories of development, envision common goals, and determine means of achieving these.[20] Kramsch sees fluid, transversal forms of decision-making operating above, below, and within the ranks of inter-state hierarchies and markets.[21] Gualini conceptualizes an institutional construct resulting from complex processes of co-evolution that have three dimensions: political-economic, institutional, and symbolic-cognitive.[22] Perkman observes the perceived need for policy coordination or the management of cross-border dependencies.[23] Pikner outlines a social infrastructure across the state borders that creates new channels for the transfer or flow of material and non-material resources.[24] Terlouw ventures that this is a new form of governance in which horizontal cross-border linkages are closely connected to vertical linkages between various administrative levels, from the local to the continental.[25] Garcia-Alvarez and Trillo Santamaria comment on the continuous process of overlapping not only of local, regional, and state governments and administrations but also of the different cultures, discourses, and objectives of territorial agents.[26] Nelles and Durand summarize that cross-border governance is a political process that is built through innovation, experimentation, error, and re-evaluation within the unique institutional constraints imposed by the fragmented international context, and that each region invents its own method of coordinating political action in its own cross-border space.[27]

In summary, the emerging literature conveys a sense of cross-border governance as somewhat more informal and fluid yet also comprehensive and reactive when compared to state-based governance structures, and as engaging agency more rapidly and perhaps more effectively. Such governance may approach institutionalization, but governance institutions are not the main vehicle for policy coordination, cross-border cooperation, and cultural interface. This new form of governance enables a social infrastructure across state borders that balances horizontal and vertical linkages, as well as a political process that is constantly evolving and innovating in the vanguard of global change but is characterized by unique constraints and conditions in a particular border space. In essence, cross-border governance may be conceptualized as a strategic action field (SAF).[28] This chapter applies the theory of SAFs to explain more fully than was once possible the emergence of cross-border governance between Canada and the US, specifically in the Pacific Northwest. The first section relates the theory of SAFs to cross-border governance between the US and Canada. The discussion then outlines the emergence of the SAF, the characteristics of the stable field, and the rupture and renegotiation of the field. The chapter concludes with an assessment of the added value gained from applying SAF theory to our understanding cross-border governance, and more generally to building theory in border studies.

The Theory of Strategic Action Fields and Cross-Border Governance between Canada and the US

The theory of SAFs was defined and elaborated in the introduction to this volume. Consequently, the discussion of the theory in this chapter will be limited to the conceptual and methodological considerations as applied to the Canada–US case study, rather than restating the theory's central elements. Fligstein and McAdam offer a roadmap to three main "states" in which SAFs are apparent:[29] field formation or emergence, the stable field, and the rupture/crisis/renegotiation of the field. This chapter explores how Canada–US cross-border governance may be interpreted by examining these states in SAF development.

To position this case study in the context of both SAF theory and the goals of this volume, which are to test, expand, and sharpen that theory, it is necessary to examine the tenets of the roadmap before proceeding with the analysis. What questions do we ask? How are these questions arranged? How does this constitute the theoretical framework for the case study?

Formation of the field, as acknowledged by Fligstein and McAdam, often emerges in "amorphous processes" that show few "empirical traces" of origins.[30] Consequently, field emergence is challenging to document explicitly, though it is still possible to conceptualize. The aim is to identify the key actors that struggled to control the emerging field, their alternative conceptions of the field, the resources they brought to the field (material, political, ideological), and their reliance on external actors, particularly state actors. What were the characteristics of the founding episode of cross-border governance? What were the principal terms of agreement? Were any governance units established to routinize and safeguard the agreement?

The stable field is more evident, but it remains a challenge to establish the boundaries of the field and discern whether those boundaries are formally prescribed or socially constructed. Also, it is necessary to identify the principal incumbents and challengers. Is the power structure a coalition or a hierarchy? Are there shared understandings about membership, acceptable forms of action, and structural rules? How strong is the consensus regarding the agreement? How do external fields help stabilize and reproduce the field? How do internal governance units serve this function? What are the "modal strategies, forms of action, and collective action frames employed by incumbents and challengers in the face of generally stable field relations?"[31]

Whereas examination of field formation and the stable field promises a more comprehensive explanation of regional cross-border governance in the Canada–US cross-border governance context, it is the final state of rupture/crisis/renegotiation that is inherently the most interesting, and potentially the most illuminating with regard to the governance of the cross-border region. Currently, in border studies, the changing nature of borders and, consequently, the transformation of cross-border structure and agency is engaging most border researchers, and the interpretation of conflicts, shocks, breaking points, and other dynamics is central to understanding how borders are changing and operating in globalization.[32] In the specific instance of cross-border governance in the Pacific Northwest, the goals are to identify how the crisis emerged, the actors and events that shaped the crisis, and the dynamics that brought about resolution. Specific questions suggested by Fligstein and McAdam are: What shock(s) initiated the crisis? What social processes mediated the crisis and mobilized challengers? With what forms of action and collective action frames do incumbents and challengers respond to the crisis? Again, what role do key external actors/SAFs play in precipitating the episode, shaping it, and forming the agreement? What are the terms of the agreement, and how do these terms alter the strategic action field? How do the crisis and agreement affect the proximate field?[33]

In approaching these states of the SAF of cross-border governance, the analysis must be mindful of and sensitive to the scaled nature of cross-border governance in the Canada–US context and in border governance generally. The scaled governance may be self-identified in discrete layers, but this identification is somewhat misleading because relating the subnational to the national state is a fluid and malleable endeavour. Also, the Pacific Northwest cross-border region must be viewed in the context of a broader, multi-regional spectrum of related yet discrete cross-border governance fields that sometimes overlap constituencies in space and time. How to conceptualize scale in globalization is one of the most difficult theoretical quandaries facing border theorists. Field theory offers a flexible conceptualization of SAFs in time and space, but the challenge remains to articulate the manifestations of these fields.

The Emergence of Cross-Border Governance in the Pacific Northwest Borderlands

Cross-border governance in the Pacific Northwest has its origins in the confluence of the regional logging industry, coastal transportation, the linkage of

Alaska to the mainland US, the Indigenous territories connected throughout the region, urban development around Puget Sound and the Georgia Strait, and Pacific Northwest culture and lifestyle (map 6.1). All of these elements, combined with a unique shared environment[34] and the distance from the national capitals in Washington, DC, and Ottawa, provided fertile conditions for the emergence of cross-border governance components soon after the border was finally agreed upon, defined, and staked out at the end of the nineteenth century.[35] Cross-border engagement expanded throughout the twentieth century, and structures and agents of cross-border governance emerged to expedite cross-border flows of people and goods, as well as cooperation.[36] Much of this field formation was localized along the border, epitomized by informal arrangements between border communities such as Abbotsford and Sumas in the Fraser Valley, White Rock and Blaine on the coast, and Osoyoos and Oroville in the Okanagan Valley (in BC and Washington respectively, in each case).

Yet despite substantial regional cooperation across the border throughout the twentieth century, it was not until the late 1980s that the BC government shifted from an inward-focused perspective on economic self-interest and a political ideology that did not foster cross-border cooperation.[37] This change of vision, combined with growing recognition of the cross-border region of "Cascadia" among both Americans and Canadians, the signing of the Free Trade Agreement (FTA) between the countries, and the further expansion of trade to Mexico under the North American Free Trade Agreement (NAFTA), marked a turning point. Additionally, leaders in business and government were gradually acknowledging that there were growing regional to global synergies and that powerful forces of convergence were operating at all scales, albeit primarily at the regional level. Clearly, this convergence provided an additional incentive to create institutions and processes for cross-border linkage and governance.[38] According to Alper and Artibise, the key actors vying for control of this emerging field initially cooperated quite well together: there was no struggle to control the emerging field, nor was there clear leadership, and moreover, there were few models of cooperation to consult. Institutionalization, therefore, was minimal. As Alper emphasizes, there were environmental Cascadians and business-oriented Cascadians, and these sectoral alignments were evident throughout the 1980s and 1990s as the field emerged.[39] The somewhat opaque yet generally acknowledged and accepted vision of a cross-border Cascadia was compelling enough to encourage cooperative governance but not sufficiently prescriptive to disenfranchise any particular cohort.

A single founding episode for the emergence of the field is difficult to discern, but two events seem to have heralded the formalization of cross-border governance and the formation of the strategic action field (SAF), or more properly fields.[40] The two events were the founding of PNWER in 1989 (the outer field) and the founding of the BC–Washington State Environmental

Cooperation Council (ECC) in 1992 (the inner field). At the outset, these fields engaged different and discrete sectors. Environmental Cascadians moved to extend sectoral representation rapidly, establishing trans-boundary NGOs (People for Puget Sound and the Georgia Strait Alliance – merged in 1995 to form the Sounds and Straits Coalition) and developing bioregional initiatives (the Georgia Basin Ecological Initiative, the Puget Sound Action Team/ Fraser Basin Council MOU, the Canada–US Joint Statement of Cooperation on the Georgia Basin/Puget Sound Ecosystem, Trans-Boundary Marine Protected Areas). Business-oriented Cascadians initiated the Cascadia Project (the Discovery Institute–US and the Cascadia Institute–Canada) as a strategic plan for environmentally sound economic development and urban management in the trans-border corridor; this initiative then spawned the Cascadian Mayor's Council, the Cascadia Metropolitan Forum, the Cascadia Border Working Group, and the International Mobility and Trade Corridor Project (IMTC), among other projects and institutions. Other examples of regional economic cooperation have been the Pacific Corridor Enterprise Council (PACE), the Pacific Northwest Economic Partnership, the Alliance of Border Communities, the BC–Washington–Oregon Rail Working Group, and the BC–Washington Corridor Task Force.[41] It appears that the founding episode not only resulted in a set of SAFs that overlapped geographically but also allowed numerous sector-specific and aligned organizations to emerge and populate the field rapidly, under a guiding vision of Cascadia and a basic commitment to sustainability.

For business-oriented Cascadians, developments seem to have been consistent with the expanded geographical vision of the cross-border region and with the need for constant innovation and renewal in the regional economy. PNWER provided legislative and business integration across the border within a "natural global business zone,"[42] and by the 1990s it had emerged as the regional organization that addressed both economic and environmental/social issues through its nine working groups: agriculture, environment, export, forest products, government procurement, recycling, telecommunications, tourism, and transportation. All the while, however, the Cascadia Project continued to lead in cross-border initiatives in transportation, border infrastructure, and regional tourism; PACE continued to advocate free trade; and the governments of BC and Washington continued to build alliances. The agreement has been to establish complementary roles and to engage and integrate the fields as one tapestry linked by the Cascadia vision.

The environmental field is populated by more organizations, institutions, and advocacy groups; however, a similar guiding spirit prevails among the various trans-boundary NGOs and bioregional initiatives. These organizations characteristically operate at more micro-regional levels and focus on specific local and regional environmental issues. The terms of agreement have enabled this relative autonomy within an acknowledged set of guiding environmental principles originating in large part within the Pacific Northwest. The terms of agreement for the BC–Washington ECC are more explicit and constraining. "The ECC is limited by a lack of authority to make and enforce rules. Neither Washington State nor BC has given up decision-making power to this regional organization. Even if there existed the political will to do so, this would be difficult, if not impossible, given the mix of federal, provincial, and state jurisdictional authorities involved."[43]

In the process of field formation, the role of federal actors is limited. According to both Artibise and Alper, Cascadians have developed a "go it alone attitude" and generally view federal officials as distant, meddlesome, and unhelpful. Not until the roll-out of the FTA and NAFTA did federal authorities nurture the field formation, and that help was generally seen as superfluous by key actors in the region. The general absence and exclusion of federal actors from the process of developing the emerging SAF may partly account for the limited struggle within the region to control the emerging field. There was broad unanimity in conceptions of the field; key actors in the cross-border region cooperatively evolved a vision and a symbolic representation of the field and then turned this vision of Cascadia into a reality.

From Cascadia to the Salish Sea: The Constantly Evolving Cross-Border Governance Field

Recently, the guiding vision of Cascadia has been overlaid with a new concept of cross-border regional identity. In 2009, a more defined spatial concept of the Salish Sea encompassing aspects of Indigeneity, coastal environment, watershed, and life zone replaced the former cross-border environmental and ecological approximation of the cross-border region.[44] Although the term Cascadia remains, it no longer serves as extensively to galvanize environmental, political, and social advocacy and policy in the cross-border region. The mature cross-border governance field remains bounded by a set of nested visions; some of these are socially constructed, like Cascadia, and others are formally prescribed, like the Salish Sea. Indeed, it appears that the SAF is being more formally prescribed as the field matures, with state and provincial boundaries framing PNWER and explicit watershed boundaries defining the Salish Sea basin. The cross-border governance field continues to operate within distinct environmental and economic frameworks, although the sectoral differentiation is more blurred, or at least traversed more readily by policy-makers.

During the 1990s, the cross-border governance field was evolving constantly, with routine engagement of federal authorities, although diverse federal agencies on both sides of the border operated within mandates and regulatory frameworks. Occasionally, cross-border fisheries management disagreements, and forest industry issues extending across the border, among other issues, would require intervention from Washington, DC, and Ottawa, but many cross-border governance concerns were handled by federal authorities in the cross-border region. For example, Integrated Border Enforcement Teams (IBETs) had been initiated by the RCMP in BC and the US Border Patrol in Washington to deal with cross-border drug smuggling before the IBETs became a policy direction across the continent.[45] This pattern of balanced federal and regional control of cross-border governance, combined with an increasingly strong voice from urban, municipal, community, and other local-level interests, appeared to work well until federal engagement was required beyond the routine, as in the case of the salmon fishery dispute.[46] The cross-border governance field in the Pacific Northwest had evolved as a viable, effective, and sustainable strategic action field.

In this SAF, it is difficult to differentiate principal incumbents and challengers. Are the federal authorities and agencies the principal incumbents, and all or some of the state and provincial authorities, mayors, and action group leaders the challengers? The distinction was difficult to establish in the decade after the field emerged, but it did become more visible when crises requiring high-level federal decisions arose. During the 1990s, these crises were relatively modest and sectoral in their impact. Consequently, a full mobilization and confrontation of incumbents and challengers in the field did not emerge until the events of 9/11, after which the strong emphasis on security distinguished formally and explicitly the roles of incumbents and challengers in the cross-border governance field. At the point, US federal agencies such as the Department of Homeland Security (DHS) began exercising the weight and reach of incumbency, and US Congressional representatives began pressing regional interests.[47] In Canada after 9/11, a similar albeit more subdued regional/national discourse ensued. In both countries, state, provincial, and local politicians were the main challengers.

Also, the pattern of balanced federal and regional control of cross-border governance operated within the coalition framework that had emerged in the field while it was being formed and as it evolved during the 1990s. Shared understandings regarding membership, acceptable forms of action, and guiding rules and principles were loose and informal, guided primarily by cooperative goals rather than by any imperative to structure the field. So the SAF of cross-border governance in the Pacific Northwest gelled without a rigid structure and without either substantial external influence or internal direction and institutionalization. "Bottom-up" strategies of governance appeared to prevail, and work, as long as no serious challenges developed within the field. Yet as border stakeholders in the region have acknowledged, field stability remained tenuous, always open to adjustment by external and internal forces, which perhaps sought but never attained acknowledged stasis. As one stakeholder put it, "Top-down and bottom-up governance are not meeting."[48]

The Events of 9/11 and the Sustained Challenges of Security Primacy

In hindsight, it is tempting to posit that the cross-border governance field, which never quite stabilized and matured during the 1990s, required a jolt to truly activate the transformation of cross-border governance that had been imminent since the emergence of the field. Although this point is debatable, it is clear from the actions and events that followed 9/11 that the sudden shock of the terrorist attacks combined with a startled nationwide reaction spurred the rapid development and institutionalization of a new order of cross-border governance between Canada and the US.[49] Also, it was acknowledged gradually that for this governance system to work effectively, some form of shared "top down" and "bottom up" governance would be necessary as new security policies were implemented in different regional contexts and settings along the diverse border between the US and Canada.[50] Furthermore, it was the Pacific Northwest cross-border region that would lead in the testing and implementation of models of cross-border governance in the wake of 9/11. Potentially, then, it is the crisis caused by 9/11 that today enables the researcher of order and change in cross-border governance between the US and Canada to analyse how and why this change has taken place. This analysis will focus on the factors that precipitated the crisis in cross-border governance, the actors and events that shaped an episode of crisis, and the interactive dynamics that brought the episode to a close. The focus is not on the events of 9/11 but rather on how 9/11 changed cross-border governance in the Pacific Northwest.

A field theory approach allows us to re-examine an already familiar story and to scrutinize how the shock to an emerging cross-border governance system altered, rationalized, and, to some extent, institutionalized the system or SAF. This re-examination is conducted by evaluating the crisis in the context of field theory and by drawing on empirical research conducted in the cross-border region in 2009–10.[51] The analysis begins with a consideration of how the field crisis emerged. This is followed by a discussion of the social processes that mediated between the destabilizing events and the actual mobilization of challengers. The analysis then identifies forms of action and collective action frames used by incumbents and challengers as they responded to the crisis. The analysis then considers the role of key external actors and SAFs in precipitating the crisis, then shaping its trajectory and eventually affecting an agreement. Finally, the terms of the new agreement are considered as well as the impact of these terms on the prior power structure.

The field crisis arose immediately after 9/11, when the evolved, informal approaches to cross-border governance were deemed inadequate by federal authorities in Ottawa and particularly in Washington, DC, and substantially enhanced security policies were implemented and enforced with renewed vigour and limited "port authority."[52] Federal authorities now took over cross-border governance, and that governance became more regulated, more militarized, more intolerant, and more secretive. This immediately disrupted the cross-border governance field in just about every facet of its operation. The entire US–Canada border snapped shut, bringing and end to long-established procedures, movements, communications, pathways, and visions. New federal regulations and procedures linked to security primacy prevailed. In the Pacific Northwest, as in other cross-border regions, problems of congestion at the border, heightened costs for crossing, uncertainty, and fear manifested themselves immediately and could not or would not be addressed adequately by federal authorities.

This crisis cried out for resolution. At first, federal incumbents closed ranks under the auspices and direction of the newly created DHS in the US and the Department of Public Safety in Canada. Legislation – the Patriot Act in the US[53] and the Public Safety Act in Canada[54] – entrenched security primacy, and the cross-border pacts between the countries such as the Canada–US Partnership (CUSP)[55] attempted to mediate the Canadian imperative for cross-border trade with the US imperative for security.[56] It became increasingly evident that entrenched federal positions, especially in the US, were expensive, disruptive, and essentially counterproductive for both regional and federal interests.[57] There had to be a better way. In the Pacific Northwest, this better way simply involved re-engaging with the emerging cross-border governance processes (and their players) that had been curtailed after 9/11. At the core of this re-energized initiative were the challengers, who had begun consistently questioning the draconian "top down" measures of a newly mandated and muscled-up DHS. These challengers, primarily elected leaders and high-level bureaucrats in Washington state and BC, regional mayors, NGO leaders, and cross-border organizers, began to mobilize soon after 9/11, but it was the implementation of rigid policies by the incumbents that did the most to drive mobilization. For example, the implementation of the Western Hemisphere Travel Initiative (WHTI) in 2007 for airports and 2009 for land and sea ports that galvanized the resolve of Washington Governor Christine Gregoire and BC Premier Gordon Campbell to embark on a project to introduce an "enhanced driver's licence" (EDL) to enable border crossings by those many Americans and Canadians in the cross-border region who lacked a passport or considered it inconvenient to carry one.[58] The EDL was rolled out quickly in BC and Washington in response to the growing concerns about wait times at border crossings and the need for an alternative to passports. Though this initiative was only modestly successful, the EDL was lauded in the cross-border region as well as at the federal level, and comparable initiatives were soon being developed in other cross-border regions.[59]

What is important to note about this EDL project is the nature of the process that mediated between the destabilizing events – 9/11 and then the WHTI –

and the actual mobilization of the challengers. The process involved the engagement of state and provincial leaders and legislators working in concert with border interest groups and a diverse set of economic interest groups whose constituencies were being increasingly impacted by the "thickening" border. Specifically, this process formed a collective action field involving the offices of Premier Campbell and Governor Gregoire, cross-border interest groups such as PNWER, BPRI, and IMTC, a multitude of state and provincial transportation agencies and chambers of commerce, and even the Vancouver Olympic Committee. Integral to the process, and ultimately to the collective action field, were the cross-border interest groups. At the macro-regional level, PNWER's engagement was crucial because it provided the well-articulated state/provincial contacts and working protocols necessary for action field deployment and maintenance. At the core of the cross-border region, the IMTC emerged as the forum of continuity and sustained action, and this made it possible to convene and enable the collective action field through the representation and the engagement in consensus of mobility, trade, security, and governance groups at multiple scales.

The IMTC was founded in 1997, well before 9/11 and the ensuing and expanding security regime. In this regard, it has provided a forum for border stakeholder interactions throughout almost two decades of rapid and extensive change in the cross-border region, and specifically in the Cascade Gateway. Many of the policy responses and solutions to problems at the border began with communication and consultation at the IMTC. The IMTC model makes stakeholder involvement work, and more important, it makes it work through consensus group representation and engagement:

> The IMTC is a U.S.–Canadian coalition of government and business entities that identifies and promotes improvements to mobility and security for the four border crossings that connect Whatcom County, Washington State and the Lower Mainland of British Columbia. Together these four crossings are called the Cascade Gateway. The goals of the IMTC project are to: 1) Facilitate a forum for ongoing communication between agencies responsible for regional, cross-border transportation, safety, and security. 2) Coordinate planning of the Cascade Gateway as a transportation and inspection system rather than as individual border crossings. 3) Improve and distribute traffic data and information. 4) Identify and pursue improvements to infrastructure, operations, and information technology.[60]

Border stakeholder consensus as enabled and articulated by the IMTC clearly makes it possible to develop and adjust border policy at the scale of the Cascade Gateway. At this scale, the IMTC also provides a vehicle for cross-border governance. Can this model work "up the line" at the regional scale, or even beyond this scale? Can the model work in other cross-border corridors and gateways? When asked these questions, respondents to a survey of almost 100 border stakeholders in the Pacific Northwest, and an equal number of interviewees in the cross-border region, were uncertain about how to achieve exceptional stakeholder engagement and consensus beyond the "Gateway," although the respondents did suggest that the model should be able to work in other rapidly changing cross-border "flow" areas.[61] The success and achievements of the IMTC as a collective action field at the local to sub-regional scale are mirrored in part by PNWER's accomplishments in cross-border governance at the macro-regional scale.[62] Yet PNWER is a collaborative governance forum with an extensive agenda, and it does not exist solely to evaluate and build better border policy. It seems that the collective action field for cross-border governance in the Pacific Northwest is articulated most effectively at the local to sub-regional scale, then thins and perhaps weakens as it extends to represent more diverse interests and extensive constituencies up the scale toward the regional and national levels.

There are times when major issues – as in the case of passports (already discussed), or the potential for a cross-border traffic cataclysm at the Vancouver Olympics in 2010 – engage a broader range of border stakeholders and serve as a catalyst for deploying cross-border governance across scales. Well before the 2010 Winter Olympics, the Vancouver Olympic Committee (VANOC)[63] raised the stakes for seeking remedies to the security/mobility conundrum at the Canada–US border in the Pacific Northwest, and particularly in the Cascade Gateway. Visions of massive traffic delays as cars and buses lined up for hours at the border were conveyed by VANOC to a concerned audience of Olympic officials and business leaders, all levels of government, and a tuned-in public. VANOC linked its campaign for enhanced cross-border mobility to IMTC and other cross-border interest groups to push for greater passenger rail access across the border and expedited bus clearance at crossing points. The result was that during the Vancouver Winter Olympics, traffic problems were anticipated, addressed, and largely minimized.[64] This success further enhanced the credibility and confidence of the collaborators engaged in the collective action field, which now appeared to extend as effectively as necessary from its core in the IMTC to regional and national engagement in cross-border governance.

Alper and Hammond found that by the late 2000s, while the vital security function of the Canada–US border had been widely acknowledged, management of that border required increased attention to customer service. Governance of the cross-border field needed to be aligned more with professionalism, efficiency, and "human decency" and less bound to a rule-bound, militaristic approach. This required more effective collaboration and coordination as well as, more fundamentally, a change in attitude among border officials. According to the same authors, the key factors for an effective border in the Pacific Northwest as identified by stakeholders were strong cross-border relationships and collaboration, efficient facilitation of traffic, adequate infrastructure, adequate staffing, a positive attitude, ensured security, and strong stakeholder involvement.[65] By 2010, mutual recognition of these key factors by both federal incumbents and regional and local challengers was shaping the trajectory of the new field. Although incumbents and challengers remained apart regarding certain approaches to security enhancement and civil liberties, and the agreement was not effectively attuned to the regional scale of the Pacific Northwest, the Beyond the Border (BTB) Accord[66] drew on many aspects of the Pacific Northwest border governance experience, and consequently contributed to an agreement that suited the region.[67]

The terms of the new agreement have been codified in the Beyond the Border Accord. That accord represents a shared vision of cooperation in managing the border. There are four key components to extending border governance beyond the border, and together they essentially govern the border both away from and at the border: (1) addressing threats early, (2) facilitating trade, economic growth, and jobs, (3) integrating cross-border law enforcement, and (4) developing critical infrastructure and cybersecurity. In the Pacific Northwest, these four pillars of cross-border governance were all part of the *de facto* agreement negotiated by the incumbents and the challengers in the inner SAF of the IMTC with the outer SAF of PNWER, as well as associated or proximate fields within and outside the region. Perhaps what is most significant about the new agreement is the geopolitical reconfiguration and definition of the field. The new agreement defined a field centred on the border but extended beyond it to encompass space and the constituencies of this space in the cross-border region, thus codifying a pre-existing geographical reality. Border governance was now acknowledged as integrated, cooperative, and aligned governance within a zone and as enabled by people, tools, and technologies operating throughout and beyond that zone. This form of cross-border governance is consistent with the simultaneously local and global realities emerging elsewhere to challenge and reshape border governance.

Reshaping Border Governance

Border governance has been reshaped by globalization.[68] Once located at the limits or edges of territorial governance, borders are now more often situated *within* bordered space, where they retain or exaggerate some of their "territorialist" function while mediating increasingly the spaces of flows around and through the boundaries. Consequently, border governance in globalization is at once more layered and complex, more unpredictable and fluid, and more denationalized and privatized.[69] In the newly evolved governance spaces of a more globalized world, there are more and stronger international governance bodies and more powerful cross-border regions where more non-state actors often predominate and prevail in governance of cross-border space. Yet while "bottom up" processes of governance continue to expand, nation-state boundaries are in many instances being hardened against unwanted flows such as illegal migration and drugs.

Clearly, globalization has reshaped cross-border governance; no longer is it a localized phenomenon with discrete characteristics and unique processes in different, separated locales; now it takes the form of sets of parallel and often connected governance systems operating in concert in an international context like the European Union, North America, or the Canada–US borderlands. In the Canada–US context, cross-border governance manifested itself in the twentieth century, when, as early as 1973, the adjacent regions of New England and the Atlantic provinces aligned in the New England Governors–Eastern Canadian Premiers Conference and established a secretariat to sustain the relationship.[70] This model would influence other regional cross-border governance constructs along the Canada–US border and ultimately guide the institutionalization of PNWER in the Pacific Northwest. Although PNWER has emerged as the "gold standard" for regional cross-border governance between the US and Canada, other regional cross-border governance constructs continue to thrive and evolve according to regional requirements, issues, and the leadership signatures of the main actors. In the Great Lakes region, where local crossing corridors prevail, "gateway" organizations thrive; Quebec has aligned with New York to participate in the Atlantic Canada–New England partnership; Prairies and Plains linkages remain subdued and localized astride the 49th Parallel. Yet, despite the heterogeneity of approaches and styles of emergent cross-border governance along the Canada–US border, the goals and tenets of governance are largely the same, and the processes, challenges, experiences, and outcomes are comparable.

Herein lies the compelling argument for applying the theory of SAFs to the analysis of cross-border governance, not only within one region like the Pacific Northwest, but also within comparable regions along the Canada–US border. The analysis of proximate fields may provide additional insights into how fields emerge, what characterizes a stable field, and how crisis impacts the field. Moreover, the comparative analysis of proximate fields may allow additional temporal and spatial insights about rates of field development, differential patterns of field emergence, scale alignments and differentiation, and the relative operation of agency. These explorations in comparability may then be extended to other binational and international contexts as illustrated in this volume. Also, the challenge of adjusting border governance to address the impacts of the COVID-19 pandemic provides an opportunity to examine the applicability of the theory of SAFs during another period of shock to the evolving system. An assessment of post-pandemic developments would allow further comparability of cross-border governance in time and space.

Although comparing and explicating the applicability and analytical power of the theory of fields is a core goal of this volume, in essence it is the greater resolution of cross-border governance within a cross-border region that draws the researcher to apply and test a theory. In this regard, the theory of fields is satisfying in the sense that processes, events, and actors in cross-border governance in the Pacific Northwest fall neatly into the compartments of the theoretical framework and are easily interpreted using the road map for analysis. Furthermore, when the road map is applied and the theory is implemented, the story of cross-border governance is more compelling and just seems to make more sense. In the Pacific Northwest, the complex interactions of multiple agents and structures of governance across an international boundary and within an envisioned cross-border region are not simplified, but rather are arrayed in conceivable and interpretable SAFs. These fields capture the essence of, and help us navigate, the complex rescaling of space, place, and time in globalization, to explain more about how cross-border governance works in a vibrant and evolving cross-border region. Yet as stated previously in this chapter, conceptualizing scale in globalization remains elusive in border theory, and although SAFs offer flexible situations in time and space to address this problem, the challenge remains to articulate the manifestations of these fields. An element of healthy questionability prevails because the application of the theory of SAFs produces some residuals although the theory itself is explicit and appears to account for a universe of possibilities.

NOTES

1 Guadalupe Correa-Cabrera and Victor Konrad, *North American Borders in Comparative Perspective* (Tucson: University of Arizona Press, 2020).

2 S. Harris, "Canada–US border rules and restrictions during the COVID-19 pandemic explained," CBC News, 20 June 2020, https://www.cbc.ca/news/business/canada-u-s-border-rules-and-restrictions-covid-19-travel-1.5619268.

3 Border Policy Research Institute (BPRI), "COVID-19 and the US–Canada Border: Retail Shopping Destinations for Canadians in Whatcom County, Updated," BPRI Publications 119 (Bellingham: Western Washington University, 2020), https://cedar.wwu.edu/bpri_publications/119.

4 BPRI, "COVID-19 and the US–Canada Border."

5 M. Sare, "Non-Governmental Organizations and Cross-Border Environmental Cooperation: Salish Sea and Baltic Sea Regions," BPRI Publications 118 (2020), https://cedar.wwu.edu/bpri_publications/118.

6 BPRI, "The Changing Landscape of Border Crossing Documents", BPRI Publications 121 (Bellingham: Western Washington University, 2020), https://cedar.wwu.edu/bpri_publications/121.

7 D. Alper, "Emerging Collaborative Frameworks for Environmental Governance in the Georgia Basin–Puget Sound Ecosystem," *Journal of Borderlands Studies* 19, no. 1 (2004): 79–88.

8 E. Gilbert, "Leaky Borders and Solid Citizens: Governing Security, Prosperity, and Quality of Life in a North American Partnership," *Antipode* 39, no. 1 (2005): 77–98.

9 V. Konrad, "'Breaking Points' but No 'Broken' Border: Stakeholders Evaluate Border Issues in the Pacific Northwest Region," *Border Policy Research Institute Research Report* 10, no. 75 (2010): 24–5.

10 Konrad, "'Breaking Points'"; see also Konrad, "Borders, Bordered Lands, and Borderlands: Geographical States of Insecurity between Canada and the United States, and the Impacts on Security Primacy," in *Borders, Fences and Walls: State of Insecurity?*, ed. E. Vallet (Aldershot: Ashgate, 2014), 85–102.

11 Konrad, "'Breaking Points," 24–5.

12 D. Alper and B. Hammond, "Bordered Perspectives: Local Stakeholders' Views of Border Management in the Cascade Corridor Region," *Journal of Borderlands Studies* 26, no. 1 (2011): 110–11.

13 E. Brunet-Jailly, "NAFTA, Economic Integration, and the Canadian–American Security Regime in the Post-September 11, 2001 Era: Multi-Level Governance and Transparent Border?," *Journal of Borderlands Studies* 19, no. 1 (2004): 71–93.

14 See BPRI) website: https://wp.wwu.edu/bpri.

15 See Borders in Globalization Project website: https://biglobalization.org.

16 E. Brunet-Jailly and P. Smith, "Introduction: Constructing a Cross-Border Cascadia Region," *Canadian Political Science Review* 2, no. 2 (2008) 1–5.

17 S. Perival, *Beyond Borders: Regional Partnerships in the Pacific Northwest*, Henry Jackson School of International Affairs, Occasional Papers on Canada–US Relations (Seattle: University of Washington, 2007).

18 Government of Canada, *The Emergence of Cross-Border Regions between Canada and the United States: Reaping the Promise and Public Value of Cross-Border Regional Relationships*, Policy Research Initiative (PRI) (Ottawa, 2008).

19 E. Mikhailova, "Theorizing on Cross-Border Governance from Emergence of the Concept to Its Current Understanding," *Public Administration E-Journal* 46 (Lomonosov Moscow State University, School of Public Administration, 2014), http://www.academia.edu/9236087.

20 J.W. Scott, "Euroregions, Governance, and Transborder Cooperation within the EU," in *Border Regions and People*, ed. M. van der Velde and H. van Houtum (London: Pion, 2000): 91–106.

21 O. Kramsch, "Reimaging the Scalar Fix of Transborder Governance: The Case of the Maas-RheinEuroregion," in *Routing Borders between Territories, Discourses, and Practices*, ed. E. Berg and H. van Houtum (Gateshead: Atheneum, 2003).

22 E. Gualini, "Cross-Border Governance: Inventing Regions in a Transnational Multi-Level Polity," *disP – The Planning Review* 39, no. 152 (2003): 43–52.

23 M. Perkman, "Policy Entrepreneurship and Multi-Level Governance: A Comparative Study of European Cross-Border Regions," *Environment and Planning C* 25, no. 6 (2007): 861–79.
24 T. Pikner, "Reorganizing Cross-Border Governance Capacity: The Case of the Helsinki–Tallin Euregio," *European Urban and Regional Studies* 15, no. 3 (2008): 211–27.
25 K. Terlouw, "Border Surfers and Euroregions: Unplanned Cross-Border Behavior and Planned Territorial Structures of Cross-Border Governance," *Planning Practice and Research* 27, no. 3 (2012): 351–66.
26 J. Garcia-Alvarez and J.M. Trillo Santamaria, "Between Regional Spaces and Spaces of Regionalism: Cross-Border Region Building in the Spanish State," *Regional Studies* 47, no. 1 (2013): 104–15.
27 J. Nelles and F. Durand, "Political Rescaling and Metropolitan Governance in Cross-Border Regions: Comparing the Cross-Border Metropolitan Areas of Lille and Luxembourg," *European Urban and Regional Studies* 21, no. 1 (2014): 104–22.
28 Neil Fligstein and Doug McAdam, *A Theory of Fields* (New York: Oxford University Press, 2012), http://doi.org/10.1007/s11186-014-9237-0.
29 Fligstein and McAdam, *A Theory of Fields*, 165–7.
30 Fligstein and McAdam, *A Theory of Fields*, 165.
31 Fligstein and McAdam, *A Theory of Fields*, 166.
32 V. Konrad, "Toward a Theory of Borders in Motion," *Journal of Borderlands Studies* 30, no. 1 (2015): 1–17.
33 Fligstein and McAdam, *A Theory of Fields*, 166–7.
34 J. Garreau, *The Nine Nations of North America* (New York: Avon, 1981).
35 V. Konrad and H.N. Nicol, *Beyond Walls: Reinventing the Canada–United States Borderlands* (Aldershot: Ashgate, 2008); V. Konrad and H.N. Nicol, "Passports for All," *Canadian-American Public Policy* 74 (Orono: University of Maine Press, 2008); V. Konrad and H.N. Nicol, "The Canada–United States Borderlands: Drawing the Line: Working across It, and Reinventing the Border," *Pennsylvania Geographer* 42, no. 1 (2009): 55–90.
36 D. Alper, "Conflicting Transborder Visions and Agendas: Economic and Environmental Cascadians," in *Holding the Line: Borders in a Global World*, ed. H.N. Nicol and I. Townsend-Gault (Vancouver: UBC Press, 2005), 222–37.
37 Alper, "Conflicting Transborder Visions and Agendas," 222–3.
38 A.F.J. Artibise, "Cascadian Adventures: Shared Visions, Strategic Alliances, and Ingrained Barriers in a Transborder Region," in *Holding the Line: Borders in a Global World*, ed. H.N. Nicol and I. Townsend-Gault (Vancouver: UBC Press, 2005), 247–8.
39 Alper, "Conflicting Transborder Visions and Agendas."
40 Artibise, "Cascadian Adventures," 240. According to Artibise, the field is actually a nested set of shared visions comprising "Main Street Cascadia," the cross-border urban corridor at the core of the field; the states of Washington and Oregon and

province of BC straddling the border; and the additional states, provinces, and territories of Idaho, Montana, Alberta, Yukon, and Alaska beyond the core.

41 Artibise, "Cascadian Adventures"; Alper, "Conflicting Transborder Visions and Agendas."

42 K. Ohmae, "The Rise of the Region State," *Foreign Affairs* 72, no. 2 (1993): 78–88.

43 Alper, "Conflicting Transborder Visions and Agendas," 231.

44 "BC waters officially renamed Salish Sea," *CBC News*, 15 July 2010, http://www.cbc.ca/news/.../b-c-waters-officially-renamed-salish-sea-1.909504; A.D. Benedict and J.K. Gaydos, *The Salish Sea: Jewel of the Pacific Northwest* (Vancouver: Sasquatch, 2015).

45 RCMP, "Integrated Border Enforcement Teams (IBETs)," https://www.rcmp-grc.gc.ca/detach/en/d/50.

46 ABC News, "Canada–US declare end to Salmon War," *ABC News*, 3 June 1997, http://abcnews.go.com/Technology/story?id=99350.

47 Konrad, "'Breaking Points,'" 25, 47–50.

48 Konrad, "'Breaking Points,'" 25.

49 J. Ackleson, "From 'Thin' to 'Thick' (and Back Again?): The Politics and Policies of the Contemporary US–Canada Border," *American Review of Canadian Studies* 39, no. 4 (2009): 336–51.

50 Alper, "Conflicting Transborder Visions and Agendas," 222–37; Konrad and Nicol, *Beyond Walls*; Konrad and Nicol, "Passports for All."

51 Konrad, "'Breaking Points.'"

52 P. Andreas and T.J. Bierstecker, eds., *The Rebordering of North America* (New York: Routledge, 2003).

53 US Government Publishing Office, *Uniting and Strengthening America by Providing Appropriate Tools Required to Intercept and Obstruct Terrorism (USA PATRIOT ACT) Act of 2001*, 115 Stat. 272, United States Statutes at Large (Date Approved: 26 October 200), https://www.govinfo.gov/app/details/STATUTE-115/STATUTE-115-Pg272/context.

54 Government of Canada, *Public Safety Act, 2002 (S.C. 2004, c. 15)*, Justice Laws website, https://laws.justice.gc.ca/eng/acts/P-31.5. See also Public Safety Canada, https://www.publicsafety.gc.ca/index-eng.aspx.

55 Government of Canada, *Creating Tomorrow's Border Together – The Canada–United States Partnership (CUSP)*, Foreign Affairs and International Trade (2007), http://geo.international.gc.ca/can-am/main/border/creating_cusp_en.asp.

56 D. Drache, *Borders Matter: Homeland Security and the Search for North America* (Halifax: Fernwood, 2004).

57 E. Alden, *Closing of the American Border* (New York: HarperCollins, 2008).

58 Konrad and Nicol, *Beyond Walls*; Konrad and Nicol, "Passports for All"; British Columbia, *Your Guide to BC's Enhanced Driver's Licence Program*, MV2657 (ICBC, 2015), http://www.icbc.com/driver-licensing/getting-licensed/Documents/edl-guide.pdf.

59 BPRI, "Western Hemisphere Travel Initiative," *Border Policy Brief* 1, no. 1 (January 2006): 47, https://cedar.wwu.edu/bpri_publications/47/; BPRI, "Border Crossing Documentation," *Border Policy Brief* 2, no. 1 (January 2007): 41, https://cedar.wwu.edu/bpri_publications/41/; BPRI, "2013/14 IMTC Passenger Vehicle Survey: Project Organization and Report of Findings," research report, July 2014, 93, https://cedar.wwu.edu/bpri_publications/93.

60 Whatcom Council of Governments (WCOG), "International Mobility and Trade Corridor Program (IMTC)" (n.d.), https://wcog.org/imtc/#:~:text=The%20International%20Mobility%20and%20Trade,Columbia%2C%20which%20together%20are%20known. See also: http://www.theimtc.com and http://www.wcog.org.

61 Konrad, "'Breaking Points,'" 48.

62 Pacific Northwest Economic Region (PNWER), "The gold standard of the US–Canada relations," (n.d.), http://www.pnwer.org.

63 Vancouver Olympic Committee (VANOC) (2010), http://www.olympic.org/vancouver-2010-winter-olympics and https://olympics.com/en/olympic-games/vancouver-2010.

64 Canada Institute, "Border Challenges and Regional Solutions: 2010 Olympics and the Pacific Northwest Experience," *Event*, Woodrow Wilson Center, 24 February 2009, https://www.wilsoncenter.org/event/border-challenges-and-regional-solutions-2010-olympics-and-the-pacific-northwest-experience.

65 Alper and Hammond, "Bordered Perspectives," 108.

66 Government of Canada, *Beyond the Border Implementation Report* (2015), https://www.publicsafety.gc.ca/cnt/rsrcs/pblctns/2015-bynd-brdr-mplmntn/index-en.aspx; US Department of Homeland Security, *Beyond the Border: A Shared Vision for Perimeter Security and Economic Competitiveness* (n.d.), http://www.dhs.gov/beyond-border.

67 Donald K. Alper, "Scholars' Views on Improving Border Policy," *Border Policy Brief* 6, no. 3, BPRI 25 (Bellingham: Western Washington University, 2011), https://cedar.wwu.edu/bpri_publications/25.

68 S. Sassen, *Deciphering the Global: Its Scales, Spaces, and Subjects* (New York: Routledge, 2007).

69 E. Brunet-Jailly, "Governance: Borders in Globalization (BIG) themes" (2014), http://www.biglobalization.org.

70 Council of Atlantic Premiers (CAP), New England Governors and –Eastern Canadian Premiers' Annual Conference (NEG/ECP), 2015, http://www.cap-cpma.ca.

7 Revisiting "Paradiplomacy" in the Quebec–US States Cross-Border Area

BRUNO DUPEYRON

Since the 1960s, globalization has generated a number of policy challenges that have required new types of governance. Sub-national actors have emerged on the international stage, contributing to the solutions to some policy problems that have challenged national governments – challenges those governments have ignored.[1] Along the Canada–US border, sub-national actors have been especially active in recent decades, and we can discern a long-standing web of cross-border relations and policies. Canada–US bilateral relations have undoubtedly shaped a large part of this matrix, but bilateral dynamics are being complemented by other levels of government, in particular by state/provincial and municipal actors. In this chapter, we focus on the Canadian province of Quebec and its cross-border partners, the US states of New York, Vermont, New Hampshire, and Maine. We will analyse how cross-border governance between these sub-national actors has evolved, considering in particular how Quebec's distinctive paradiplomacy may be influencing cross-border governance initiatives.

Defining Paradiplomacy

A growing body of literature has analysed the expanding role of sub-national actors in the international sphere using the notion of "paradiplomacy." That word can generally be defined as "sub-state units [that] engage to different degrees and in various modes with external actors, comprising other regions, third states, international networks and supranational organizations."[2] Dickson's definition is broad enough to include two main categories of paradiplomacy. Kaiser shows that US states have developed economic external activities, unlike other jurisdictions that have pushed additional interests – for instance, cultural recognition, capacity building, or projects of political autonomy or even independence.[3] In the case of Quebec, economic and trade interests have been complemented by national and identity objectives. Although Dickson's broad definition is a helpful place to start, a more specific definition of paradiplomacy is needed.

A more accurate definition of paradiplomacy reveals several approaches that seek to make sense of this phenomenon.[4] Thus, Kuznetsov proposes a functional definition of paradiplomacy, suggesting that it "is generally referred to in the literature as the involvement of the constitutional units (regions) of national states in international affairs."[5] He provides examples of specific functions: "they own trade and cultural missions abroad, sign treaties and agreements with foreign state and non-state actors, they participate in international networks of regional cooperation and they sometimes even challenge the official foreign policy of their central governments through their statements or actions."[6] He suggests that the spectrum of sub-national units' paradiplomatic functions is broad, but he also notes that these functions are political and can challenge national states' foreign policy goals. Finally, he goes a step further to show that the core function of paradiplomacy is to articulate private and public interests between the sub-national and international levels, as these interests are often ignored in international forums dominated by states.[7]

However, it is somewhat vague to refer to paradiplomacy as the activities of sub-national actors "in international affairs."[8] Duchacek proposes a typology of paradiplomacy that allows us to define that term at three different scales: cross-border, trans-regional, and global. This typology is useful to us, since our focus in this chapter is on the cross-border level. It also serves to remind us that activities at the trans-regional and global levels, not analysed in this chapter, complement cross-border paradiplomacy.[9]

Nossal, Roussel, and Paquin distinguish between paradiplomacy and "protodiplomacy."[10] Paradiplomacy refers to international activities conducted by sub-national entities, generally in alignment with the diplomatic efforts of the federal/central government; an example is the international activities of US states that have trade offices abroad,[11] and of Canadian provinces that have significant international relations (e.g., British Columbia, Alberta, Ontario, and Quebec). In this vein, Cazé shows how city-twinning can serve as another tool in the paradiplomatic repertoire.[12] By contrast, protodiplomacy refers to international activities implemented by sub-national entities in order to advance diplomatic objectives, such as recognition by other states, which is likely to be dissonant with the diplomacy conducted by the federal/central government.[13] Quebec is used as a case study to show how paradiplomacy and protodiplomacy can be implemented simultaneously: paradiplomacy has served to strengthen Quebec's economic and trade interests, along with its identity; between 1976 and 1983, and between 1994 and 1995, however, episodes of protodiplomacy emerged as the Parti Québécois took steps to support its *souverainiste* policies on the international stage.[14] Other examples of protodiplomatic activities are provided by Fry: Catalonia and the Basque Country in Spain, and the Flemish region in

Belgium.[15] This distinction between paradiplomacy and protodiplomacy is also captured by Lecours and Moreno when they write that "paradiplomacy, at least in its most developed form, needs to be re-conceptualized through a theoretical linkage with substate or stateless nationalism."[16] They argue that nationalism is a key explanatory factor if we want to understand how regional/provincial governments "seek international agency" and develop international activities.

The Significance and Limitations of Paradiplomacy

The factors that explain paradiplomacy in North America have generated minor disagreements in the literature, which highlights various theoretical and methodological perspectives. First, regional integration (NAFTA, now USMCA) has helped expand trade and increase investment between Mexico, the US, and Canada.[17] Thus, free trade has been analysed as a prevailing factor that has promoted integration in North America among those three countries, and this has been emulated by sub-national entities, especially in borderlands through cross-border activities. As a side note, the contributors to this volume show that the legal and illegal circulation of goods and services in North American borderlands predated NAFTA.[18] Some scholars disagree that free trade is the main explanation for the emergence of paradiplomacy. Truly, sub-national actors have been confronted along border areas with a multitude of policy issues, such as cross-border pollution, economic and forced migration,[19] water management,[20] policing,[21] cross-border mobility, and cross-border infrastructure. Martínez contends that as federal/central governments have failed to respond adequately to these challenges, sub-national actors have stepped forward to provide policy answers, including through paradiplomatic modes of resolution, and have contributed to the emergence of new forms of governance.[22] These responses have been made possible as states have begun to decentralize and fragment. The relative ease of collaboration between levels in federal systems in North America explains how sub-national actors have been able to create various cross-border governance mechanisms – most of them policy forums – to tackle joint policy issues. Vengroff and Rich point to other contributing factors that suggest how paradiplomacy emerged in Canada, for instance, globalization and nationalism.[23]

Some authors discuss how the concept of paradiplomacy may face theoretical and/or empirical limitations. Lecours and Moreno maintain that federalism has not been a decisive factor in the emergence of paradiplomacy; instead, they suggest that nationalism is the central explanation for why sub-national actors, primarily within multinational states, develop international activities.[24] Chaloux and Paquin,[25] followed by Dickson,[26] show how paradiplomacy differs from multi-level governance: both concepts attempt to make sense of the international activities of sub-national actors, but multi-level governance focuses on the governance dynamics between levels of government, in particular within the European Union. Even so, it is possible to transpose the notion of multi-level governance to other regional areas, for instance in North America, and doing so helps explain the emergence of cross-border governance entities as well as the ensuing dynamics in their relations.[27] For his part, Hocking rejects the concept of paradiplomacy, contending that the state has only a single diplomatic system, one that is based on "cooperation imperatives" between central and sub-national governments.[28] Dickson writes that theory-building for students of paradiplomacy is urgently needed: while paradiplomacy is a useful concept when describing the various international activities of sub-national entities, it is necessary to analyse their political agency. He adds that it is imperative to address the significance of this political agency within academic disciplines such as comparative politics and international relations. He suggests a few research questions for paradiplomatic scholars – for instance, "How do sub-state governments articulate their perceived legitimacy in the international domain? In what ways is a regional international agency qualitatively different from the agency of state-level actors?"[29] Finally, we point out that the notion of paradiplomacy is helpful, for it situates the international activities of sub-national actors in a multi-scalar context that is still heavily influenced by nation-states and allows us to focus on cross-border paradiplomacy. Nonetheless – and here we agree with Dickson – the internal and external dynamics of cross-border paradiplomacy, and its governance manifestations, remain quite fuzzy. To unpack the limitations of the notion of paradiplomacy, the theory of fields will be used, for it allows us to scrutinize how Quebec's modulations in its approaches to paradiplomacy influence cross-border governance on its sector of the Canada–US border.[30]

Methodology

This chapter takes a qualitative approach, using primary and secondary sources. Primary sources mainly included documents available from provincial and state government websites. Secondary sources were drawn from the scholarly literature in the sub-field of paradiplomacy and related disciplines interested in cross-border cooperation and cross-border governance. Additional secondary sources included grey literature from executive and legislative bodies. We also conducted twenty-three telephone and Skype semi-structured interviews with Canadian and US stakeholders. Since the focus of this study was the distinct role of Quebec in the field of cross-border governance, around half of those interviews were with Québécois research participants (provincial civil servants, as well as stakeholders from the public and private sectors). The rest were public and private actors from New York, Vermont, New Hampshire, and Maine.

There is an imbalance between Canadian and US stakeholders; even so, saturation was reached for both categories of research participants.

Structure of the Chapter

Cross-border governance between Quebec and US states is multifaceted and multi-level, for it implies the management of shared border issues such as trade, the environment, security, and people's mobility. It also involves an articulation between the international priorities of the Canadian federal government and Quebec's paradiplomatic objectives, which implies maintaining stable relations with Washington and each neighbouring US state, notwithstanding occasional crises. To understand how this articulation operates, we conceive a multi-level web of intersecting fields. Also, we focus on the dynamics among incumbents, challengers, and internal governance units within the field of cross-border governance and show that Canada's diplomatic and paradiplomatic agendas have been instrumental to the stabilization of the Quebec–US cross-border governance field in terms of a number of bilateral issues, such as ongoing border security policies, recurring US protectionist policies, and recent mobility restrictions arising from COVID-19.

This chapter has three sections. After a brief overview of the analytical tools borrowed from the theory of fields, we will analyse how the field emerged, stabilized, and then experienced limited periods of crisis. In the conclusion, we highlight how the theory of fields represents a valuable theoretical complementary framework to the sub-field of paradiplomacy.

Which Analytical Instruments Should We Borrow from the Theory of Fields to Analyse the Field of Cross-Border Governance and Supplement the Notion of Paradiplomacy?

The analytical toolbox offered by Fligstein and McAdam is quite substantial. Defining a strategic action field (SAF, or field) is fairly easy: Fligstein and McAdam suggest that when two or more organizations or groups are trying to achieve similar goals, and when each, in doing so, must consider what the other organizations are doing, we are witnessing a possible field formation.[31] The next task when defining the field is perhaps more difficult: it requires us to determine which actors can be considered members of the field and which actors cannot be. Fligstein and McAdam suggest that groups that "routinely take each other into account in their actions"[32] can be considered field members. Of course, this perspective tends to exclude peripheral members that are not routinely involved in the field but that play a significant role in adjacent or dependent fields. In this context, it is crucial to define the field of cross-border governance in relation to proximate fields, for example, the Canadian and US federal governments. Back to our case study: Quebec and its neighbouring US states share a history of cross-border work dating back the 1960s, with routine interactions between provincial and state political officials and public administrations. This cross-border work is inevitably tied, however, to the unilateral and bilateral actions of federal governments – for example, to the heightened border security measures in 2001 in the wake of the 9/11 terrorist attacks, and in 2020 to the measures taken to control the COVID-19 pandemic. As we will see later, other stakeholders are also active in the field on each side of the border – for instance, business actors – and may have some influence at least on their respective sub-national governments. But should we view them as field members? The non-routinized interactions with established field members lead us to posit that those stakeholders belong to adjacent fields but still play a significant role, thanks to their links with political and administrative actors. The third step in the definition of the field is to determine the relative positions of field members. According to Fligstein and McAdam, they can be incumbents, challengers, or internal governance units. In this specific case study of the cross-border governance field, it is not obvious who the challengers are. That said, and as we will explicate later, the position of incumbent occupied by provincial and state actors can at times be downgraded to that of challenger, temporarily or permanently, for instance, when the accepted rules are questioned. We will argue that that is what happened temporarily with Quebec during the two protodiplomatic episodes.

Once we have defined the field, Fligstein and McAdam's theory of fields allows us to analyse change and stability as these affect that field.[33] They suggest that researchers should focus on three "states" of the field: how it was formed, how the settled or stable field is reproduced, how episodes of crisis destabilize the field, and how field stability is re-established. This provides a set of analytical lenses to analyse change and stability in paradiplomacy.

First, scrutinizing the emergence of the field compels us to pay attention to several issues: Who were the central actors who pushed to create and take control of the field? Were there alternative perspectives about the emerging field? Was there an initial struggle to make the field emerge, and if there was, what resources were brought by the different actors and how did the struggle unfold? Were specific rules established after the field was settled? Were internal governance units created at the end of this episode of formation?[34] Applied to our case study, these questions will help us understand, for instance, whether there was an initial shared view of cross-border governance for Quebec and the US states or an initial struggle.

Second, examining a settled and stable field presents specific challenges: What are the limits of the field, and how have they been constituted? Who are the main incumbents and challengers? Is the field structured hierarchically or collaboratively? What are the main consensual policies, practices, and representations that the main actors share? What are the main internal governance units, and how do they serve to stabilize the field? Analysing the stable field of cross-border governance through this second set of lenses is crucial, for example, to identify how the field is structured, to determine the material and symbolic resources that the main field members bring and receive, and to understand how internal governance units have been designed and represent an essential component of routine interactions within the field.

Finally, the phase of "rupture/crisis/resettlement" is undoubtedly the most stimulating for researchers. What are the factors, both external and internal, that provoke a field crisis, and how do they affect the intensity of each crisis? Are challengers mobilized when shocks destabilize the field? What role is played by adjacent fields and state and non-state actors in producing the crisis, instrumentalizing it, and driving the resettlement of the field?[35] These questions will help us understand how major and minor shocks have affected the field of cross-border governance, as well as the role played by internal and external actors in heightening or resolving the crisis. Next, we look at the evolution of a field that is mostly stable.

Evolution of the Field of Cross-Border Governance: A Stable Field, Created by US Incumbents

The Province of Quebec and the neighbouring US states – New York, Vermont, New Hampshire, and Maine – became active in paradiplomatic activities in the 1960s, with similar objectives (trade, energy, environment), but also with distinct goals (which for Quebec were constitutional, that is, to defend its distinct identity within Canada and to project its interests abroad). In this context, the evolution of the field of cross-border governance reveals three fundamental elements: during the formation of the field, Quebec (along with some other provinces) was accepted into several US policy forums, which established that field's foundations. The stable field has relied essentially on common interests, strengthened by NAFTA (now USMCA) in the mid-1990s, and by regional integration discourses.

The formation of a field of cross-border governance has two main drivers. The first of these includes various policy forums that were created by US states (executive or legislative branches) over several decades and that later accepted one or more Canadian provinces as members or associate members. When US states welcomed Canadian provinces, including Quebec, into their existing networks, this turned those networks into cross-border forums. US policy forums can be viewed as a proximate field that was instrumental in the creation of the field of cross-border governance. For instance, an inter-state compact to prevent forest fires along the Québécois segment of Canada–US border was concluded in 1949 by seven US states and was expanded to Quebec in 1969.

Similarly, the Great Lakes Commission was founded in 1955 by the Great Lakes Basin Compact, comprising eight US states, in order to focus on shared economic and environmental issues. In 1999, the Declaration of Partnership with Ontario and Quebec extended associate member status on the Great Lakes Commission to the provincial governments of Ontario and Quebec. Finally, the Council of State Governments is a regional forum, established in 1933, that facilitates the exchange of ideas between state policy-makers, business leaders, and academic experts and serves the three branches of government. One of its regional offices is the Eastern Regional Conference, founded in 1937, comprising today eighteen regional partners, thirteen US states, and five Canadian provinces. Table 7.1 provides an overview of the main organizations and agreements that play a cross-border role in the Quebec–US borderland.

The second source of the formation of the field is related to the fact that only a few cross-border organizations were created jointly by Quebec and its neighbours, for instance, the Conference of New England Governors and Eastern Canadian Premiers' Annual Conference in 1973. In summary, the emerging relations within an existing proximate field and the growing interest of Quebec in paradiplomatic activities, including cross-border cooperation, helped create the field of cross-border governance. Also, we could suggest that the field was essentially created by US states as incumbents, with Quebec as subaltern incumbent and/or incumbent (along with other Canadian provinces). in rare occasions of co-creation.

The stability of the field has been based on shared interests, mainly trade, environment, and water resource management. Other policy sectors have been studied, for instance the policing sector. Dunton and Kitchen note that Sûreté du Québec is engaged "in technical and operational cooperation in public safety and security with different partners [focusing] primarily on improving police practice and learning from other police forces"[36] with US and European partners. Morin and Poliquin take a broader perspective, suggesting that paradiplomatic activities in the policing and border security sectors may lead to a "Quebec security paradiplomacy."[37] Before examining some examples of this field stability, it is interesting to note that Quebec's Ministry of International Relations and Francophonie (MRIF) currently labels the province's relations with US actors "bilateral relations," encompassing relations with cross-border organizations, trans-regional entities, and a number of associations and forums.[38] By contrast, and not surprisingly, Washington holds that only Ottawa represents Canada internationally[39] and, therefore, that bilateral relations exist only with Canada.

Beyond this controversial choice of words, Quebec and its neighbouring US states share key trade interests, and not just with each other. Quebec's main trade priority is the US, not France or the Francophonie: more than 70 per cent of Quebec's exports go to the US.[40] Likewise, Canada is the largest market

Table 7.1. Internal governance units in the field of cross-border governance

Internal governance units	Creation, current members (in 2019)	Policy sector(s)	Quebec	New York	Vermont	New Hampshire	Maine
Great Lakes Commission (a)	1955, 8 members + 2 associate members	Eco., env.	Y (associate member since 1999)	Y (member)			
Council of State Governments – Eastern Regional Conference (b)	1937, 18	Multiple sectors	Y (Quebec National Assembly affiliated as international member since 1990)	Y	Y	Y	Y
Conference of New England Governors and Eastern Canadian Premiers' Annual Conference (c)	1973, 11	Eco., trade, env., & climate change. Transp. energy security	Y		Y	Y	Y
The Conference of Great Lakes and St. Lawrence Governors and Premiers (d) (formerly Council of Great Lakes Governors, created in 1983 by 6 US states, joined by Quebec as associate member in 1997 (with Ontario)	2015, 10	Trade, eater manag., Env., Tourism	Y	Y			
Environmental Cooperation Agreement on the Management of Lake Champlain	2015 (2003, 2008, 2010), 3	Env.	Y	Y	Y		
Pacte des États du nord-est sur la protection contre les feux de forêts (formerly Convention pour fins de protection des forêts contre l'incendie dans le territoire boisé adjacent aux lignes frontières du Québec et de certains États américains)	2013 (1949), 8	Forest protection	Y (joined in 1969)	Y	Y	Y	Y

Source: Data compiled by the author from organizations' websites: (a) https://www.glc.org; (b) https://csg-erc.org; (c) https://www.coneg.org/neg-ecp; (d) https://gsgp.org.

Table 7.2. Foreign presence to promote interests on the other side of the border

Incumbent	Foreign presence
Quebec	9 foreign offices (délégations) in the US, 5 of them in the US Northeast (Washington, Boston, Chicago, New York, Philadelphia)
New York	6 foreign offices, 1 in Montreal
Maine	No foreign office, but there is a Canada Desk within Maine's International Trade Center
Vermont	No office, but attends trade shows. Canada is Vermont's largest market in export volume (https://ustr.gov/map/state-benefits/vt)
New Hampshire	No office, but Canada was the 2nd top market in export volume in 2020 (https://www.nheconomy.com/office-of-international-commerce/new-hampshire-export-statistics)

Source: Data compiled by the author.

in export volume for New York, Maine, and Vermont and the second-largest market for New Hampshire (see Table 7.2). These mutual interests in the trade sector explain why all Québécois premiers have increased their number of visits to the US.[41]

Those trade interests are also visible when we examine how each jurisdiction seeks to promote economic actors and attract investment. Some of them attend trade fairs, while others have a permanent presence in specific cities abroad (see table 7.2). New York has one foreign office in Montreal, focusing on trade and investment. Maine, Vermont, and New Hampshire do not have foreign offices in Canada, even though Canada is their first or second largest market in export volume. Conversely, out of the thirty-two foreign offices ("délégations") that Quebec maintains in eighteen countries,[42] nine are in US cities, five of these in the northeast US (Washington, Boston, Chicago, New York, Philadelphia). Those offices play a quadruple role: they support businesses, workers, artists, and higher education organizations, they promote Quebec to their counterparts in the same sectors, they cultivate relations with governments, and they gather strategic information for Quebec policy-makers.

These Quebec offices have been tolerated by Washington as long as Quebec does not try to play the role of a sovereign state. From Ottawa's perspective, these offices have been useful, for they serve as complementary channels for delivering messages to US policy-makers, as happened during the renegotiation of NAFTA, when the US threatened to terminate that treaty. Also, they complement the work of internal governance units and translate the Québécois paradiplomacy that has generally been consensual among the province's policy-makers.[43]

In the environmental sector, a regional Climate Change Action Plan (CCAP) was adopted by the Conference of New England Governors and

Eastern Canadian Premiers[44] in 2001. CCAP was one of the first cross-border initiatives to reduce greenhouse gas (GHG) emissions and to mitigate the effects of climate change through adaptation. Although NEG-ECP claimed that it had been able to achieve its 2010 GHG emissions reduction goal, it also recognized in 2015 that the production and consumption of energy required significant changes. In this regard, Resolution 39–1 had two main goals: first, it called for an objective for 2030 of reducing regional GHG emissions by at least 35 to 45 per cent below 1990 levels; and second, it required an update of CCAP in order to help the region meet its GHG reduction goals. In 2018, the Climate Change Steering Committee submitted the "2017 Update of the Regional Climate Change Action Plan," a follow-up to the 2001 initiative and a response to Resolution 39–1.[45] This plan called for increased collaboration in several areas (e.g., energy, transportation, natural resources) at the cross-border level so as to reduce GHG emissions, along with other initiatives at different scales. In 2018, Resolution 42–1: Resolution Concerning Adaptation was adopted.[46] The Committee on the Environment coordinates the work of several committees and working groups, which included in 2019 the aforementioned Climate Change Steering Committee, as well as the Ecological Connectivity Working Group and the more recently created Adaptation Working Group. Most of these climate change initiatives are symbolic and have limited resources; even so, NEG-CEP supports collaborative efforts among partners and helps keep the field committed to a complex and long-term policy issue.

In the water resource management sector, US states and Canadian provinces have made incremental progress in institutionalizing cross-border governance. The case of the Conference of Great Lakes and St Lawrence Governors and Premiers shows that informal relations between US and Canadian provinces allowed them to focus on cross-border water issues, though the US Congress refused to recognize Ontario and Quebec as official parties in the 1968 Great Lakes Basin Compact.[47] This did not impede cooperation at the sub-national level, which contributed in 1983 to the creation of the Council of Great Lakes Governors and in 1985 to the adoption by the Council, Quebec, and Ontario of the Great Lakes Charter. That charter explicitly referred to the joint interests in the Great Lakes watershed and their economic development implications.[48] In 1997, Quebec and Ontario officially became associate members. In 2005, two milestones were achieved: the signing of the Great Lakes–St Lawrence River Basin Sustainable Water Resources Agreement, a voluntary agreement, and the Great Lakes–St Lawrence River Basin Water Resources Compact, a legally binding agreement. In 2015, the Conference of Great Lakes and St Lawrence Governors and Premiers replaced the Council, uniting the chief executives as equal partners.[49] Johns and Thorn show that various factors – economic opportunities and threats, institutional factors, and intergovernmental relations in each country – explain the recent cross-border involvement of US states and Canadian provinces in the Great Lakes basin, and thus the stability of the field.[50]

The main international focus of Quebec in the mid-1960s was on France–Quebec relations, as French president Charles de Gaulle fully supported not only Quebec's extensive ties with France and the francophone countries but also Quebec's independence project as a means to weaken US–British relations. In this vein, Paul Gérin-Lajoie, Quebec's vice-premier, made an important speech on 12 April 1965 in which he enunciated the "Gérin-Lajoie doctrine." That doctrine supported the external projection of Quebec's domestic powers in areas where it had provincial jurisdiction and shared jurisdiction with the federal government.[51] Consequently, this doctrine rejected the federal government's monitoring of the international activities of the provinces. This doctrine had two main facets, political and legal. Politically, Gérin-Lajoie declared that Quebec had a responsibility, if not an obligation, to consider international relations when formulating and implementing its domestic policies. This doctrine has been accepted by both the Liberal Party and the Parti Québécois, which usually govern in Quebec. From a legal perspective, the doctrine asserted the legal "personhood" of Quebec, that is, its right to exercise its provincial competencies on the international stage and sign international agreements. In addition to this, Quebec negotiates with the federal government international instruments that Quebec will implement.[52] These elements have helped cement Quebec's relations with US sub-national actors.

A Field Destabilized by Significant Exogenous Shocks and Limited Internal Episodes of Rupture

Several episodes of rupture have destabilized the field. Those episodes can be divided into two categories: shocks external to the field, and shocks within the field. External shocks have encompassed three main issues: border securitization policies enacted after the 9/11 attacks; trade uncertainties related to the Trump administration's insistence on renegotiating NAFTA, which included resorting to tariffs to pressure Canada (2017–20); and the COVID-19 pandemic that led to the closing of the US–Canada border for "non-essential travel" (2020). Internal shocks refer to two separate shifts by Quebec in order to conduct protodiplomatic efforts, in line with domestic *souverainiste* politics: one occurred between 1976 and 1983, the other one between 1994 and 1995.

In 1969, Canadian prime minister Pierre Trudeau famously said that living next to the US was in some ways like "sleeping with an elephant. No matter how friendly or temperate the beast, one is affected by every twitch and grunt."[53] As a result of this structural asymmetry, Canada–US relations fundamentally changed after 9/11. Despite Canadian efforts to meet US security demands against terrorism, Paul Cellucci, the US Ambassador to Canada, bluntly stated in 2003 that "security trumps trade."[54] In this context, the first major external shock that reshaped the Canada–US border happened after the 9/11 attacks, at which time the entire border was reframed as a national security threat by the White House. The variegated effects of border securitization have been studied by border, migration, and forced-migration scholars.[55] For the next two decades, the border governance field had no alternative but to include the border security variable into its agenda. For instance, in 2015, the 39th Annual NEG-ECP Conference adopted Resolution 39–2, which called for prompt ratification of the pre-clearance agreement (it would be signed on 16 March 2015 by Ottawa and Washington), as well as for US and Canadian customs pre-clearance and clearance at Central Station in Montreal.[56] The second external shock relates to the Trump administration's impact on border issues. According to Gagnon and Cloutier-Roy, who studied how Donald Trump impacted states bordering Ontario and Quebec on several policy issues in 2018, the Trump administration's agenda, especially regarding Canada–US issues, was adopted by numerous local actors.[57] But does that mean that this agenda, whose key issue was the renegotiation of NAFTA, influenced the cross-border governance field? Indeed, the cross-border governance field feared that the aggressive negotiation strategy followed by the Trump administration would damage shared interests within the region in the mid- and long term. Several statements, resolutions, and declarations released by cross-border organizations focused more strongly than ever on stable trade relations in the cross-border region. For instance, NEG-ECP released several resolutions between 2017 and 2019 that referred to "trade integration and the benefits of cross-border trade,"[58] to "NAFTA,"[59] and to "business and trade."[60] At the same time, NEG-ECP declared its political and policy differences with the Trump administration related to climate change, passing several resolutions on this issue.[61]

The effects of the COVID-19 pandemic in the cross-border area have been felt in several ways. First, Canada and the US agreed to close their common land border to non-essential travel. That did not mean the border would be entirely closed – the flow of goods by land, vital for both economies, would not be stopped. Cross-border commutes related to grocery shopping, studies, and work were still allowed as well. Several sectors *were* affected by those restrictions, even after they were lifted (e.g., tourism and culture in border areas). Moreover, leaked documents reveal that US Customs and Border Protection (CBP) had asked the US Department of Defense to deploy more than 1,500 troops to the southern and northern borders to support border enforcement during the COVID-19 pandemic. Finally, several cross-border organizations decided to cancel or reschedule their annual meetings in 2020, due to travel restrictions as well as the risks associated with the pandemic. Online meetings will likely replace in-person ones for a while, as with many other sectors. It is not certain how the pandemic will affect the border in the long term.

Next, we examine the internal shocks that emanated from electoral victories of the Québécois *souverainiste* party between 1976 and 1983 and between 1994 and 1995. The Parti Québécois (PQ), elected with a large majority in 1976 under René Lévesque, had Quebec independence at the top of its agenda. To reassure the US, the PQ had to guarantee that the interests of the US would not be affected by the possibility of independence north of the border. To that end, Lévesque travelled to New York in January 1977 with his finance minister. That trip turned into a fiasco for the PQ government. Instead of reassuring investors, Lévesque ignited serious concerns about the impact on the US of the possible independence of Quebec, for instance by mentioning explicit nationalizations, hedging on whether Quebec would avoid default on its debts, and so on. The Canadian federal government responded the following month, in February 1977, when Prime Minister Pierre Trudeau addressed the US Congress. There, Trudeau sought to reassure US interests and pointedly emphasized Canada's unity. President Jimmy Carter supported Ottawa by insisting that the US preferred stability with a united Canada, adding, however, that it was a decision for the Canadians to make and that the US government would respect that decision. In this context of bilateral mutual understanding, the PQ government launched "Operation America" to convince Americans that Quebec was a trustworthy ally and business partner. In May 1980, the results of the Quebec independence referendum, which the PQ lost, sealed the end of PQ's protodiplomatic efforts.[62]

In 1994, the PQ returned to power in Quebec, promising a speedy referendum on independence. Over the following months, the PQ launched a second phase of protodiplomacy, seeking the support of Paris. In parallel, Ottawa sought the help of Washington. The Clinton administration responded more forcefully than Carter, signalling that an independent Quebec might not automatically be able to join NAFTA. In October 1995, the referendum failed by a narrow margin. This marked the end of the second phase of protodiplomacy and the return to a tradition of paradiplomacy, at least for the next twenty-five years. During these two periods of protodiplomacy, the field of cross-border governance was affected in such a way that Quebec temporarily became a challenger. For instance, in 1978 and the following years, Lévesque used NEG-ECP to promote the interests of Quebec, particularly in the energy export sector. This approach helped modify NEG-ECP, leaving it more vulnerable to internal divisions. This happened in 1981, when Quebec decided to boycott the annual NEG-ECP conference in Newfoundland. This boycott was not directed specifically against NEG-ECP, but rather against Canadian federal legislation in the energy sector that had negative consequences for Quebec. The absence of Quebec allowed the Province of Newfoundland and Labrador to start its own negotiations about energy exports with nearby US states.[63] After 1995, the successive

Québécois governments, essentially PQ and Liberal governments, followed the line of paradiplomacy.[64] This enabled Quebec to return to the cross-border governance field as an incumbent.

Concluding Remarks: Making Sense of the Field and Its Surroundings

A significant facet of Quebec's paradiplomatic efforts plays out in the Quebec–US borderlands. Quebec's commitments in the cross-border governance field must be viewed as a sub-field of its paradiplomacy, aimed at acquiring material and symbolic resources. The presence of Quebec in governance structures serving as IGUs is visible in a small number of organizations that focus on cross-border policy issues, such as the Council of Great Lakes Governors and the Conference of New England Governors and Eastern Canadian Premiers. Those cross-border governance organizations cover several policy sectors such as the environment, water management, trade, transportation, and infrastructure. The US is a vital partner, given that Quebec exports 70 per cent to its southern neighbour. This dependence leaves Quebec vulnerable if the US administration decides to take protectionist measures against Canada, which it could do even after the conclusion of the USMCA. In this context, preserving and consolidating trade, political, and academic relations with several levels of government in the US is essential for Quebec. In the field of cross-border governance, Quebec is a late incumbent, but still an incumbent, and at times a challenger. Surprisingly, other Québécois and US stakeholders, in particular in the private and not-for-profit sectors, occupy a grey area, as neither incumbents nor challengers. This raises the question of the role of adjacent fields, and under what circumstances actors that are positioned in an adjacent field have sufficient material and/or symbolic resources to influence incumbents in another field.

Although paradiplomacy and protodiplomacy represented central conceptual lenses in this chapter, the theory of fields has been essential for analysing how a field of cross-border governance emerges, stabilizes, and at times destabilizes. It was also useful to examine how PQ governments with an independence agenda lost their incumbent status and became challengers for limited periods of time. This echoes what has been observed in other borderlands, for instance on the French–Spanish border, when the election of the far right party in a French region led to a boycott of the main IGU by other partners.[65] Yet the absence of stable challengers is surprising in the field. It can perhaps be explained by how the field first emerged, centred originally around US states and then expanding toward Canadian provinces. As we have noted, the US and Canadian federal governments belong to powerful adjacent fields and thus are included in the cross-border governance field.

What are the implications of Quebec's relations with external governments with respect to other cases that do not face sub-state identity issues? As Quebec contributed to the emergence of a field of cross-border governance, its paradiplomatic activities were innovative in North America. Other Canadian provinces found in the Quebec case useful blueprints they were able to adapt to their own paradiplomatic contexts, in order to focus on specific policy sectors. At the same time, Quebec's controversial protodiplomatic actions drew a clear red line regarding what was *not* acceptable by federal states – that is, stepping on bilateral state responsibility. In addition, Quebec's paradiplomatic ministry, the Ministère des Relations internationales et de la Francophonie, is meticulously modelled after foreign affairs ministries, with clearly defined international objectives. This represents a major departure from the design of sub-state jurisdictions, which often engage in what are at best amateurish and unstructured international and transnational initiatives.

NOTES

1 Roberto Zepeda Martínez, "The Paradiplomacy of Subnational Governments in North America," *Ánfora: Revista Científica de la Universidad Autónoma de Manizales* 25, no. 44 (2018): 20, https://www.redalyc.org/journal/3578/357856333004/html.
2 Francesca Dickson, "The Internationalisation of Regions: Paradiplomacy or Multi-level Governance?," *Geography Compass* 8, no. 10 (2014): 690, https://doi.org/10.1111/gec3.12152.
3 R. Kaiser, "Paradiplomacy and Multilevel Governance in Europe and North America: Subnational Governments in International Arenas," *Participation* 27, no. 1 (2003): 17–19.
4 Zepeda Martínez, "The Paradiplomacy of Subnational Governments," 29–30.
5 Alexander Kuznetsov, *Theory and Practice of Paradiplomacy: Subnational Governments in International Affairs* (New York: Routledge, 2014), 2, https://doi.org/10.4324/9781315817088.
6 Kuznetsov, *Theory and Practice of Paradiplomacy*, 3.
7 Kuznetsov, *Theory and Practice of Paradiplomacy*, 3.
8 Kuznetsov, *Theory and Practice of Paradiplomacy*, 2.
9 Ivo Duchacek, "International Competence of Subnational Governments: Borderlands and Beyond," in *Across Boundaries: Transborder Interaction in Comparative Perspective*, ed. Oscar Martínez (El Paso: Texas Western Press, 1986), 11–28.
10 Kim Richard Nossal, Stéphane Roussel, and Stéphane Paquin, *The Politics of Canadian Foreign Policy* (Montreal and Kingston: McGill–Queen's University Press, 2015).
11 André Lecours and Luis Moreno, *Paradiplomacy and Stateless Nations: A Reference to the Basque Country* (Montreal: Concordia University and Spanish National Research Council [CSIC], 2001): 2–3.

12 Nathan Henrique Alves Cazé, *Paradiplomacy within the Globalization Debate: The Tendencies of Subnational Governments' Engagements in Transnational City Twinning between 2010 and 2014* (Brazil: Universidade Católica de Brasília, 2015), https://repositorio.ucb.br:9443/jspui/bitstream/123456789/8392/1/NathanHenriqueAlvesCazeTCCGraduacao2015.pdf.
13 James T. McHugh, "Paradiplomacy, Protodiplomacy, and the Foreign Policy Aspirations of Quebec and Other Canadian Provinces," *Canadian Foreign Policy Journal* 21, no. 3 (2015): 238–56, https://doi.org/10.1080/11926422.2015.1031261.
14 Nossal, Roussel, and Paquin, *The Politics of Canadian Foreign Policy*, 356–71.
15 E.H. Fry, "Federalism and Foreign Relations," in *The Encyclopedia of Political Science*, ed. George T. Kurian, James E. Alt, Simone Chambers, Geoffrey Garret, Margaret Levi, and Paula D. McClain (California: CQPress, 2011): 573–74, cited in Zepeda Martínez, "The Paradiplomacy of Subnational Governments."
16 Lecours and Moreno, *Paradiplomacy and Stateless Nations*, 2.
17 Zepeda Martínez, "The Paradiplomacy of Subnational Governments."
18 See the chapters by Staudt and Cruz, Payan, and Konrad in this book.
19 Mathilde Bourgeon, Thalia D'Aragon-Giguère, and Élisabeth Vallet, "Les Flux Migratoires à la Frontière Québéco-Américaine," *Québec Studies* 64 (2017): 141–56, https://doi.org/10.3828/qs.2017.20.
20 Annie Chaloux and Stéphane Paquin, "Green Paradiplomacy and Water Resource Management in North America: The Case of the Great Lakes–St Lawrence River Basin," *Canadian Foreign Policy Journal* 19, no. 3 (2013): 308–22, https://doi.org/10.1080/11926422.2013.845582; Carolyn M. Johns and Adam Thorn, "Subnational Diplomacy in the Great Lakes Region: Toward Explaining Variation between Water Quality and Quantity Regimes," *Canadian Foreign Policy Journal* 21, no. 3 (2015): 195–211, https://doi.org/10.1080/11926422.2015.1035296; Daniel Macfarlane, "Watershed Decisions: The St Lawrence Seaway and Sub-National Water Diplomacy," *Canadian Foreign Policy Journal* 21, no. 3 (2015): 212–23, https://doi.org/10.1080/11926422.2015.1051069.
21 Caroline Dunton and Veronica Kitchen, "Para-Diplomatic Policing and Relocating Canadian Foreign Policy," *International Journal* 69, no. 2 (2014): 183–97, https://doi.org/10.1177/0020702014525903.
22 Zepeda Martínez, "The Paradiplomacy of Subnational Governments," 29.
23 R. Vengroff and J. Rich, "Foreign Policy by Other Means: Paradiplomacy and the Canadian Provinces," in *Handbook of Canadian Policy*, ed. P. James, N. Michaud, and M.J. O'Reilly (Toronto: Lexington Books, 2006), 105–30, cited in Zepeda Martínez, "The Paradiplomacy of Subnational Governments."
24 Lecours and Moreno, *Paradiplomacy and Stateless Nations*.
25 Chaloux and Paquin, "Green Paradiplomacy."
26 Francesca Dickson, "The Internationalisation of Regions: Paradiplomacy or Multi-level Governance?," *Geography Compass* 8, no. 10 (October 2014): 690–1, https://doi.org/10.1111/gec3.12152.

27 Chaloux and Paquin, "Green Paradiplomacy," 311.
28 Brian Hocking, *Localizing Foreign Policy: Non-central Governments and Multi-layered Diplomacy* (New York: St Martin's Press, 1993).
29 Dickson, "The Internationalisation of Regions," 698.
30 Neil Fligstein and Doug McAdam, *A Theory of Fields* (New York: Oxford University Press, 2012), http://doi.org/10.1007/s11186-014-9237-0.
31 Fligstein and McAdam, *A Theory of Fields*, 167.
32 Fligstein and McAdam, *A Theory of Fields*, 167–8.
33 Fligstein and McAdam, *A Theory of Fields*, 170–8.
34 Fligstein and McAdam, *A Theory of Fields*, 165.
35 Fligstein and McAdam, *A Theory of Fields*, 166.
36 Dunton and Kitchen, "Para-Diplomatic Policing," 187.
37 David Morin and Myriam Poliquin, "Governing from the Border? Quebec's Role in North American Security," *American Review of Canadian Studies* 46, no. 2 (2016): 266, https://doi.org/10.1080/02722011.2016.1185594.
38 Ministère des Relations Internationales et de la Francophonie (MRIF), « Bilateral Relations, » Government of Québec (2019), https://www.mrif.gouv.qc.ca/en/relations-du-quebec/ameriques/etats-unis/relations-bilaterales.
39 Louis Balthazar and Alfred Hero, *Le Québec dans l'espace américain* (Montréal: Québec-Amérique, 1999).
40 Institut de la Statistique du Québec, "Québec's International Exports up in 2017," (2018), https://www.stat.gouv.qc.ca/salle-presse/communique/communique-presse-2018/fevrier/fev1828_an.html.
41 Nossal, Roussel, and Paquin, *The Politics of Canadian Foreign Policy*.
42 Ministère des Relations Internationales et de la Francophonie (MRIF), "Rapport Annuel, 2018–2019" (2019), 5, https://performance.gouv.qc.ca/fileadmin/documents/RAG/MRIF_RAG_2018-2019.pdf.
43 Nossal, Roussel, and Paquin, *The Politics of Canadian Foreign Policy*, 2015.
44 New England Governors and Eastern Canadian Premiers (NEG–ECP), Committee on the Environment and the Northeast International Committee on Energy, "Climate Change Action Plan 2001" (August 2001), https://www.coneg.org/wp-content/uploads/2019/01/ClimateChange-Action-Plan-August-20011.pdf.
45 Conference of the New England Governors and Eastern Canadian Premiers, "2017 Update of the Regional Climate Change Action Plan" (2019), https://www.coneg.org/neg-ecp-regional-climate-change-initiative/ and https://www.coneg.org/wp-content/uploads/2019/01/2017-rccap-final.pdf.
46 Coalition of Northeastern Governors (CONEG), "Committee on the Environment (COE)," 13 August 2018, https://www.coneg.org/neg-ecp/committees/committee-on-the-environment-coe.
47 Chaloux and Paquin, "Green Paradiplomacy."
48 Council of Great Lakes Governors, "The Great Lakes Charter – Principles for the Management of Great Lakes Water Resources" (1985), https://gsgp.org/media/j1zcl0x2/greatlakescharter.pdf.

49 Conference of Great Lakes and St. Lawrence Governors and Premiers, "History Great Lakes Governors and Premiers" (2020), https://gsgp.org/about-us/history/.

50 Johns and Thorns, "Subnational Diplomacy in the Great Lakes Region," 207–8.

51 See Table 1 for a summary of the constitutional division of powers in Canada in Zepeda Martínez, "The Paradiplomacy of Subnational Governments," 25.

52 Nossal, Roussel, and Paquin, *The Politics of Canadian Foreign Policy*, 2015; Ministère des Relations internationales et de la Francophonie (MRIF), Doctrine Gérin-Lajoie (2016), http://www.mrif.gouv.qc.ca/fr/ministere/historique/doctrine-paul-gerin-lajoie/50-ans-doctrine.

53 "Pierre Trudeau's Washington Press Club Speech," *CBC News* (1969), https://www.cbc.ca/player/play/1797537698.

54 Greg Anderson, "David and Goliath in Canada–US Relations: Who's Really Who?," *Canadian Foreign Policy Journal* 25, no. 2 (2019): 115–36, https://doi.org/10.1080/11926422.2018.1542604.

55 Matthew B. Sparke, "A Neoliberal Nexus: Economy, Security, and the Biopolitics of Citizenship on the Border," *Political Geography* 25, no. 2 (2006): 151–80, https://doi.org/10.1016/j.polgeo.2005.10.002; Victor Konrad and Heather Nicol, *Beyond Walls: Reinventing the Canada–United States Borderlands* (London: Routledge, 2008); Heather N. Nicol, "The Wall, the Fence, and the Gate: Reflexive Metaphors along the Canada–US Border," *Journal of Borderlands Studies* 27, no. 2 (2012): 139–65, https://doi.org/10.1080/08865655.2012.687213; Susan L. Bradbury, "The Impact of Security on Travelers across the Canada–US Border," *Journal of Transport Geography* 26 (2013): 139–46, https://doi.org/10.1016/j.jtrangeo.2012.08.009; Jane Helleiner, "Unauthorised Crossings, Danger, and Death at the Canada–US Border," *Journal of Ethnic and Migration Studies* 39, no. 9 (2013): 1507–24, https://doi.org/10.1080/1369183X.2013.815431; Morin and Poliquin, "Governing from the Border?"; Elisabeth Vallet, *Borders, Fences, and Walls: State of Insecurity?* (New York and London: Routledge, 2016); Bruno Dupeyron, "'Secondary Foreign Policy' through the Prism of Cross-Border Governance in the US–Canada Pacific Northwest Border Region," *Regional and Federal Studies* 27, no. 3 (2017): 321–40, https://doi.org/10.1080/13597566.2017.1343722; Matthew Longo, "From Sovereignty to Imperium: Borders, Frontiers, and the Specter of Neo-Imperialism," *Geopolitics* 22, no. 4 (2017): 757–71, https://doi.org/10.1080/14650045.2017.1355785.

56 New England Governors and Eastern Canadian Premiers (NEG-ECP), "Resolution 39–2: Resolution Concerning the Canada–US Preclearance Agreement and the Customs Preclearance Project for Central Station in Montreal (2015), https://www.coneg.org/wp-content/uploads/2019/04/39-2-Preclearance-Agreement.pdf.

57 Frédérick Gagnon and Christophe Cloutier-Roy, "Ephemeral or Durable? Donald Trump's Impact on Canada–US Issues in the Great Lakes Heartland and Northeast Borderlands," *Canadian Foreign Policy Journal* 26, no. 2 (2019): 182–96, https://doi.org/10.1080/11926422.2019.1696848.

58 NEG-ECP, "Resolution 41–1: Resolution Concerning Trade Integration and the Benefits of Cross-Border Trade" (2017), https://www.coneg.org/wp-content/uploads/2019/01/41-1-Cross-Border-Trade.pdf.

59 NEG-ECP, "Resolution 42–4: Resolution Concerning NAFTA" (2018), https://www.coneg.org/wp-content/uploads/2018/12/42-4_en.pdf.

60 NEG-ECP, "Resolution 42–3: Resolution Concerning Business and Trade" (2018), https://www.coneg.org/wp-content/uploads/2018/12/42-3_en.pdf.

61 NEG-ECP, "Resolution 41–2: Resolution Concerning the Regional Climate Change Action Plan" (2017), https://www.coneg.org/wp-content/uploads/2019/01/41-2-Regional-Climate-Change-Action-Plan.pdf; "Resolution 42–1: Resolution Concerning Adaptation" (2018), https://www.coneg.org/wp-content/uploads/2018/12/42-1_en.pdf; Conference of the New England Governors and Eastern Canadian Premiers, "2017 Update of the Regional Climate Change Action Plan" (2019); CONEG, Committee on the Environment, 2018.

62 Nossal, Roussel, and Paquin, *The Politics of Canadian Foreign Policy.*

63 Lise Bissonnette, "Orthodoxie fédéraliste et relations régionales transfrontières, une menace illusoire," *Études internationales* 12, no. 4 (1981): 635–55, https://doi.org/10.7202/701272ar.

64 Nossal, Roussel, and Paquin, *The Politics of Canadian Foreign Policy.*

65 Bruno Dupeyron, *L'Europe au défi de ses régions transfrontalières. Expériences rhénane et pyrénéenne* (Bern: Peter Lang, 2008).

PART TWO

Cross-Border Governance in Europe: A Steady but Contested Multi-level Governance

8 Actors and Policy Outcomes in the Pyrenees–Mediterranean Euroregion: From the Emergence to the Stabilization of the Field (1990–2020)

ANDREA NOFERINI

This chapter seeks to exploit the potential of the strategic action field (SAF) framework[1] to analyse the Euroregion Pyrénées-Méditerranée (EPM), a cross-border entity on the Franco-Spanish border. The border between Spain and France, one of the oldest in Europe, presents a dense set of formal cross-border fields in policy areas that have an impact on its citizens' welfare. In 2004, five sub-national authorities (SNAs) from two distinct sovereign states – France and Spain – created the EPM with the ambitious goal of transforming the cross-border territory into "a sustainable development cluster in the northwestern Mediterranean region based on innovation and the social and economic integration of the territory."[2] With a population of more than 15 million relatively wealthy European citizens, EPM is today a recognized cross-border organization involved in sectors such as economic development, research and innovation, culture, education, sustainability, and transportation.

EPM constitutes a formal attempt to build up some model of shared cross-border governance that goes beyond traditional state-centric models. In this respect, it can be conceptualized as a SAF in which SNAs interact with one another based on a shared understanding (not always consensual) of the field's purpose, which is to promote the cross-border space in European and national arenas where central governments and EU institutions are depicted as the lead actors.

Cross-border cooperation has been defined in different ways,[3] but it is basically "an institutionalized collaboration between contiguous sub-national authorities across national borders."[4] In the European context, Euroregions are operational instruments charged with responsibility for propelling and coordinating cross-border initiatives. No official definition of the term "Euroregion" exists,[5] but generally speaking, Euroregions are formal organizations led by administrators at the regional or local level.

The Euroregional phenomenon exploded in the 1990s as the result of pressure on central governments. From a functional perspective, globalization and the European project of a single market helped shift the focus toward border territories, where the free circulation of goods, services, and people could be delayed or halted if obstacles were not removed. From a political perspective, decentralization trends across Europe contributed to the consolidation of democratically legitimate SNAs, some of which were endowed with legislative powers and political autonomy. Usually neglected by central governments, SNAs found in the European Commission (EC) a strategic ally that provided them with legitimacy, as well as technical and financial assistance in the first pioneering cross-border initiatives.

Recent studies count more than 300 Euroregions; about 150 are actually functional.[6] The rise of the Euroregional model is evidence of the vitality of European cross-border cooperation today. The literature, however, shows great variation regarding the role, success, and impact of the Euroregions. Scholars of multi-level governance place cross-border cooperation in the wider context of EU regional policy and public policy analysis. They privilege a functional logic by which SNAs lobby for European funding and institutional visibility.[7] On the negative side, it is reported that Euroregions rely on EU funds and often do not survive after those dry up. The literature on international relations focuses on the external dimension of cross-border cooperation and is primarily interested in understanding why, how, and with what results regional (and local) governments engage in paradiplomacy by challenging the gatekeeper position of central governments.[8] Border and “new regionalism” studies suggest that SNAs with nationalistic claims and strong territorial identities are more likely to engage in external actions but with a high degree of politicization.[9] This can lead to increased hostility among central governments toward cross-border activities by SNAs, even in neutral cases where a functional logic should prevail.

Focusing on EPM can shed light on the dynamics of cross-border governance for several reasons. First, since EPM involves SNAs from two sovereign states with different administrative, political, and institutional cultures, the analysis can help unpack the impact of the above-mentioned asymmetries on the development of cross-border initiatives. Second, because of a historical common past (some of the territories that EPM currently includes had already been grouped under the Crown of Aragon), the eastern Pyrénées are perceived as a relatively cohesive cross-border field with shared values and beliefs and a relatively fluid economic space. Nevertheless, the political border between France and Spain has been an obstacle to the development of integrated cross-border activity. Third, because Catalonia plays an active role, the EPM project has been highly politicized from the beginning. The resulting political “tint,” however, has not prevented this cross-border structure from surviving various dramatic shocks, such as the premature withdrawal of a partner,[10] a change in the legal structure in 2009–10, the Catalan secessionist movement since 2012, a territorial reform in France in 2016, and the suspension of Catalan autonomy in 2017.

Despite these external shocks, the field has stabilized, and EPM has entered an incisive phase characterized by the reduction in the number of SNA members (from five to three), a simplification of the organizational structure, and a new political agenda. The reasons for EPM's resilience are hardly explained by the analytical categories of the literature mentioned above. True, EPM today competes for EU funding, and the Euroregion has long been financed by the respective regional governments. Not even the financial crisis of 2007 and the consequent austerity measures applied by EU institutions and national governments have led regional governments to withdraw. Equally controversial is EPM's resilience in the face of the political challenge represented by Catalan secessionism. In 2018, the Spanish central government, led by the conservative Mariano Rajoy, applying Article 155 of the Constitution, closed *de facto* all Catalan official delegations and offices abroad. But EPM was not disturbed; indeed, it was allowed to continue its activities.

By treating EPM as an SAF that adjusts over time, moving back and forth along a continuum, the chapter offers an alternative view of the cross-border field. In this sense, the SAF approach is useful with respect to institutional theory, because it views fields as only rarely organized around a consensual and shared understanding of the field. Actors are constantly in motion, making ongoing adjustments to the field conditions. Through this actor-centred and dynamic perspective, the chapter can trace the permanent and continuous processes of adjustment that have characterized EPM's development from emergence to stabilization.

The research combines qualitative and quantitative analyses. The bibliographic references come from EU integration studies, border studies, and international relations. Primary sources include legal and official texts, administrative documentation, political declarations, and position papers generated by the regional authorities that lead the EPM project as well as by national and European institutions. Primary data come from two different databases and from fieldwork between 2013 and 2017 under the BORDERGOV research project. The two databases were developed by two parallel projects led by the Universitat Autònoma de Barcelona and financed by the Spanish government.[11] For the fieldwork, the profiles to be interviewed were selected according to their formal role and position in the field. They are civil servants and public officials who hold responsibilities within the EPM structure and in the regional governments that lead the Euroregion. The sample has been progressively widened to include experts, specialists, and other stakeholders who have interacted with EPM.

Section 2 of this chapter introduces cross-border cooperation in the context of European integration by complementing the SAF approach with traditional streams of literature that deal with borders and the mobilizations of SNAs in the international and European scenarios. Section 3 contextualizes the eastern side of the Franco–Spanish border by presenting the most relevant characteristics of the EPM territory. This section focuses on the impact of the "border effect" on the entire area. Section 4 illustrates the conditions that in the 1980s and 1990s contributed to the emergence of the field in the early 2000s. Section 5 illustrates the three main stages of the EPM: emergence, stabilization, and the current situation. The narrative follows the timeline of events, and SAF analytical tools and references have been framed directly within the text. Section 6 presents some analytical remarks regarding the interpretation of the field. Section 7 presents this study's conclusions.

Cross-Border Cooperation in the EU as a Strategic Action Field

Europe and its national states have around forty internal land borders.[12] Internal borders pose challenges to integration processes because they increase transaction costs and raise additional obstacles to the free movement of workers, persons, goods, and ideas. Cross-border cooperation is thus seen an instrument for weakening or eliminating the negative effects of borders.[13] Its goals are to tackle common challenges identified jointly in the border territory and to facilitate the striking of cooperation agreements among actors.

Given that all fields are embedded in a complex web of other fields, cross-border cooperation in Europe can be conceived as a sub-field of the EU integration process and of EU member-states' fields. In formal terms, as Euroregions are framed within the formal regulation of EU Cohesion Policy, cross-border cooperation is a *dependent* field of the wider EU integration field.[14] Moreover, SNA dependence arises from the formal and legal authority of the central governments regarding the degree of autonomy assigned to SNAs as well as from reliance on EU institutions for resources. Notwithstanding this reliance, the processes of European integration differ from those of cross-border cooperation. If SAFs can be defined as socially and politically constructed arenas within which actors with different endowments vie for advantage,[15] then cross-border cooperation and EU integration represent two different fields. The EU itself as a political order is embedded in complex webs of other fields. EU policy-making relies on a dense system of interdependent fields in which national governments bargain with supra-national institutions regarding how much national sovereignty to devolve. The process of European integration constitutes a search for a delicate balance between intergovernmental and supra-national logics. Supporters of liberal intergovernmentalism claim,[16] correctly, that national governments are the dominant actors (incumbents), given that they wield greater influence within the field and impose the political goals of the EU through the EU Council of the Ministries.

The EC and the European Parliament are, for their part, *challengers* in the field, in that they occupy a less privileged niche and the degree of their influence varies depending on the policy sector. Here, neofunctionalist[17] logics perfectly fit with the SAF approach in explaining, for example, the increasing relevance of the former two supra-national institutions in the current EU political arena. By recognizing the dominant logic of incumbent actors, the EC and the European Parliament have helped articulate alternative visions of the field. The EC has usually been viewed as having the capacity and skill to assume the role of "institutional entrepreneur."[18]

Regarding the actors, cross-border cooperation fields depart from the European integration project in many aspects. First, national governments remain the incumbent actors, but the main challengers are now public stakeholders acting at the sub-national level (regions, towns and cities, local authority associations, etc.) or, to a lesser extent, private stakeholders (associations, businesses, frontier workers, chambers of commerce, etc.). Second, the logic of the field and actors' priorities vary considerably with respect to the fundamentals of the EU integration process. Far from the rhetoric of an "ever closer union among the peoples of Europe," the pioneering experiences of cross-border cooperation among local actors along the Dutch–German and Franco–German–Swiss[19] borders in the late 1950s were pragmatic, that is, oriented toward solving problems. Local administrations were not looking to "overcom[e] national frontiers to heal the scars of history"; rather, they were seeking practical solutions to border problems that arose when national frontiers were crossed in daily life.

Finally, European integration and cross-border cooperation evolved in fundamentally different ways. European integration grew out of tensions stemming from a deepening/widening divide. In seven enlargement stages, national-based governance models have been partly Europeanized, and, in some areas (trade, competition, economic governance), policy convergence has occurred. By contrast, cross-border cooperation seems to be marked by three characteristics: singularity, diversity, and complexity.[20] Each cross-border region has a unique history and distinctive geographical and political features. There is, therefore, no single field of cross-border cooperation; there are, rather, as many fields as there are border regions.

Sub-National Authorities as Skilled Actors in the Cross-Border Cooperation Field

The first cross-border experiences in Europe date back to the late 1950s, but the explosion of cross-border cooperation agreements happened in Europe in the 1990s, with the creation of the European Common Market.[21] With the deepening of the integration process, the EC assigned cross-border territories the role of "laboratory" areas for European integration. The 1988 reform to Cohesion Policy, the introduction in 1990 of the Community Initiative INTERREG, and the 1993 Maastricht Treaty (which established the Committee of the Regions) inserted into the European political agenda the "regional question," that is, the question of the role SNAs would play in EU policy-making.

Thus, the 1990s opened a window of opportunity for sub-national mobilization conceived as the participation of SNAs in EU policy-making. Globalization, Europeanization,[22] and decentralization were among the most relevant phenomena that enhanced the role that territorial units would play across Europe. Nation-state dominance may have been the rule until the early 1980s, but neofunctionalists and multi-level governance arguments[23] now started to focus attention on the novel fact that in some areas of EU policy-making, decisions depended on the mutual relations among different levels of government (EU, national, sub-national, local) as well as on the participation of a new array of civil society actors. Several approaches to "the Europe of regions" in political science,[24] international relations, border studies,[25] and comparative politics emphasized the role of SNAs in European integration. For these scholars, politically endowed regions represented the "ideal" level of governance for establishing a united Europe that would be close to the people. The presence of these new actors required a qualitative shift in EU policy-making and politics that, according to some, had become plural, open, and less hierarchical – in a word, multi-level.[26]

In this context, SNAs began acting in ways that blurred the domestic/international divide. The proliferation of international networks of territorial actors, the establishment of regional offices and delegations abroad, and the creation of Euroregions are examples of this renewed role for SNAs in international fields. The drivers for cross-border initiatives were diverse, with much depending on the actors involved and the characteristics of the border territory. For some, Euroregions were functional organizations aimed at increasing the economic competitiveness of cross-border areas by focusing, for example, on communication and transportation infrastructure. For others, cross-border cooperation was more political, framed within the broader area of external action, along with decentralized cooperation and international lobbying. From this perspective, Euroregions were instruments for projecting regional identity onto international scenarios in order to capture European funding or increase their political visibility.

The variety of the experiences makes any generalization difficult. Nevertheless, the empirical evidence indicates that very few Euroregions were able to establish and implement new and effective cross-border integrative strategies better than more classic planning instruments. Also, Euroregions were usually propelled by public administrators, with the involvement of actors from civil society; NGOs and business interests were scarce and of low intensity. Even after a strategic plan was agreed to at the cross-border level, controversies among SNAs and the rest of the territorial stakeholders, as well as external shocks, often delayed or halted implementation.

But by pursuing less ambitious goals, Euroregions succeeded in occupying some relevant space in cross-border governance. Many organizations were able to act as normative and policy referents in cross-border areas, especially when it came to lobbying EU institutions and providing institutional and financial resources to Euroregional actors. In sum, Euroregions achieved positive results when cross-border fields presented some enabling conditions, such as a base level of administrative and financial capacity among their members, consistent political commitment, and the external support of EU institutions. Also, resources matter. The management of cross-border cooperation fields is complicated, and only sufficiently endowed SNAs can afford to carry out strategic actions aimed at shaping cross-border coalitions. When adequate economic, institutional, and administrative capacities are lacking, Euroregions remain weak, as well as instrumental to a limited and temporary goal. Also, cross-border initiatives must be supported by the presence of strong and constant political commitment. When elections or political changes alter actors' preferences and understandings of the field, Euroregions are negatively affected. Political instability can open a field crisis when, for example, a new political coalition does not adequately support Euroregional initiatives. Moreover, political divergence can produce an impasse when challengers fail to (a) mobilize partners to help them build up a political coalition, or (b) pool resources for some common interest. Moreover, when SNAs present relevant asymmetries in their respective legal responsibilities, cross-border joint initiatives must overcome additional obstacles; whether they can do so depends on the will of central governments.[27] Finally, as the stability of any given field is a function of its relations with other fields, the continuous support received by EU institutions enhances the sustainability of most Euroregions. Since 2007, cross-border cooperation has been an official goal of Cohesion Policy programming; across more than five stages of the INTERREG initiative[28] (1990–2020), the EC has contributed so far to the stabilization of the cross-border cooperation field.

The Border Effect in the Eastern Pyrénées

With twelve different and often overlapping cross-border structures today, the entire French–Spanish border constitutes a dynamic field. In this sense, "French–Spanish cross-border structures can be conceived as sub-national fields that emerge when regional and/or local stakeholders cooperate across the national boundary in order to jointly face common challenges."[29] According to the scale, cooperation across the border can follow one of two different models. The first accounts for cooperation fields led by municipalities and supra-local administrations. The second involves SNAs and entails a more top-down approach aimed at setting ambitious and comprehensive cross-border joint initiatives.[30]

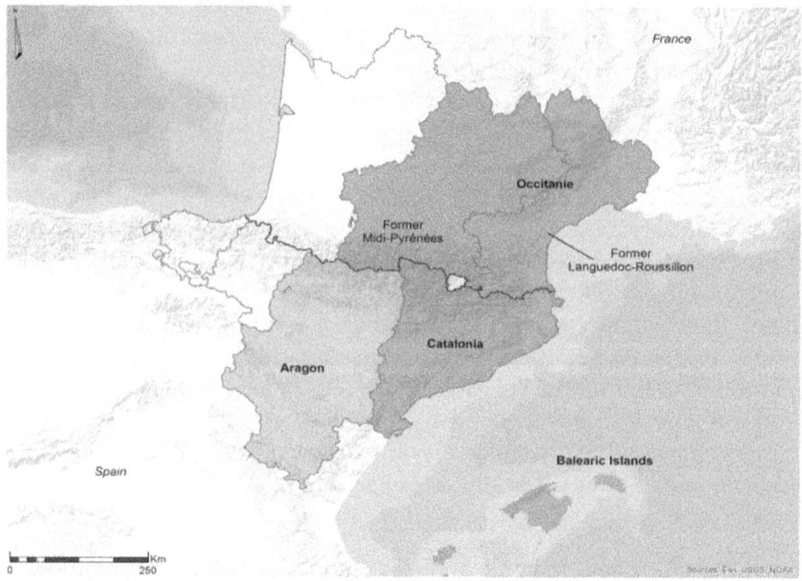

Map 8.1. The EPM on the Franco-Spanish border

Sources: Andrea Noferini and Matteo Berzi.

On the southeastern side of the border, the EPM is the most visible example of the second cooperation model. Geographically, the EPM covers an extensive territory of 109,830 km^2, characterized by a dense network of cities in a wealthy industrialized area that is home to more than 15 million French and Spanish citizens.

The territory is geographically quite diverse, and encompasses an important coastal area with large urban agglomerations such as Barcelona, Gerona, Toulouse, and Montpellier. It is also one of the most densely populated regions in Europe. It has many universities and research laboratories, a modern economy with great potential in IT, electronics, and biotech, and a modern agricultural sector as well as a growing tourism industry.

Cultural and historical links contribute to the view that the entire geographical area is a cohesive space. The territory presents some common traits, such as close business relationships and an interdependence of productive sectors, as well as common social and cultural values.[31] For more than five centuries, the Valencian Community, Aragon, Catalonia, the Balearic Islands, the Kingdom of Andorra, and the French *departementes* of Languedoc-Roussillon and Midi-Pyrénées shared political institutions under the Crown of Aragon.[32] Federal

Table 8.1. Main territorial and socio-economic figures of the EPM

	Aragon	Catalonia	Balearic Islands	Midi-Pyrénées (NUTS 2013)	Languedoc Roussillon (NUTS 2013)	EPM	EU
Area (km^2)	47,719	32,106	4,992	45,348	27,376	109,822	4,422,773
Population (millions)	1.3	7.44	1.15	3.04	2.81	15.7	511.52
Density (inh/km^2)	27.8	232.3	229.9	66.8	102.5	131.9	117.5
GDP (millions of euros)	34,368	213,766	28,651	92,816	68,417	438,018	14,907,852
GDP per capita (euros)	26,328	30,900	27,000	27,400	22,800	26,900	29,121
Unemployment rate (%)	11.7	13.4	12.4	7.2	12.2	11.4	7.6
People at risk of poverty (%)	18.7	17.9	19.1	14.6	19.6	17.8	17.3

Sources: Eurostat and national statistical offices. Last available data from 2018.

and consensual relations characterized the political philosophy of the Aragon Crown, allowing different territories to maintain their own norms, institutions, and symbols.[33] Nevertheless, modern and contemporary political history progressively widened the distance between those communities. In the eighteenth century, Spanish dynastic wars ruptured the territory's unity, splitting the traditional Catalan territory between Spain and France. Later, the Franco regime in Spain (1939–75) reduced any cross-border social and economic interaction for decades, increasing the border effect in the territory. Basically, cross-border relations could not start again until the late 1980s, when democratic Spain joined the European Economic Community.

The highly centralist construction of the French and Spanish states did not favour peripheral territories. The "radial state" approach[34] in this region usually favoured connections between a territory and its capital. Thus, the Spanish and French states governed their territories from the perspective of Paris and Madrid, and this consigned regions such as Languedoc-Roussillon, Midi-Pyrénées, the Balearic Islands, and Catalonia to a secondary role in large state investments and infrastructure policies, as well as in education and health care.[35] The lack of an adequate internal transportation network limited, for example, internal accessibility within the cross-border area.[36]

As the political frontier delimits not only territories but also politico-administrative systems, SNAs from both sides of the border are imbued with a specific and nationally based regulatory and institutional environment. Relevant administrative and political asymmetries among the SNAs that form EPM reduced, in some cases, the possibility of cross-border joint initiatives. According to the Article 137 of the Constitution of 1978, Spain is a unitary state in which sub-national authorities' autonomy is constitutionally recognized. Spain is a quasi-federation in which autonomous communities (ACs) have broad autonomy since, as a rule, responsibilities not expressly assigned to the central state by the Constitution are devolved to ACs. For example, Spanish ACs are responsible for education (since 2000), health care (since 2002), public safety, planning, urban development and housing, transportation, environmental protection, agriculture, culture, and social assistance. Compared to the rest of Europe, Spanish ACs enjoy exceptional autonomy resembling that of federal (or quasi-federal) arrangements.

France, by contrast, belongs to the group of OECD countries that are moderately decentralized. After a number of waves of decentralization reforms (the 1982–3 decentralization laws; the 2003–4 law; the 2010 and 2015 territorial reforms), France's territorial structure was substantially modified. Then in 2015, the law of the Delimitation of Regions forced the consolidation of regions, which now numbered thirteen instead of twenty-two. This last reform assigned to the regions the role of principal state interlocutor for economic development and social cohesion. More recent reforms have clarified the distribution of functions across French levels of government. Today, French regions largely oversee regional economic development, territorial planning, environmental protection, regional transportation, high schools (*lycées*), and vocational training.[37]

Finally, it is worth noting that Spanish and French sub-national authorities are involved in similar policy sectors, yet the two vary considerably in terms of their autonomy in given policy domains. For example, Spanish ACs enjoy strong control over regional health care systems and education, whereas in France both policy fields are still centralized and under the strict control of Paris. According to the Regional Authority Index,[38] Spain is the second most decentralized country in the world, below Germany but above Belgium, Switzerland, and Canada.[39] Within Spain, though it does not enjoy the fiscal autonomy of Navarre and the Basque Country, Catalonia ranks in the top tier, behind Quebec and US states, but above Scotland in the UK and Wallonia in Belgium. In France, the *départmentes* have much less regional power. The French state's Jacobin tradition has historically privileged equality among territories to the detriment of autonomy in administration, which was long considered synonymous with discord and territorial competition.

EPM as an SAF: From Emergence to Stabilization (1990–2018)

Enabling Conditions for the Field in the 1990s

Except for some earlier isolated initiatives undertaken by municipalities, contemporary cross-border cooperation along the Franco-Spanish border arose in the 1980s.[40] That decade established the conditions that would later enable SNAs to engage in cross-border initiatives. In 1978, with the promulgation of a new constitution, Spain became a democracy and devolved political autonomy to newly constituted ACs. Then in 1982, following the first decentralization law of that year, the French government began a process of devolving authority. More responsibilities were assigned to the *départements*,[41] and a new institution for regional cooperation was created within the territorial organization of the French state – the Regional Council.[42]

Another enabling condition came from external actors at the international level. In 1980, the Council of Europe adopted the Madrid Convention, which set the first regulatory framework for promoting cross-border initiatives among local and regional actors. That convention was intended to encourage and facilitate the crafting of cross-border agreements between local and regional authorities within the scope of their respective powers. Such agreements covered regional development, environmental protection, improvements to public services, and the like, and involved setting up transborder associations or consortia of local authorities. In 1990 and 1994 respectively, Spain and France ratified the convention, which was later modified by three further protocols (1995, 1998, 2009). Finally, a decade later, the EC and reforms to the Cohesion Policy in 1989 provided the necessary technical and financial assistance for the development of the first cross-border initiatives. The well-known INTERREG program, established in 1990, was a turning point for cross-border cooperation across Europe.

Under this promising scenario, French and Spanish SNAs took their first steps in the cross-border field. The Pyrénées Working Community (CTP), set up in 1983, included the *départementes* of Aquitaine, Midi-Pyrénées, and Languedoc-Roussillon in France and the ACs of Catalonia, Aragon, Navarre, and the Basque Country in Spain, as well as the Principality of Andorra. The CTP was strongly supported by Catalonia's conservative leader, Jordi Pujol y Soley, who governed that region for more than two decades. Its CTP's main objective was to develop the Pyrenean region by promoting exchanges between territories and actors spanning the mountain range with the goal of propelling actions with cross-border scope.[43]

In the 1990s, pressure to consolidate the field increased throughout the cross-border area, but the actors' positions and interests were confused and in some cases antagonistic. The debate reflected the different (and in some cases alternative) views that challengers held regarding the nature of the cross-border space and which cross-border governance models could benefit their respective interests the most. The challengers (here, regional governments and even cities) had roughly the same understanding of the field. Cross-border cooperation was conceived as a new field to be explored under the legal and normative umbrella provided by EU institutions and under the benevolent attitude of central governments (the incumbents). Reflecting their efforts to adapt their territorial structures and policies to the challenges of economic globalization and integration, the both French and Spanish states were more prepared to accept alterations to the international/national gate and allowed SNAs some incursions into the field of cross-border cooperation.

Unresolved geographical tensions among the challengers related to the scale of cooperation prevented the formation of the field in this decade.[44] In the 1990s, two distinct projects led by different actors seemed to be competing for dominance in the field. The first was territorially based and was launched by regional governments. The second was promoted by municipalities and relied on a network governance model. Regarding the first, the regional presidents of Catalonia, Languedoc-Roussillon, and Midi-Pyrénées signed the Charter of the Euroregion in Perpignan in 1991. This cooperation agreement, which was largely political and not formally binding, set two essential objectives: to facilitate exchanges between economic, social, and cultural actors in the three regions, and to strengthen the role of the Euroregions in Europe. The former goal was intended to rebalance Europe to the benefit of its southern regions.

This novel attempt to create a Euroregion comprising Catalonia, Languedoc-Roussillon, and Midi-Pyrénées failed for lack of political commitment and because of strong differences among the promoters. A crisis arose in 1998 when Jacques Blanc, the president of Languedoc-Roussillon, formed a government (his third) that included deputies from the far-right Front National, causing a split in the Euroregion. As a result of these political divergences, the activities of this first Euroregion slowed to a halt, not to be reawakened until the early 2000s.[45]

The second initiative, promoted in 1991 by local actors, was the C6 network, a cluster of cities that included Barcelona, Montpellier, Palma de Mallorca, Toulouse, Valencia, and Zaragoza. In the context of municipal diplomacy and the external actions of non-state actors, the C6 network reflected a different interpretation of the cross-border space between Spain and southern France. Led by the municipality of Barcelona – run at the time by Pasqual Maragall, a socialist – the C6 network focused on local governments and urban areas as promoters of joint governance mechanisms in the cross-border space. This network did not prosper; even so, the C6 is viewed today as EPM in its embryonic stage, since the same the six cities would later be part of the EPM project.

The competing views about how to interpret the cross-border field reflected what some scholars have described as a choice between a Europe of Regions and a Europe of Cities.[46] At this initial stage of the field, while regional governments (especially Catalonia) were committing themselves to exploring the potential for a cross-border entity in the western Mediterranean, cities oriented their strategies toward the formation of international networks that could improve their visibility and role at the international level.

Field Emergence: EPM in Practice (2004–2010)

It is difficult to identify a single episode that brought about the emergence of the field. That said, EPM was formally established by declaration in October 2004. The founding members were three Spanish ACs (Aragon, Catalonia, the Balearic Islands) and two French *départmentes* (Midi-Pyrénées and Languedoc-Roussillon). Though formally open to all administrations and all types of actors, including institutions, firms, and civil society groups, EPM was based on a political agreement among the five sub-national governments. The goal was to create a pole of development in the northwestern Mediterranean.[47] The founding declaration laid out four objectives: (a) to transform the Euroregion into a leading economic space based on research and technological innovation; (b) to create a dense infrastructure network for its population; (c) to become a space of cultural and human interchange; and (d) to promote sustainable development based on social and territorial inclusion.

The early 2000s opened a new window of opportunity for SNAs on both sides of the border. In France, a new decentralization reform was approved in 2003 that would further empower territorial authorities. In Spain, the socialist government of José Luis Rodríguez Zapatero opened the path to participation by Spanish ACs in some EU institutions by including AC representatives in the Spanish national delegation to the EC.[48] Nevertheless, boundaries were still contested in EPM, and some controversies persisted.

In 2003, when Pasqual Maragall, the former mayor of Barcelona and newly elected president of the Generalitat, was setting the basis for the institutionalization of the new Euroregional project, Valencia and the Principality of Andorra (a national state) were folded into the territory of EPM. Maragall maintained a pro-European attitude, and his objective was to draw Catalonia and the Mediterranean on the European political map. At first, Catalonia was supported in this by Aragon and the two French *départmentes*, all of which were governed by socialist or centre-left parties. The Balearic Islands and Valencia – governed at the time by the conservative Partido Popular – received the proposal with less enthusiasm. Being among the peripheral and maritime group of regions of Europe, the Balearic Islands finally agreed to join the initiative in terms of a functional commitment to EPM – that is, the Euroregion as an instrument for islands to mitigate the effects of their insularity. Valencia's regional government refused to take part in the project, for three reasons: (1) EPM did not fully respond to the economic and functional interests of Valencia; (2) EPM was perceived as being led by Catalonia, which would relegate Valencia to a subordinate role; and (3) influential regional actors in Valencia were considering their own alternatives to EPM. The best known of these was a cooperative project to be called the Mediterranean Arc, which in theory would unite Valencia, the Balearic Islands, and Catalonia to Murcia and Madrid.

Tensions rose when the debate over the field's boundaries reached the national level.[49] During a political meeting in the Balearic Islands, José María Aznar, the Spanish president, labelled the EPM project an attempt to modify – illegally – the territorial order established by the Spanish Constitution. Aznar's attitude toward any external actions by Spanish ACs was negative, and he interpreted Maragall's proposals as an attempt to reawaken the "Catalan Countries" by challenging Madrid's role as Spain's gatekeeper in the domain of international relations. Territorial reconfiguration did not result in EPM's abandonment even after the Euroregion was officially founded. In May 2006, Aragon suspended its participation after a political dispute with the Catalan government over some contested artworks.[50]

In terms of internal governance, EPM initially adopted an informal organizational structure based on thematic working groups composed of political representatives and technical experts from the various member regions. At this point, EPM enjoyed neither legal personality nor financial autonomy. The presidents of the member regions agreed on EPM's general political strategies, and an EPM secretariat located in Barcelona supported the presidency by handling administrative and executive tasks. A rotating presidency would ensure political momentum and guarantee that EPM would have external representation at the institutional and political levels.[51] A turning point came in 2009, when EPM adopted the EGTC instrument, a European legal tool and framework that endowed the Euroregion with a legal standing, thus allowing it – among other things – to buy and sell goods and hire staff. The European Grouping for Territorial Cooperation (EGTC), which covered all member-states, was designed to facilitate and promote cross-border, transnational, and interregional cooperation; this mainly meant helping to implement projects initiated by regional or local authorities and co-financed by the EU, with or without EC funding. Within the EPM, the EGTC began to operate in 2010 as an "instrumental arm" of the Euroregion, not as a legal substitute for EPM.

At first, weak administrative capacity, bureaucratic asymmetry, structural changes, and some internal shocks, such as the premature departure of one of the members in 2006, weakened the impact of EPM activities in the cross-border area. Empirical studies show that while perceptions varied among stakeholders, in general EPM was a relatively well-known subject in the cross-border territories in 2008.[52] Nevertheless, the role of the Euroregion was still confused. French actors, for example, identified networking as among EPM's most relevant objectives (90.7 per cent in Midi-Pyrénées, 80 per cent in Languedoc-Roussillon). On the Spanish side, networking was perceived as less relevant (50.5 per cent in Catalonia, 42 per cent in Aragon, 38.6 per cent in the Balearic Islands) and as subordinate to the more political goal of exercising influence at the EU level.

Field Consolidation and Policy Outcomes of the EPM (2010–2020)

In 2015, EPM celebrated its tenth anniverary with an event at the Committee of the Regions, in Brussels. Political representatives of the four governments reaffirmed their commitment to the Euroregion by adopting the official rhetoric of that time: "to stimulate innovation," "for employment, especially among young people," and "to get closer to the Euroregion citizens." By 2010, with the founding of the EGCT – which conferred on the Euroregion legal personhood and the capacity to act on its own behalf – the role and impact of the EPM in the cross-border area strengthened notably. This allowed EPM to lead or participate in various relevant projects partly financed by EU institutions and/or regional administrations. Between 2010 and 2013, the CREAMED project – with a budget of €1.5 million – set out to bring together business incubators[53] from the four regions to stimulate innovation and exchanges among SMEs, as well as to foster complementarity in approaches to business incubation and the development of firms in an international environment. More than 1,400 innovative businesses were assisted in the fields of biotech, health, renewable energy, agro-industry, tourism, ecommerce, electronics, and mechanics. As a positive spillover, economic development and innovation strategies in EPM are now closer to the EU 2020 strategy.

During this period, a second relevant role for EPM was to provide institutional and financial support to Euroregional actors (civic society and business) interested in cross-border projects in the areas of culture, environment, tourism, and climate change.[54] With regard to higher education, research, and innovation, for example, the EUROCAMPUS project brought together more than 510,000 students and 45,000 researchers belonging to the universities in the four territories. Its activities included the creation of an interactive and regularly updated Web portal dedicated to tertiary education, a reciprocal mobility program in the four regions (studies or company internships in the neighbouring territories), and the promotion of university double-degrees. EPM's commitment to this field seemed to be confirmed today thanks to another project, eHealth EUROCAMPUS, which trained health care professionals in information and communication technologies. This three-year project (September 2016 to August 2019) was fully funded by the EC with €430,000 under the Erasmus+ program.

In terms of governance, EPM grew both more complex and more fragmented, reflecting the presence of different political principals. Because the secretariat was based in Barcelona, Catalonia was assured some control over EPM's political and institutional functions. More technical and operational tasks were decentralized to Toulouse, the largest city in Midi-Pyrénées, where the EGCT headquarters was established.

As the EGCT expanded, it acquired more and more power over EPM's internal governance. As proposed by the French SNAs, the EGCT director strengthened his power and autonomy relative to the EPM secretary. Meanwhile, an EPM office was opened in Brussels. The EPM delegation in Brussels acted on behalf of the four member regions to ensure the visibility of the Euroregion and its EGTC in dealings with European institutions and actors involved in the EU's Cohesion Policy. As could be expected, fragmentation undermined cross-border policy coherence, and internal political controversies (or simply different understandings of issues) reduced EPM's impact.

The 2015 territorial reform in France merged two French *départmentes*, Midi-Pyrénées and Languedoc-Roussillon, thus forming a new region, called Occitanie. EPM was formally obliged to adjust its foundational statute so as to recognize the new status of the former two partners. This external shock repesented an opportunity to remodel the internal governance structure to address some duplication and heighten the organization's impact in the cross-border area. The EPM simplified its internal governance by placing its executive

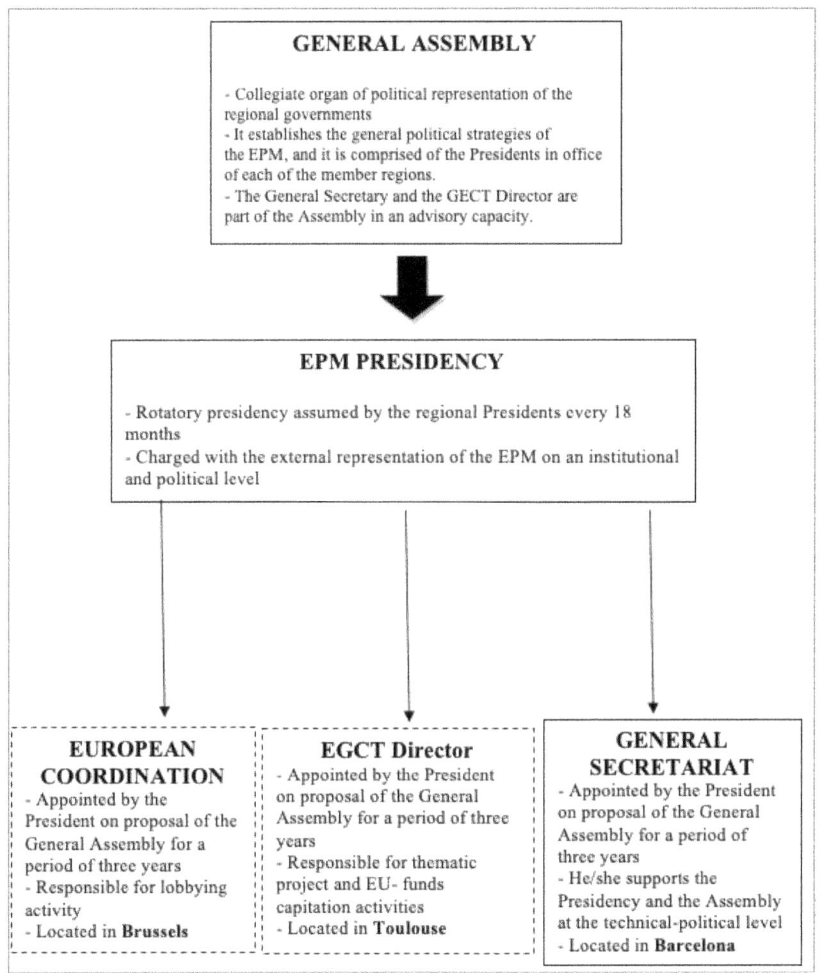

Figure 8.1. EPM governance structure, 2010–2016

Source: Author's elaboration.

functions in the hands of the EGCT director. However, the EGCT director was now accountable to the assembly, and political control over him was strengthened. His role was to oversee the EGCT's activities under the aegis of political guidelines crafted by the assembly and by delegation of the president. Finally, the EGCT headquarters and main structure, which from then on would coincide with the EPM organization, was moved to Perpignan, near Toulouse.

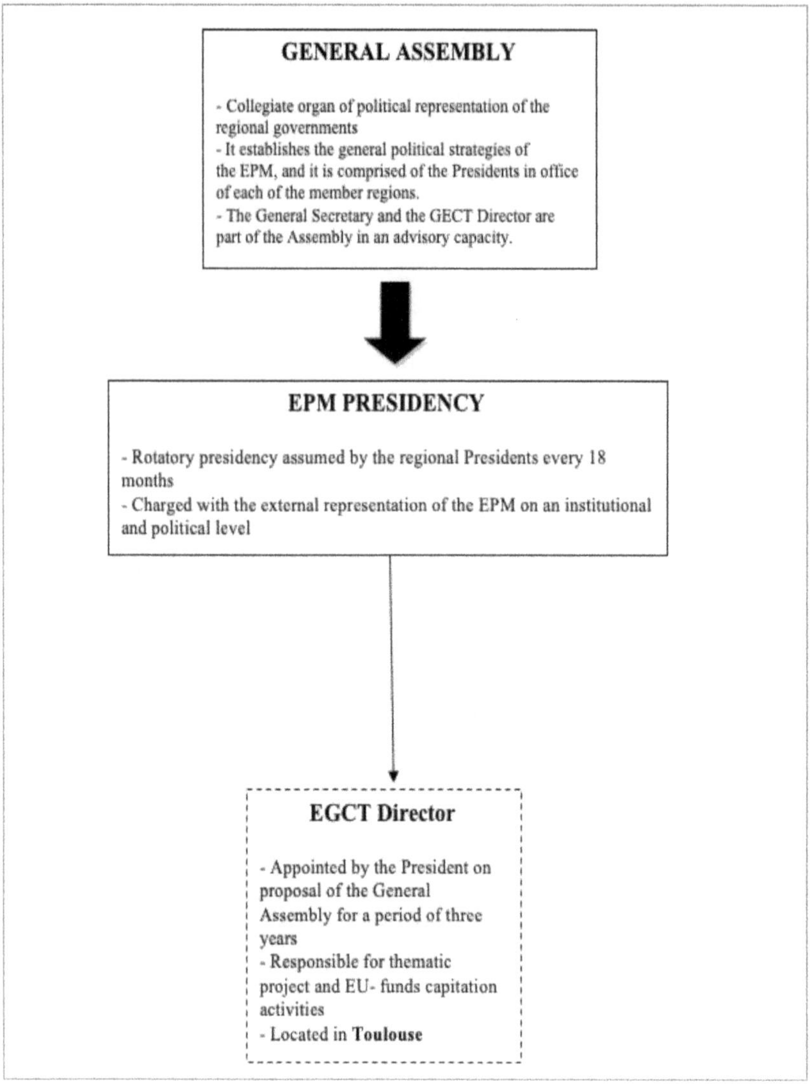

Figure 8.2. EPM governance structure since 2020

Source: Author's elaboration.

Field Interpretation and Final Remarks

In terms of field contextualization, the previous sections showed how cross-border cooperation in the southwestern Mediterranean and in the EU in general can be interpreted as a sub-field of a complex web of other fields, each one of which may present a specific configuration. Figure 8.3 illustrates this interdependence among fields. In the case of the EPM, the visualization synthesizes several relevant interconnected fields.

The analytical demarcation of a social, political, and institutional field is a delicate phase of a research design, and an indeterminate number of fields can exist – indeed, as many fields as the researchers can select and justify. This is probably one of the main limitations of the SAF approach. Still, dependence on multiple "principals" (incumbents) has been common to many Euroregions. In cross-border cooperation fields, the role of EU institutions was decisive in providing financial assistance and institutional legitimacy to more skilled SNAs that were interested in some form of cross-border cooperation. In the EPM field, the constitutional requirements and political cultures of the two sovereign states framed the range of autonomy assigned to SNAs across the domestic/international divide. Without the benevolent attitude of the Spanish and French central governments, which in the 1990s ratified the Convention of Madrid aimed at facilitating cross-border agreements between local and regional authorities, cross-border cooperation among SNAs would have remained informal and of lower intensity. In France and Spain, cross-border cooperation was driven by national and European authorities, and this enabled cross-border initiatives that focused on cooperation between territorial authorities. SNAs were the challengers, exploring the scenario in search of rewards and a more effective defence of their territorial interests. Interestingly, the SAF approach is consistent with findings from other academic literatures when they claim that more effective strategies for external and cross-border action at the sub-national level were framed in collaboration with (not against) gatekeepers' central governments.[55]

Regarding the challengers in the EPM field, the key actors were SNAs with some political commitment, which played a role in the novel scenario of cross-border cooperation and, in general, in the European and international arenas. In this fertile environment, SNAs attempted to elevate their strategies at the cross-border level, using the EPM organization as a platform for seeking either funding or visibility beyond national boundaries. As the emergence of the field showed, however, some influential actors in the border area expressed alternative understandings of the field's nature and goals. Catalonia was surely the government that conferred the highest political and identity value to the Euroregional project. This happened not because the Catalan government exercised strict control over EPM's autonomy but because in Catalonia all aspects of

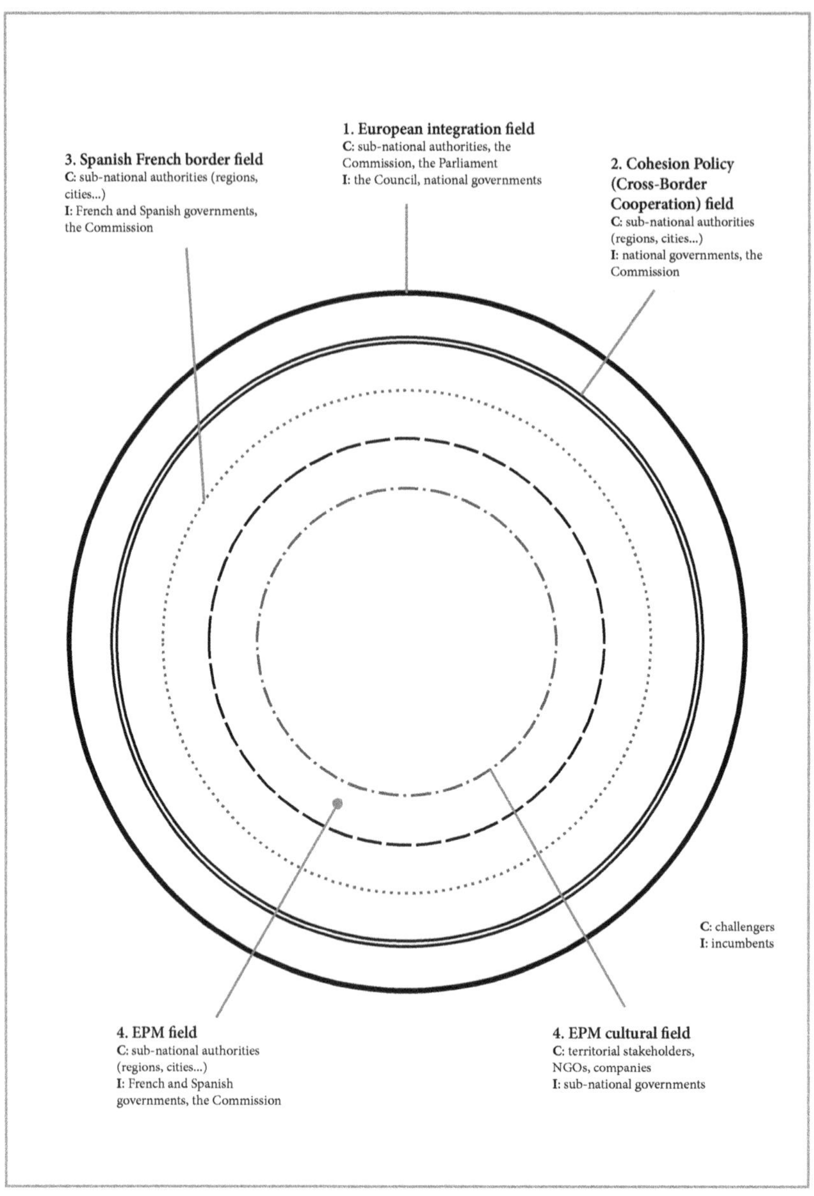

Figure 8.3. European integration and cross-border cooperation as fields of fields

Source: Author's elaboration.

external actions were immediately politicized. Thus, EPM was included from the beginning among the possible instruments for strengthening Catalonia's presence in the Mediterranean area. The Balearic Islands and Aragon as well as Valencia took a more functional approach to the Euroregion and were more focused on transportation networks, overcoming insularity, and increasing their expertise and institutional capacities at the EU level. In France, especially after the 2003 decentralization reforms, SNAs were incentivized to widen their actions at the European level. Usually weaker and less endowed than Spanish ACs, French regions and *départmentes* saw the possibility of joining more skilled regional governments as an advantage in the competition for EU assistance. For Languedoc-Roussillon, EPM served the strategic aim of converting the territory into a "bridge" between the south and the Continental Europe.

Examining the field over time (from emergence to stabilization), the SAF approach suggests that politics may have an impact, but not a linear one. Partisan alignment is a relevant dimension but not always determining. Table 8.1 presents the mandates of the presidents of the SNAs involved in EPM and their political affiliations between 1990 and 2020.

As regional presidents own the EPM presidency on a rotating basis, they exercise a dominant role in the organization, and members' political alignments are usually a key variable that can help propel (or arrest) EPM activities. The longitudinal analysis indicates that French SNAs have greater political stability, in contrast to Spanish ACs, which must contend with more frequent changes in political majorities. Also, if it is true that EPM's genesis was facilitated by the dominance of centre-left parties in the cross-border areas, the partisan logic explains neither the participation of the Balearic Islands (which in 2003 were governed by the conservative Partido Popular) nor the political changes that occurred in Catalonia. Probably, the consensual nature of the field – key decisions were taken in the General Assembly by vote – mitigated the negative effects of partisan misalignment as well as of changes in incumbent majorities.

Finally, starting in 2012, the field was racked by the "Catalan question," the political controversy that openly threatened the constitutional indivisibility of the Spanish parliamentary monarchy, thereby raising the possibility that Catalonia would secede from Spain and become an independent state. Catalan independence is a complicated issue, whose analysis exceeds the aims of this chapter. Its impact on the cross-border area is still ambiguous, but it is probably one of the most puzzling aspects of the field scenario. First, because of its relevance and pervasiveness, the independence process monopolized the debate in Catalonia and steered nearly all governmental resources, especially those related to the external actions and foreign relations of the regional government, toward the internationalization of the "Catalan question." We therefore expected the Catalan government to engage in some political exploitation of EPM's centrality in the cross-border areas. Surprisingly, and except for

Table 8.2. President of SNAs 1999–2020

Aragon			Balearic islands			Catalonia			Languedoc- Rossellon			Mide-Pirenees		
Marcelino Iglesias	1999–2003	PSOE	Francesc Antich	1999–2003	PSOE	Jordi Pujol	1980–2003	CiU	Jacques Blanc	1986–2004	UDF, UMP	Martin Malvy	1998–2015	
	2003–2007	PSOE	Jaume Matas	2003–2007	PP	Pasqual Maragall	2003–2006	PSC	Georges Frêche	2004–2010	PS, puis divers gauche			
	2007–2011	PSOE	Francesc Antich	2007–2011	PSOE	José Montilla	2006–2010	PSC						
Luisa Fernanda Rudi	2011–2015	PP	José Ramón Bauzá	2011–2015	PP	Artur Mas	2010–2016	CiU	Christian Bourquin	2010–2014	PS, puis divers gauche			
Javier Lambán	2015–	PSOE	Francina Armengol	2015–	PSOE	Carles Puigdemont	2016–2017	CDC	Damien Alary	2014–2015	PS			
						Quim Torra	2018–	JxS	**Occitanie** (since 2016)					
									Carole Delga	2016–	PS			

Source: Author's elaboration.

some minor episodes, partisan politics did not strongly impact EPM activities, and Catalan politicians largely insulated the cross-border area from the most controversial aspects of the independence process. It is still worth clarifying whether this was part of a strategic position adopted by the Catalan authorities or a pragmatic choice not to insert the policy issue into a territory dominated by a centralist state like France, which is profoundly sceptical of any kind of territorial claims.

A second critical episode occurred at the end of 2017. After the celebration of an illegal referendum and after secessionist Catalan MPs (rhetorically) voted to establish an independent republic, in October 2018 Spain's prime minister, Mariano Rajoy, with the support of the Spanish Parliament, took control of Catalonia's principal institutions by dissolving the regional parliament and announcing elections. By invoking Article 155 of the Spanish Constitution and flexing the state's legal and physical monopoly of power in an unprecedented way, the central state *de facto* suspended Catalan autonomy; among the first measures it took after that, it ordered the Catalan government's international "embassies" to shut down. Moreover, and against some of the expectations expressed by Catalan secessionist leaders, the EU, the UK, Germany, and the US all said they would not recognize Catalan independence and declared their support for Madrid to preserve Spanish unity.

Despite all this, EPM, whose political control was under the direct control of the Catalan "ministry of foreign affairs," only weakly intervened. In 2017, for example, EPM maintained its commitment to the European project SPIN (SPort for Inclusion), a project to promote the social inclusion of immigrant populations through grassroots sports and sport for all in Catalonia, the Balearic Islands, Languedoc-Roussillon, Midi-Pyrénées, and Piemonte. Then in June 2018, the EPM General Assembly was held at the headquarters of the new Catalan government. Finally, in 2019, EPM was among the founders of a challenging Euro-Mediterranean initiative – the Mediterranean Cooperation Alliance, a new "network of networks" that brought together the Inter-Mediterranean Commission of the Conference of Peripherical and Maritime Regions (regions), Arco Latino (supralocal level), MedCities (municipalities), and the Euroregion Adriatic (an Euroregion). The main goal of this multi-level political platform is to increase the effectiveness of public policies in the wide area of the Mediterranean within the framework of the European Green Deal and the Sustainable Development Goals. With the explosion of the COVID-19 pandemic in 2020, this alliance as a network of networks is an example of solidarity in a time of health crisis.

To conclude, neither changes in the political colours of regional governments nor dramatic external shocks, such as intervention by the Spanish central government in Catalan political institutions, seem to have arrested the development of EPM activities. Against more traditional institutional explanations, this finding is interesting, for it can improve the analysis about how much and in what direction politics impact cross-border organizations. In the case of EPM, functional logics and a shared understanding of the main goals of the cross-border organization – basically it is a vehicle for collective claims at the EU level either for funding or for visibility – allowed EPM to survive and to overcome internal and external threatens that, in other territories, would have led to the failure of many cross-border projects.

NOTES

1 Neil Fligstein and Doug McAdam, *A Theory of Fields* (New York: Oxford University Press, 2012), http://doi.org/10.1007/s11186-014-9237-0.

2 From the Founding Declaration of the Euroregion Pyrénées–Mediterranean (EPM), *L'Eurorégion, un futur partagé*, 29 October 2004, https://www.euroregio.eu/en/euroregion/documentation and https://www.euroregio.eu/wp-content/uploads/041029_declaration_constitutive_epm_fr.pdf.

3 M. Perkmann, "Cross-Border Regions in Europe: Significance and Drivers of Regional Cross-Border Co-operation," *European Urban and Regional Studies* 10, no. 2 (2003): 153–71, http://doi.org/10.1177/0969776403010002004; L. De Sousa, "Understanding European Cross-Border Cooperation: A Framework for Analysis," *Journal of European Integration* 35, no. 6 (2013): 669–87, http://doi.org/10.1080/07036337.2012.711827; E. Nadalutti, "Does the 'European Grouping of Territorial Co-operation' Promote Multi-level Governance within the European Union?," *Journal of Common Market Studies* 51, no. 4 (2013): 756–71, http://doi.org/10.1111/jcms.12014; Association of European Border Regions (AEBR), *Practical Guide to Cross-Border Cooperation*, 3rd ed. (2000), https://www.aebr.eu/files/publications/lace_guide.en.pdf; European Commission, *European Territorial Cooperation: Building Bridges between People* (Brussels: EU Publications Office, 2011), http://doi.org/10.2776/40850; Bruno Dupeyron, *L'Europe au défi de ses régions transfrontalières: expériences rhénane et pyrénéenne*, vol. 556 (Frankfurt am Main: Peter Lang, 2008).

4 X. Oliveras González, A. Durà Guimerà, and M. Perkmann, "Las regiones transfronterizas: Balance de la regionalización de la cooperación transfronteriza en Europa (1958–2007)," *Documents d'Analisi Geografica* 56, no. 56 (2010): 21–40, http://doi.org/10.1080/03066150.2013.876996.

5 E. Medeiros, "Euro–Meso–Macro: The New Regions in Iberian and European Space," *Regional Studies* 47, no. 8 (2013): 1249–66, http://doi.org/10.1080/00343404.2011.602336.

6 A. Durà, F. Camonita, M. Berzi, and A. Noferini, *Euroregions: Excellence and Innovation across EU Borders: A Catalog of Good Practices* (Barcelona: Department of Geography, UAB, 2018), https://ddd.uab.cat/record/189399.

7 L. Hooghe and G. Marks, *Multi-Level Governance and European Integration* (Lanham: Rowman and Littlefield, 2001); Hooghe and Marks, "Gobernanza estatocéntrica y gobernanza multinivel," in *Gobernanza Multinivel en la Unión Europea*, ed. F. Morata (Valencia: Tirant lo Blanch, 2004); C. Jeffery, "Sub-National Mobilization and European Integration: Does It Make Any Difference?," *JCMS: Journal of Common Market Studies* 38, no. 1 (2000): 1–23; R. Leonardi, *Cohesion Policy in the European Union: The Building of Europe* (London: Palgrave Macmillan, 2005).

8 Ivo Duchacek, "Perforated Sovereignties: Towards a Typology of New Actors in International Relations," in *Federalism and International Relations: The Role of Subnational Units*, ed. Hans J. Michelmann and Panoyatis Soldatos (Oxford: Clarendon Press, 1990); F. Aldecoa and M. Keating, *Paradiplomacy in Action: The Foreign Relations of Subnational Governments* (London and New York: Routledge, 1999).

9 M. Keating, *State and Regional Nationalism: Territorial Politics and the European State* (Hemel Hempstead: Harvester Wheatsheaf, 1988); M. Keating, *The New Regionalism in Western Europe. Territorial Restructuring and Political Change* (Cheltenham: Edward Elgar, 1998).

10 Aragon left the EPM in 2006.

11 "Territorial Cooperation in Spain and the EU: Comparing Institutional Capacities for the Governance of Cross-Border Areas" (COOP-RECOT I); "Territorial Cooperation in Spain and the EU: A Selection of Guiding Experiences for Excellence and Innovation in the 2014–2020 Period" (COOP-RECOT II).

12 With the aim of strengthening the Union's economic, social, and territorial cohesion, Article 174 of the Treaty on the Functioning of the European Union formally recognizes the challenges faced by border regions and stipulates that the Union should pay particular attention to these regions.

13 European Commission, Overcoming Cross-Border Obstacles to Boost Growth in EU Border Regions" (2017), http://europa.eu/rapid/press-release_MEMO-17-3271_en.htm.

14 In a classical Russian-doll structure, EU member-state fields are at the same time a collection of regional fields.

15 P. Bourdieu and L.J. Wacquant, *An Invitation to Reflexive Sociology* (Chicago: University of Chicago press, 1992); Fligstein and McAdam, *A Theory of Fields*, 2012.

16 A. Moravcsik, "Preferences and Power in the European Community: A Liberal Intergovernmentalist Approach," *JCMS: Journal of Common Market Studies* 31, no. 4 (1993): 473–524; Moravcsik, "Liberal Intergovernmentalism and Integration: A Rejoinder," *JCMS: Journal of Common Market Studies* 33, no. 4 (1995): 611–28.

17 P.C. Schmitter, "Ernst B. Haas and the Legacy of Neofunctionalism," *Journal of European Public Policy* 12, no. 2 (2005): 255–72.

18 Walter W. Powell and Paul J. Di Maggio, eds., *The New Institutionalism in Organizational Analysis* (Chicago: University of Chicago Press, 1991), 1–38; M.A. Pollack, "Delegation, Agency, and Agenda Setting in the European Community," *International Organization* 51, no. 1 (1997): 99–134; G. Majone, "The European Commission as Regulator," in *Regulating Europe* (New York and London: Routledge, 2002), 77–96.

19 The first experiences were Euregio (1958), Regio Basiliensis (1963), and SaarLorLux (1968).

20 B. Wassenberg, R. Bernard, and J. Peyrony, *Territorial Cooperation in Europe – A Historical Perspective* (Brussels: EC, 2015), http://doi.org/10.2776/374386.

21 For a historical review of cross-border cooperation in Europe, see Durá, Oliveras, and Perkmann, "Las regiones transfronterizas: Balance de la regionalización de la cooperación transfronteriza en Europa (1958–2007)," 2010; and Wassenberg, Bernard, and Peyrony, *Territorial Cooperation in Europe*.

22 K. Featherstone and C.M. Radaelli, eds., *The Politics of Europeanization* (Oxford: Oxford University Press, 2003).

23 Proponents of MLG have contend that European policy-making can be characterized by the presence of a "multiplicity of politically independent but otherwise interdependent actors at different levels of territorial aggregation engaging in more-or-less continuous negotiation/deliberation/implementation in a context which does not assign exclusive policy competence or assert a stable hierarchy of political authority to any of these levels." Philippe C. Schmitter, "Neo-Neofunctionalism," in *European Integration Theory*, ed. Antje Wiener and Thomas Diez (Oxford: Oxford University Press, 2003).

24 Angela K. Bourne, "The Impact of European Integration on Regional Power," *Journal of Common Market Studies* 41, no. 4 (September 2003), https://doi.org/10.1111/1468-5965.00437; Jeffery, "Sub-National Mobilization."

25 E. Brunet-Jailly, "Theorizing Borders: An Interdisciplinary Perspective," *Geopolitics* 10, no. 4 (2005): 633–49; O.T. Kramsch and B. Hooper, eds., *Cross-Border Governance in the European Union* (London and New York: Routledge, 2004), https://books.google.es/books/about/Cross_Border_Governance_in_the_European.html?id=-3MQzSXosZYC&redir_esc=y.

26 Simona Piattoni, *The Theory of Multi-level Governance: Conceptual, Empirical, and Normative Challenges* (Oxford: Oxford University Press, 2010).

27 Mission Opérationnelle Transfrontalière (MOT), Working Group on Innovative Solutions to Cross Border Obstacles, Background Report (2017), http://www.espaces-transfrontaliers.org/fileadmin/user_upload/REPORT_20170628_WG_on_Innovative_Solutions_to_Cross-Border_Obstacles.pdf; MOT, Working Group on Innovative Solutions to Cross-Border Obstacles, Main Report (2017), http://www.espaces-transfrontaliers.org/fileadmin/user_upload/REPORT_20170628_WG_on_Innovative_Solutions_to_Cross-Border_Obstacles.pdf.

28 The INTERREG initiative has run through several different phases: INTERREG I (1989–93, programming period), INTERREG II (1994–99), INTERREG III (2000–6), INTERREG IV (2007–13), and INTERREG V (2014–20). At the same time, each INTERREG comprises three strands of action and funding: INTERREG A (cross-border cooperation), INTERREG B (transnational cooperation), and INTERREG C (interregional cooperation).

29 See Matteo Berzi's chapter in this volume.

30 Francesc Morata and Andrea Noferini, *Gobernanza y capacidades institucionales en la Frontera Pirenaica*, XI Congreso Español de Ciencia Política y de la Administración, Panel "Procesos políticos en la Unión Europea en tiempos de crisis: respuestas de distintos actores en una gobernanza multinivel" (2014); C. Colomb, F. Morata Tierra, A. Durà Guimerà, and X. Oliveras González, "The Multi-Level Geographies of Trans-Boundary Cooperation, Territorial Development, and Europeanisation in South-West Europe. The Case of Catalonia," in *Territorial Policy and Governance: Alternative Paths*, ed. I. Deas and S. Hincks (London: Routledge, 2017), 92–123.

31 Francesc Morata, "La costruzione istituzionale delle Euroregioni," *Le Istituzioni del Federalismo* 7 (2007): 7–39. https://www.regione.emilia-romagna.it/affari_ist/supplemento_4_07/Morata.pdf; Fabiola Mota and Andrea Noferini, "Evidence from Structural Funds Implementation in Two Spanish Regions," in Simona Milio, *From Policy to Implementation in the European Union: The Challenge of a Multi-Level Governance System*, Library of European Studies no. 13 (London: I.B. Tauris, 2010); Francesc Morata and Andrea Noferini, "The Pyrenees–Mediterranean Euroregion Functional Networks: Actor Perceptions and Expectations," in *Europe's Changing Geography: The Impact of Inter-regional Networks* (New York: Routledge, 2013).

32 The Crown of Aragon comprised, at its zenith, territories today located in eastern Spain, the Balearic Islands, part of southern France, Corsica, Sardinia, Sicily, southern Italy, and part of Greece.

33 Today, this historical legacy is recognized in the geographical space of the "Catalan Countries" (*els paisos Catalans*), the linguistic cultural area where Catalan is still spoken in France, Andorra, and Spain.

34 <full cite please> Bel 2010; Dennis Rumley and Julian V. Minghi, *The Geography of Border Landscapes* (London: Routledge, 1991), https://doi.org/10.4324/9781315746593.

35 Xavier Oliveras González, "La cooperación transfronteriza en la Cerdanya (frontera España-Francia)," *Boletín de la Asociación de Geógrafos Españoles* 62 (2013).

36 Alfons Bayraguet, *L'estructura econòmica de l'Euroregió Pirineus Mediterrània* (Barcelona: Consell de Treball, Econòmic i Social de Catalunya, 2005).

37 At the intermediate level, the suppression of the departments, mentioned at some point in the reform process, has been abandoned, and discussions are reported to 2020. Thus, French departments are still responsible for social solidarity and

territorial cohesion, including services such as social welfare for families, the elderly, the disabled, secondary schools, and support to rural municipalities.

38 The Regional Authority Index (RAI) measured the authority of regional governments in eighty-one democracies or quasi-democracies on an annual basis between 1950–2010. The dataset encompasses subnational governments with an average population of 150,000 or more. Regional authority is measured along ten dimensions: institutional depth, policy scope, fiscal autonomy, borrowing autonomy, representation, lawmaking, executive control, fiscal control, borrowing control, and constitutional reform. Primary sources (constitutions, legislation, statutes) are triangulated with secondary literature and consultation with country experts to achieve reliable and valid estimates.

39 Liesbet Hooghe, Gary Marks, and Arjan H. Schakel, "Measuring Regional Authority," *Regional and Federal Studies* 18, nos. 2–3 (June 2008): 111–21.

40 X.O. González, "La cooperación transfronteriza en la Cerdanya (frontera España-Francia," *Boletín de la Asociación de Geógrafos Españoles* 62 (2013): 25–48.

41 *Départements* are one of three levels of government below the national level ("territorial collectivities"), between the regions and the *communes*. There are ninety-six departments in metropolitan France and five overseas departments. According to the EU statistical classification, French departments, as well as Spanish *diputaciones* (provinces), are included in the NUTS III category.

42 *Conseils régionaux* (regional councils) were created in 1972. Originally, they were simply consultative bodies consisting of the region's parliamentary representatives plus an equal number of members nominated by the departments and municipalities. The decentralization program of 1982–83 provided for direct elections, which began in 1986 and increased the powers of the councils.

43 In 1993, this community became an association; then in 2005 it was transformed into a *consorcio*, a legal entity under Spanish public law. This status notably allowed it to become the managing authority of the Franco-Spanish cross-border cooperation program POCTEFA for the 2007–13 and 2014–20 periods.

44 Francesc Morata, "The Euro-Region and the C-6 Network: The New Politics of Sub-National Cooperation in the West-Mediterranean Area," *Political Economy of Regionalism* (1997): 292–305.

45 M. Duran, *Mediterranean Paradiplomacies: The Dynamics of Diplomatic Reterritorialization* (Hotei, 2015).

46 P.J. Taylor, "So-Called 'World Cities': The Evidential Structure within a Literature," *Environment and Planning* 31, no. 11 (1999): 1901–4.

47 Morata and Noferini, "The Pyrenees–Mediterranean Euroregion Functional Networks actor perceptions and expectations," 2013.

48 Andrea Noferini, "The participation of subnational governments in the council of the EU: Some evidence from Spain," *Regional & Federal Studies* 22., no. 4 (2012): 361–385.

49 The partisan alignment between the central government and the Valencia government was -according to some interpretations- one additional reason for the refusal expressed by the conservative Valencian government in joining the EPM.
50 See Thomas Perrin's chapter in this volume.
51 The Meeting of Presidents which took place in Toulouse on February 10, 2006, ratified the principle of the 18 months rotating presidency of the EPM.
52 Noferini and Morata, "The Pyrenees–Mediterranean Euroregion Functional Networks."
53 Led by the EPM, the project nées-Méditerranée in collaboration with the Réseau de Pépinières d'Entreprises de Midi-Pyrénées (REZOPEP or the Network of Midi-Pyrénées company incubators), the Réseau des Pépinières d'Entreprises de Languedoc-Roussillon (SYNERSUD or the network of Languedoc Roussillon business incubators), the Département d'Entreprises et Travail de la Generalitat de Catalunya (the Department of companies and work of the Generalitat of Catalonia) ,and the Parc d'Innovation Technologique des Baléares (PARCBIT or the Technology innovation cluster of the Balearic Islands).
54 See Thomas Perrin's chapter in this volume.
55 M. Tatham, "Networkers, Fund Hunters, Intermediaries, or Policy Players? The Activities of Regions in Brussels," *West European Politics* 40, no. 5 (2017): 1088–108, http://doi.org/10.1080/01402382.2017.1303246; Tatham, "'With or Without You'? Revisiting Territorial State-Bypassing in EU Interest Representation," *Journal of European Public Policy* 17, no. 1 (2010): 76–99.

9 Cross-Border Islands Governance: A Field Analysis of the Italy–Malta INTERREG Program

FRANCESCO CAMONITA

This chapter employs a strategic action field (SAF) framework to analyse governance in the case study of the Sicily–Malta border region within the European framework of territorial cooperation. The cross-border region made up of two islands in the geographical centre of the Mediterranean Sea is younger than other border regions on the continent (it has only been active since 2004). Furthermore, it does not have a European political cross-border governance platform such as a Euroregion. Instead, it relies on the institutional apparatus provided by the INTERREG cross-border program agreed to by the Italian and Maltese state-level governments (Operational Program [OP] INTERREG Italy–Malta). Even so, there are grounds to test and expand Fligstein and McAdam's SAF theory regarding the basic institutional structure that has been built between the micro-island state and the much larger island-region. To do this, we will be utilizing the extensive fieldwork undertaken by the author in the border region in 2017 and 2018.[1]

The identification of powerful incumbents (i.e., the governments of the two islands, which avail themselves of the governance units of the INTERREG program) and the presence of very weak and isolated challengers (i.e., the Sicilian regional deputy, who failed in his attempt to establish a new Euroregional structure) provide a rationale for what is a "crystallized" SAF. The clear lack of shocks powerful enough to disrupt the existing INTERREG SAF can and should be interpreted as a call for challengers to organize themselves, if they are to bring any substantial changes to the field.[2] Thus, in terms of structure, this chapter begins by discussing the implications for European cross-border cooperation (CBC) and political governance platforms such as the Euroregions. It then explores the history and features of the Italo-Maltese field and maps out, as completely as possible, the actors involved in the process. In these sections, the aim is to identify the relevant incumbents, challengers, and governance units in terms of SAF theory. Also, the operationalization of new SAF functional terminology (functionality vs effectiveness; field participants) is introduced, providing new insights into the already existing framework. This leads to an analysis of the theoretical features of SAF and of the actions required of challengers to bring change to this particular field. Regarding methodology, this study relies on a qualitative analysis of twenty-four interviews conducted on both islands, which used semi-structured questionnaires. The rest of the data are provided by institutional documents and the small handful of academic studies published about the topic.

The European Background on Cross-Border Cooperation

European territorial cooperation (ETC) policies are among the most advanced forms of subnational cooperation in the international arena. Cross-border, trans-national, and inter-regional initiatives are funded by the European Union's (EU) INTERREG program, albeit through a rather modest (at least in macro-economic terms) seven-year budget. Furthermore, thanks to the sixty CBC programs approved for the 2014–20 EU funding period, almost all internal borders of the EU have been covered in some way by the INTERREG V-A strand of ETC. In their entirety, these programs serve as a stimulus for the realization of cross-border projects or the activation of pioneering trans-frontier services for the 135 million EU citizens living along member-states' borders.[3]

Today, innovation brought about by ETC policies is not limited to the presence of financially stable European programs. These initiatives can nurture new governance structures that defy the separation logic of borders in favour of joint management of allotted resources. Thus, the functional logic of all this lies in multi-level governance, demonstrating that the EU encourages subnational authorities and willing non-governmental actors (including NGOs) to participate in governance processes across sectors and administrative levels.[4] When the theoretical concept is translated into cross-border policy, the first multi-level commitment of the participating territorial actors is found in INTERREG-based institutions and aims at funding CBC projects. On a more advanced level (and more so in the presence of a vast borderline with many cross-border networks), different groups of territorial actors may decide to sign individual agreements in order to establish common representation platforms across the border. One of the most commonly employed forms of European cross-border association is the Euroregions. In general terms, these are cross-border governance organizations established voluntarily to better qualify for European funding and for the further alignment of policies across the territories.[5] In a pilot research project, some European members of the BORDERGOV network underwent a comprehensive cataloguing and classification of Euroregional experiences throughout the EU territory (COOP-RECOT II).[6] The results were encouraging: there were 158 active Euroregional structures on European borders. The same project found an abundance of cross-border "equipment" (such as a binational hospital in the Pyrenees and a trinational airport between France, Switzerland, and Germany), as well as some interesting examples of cross-border nature parks jointly managed across borders.[7] Notwithstanding, to suggest that Europe has achieved "heaven status" for CBC would be a gross misconception. First, European CBC still suffers from enduring legal, administrative, and technical obstacles. Second, with CBC experiences localized across the European map, geographical localization foretells the continued presence of an already well-known and unfortunate trend in economics, that being, a tangible North–South divide in terms of outcomes and performances. However, RECOT research did identify some excellent Euroregional CBC practices in Central and Western Europe, as well as a solid presence of such practices in Northern Europe.[8]

We should avoid "Mediterranean Syndrome" bias, which blames the lack of policy efficiency in that region "on specific endemic characteristics of the socio-political institutions hindering implementation and enforcement."[9] Still, it must be acknowledged that Europe's cross-border regions and their institutional settings have not reached a deeper stage of involvement, and that the corresponding authorities have not felt (perhaps yet) the need to explore new paths of political collaboration. Take the example of Italy, which has been involved in eight cross-border INTERREG programs[10] but does not present an equal number of Euroregional structures. It is in this context that the Sicily–Malta region is found. Thus, the purpose of this study is to unveil the dynamics of areas that are still locked into what we might call *proto-Euroregional* structures. To that end, we will employ theoretical lenses such as the multi-level governance toolkit and the SAF framework.[11] This terminology is deployed insofar as we are dealing with the existence of an INTERREG management structure that is dedicated in the main to administering European funding. Naturally, its functions still include political choices in selecting an operational strategy and assigning budgets for the execution of cross-border projects. However, this research stresses that there is an overall lack of political vision and identity-building for the cross-border region at hand, which is rarely even mentioned as such by actors in the field. We begin our analysis of the INTERREG Italy–Malta SAF by analysing its chronological stages.

Field Formation and Emergence: Origins of the INTERREG Italy–Malta Program

Historical Antecedents of the Field: Italy–Malta Relations

Before analysing the events surrounding the launch of the Italy–Malta INTERREG program, it would be useful to summarize the past ties between the two countries over the centuries.[12] Sheer geopolitical size has certainly had an impact on those ties, so much so that Italian politics and culture (well before there was an Italian state) have profoundly affected developments in Malta. It would hardly be an overstatement to assert that up until the sixteenth century, most historical events were felt by Malta and southern Italy in common. The Roman, Arab, Franco-Norman, and even the Catalan–Spanish hegemons all dealt with the two islands as if they were one. Their destinies did not begin to diverge until 1530, when Charles V of Spain gave the Maltese islands as a gift to the Knights of St John. True, this transfer of power did not end commercial and cultural relations between the two; but true, as well, that change in leadership did steer Malta's future down a path distinct from that of its neighbour. In the late eighteenth century, after three long centuries of relatively great prosperity provided by the wealthy Knights, Napoleon, on his way to Egypt, cast them out and absorbed Malta in the new French empire. French dominion, however, was not destined to last. The local population was outraged by the French forces' disrespect of Christian traditions; this led the British to intervene and take the archipelago under the protection of their empire. Until well into the twentieth century, Malta would be a British colony.[13] It developed economically and politically under the British, who brought democratic developments such as a constitution (frequently revised), a legislature, and a party system of government.[14] An examination of Maltese politics makes it clear that Italy's cultural presence had a strong impact on the island, including its politics, which were deeply polarized. The right-wing Nationalist Party and its intellectual class had deep roots in Roman Catholic values (which included a church-controlled education system modelled after Italy's – the Maltese identified themselves as Latins). However, closer political relations between Malta and the Italian state were interrupted by enmity between Fascist Italy and British Malta during the Second World War.

Soon after the war, Britain's colonial empire began to disintegrate. Meanwhile, the Maltese quickly restored their friendship with the Italians, reflecting the political, commercial, and even touristic facts on the ground.[15] Malta achieved formal political independence from the UK in 1964, became a republic in 1974, and separated itself militarily from Great Britain in 1979. By that point, Malta realized that it would need to depend on other countries for its defence;[16] meanwhile, Italy was entering a new phase of political maturity, which included a stronger foreign policy that looked beyond the European Community (EC).[17] In the 1980s, acting independently of the EC, the Italian government sealed a special agreement with Malta. Under that agreement, Malta declared its neutrality, and in return, Italy provided financial assistance to help its neighbour modernize.[18] Over the next twenty years, Italy and Malta signed four cooperation protocols, under which Italy provided its much smaller neighbour with US$618 million[19] for development projects, which helped transform the small nation into a modern state.[20]

But the bilateral alliance between Italy and Malta did not last. By the end of the Cold War, the island-state was reviewing its relationship with the EC. Until this point, contacts between the two had revolved largely around generic trade agreements and Malta's tendency to embrace Britain's scepticism toward Europe. Noting that the soon-to-be European Union (EU) intended to unify Europe, the Maltese began to debate their country's future. On one side were left-wing Eurosceptics who wanted Malta to remain neutral; on the other were right-wing nationalists who were open to joining the European political family both in economic terms and in terms of cultural identity.[21] The national debate was extremely intense, but in the end, both political parties accepted that joining the EU was Malta's only viable option, and it applied for membership in July 1990. Once all the necessary structural preparations were completed, the Maltese government held a referendum on 8 March 2003, seeking popular ratification to join the EU. The result: 91 per cent of voters cast a ballot, and 53.6 per cent of them were in favour. On 1 May 2004, Malta became an EU member, along with Cyprus and a number of Eastern European countries. It was now possible for Malta to access substantial amounts of European regional funding under the provisions of Cohesion Policy.

The Origins of the INTERREG Italy–Malta Field and Its Consolidation: The 2004–2006 "Experimental Phase"

The events just described were instrumental in shaping Malta's relations with Sicily. We emphasize here the coincidence that Malta joined the EU just as Europe was initiating its CBC program. A fundamental feature of this case study is that in this cross-border region, there was a lack of political vision that might have reinforced such a project between the two islands. In fact, a direct comparison with the political history of the case at hand and cross-border governance platforms elsewhere in Europe cannot be done. Rather, the present case must be understood in the context of a brand-new EU member-state exploring all avenues to acquiring European funding.[22] Although not explicit, the notion of tapping into INTERREG funds, in the context of Siciy's proximity, can be deduced from the words of two Maltese officials we interviewed:

> A: It all started with Sicily … it might have been that Malta doesn't have any actual borders. The only nearest European sort of a part of a member state is Sicily so it might have been this reason as well, and all those agreements that we had before were mainly with Italy from the Italian protocol fund and it was much before the accession.
>
> B: And there's also the definition that we took from the European commission and the 150-km border rule. So, automatically, this was between our region and this one … Of course if there were other islands in the 150-km area, it could be that

> we could have other cross-border programmes, so this is the reason why we have this only cross-border one.[23]

Unfortunately, it proved impossible to find the original personnel involved in the program negotiations. Whether at the Sicilian, Maltese, or European level, either they had all either been replaced or they were not in charge of the political negotiations at the time. However, we were able to gather enough information from current officials to identify key actors in the process. From their accounts, it seems that by 2003, after the Maltese referendum, Maltese governmental actors expressed an immediate interest in further EU funding. The timing was certainly not ideal, for the seven-year EU budget for the period was enclosed within a 2000–6 window. However, the EC was holding around €7.5 million that had not been allocated during the previous distribution of the INTERREG IIIA program. The chance to be almost automatically entitled to a first tranche of European funds was an opportunity not to be wasted by either Malta or its new "dance partner," Sicily. Political decisions about how the program would be managed were made swiftly in the context of Malta's newcomer status. Managing authority was entrusted to the Sicilian regional government as the most experienced partner of the two in the field of European planning. The Italian national government would be present as second-level control and approver of all final decisions. Even so, this allowed for a great deal of regional flexibility in the negotiations. Joint planning was a new experience for both partners, and there seems to have been uncertainties early on regarding the degree of cooperation between the island state and the island region. This led to some confusion, for Malta, which was a state in its own right, was cooperating with Sicily, which was not and so did not hold a state's authority. Furthermore, it seems that the two quickly became exhausted as they struggled to find sufficient common ground to produce a cross-border program. This meant somehow avoiding overlap with the European Regional Development Fund (ERDF). All of this is partly explained by hardships all partners faced (whether at the European, national, or regional level) when developing European cross-border maritime strategies. This was even more so in the case of two islands separated by a maritime border – here, by the Malta Channel, which is around 92 kilometres wide.

Be that as it may, the INTERREG IIIA program was launched in 2004, and set out to complete thirteen pilot cross-border projects.[24] Most likely because of the time pressure exerted by operational limits, all of these activities focused on cultural exchanges, good practices, and more generically on the initial construction of actors' networks across the border. In the words of the EC representatives:

> Especially in this first moment [of the CBC], Malta was able to strengthen its capacity building in terms of cooperation processes and Sicily was able to understand

> how to interface with a new member-state that was completely new to European policies and legislation. If you look at older reports, you will realize that the first two years [2004–6] were mostly needed for institutional networking and the construction and build-up of both networks and capabilities much needed during the following years … 2004–6 was a period of "institution-to-institution" collaboration strongly focused on public sector cooperation.[25]

The execution of the OP encountered a number of obstacles and delays. The Maltese (both public institutions and private actors conducting the projects) were soon dismayed by the complications injected by Europe's project management bureaucrats. Even so, in Fligstein and McAdams's terms, the events of 2004–6 can be viewed as the stage of field formation and emergence. Under the auspices of the EC, which wanted to foster territorial cooperation, CBC networks and activities were established, and this prepared the ground for an SAF comprising the two islands. We now turn our attention to the chronology of the SAF process. Namely, we refer to the stable field in place and its governance in the Italo–Maltese cross-border region.

The Stable Field: Governance, Operational Capacity, and Actors in the INTERREG Italy–Malta Program

This section focuses on SAF actors shaping the INTERREG Italy–Malta program. The information in this section was gathered from semi-structured interviews and official documents.[26] Also included are hindsights from the work of Custro[27] and a preliminary paper produced by the author during field research in Sicily.[28]

The Governance Structure of the SAF: Mapping the Incumbents, Governance Units, and the Broader Field Environment

To decipher the governance structure of the INTERREG program, see the interpretation of the scheme as illustrated in figure 9.1. Out of the dense web of relationships among different actors and their configurations, we can separate four institutional levels for classification purposes. The first one stands at the European level and includes the participation of the Commission's Office for Macro-Regions, ETC and Programme Implementation within the Directorate-General for Regional and Urban Policy (DG Regio) Department (Unit Office dedicated to the supervision of Italy and Malta). Although external to daily operations, the office's involvement in all the fundamental decisions is closely related to its responsibility as a funding entity for CBC activities. The EU personnel hold a mediating position in the debate between partners during the writing of the operational program to be submitted for approval. Later, they

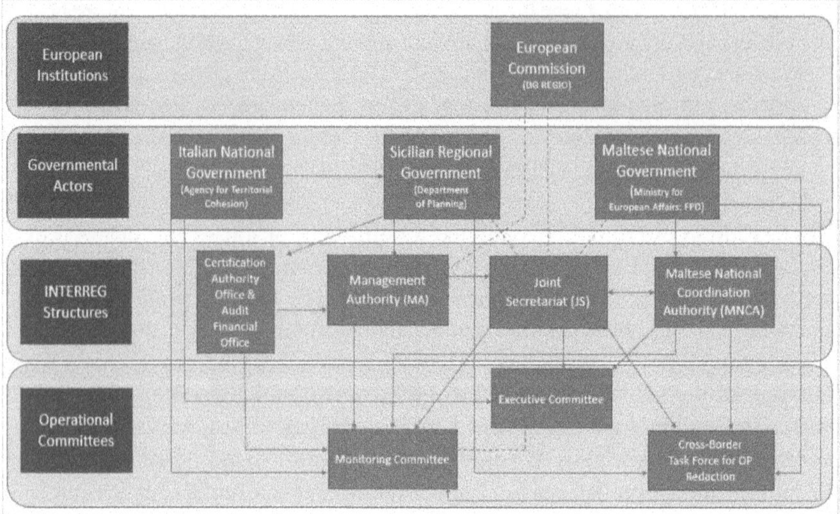

Figure 9.1. Monitoring Committee

Figure SEQ Figure * ARABIC 1: Governance Scheme of the INTERREG Italy-Malta Programme

Source: Author's elaboration

constantly monitor operations through the revision of yearly status reports produced by the OP authorities (i.e., state of activities and financial accounts). Furthermore, responsible staff can participate in INTERREG program events and, at times, at meetings of the Monitoring Committee (see above).

The second level represents the core governmental actors in the political partnership for the execution of the cross-border program. The Italy–Malta INTERREG OP is first and foremost an agreement between the Italian and Maltese states, but in the case of the former, there is a clear delegation of powers and responsibilities to the Italian regional authorities closest to the border. The Italian government participates in the work of the OP solely through its Agency for Territorial Cohesion. Acknowledging the management role entrusted to the Sicilian regional government, the corresponding Office VI – Operational Programs of Co-Financed Territorial Cooperation, International Activities, and Bilateral Cooperation (Projects and Instruments Area) mainly conducts the functions of monitoring and approving program operations. A very different role is assumed by the Maltese government, which does not count on a hierarchical territorial system of sub-national authorities for administration of the OP. Due to the country's small size and the inclusion of the entire archipelago in the eligibility criteria for CB activities, the Ministry for European Affairs and its internal Funds and Programs Division (FPD) accounts directly for, and participates in, decision-making. Interestingly, the Italo-Maltese structure reflects an atypical case of CBC between a state and a region, for it is unusual to see the latter assuming the management position. It is in fact the Sicilian regional government that holds the Managing Authority (MA) office within its Department of Planning in the Service for European Territorial Cooperation and Decentralized Development Cooperation office. Thus, the headquarters in Palermo hosts an overall majority of the INTERREG-generated structures encompassed in the third grouping of actors. In the case of the Certification and Audit Authorities, the Sicilians chose not to develop new structures, instead entrusting all relevant financial controls to the offices charged with supervising other regional programs (such as the ERDF). The MA role is carried out in the Operational Unit Italy–Malta office. Among other things, it plays a leading role on the program's Monitoring Committee, overseeing all decisions and records related to monitoring, evaluation, financial management, verification, and auditing. On its account, the Joint Secretariat (JS) of the OP is the designated office for assisting the Managing Authority in daily task development. It collects financial, physical, and statistical data regarding the program and the assigned cross-border projects, while also taking a lead role in project proposal evaluation and after-the-fact monitoring and assessment. Lastly, the parties involved have established one further structure on Maltese territory (hosted within the FPD Department) as a practical solution to the separation imposed by a maritime border (the Maltese National Coordination Authority, MNCA). Its main functions are those typical of an antenna office of the INTERREG program, insofar as the small staff involved support OP monitoring and implementation with all the Maltese partners.

Once we examine the components of the fourth and final level of the Operational Committees, however, we find that task separation is murky. One can speculate that the CBC program's small size and the presence of relatively few personnel together stimulate the occurrence of overlapping decision-making gatherings across the border. Thus, the Monitoring Committee becomes the common platform, with its twelve voting members coming from all the participating structures (the Italian Agency for Territorial Cooperation and the Maltese FPD; the Sicilian Regional Government through the MA and the Certification/Audit offices; the JS and the Maltese MNCA), who meet at least once a year to discuss and approve the different stages of the OP. The Executive Committee is a much smaller platform, one in which the two operative branches of the OP (the Palermo-based JS and the MNCA) have the opportunity to discuss directives from the Monitoring Committee and proceed to the evaluation and assessment of CBC projects. Lastly, the Cross-Border Task Force is part of an interesting experiment already used in other European contexts and here developed to improve the content of the INTERREG program. Following European institutional concerns regarding the elaboration of strongly territorial-based strategies, this Sicilian–Maltese Committee was created in preparation for the 2014–20 planning period. By directly involving representatives of the two islands' governments and other public and private actors, the INTERREG offices sought to gain real feedback on CBC experiences to elaborate later strategies. Although in line with the delegation of competences described, the Italian national government was, remarkably, not involved in the process. Regardless, it is obvious that such a governance tool is activated only when the INTERREG personnel are preparing to draft a new program (thus, on a seven-year basis).

How can the previously described scenario be interpreted within a SAF perspective? Any considerations regarding European CBC fields should begin with the presence of the supra-national political structure that is both warden and sponsor of such cooperation, namely, the EU. Given its extraordinary political complexity, the EU fits the theoretical concepts elaborated by Fligstein and McAdam regarding the existence of multiple nested fields and a common broader field environment.[29] However, we also require a small effort in theory-stretching to picture the broader European scenario. Even when focusing our attention on a field dedicated solely to ETC, the Sicilian–Maltese SAF only emerges out of a huge grouping of cross-border SAFs (be they INTERREG, Euroregions, proto-Euroregional territories, or other cooperation structures). Accordingly, all of them would still be dependent on decisions generated in other SAFs, such as the ones made in the Brussels offices that oversee the programs. In turn, the offices of the Commission would themselves depend on the SAF generated by the EU's seven-year budget negotiations at the upper level of the EU's decision making. Leaving aside further speculations that could muddy the waters, the Sicilian–Maltese SAF stands out in terms of the relative ease of identifying key players. In the straightforward political agreement inscribed by the INTERREG Sicily–Malta program, it is indeed the Maltese national government and the Sicilian regional government (albeit overseen by the third party of the Italian national government) that represent the incumbents in the cross-border field. Therefore, under the external and somewhat impartial role of the Commission as external incumbent of all INTERREG SAFs, the governmental actors of the Sicilian-Maltese case make all the decisions in shaping the direction of cooperation and the attribution of resources for the projects. Finally, they make use of the local INTERREG offices and the operational committees, which are naturally identified as the governance units of our field for decision-making compliance.

Stretching the Theory: Functionality vs Effectiveness of the Sicilian-Maltese SAF

Before proceeding to analyse the challengers, there is a need to further stretch the analytical framework to understand the dynamics of the SAF at hand. The explanatory mechanism provided by Fligstein and McAdam seems limited if one's goal is to describe elements such as the true objectives of the field and the daily obstacles to its performance.[30] Thus, in line with the general purposes of this volume, referring to further testing of the SAF in new contexts, it was decided to introduce the new operational concepts of functionality and effectiveness. Regarding the field's *functionality*, we understand this to be the general purpose behind the actions of the governance units oriented by the incumbents' political will. It is also possible to determine the objectives of the field and the reasons it exists. The idea of *effectiveness*, for its part, is formulated as a theoretical concept measuring the obstacles compromising the field's functionality. By counterbalancing expected outcomes and technical hurdles, we expect to introduce extra elements of evaluation to the global performance of the SAF at hand.

The main objective of the governance units in the Sicily–Malta OP involves the elaboration of a joint CBC strategy to be carried out through projects within a seven-year financial period. There are, however, important limitations regarding the choice of sectoral policies to which the activities may be dedicated. As the funding entity, the EU imposes a first set of thematic priorities in line with the guidelines of pan-European strategies such as the former Lisbon Strategy and Europe 2020. So even if the two archipelagos find a common interest in a sector like tourism, this cannot be directly addressed as a strategic axis; rather, it can only be incorporated into secondary priority guidelines. In the 2014–20 period, the case study established a thematic concentration around research and innovation, environmental protection, and economic competitiveness. Furthermore, calls for projects can only be ratified once the Commission has approved the cross-border strategy. The Sicilian–Maltese program does not make an exception in this regard, although the modality of the call for projects has undergone a series of reforms.[31] Following the example of other European OPs, once a call for projects is launched, several partnerships of actors will respond with their own applications for project funding. Thus, the policies sought by the field are translated as projects executed by networks of stakeholders working across the border. We choose to define such executing agents as *field participants* in our operationalization of the theory. In our view, participants are all those public and private actors who, though not directly involved in the field's power relationships, willingly contribute to its strategy by securing funding for activities. These then follow the classical European project management approach, which involves project monitoring and the production of outputs and deliverables.

Two further features of field functionality derive from the eligibility of territorial actors in the cross-border area and the financial expansion the program underwent between 2007–13 and 2014–20. While the Maltese state has always been eligible, participation in the INTERREG program was initially limited to five of Sicily's nine provinces. These were the ones directly facing the sea border with Malta. The two main industrialized provinces of Catania and Palermo were initially allowed limited participation (20 per cent of a total project's costs). The two remaining provinces (Enna and Messina) were ineligible for funding. The reasons for this may lead to speculation insofar as they might have been conceived as stimulating the less developed territories in the southern part of the island. Subsequent opening to the entire Sicilian region has been most likely due to the strong role of Catanese and Palermitan actors (emerging from the most industrialized and urbanized areas) and from the desire to avoid territorial discrimination among all Sicilian provinces. A further opening argument was likely provided by the Commission's formula for calculating the total amount of INTERREG funding. By setting a standard proportion between inhabitants and territory, the enlargement of the program contributed to augmenting the initial amount from €30,148,017 (2007–13) to €43,952,171 (2014–20).

Let us now turn our attention to the concept of field effectiveness to review the obstacles of the field in more detail. We propose to do so by elaborating on issues that arose during the interviews with incumbents and governance units. The list includes the Commission office responsible for overseeing Sicilian–Maltese CBC, the JS, and the MNCA (here grouped as INTERREG local authorities for purposes of anonymity). The most striking obstacle when considering the realities of the Sicily–Malta OP relates to the delay accumulated over the years in program execution. As a matter of fact, in its two and a half funding periods, the OP has experienced frequent postponing of both the strategy's approval and the final justification for project expenditures. Even with regard to the current 2014–20 period, at the time of fieldwork execution (2017–18), there have been significant two-year delays in calls for projects. However, beyond blindly accusing the responsible authorities, we must point out some important structural conditions that explain this scenario. First, the governance units we interviewed remarked on the hardship of a one-size-fits-all policy in the management and administration of INTERREG programs. In their view, a budget cut and poorly staffed OP should not be dealing with administrative obligations on the same level as much larger territorial programs of the EU. In their own words, "the designation of a managing authority handling €200–€300 million is one thing and the one of a MA handling €40 million is quite another thing."[32] They observed that especially when dealing with small expenditures, a simplified cost option could help dispel intricate bureaucratic procedures committing authorities and partners to time-wasting efforts. Furthermore, they would claim that the accumulation of frequent reports and evaluation procedures does not help insofar as it only slows down the entire process. Second, and as a recurring argument from the very origins of the field, the difficulties of elaborating a cross-border strategy between the two islands still affect the current outcomes of cooperation. The very same

2014–20 strategy suffered through more than a year of revisions due to a negative EC verdict on the strategy. Indeed, their continuous request for more thematic concentration in the expected program results led to resubmissions and a final approval only in October 2015. The local authorities are well aware of the situation, but they express a certain uneasiness in differentiating their activities from other European programs:

> We try to touch all those themes that cannot be directly funded under ERDF, otherwise we may as well get crazy, there would be overlapping, and it would be a mess. The commission's opinion is that there should be complementarity, but there is a subtle distinction between overlapping and complementarity; from here we had to make a choice, we have few financial resources and then you also have to go and find your own place in the world.[33]

The argument certainly implies increased difficulty in cooperation across maritime borders. A third hindrance to field functionality was present in the endemic behaviour of Italian institutions. Some of the European and Italian authorities who were interviewed complained about a clear lack of long-term sustainability in both national and regional levels of European planning. They are not alone in their judgment, as stated in a recent academic contribution by the former director of Sicily's European Planning Department. Robert Leonardi indicates that even the Italian government faced an almost two-year delay in the approval of its national-level strategies for the 2014–20 period. Furthermore, at the Sicilian level, the autonomous region has been criticized for engaging in sectorized planning; clearly lacking is an integrated strategic approach beyond the individual funding framework.[34] This could be connected to the frequent episodes of political instability that have long beset the Italian and Sicilian governments. In such a climate of uncertainty, constituencies always bet on self-concluding strategies rather than integrated approaches and continuity. Finally, a fourth obstacle in program execution arises from the OP's multi-level governance framework. In terms of institutional collaboration, the complementarities among greater territorial size (Sicily), sovereign power (Malta), and cultural similarities generally allow for harmonious relations between the two parties: "One [is] like larger than the other but we don't think that there is any difference …We don't consider ourselves to be bigger or more important than them. It's never come to our mind as a problem … We feel like two islands on the same level cooperating with each other."[35]

However good the intentions, serious issues seem to be hiding beneath the different territorial competences of the two islands. More specifically, there are important limitations regarding the degree of action that Sicily can achieve from its position under Italian authority. This holds true despite its special regional autonomy statute. Let us take as an example the recent removal of the transport and infrastructure axis from the 2007–13 and 2014–20 INTERREG strategies. This was mostly due to the paucity of funding provided by the program, but also partly the result of a complex governance process that grants national Italian actors authority over decisions. A similar case would arise around 2016, when the EU institutions called for all European programs to invest in immigration-related activities in response to the refugee crisis. Even when Malta was willing to discuss such a delicate issue at the cross-border level, the Italian authorities retained total control over that issue and forbade Sicily from acting. In a third example involving a cross-border project established by agreement between the two islands, this one regarding mutual assistance and disaster relief (SIMIT project), the pact between the two islands' civil protection agencies was long delayed because the Italian national authorities took it on themselves to review the document before ratification.

Of course, all of the above should not imply a total logjam within the SAF. Overall, we estimate that the official functionality of the field is being compromised by a set of structural obstacles that limit, at the present time, its potential effectiveness. Yet this did not prevent the Italy–Malta program from funding twenty-three cross-border projects between 2007 and 2013. There have been some successful examples of cooperation in developing joint solutions to common issues. Some examples: the VAMOS SEGURO project involved the construction of a cross-border project to surveille the Mount Etna volcano (acknowledged in 2013 by the EC as a European best practice in the risk prevention sector); the PROMED, VINENERGY, and T-CHEESIMAL initiatives improved local products such as cheeses and wines through greener technologies; the IMAGENX cross-border medical research network was dedicated to advancing the fight against breast cancer; and, finally, the CALYPSO project constructed a system of cross-border antennae to monitor oil spillage in the Malta Channel. This last project was even considered for replication in the maritime Italy–France INTERREG of the northern Mediterranean. Supposedly, some among academic and institutional circles held private doubts about the effectiveness of a maritime cross-border region.[36] Nonetheless, the examples provided show the added value of these initiatives as well as their capacity to push actors to pursue joint initiatives to address common problems.

Insufficient Shocks and Isolated Challengers: Completing the SAF Mapping

An interesting feature of SAF theory is that it identifies the power relations (and their shifts) between incumbents and challengers. When we examine a strongly institutionalized INTERREG program sponsored by European funding, a first level of analysis might rashly conclude that there is no space for altering the balance of power among the actors. Indeed, none of the individual episodes listed below had managed to modify the field by the end of contention periods. However, after identifying the shocks and the very few challengers within the SAF, we suggest an alternative vision of the field that could help break the status quo in the border region. To produce this section, we extend the range of interviews to other types of actors we encountered during the fieldwork (i.e., Members of the Sicilian Regional Assembly and the Consul of Malta in Catania).

In pursuing events that could summon episodes of contention in the field, we identified four weak shock incidents within the SAF. We classify two of them as endogenous (i.e., as happening within the existing governance units) and two as exogenous (i.e., external to both the incumbents and the governance units). The first endogenous shock to partly shake the SAF's balance was the death of the previous coordinator of the INTERREG Italy–Malta program in 2016. In terms of SAF theory, Dr Antonio Piceno's social skills were instrumental in establishing the INTERREG program. In the generous words of his own colleague, "we are what we are nowadays thanks to him … It was always his expertise, and even before the Italy–Malta program, he was director of the special office for international cooperation taking care of projects in developing countries. When he started dealing with cross-border themes, he already knew what it was all about … He surely avoided the intromission of local politics into our programmes."[37] The importance of Piceno's role was evident in the daily operations of the governance units. Thus, his death led to a months-long slowdown of the OP's activities and to a restructuring of positions in the JS. Even so, the loss of a founding father of the program was not enough of a shock to bring down the institutional agreements he had helped develop.

The second endogenous shock is interesting because it departs from standard SAF rhetoric. In fact, it shows us that even within a coalition of incumbents, some amount of contention is possible. According to the sources, once the draft negotiations started for the 2014–20 period, the Maltese government began suggesting that the time had come for a switch to the Managing Authority role for a fully Europeanized Malta. The issue never took the form of a political debate; before that could happen, it was quelled through an agreement between the two incumbents. An interesting clause in that agreement stated that a fourth member, of Maltese nationality, would be included in the JS. Unfortunately, it seems that they were unable to find a suitable person for the job, or one who was willing to move to the Sicilian capital of Palermo. By the time this research was ending, the Sicilian government had hired a fourth Italian candidate for their office.

In terms of exogenous shocks, we first identified a future development in the field that could have brought significant changes to the SAF. Due to the high-level diplomacy of EU-budget negotiations, some among the INTERREG local authorities expressed concern about a significant reduction in post-2020 European funding. Many factors could determine this choice: Malta's final exit from priority 1 target funding due to its prosperous development; a further cohesion funding redistribution toward Eastern Europe; the absence of British quotas due to Brexit; and, finally, certain preliminary discussions among Brussels INTERREG authorities for a reduction and merging of programs, particularly in the maritime context.[38] Finally, this research was instrumental in discovering a fascinating (although unfruitful) double attempt to establish political governance platforms in the cross-border region. These were produced around 2011–12 on both sides of the border, but both attempts failed in their preliminary stages and were too weak to produce significant changes. On the Sicilian side, the regional deputy Massimo Ferrara from Italy's Partito Democratico (PD) relied on the assistance of Dr Antonio Matasso, a university professor who had previously collaborated in the Tyrol–South Tyrol Euroregion in northern Italy. Understanding the benefits of a Euroregional structure for CBC, Mr Ferrara politically backed Dr Matasso's proposal for submitting draft legislation on a Sicily–Malta Euroregion. Unfortunately, the project failed to impress the political groups in the Sicilian assembly. Following the line of reasoning already cited in the previous section, the interviewee openly criticized the lack of vision of the regional parliament connected to the government. In his view, they seemed to be dealing much more with regional budgets and political (in)stability than with European strategies. The same would happen one year later, when a Maltese minister expressed some informal interest in proposing a locally based CBC platform between the two islands to the Sicilian city council. Once again, this proposal never left the realm of idle talks, and apparently neither the deputy and his assistant nor the Maltese functionary (whose name was not cited during the interviews) were even aware of each other's intentions. This last shock, however weak in its intent, is of great significance in revealing the very few and isolated challengers to the current Italo-Maltese SAF. In their actions, one can perceive a will to introduce new governance units in the field to promote increased effectiveness for the CBC. Unfortunately, the current situation places them in an unfavourable position in which alterations of the status quo may initially seem unlikely. The full mapping of the INTERREG Italy–Malta SAF (as shown in figure 9.2) provides a clear scenario in which the field is "crystallized" into perpetual dependence on the INTERREG program dynamics and channelled into a strict top-down process. In such a context, decisions made at the level of incumbents are then directly transmitted to the governance units. In turn, these units implement the decisions by granting resources to the field participants for the actualization of strategy through individual projects. In the current interpretation of

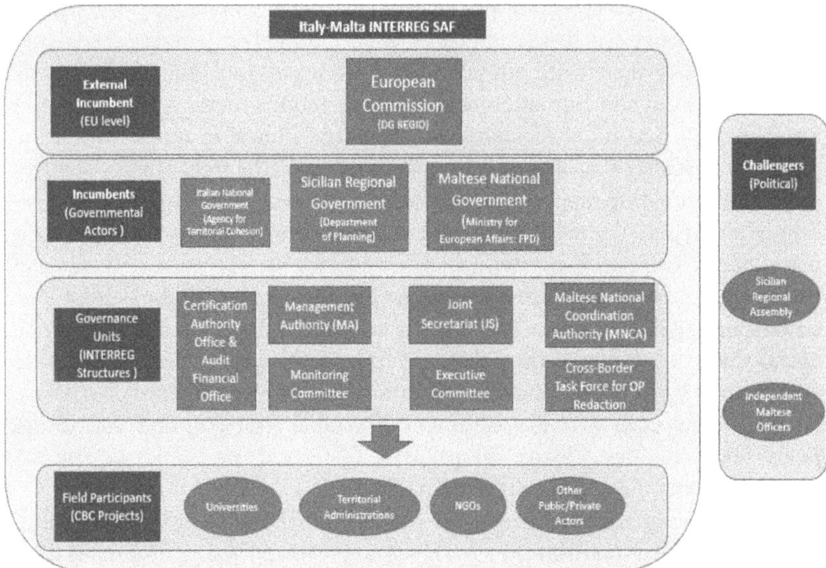

Figure 9.2. INTERREG Italy–Malta SAF

Figure SEQ Figure * ARABIC 2: Structure of the INTERREG Italy-Malta SAF.

Source: Author's Elaboration

the Italo-Maltese field, the isolated challengers seem completely alien to the dynamics and are cut off from the SAF cycle.

Conclusions: Expanding SAF Theory and Formulating an Alternative Strategy between Challengers and "Field Participants"

From a theoretical point of view, application of the SAF framework to the Italy–Malta OP has proven to have a certain degree of analytical potential in identifying power relations and the collective roles of all the actors involved in CBC processes. Indeed, the analysis has helped generate the picture of a field currently "crystallized" in its current dynamics. By virtue of the opportunities provided by the INTERREG European program, the governments of the two islands have acquired full incumbent status and have stood under the guidance of the Commission as external incumbent and sponsor of the process. Furthermore, the incumbents rely on official INTERREG structures acting as shock-resistant governance units. In turn, the entire SAF has not been disturbed by the few isolated political challengers, which are cut off from its daily operations.

However, this research was also instrumental in highlighting some limitations of the theory, which were adjusted by conceptually expanding the framework. First, SAF theory did not provide the necessary tools for evaluating the purposes behind the formation and daily operations of an SAF field (field functionality). Second, it did not show sufficient interest in underscoring the potential obstacles that may hinder full capacity of the field (field effectiveness), thus providing rationale to the challengers to contend. Third, a new conceptual focus was required to evaluate the presence of what we termed field participants. This was generated when considering an SAF entrusted with the financial capacity to mobilize other agents for the purposes of the field. In our understanding of European CBC, field participants represent public and private agents that are external to the field's governance processes yet fundamental in contributing to its effectiveness through the execution of CBC projects. These are in turn necessary for the fulfilment of general strategies and thus of the fields' functionalities. Clearly, the presence of such actors cannot be ignored when observing the role they play in the field's development.

It is also important to consider that while the selection of a case study based on a cross-border maritime region has not prevented the conceptualization of CBC fields, it has nonetheless highlighted some of the obstacles surrounding multi-sectoral cooperation, which is often easier to plan via land. Take, for example, the multiple obstacles encountered in the production of a common cross-border strategy, and the specific need to develop a further INTERREG antenna (the MCNA) on the island of Malta. While this does not diminish the potentially added value of European cooperation, it certainly underscores the need for an even stronger political motivation on the part of all key actors if they are to bring about real changes in the field.[39] This last point is also instrumental in suggesting that the current status quo (i.e., a "crystallized" SAF for the Sicily–Malta Region) may not be the only possible scenario for CBC between the two Mediterranean islands. In terms of our analytical framework, the biggest issue that currently prevents a shift in power dynamics relates to the exclusion and lack of organizational support of individual challengers. Two solutions are therefore proposed for increasing effectiveness in the field. First, an ontological separation must be considered in breaking off from the INTERREG-driven logic that permeates the whole process. The analysis carried out in this chapter implicitly assumed that the concept of an INTERREG Italy–Malta SAF overlaps with the one of the Sicily–Malta Cross-Border Region. While this may be true for the moment, the exit from a proto-Euroregional stage based purely on INTERREG structures and the introduction of a political cross-border governance platform may be key to reintroducing challengers in the game. By extending the dimension of the field beyond the operational area of the INTERREG, new spaces for cross-border action would be opened for increasing CBC effectiveness. The presence of a Euroregion could be instrumental in downplaying the EU funding exploitation scenario and in recovering the vision of an integrated European islands' border region. At the very least, the solution would provide a multi-level governance framework for a heightened Sicily–Malta debate beyond CB projects. Furthermore, challengers would be given a new political arena in the quest for further acknowledgment. Thanks to the opportunities for participation provided by Euroregional structures, there is indeed space for involving a wide array of public and private actors in the cross-border scenario. Ideally, the initial process should push challengers toward a quest for new allies among those who already possess expertise in cross-border planning. No better candidates are present than the most successful field participants, who have already executed cross-border activities in the area. For example, in the great majority of the 2007–13 projects, universities played a fundamental role in successful projects. Furthermore, their cooperation stands on solid links forged in the academic world and at times predating the INTERREG opportunities. Following the model of other multi-level Euroregions, it is easy to consider a deeper inclusion of public territorial actors, especially on the much larger Sicilian island. Involving the most active municipalities (such as the more industrialized Catania and Palermo), revitalizing the role of the stranded Sicilian provinces (which underwent a power-stripping reform in 2014), or involving the historically significant local authorities from Malta may just be some of the possible options at hand. In the current "crystallized" scenario, Sicilian–Maltese CBC may well continue to be downplayed as a smaller addition to EU individual regional funding (i.e. ERDF). In our view, it is now up to new socially skilled individuals to break the SAF's glass, restore shifting dynamics, and generate proactive coalitions of challengers. It is indeed up to them to bring about a change capable of imposing a renovated political project for the Sicily–Malta Cross-Border Region.

NOTES

1 The substantial fieldwork was conducted thanks to funding associated with a Spanish FPI scholarship (BES-2014–068387) granted to the former PhD candidate and to special funding for a research stay at the University of Palermo (Italy) and in Valletta (Malta). A first draft of this chapter has been included in the following doctoral dissertation: F. Camonita, *A Methodology for the Design of Euroregional Cross-Border Organizations and Its Application in the Sicily–Malta Cross-Border Region* (Autonomous University of Barcelona, Department of Geography, 2019).

2 At the time of the final editing of this research, it is undoubtedly true that much has happened to maritime cooperation and cooperation across borders in general. The former has been the subject of EU debates over the cessation of maritime CBC programs and their incorporation into INTERREG transnational ones (see

Christiaan van Lierop, *European Territorial Cooperation (Interreg) 2021–2027*, European Parliamentary Research Service, EU Legislation in Progress 2021–27 MFF [2021], https://www.europarl.europa.eu/RegData/etudes/BRIE/2018/628228/EPRS_BRI(2018)628228_EN.pdf). The latter has thus far suffered a temporary slowdown due to the conditions imposed by the recent COVID-19 pandemic. Notwithstanding, it would seem that a sufficient amount of lobbying from European actors involved in maritime CBC has prevented such an outcome (see Conference of Peripheral and Maritime Regions [CPMR], *The Future of INTERREG: 10 Messages from the CPMR*, Technical Note, [2018]: 9–11, https://cpmr.org/wpdm-package/the-future-of-interreg-10-messages-from-the-cpmr/?wpdmdl=17990&ind=1529396962494). In the provisional legislative agreement on the Multi-Annual Financial Framework (MFF) 2021–27 approved on 7 December 2020, the EU institutions formally maintained a cross-border maritime cooperation strand in European cooperation (EP, 2021). Considering the recent political debate, we reckon the results of this research to be even more relevant to the field of cross-border maritime and island cooperation in Europe.

3 European Commission, *European Territorial Cooperation: Building Bridges between People* (Brussels: EU Publications Office, 2011), https://doi.org/10.2776/40850; European Commission, *Interreg: European Territorial Cooperation*, europa.eu (n.d.), https://ec.europa.eu/regional_policy/it/policy/cooperation/european-territorial.

4 See I. Bache and M. Flinders, *Multi-Level Governance* (Oxford: Oxford University Press, 2004); L. Hooghe and G. Marks, *Multi-level Governance and European Integration* (Lanham: Rowman and Littlefield, 2001), https://www.amazon.co.uk/Multi-Level-Governance-European-Integration-Europe/dp/0742510204; Hooghe and Marks, "Gobernanza estatocéntrica y gobernanza multinivel," in *Gobernanza Multinivel en la Unión Europea*, ed. F. Morata (Valencia: Tirant lo Blanch, 2004); A. Noferini, M. Berzi, F. Camonita, and A. Durà, "Cross-Border Cooperation in the EU: Euroregions amid Multilevel Governance and Reterritorialization," *European Planning Studies* 28, no. 1 (2020): 35–56, https://doi.org/10.1080/09654313.2019.1623973; and S. Piattoni, *The Theory of Multi-Level Governance: Conceptual, Empirical, and Normative Challenges* (Oxford: Oxford University Press, 2010).

5 M. Perkmann, "Building Governance Institutions across European Borders," *Regional Studies* 33, no. 7 (1999): 657–67; Perkmann, "Cross-Border Regions in Europe: Significance and Drivers of Regional Cross-Border Co-operation," *European Urban and Regional Studies* 10, no. 2 (2003): 153–71, https://doi.org/10.1177/0969776403010002004.

6 "Territorial Cooperation in Spain and the EU: A Selection of Guiding Experiences for Excellence and Innovation in the 2014–2020 Period" (COOP-RECOT II, 2014–2017; CSO2013–45257-P).

7 A. Durà, F. Camonita, M. Berzi, and A. Noferini, *Euroregions: Excellence and Innovation across EU borders: A Catalogue of Good Practices* (Barcelona: UAB, Department of Geography, 2018), https://ddd.uab.cat/record/189399.

8 Durà et al., *Euroregions*, 93–5.

9 See C. Koutalakis, *Making European Policies Work in the South: Explaining Non-Compliance in Italy and Greece* (Athens, 2002), http://userpage.fu-berlin.de/~europe/forschung/dfg/projektantrag_mc.pdf; A. La Spina and G. Sciortino, "Common Agenda, Southern Rules: European Integration and Environmental Change in the Mediterranean States," in *European Integration and Environmental Policy*, ed. J.D. Liefferink, P.D. Lowe, and A.P.J. Mol (London: Bellhaven, 1993); G. Pridham, "Environmental Policies and Problems of European Legislation in Southern Europe," *South European Society and Politics* 1, no. 1 (1996): 47–73, https://doi.org/10.1080/13608749608454716; and G. Pridham and M. Cini, "Enforcing Environmental Standards in the European Union: Is There a Southern Problem?," in *Environmental Standards in the EU in an Interdisciplinary Framework*, ed. M. Faure, J.A.E. Vervaele, and A. Weale (Antwerp: Maklu, 1994): 251–77, https://searchworks.stanford.edu/view/3329363.

10 European Commission, "European operational programmes with Italian presence" (n.d.), https://ec.europa.eu/regional_policy/en/atlas/programmes/?search=1&keywords=&countryCode=IT®ionId=ALL&themeId=ALL&programType=ALL&objectiveId=ALL&periodId=3.

11 For further theorization on proto-euroregional structures, see also F. Camonita, "Passer par l'étape proto-eurorégionale: le cas de la région transfrontalière Sicile-Malte," *Sud-Ouest Européen* 48 (2019): 99–113.

12 The following historical summary will quickly shift the focus from Sicilian–Maltese relations to more Italy/Malta-based international relations. Furthermore, it will provide an account regarding the relatively recent entry of Malta into the EU compared to Italy. While this provides useful insight as a prologue to the INTERREG SAF, a separate line of research was opened by the author to reconstruct an in-depth multisectoral comparison of the two island territories. See Camonita, "Passer par l'étape proto-eurorégionale."

13 B. Blouet, *The Story of Malta*, 6th ed. (La Valletta: Progress Press, 1997); S. Goodwin, *Malta, Mediterranean Bridge* (Westport: Bergin and Garvey, 2002), http://books.google.com/books?hl=en&lr=&id=up9Fy-NBiLAC&pgis=1.

14 M. Harwood, *Malta in the European Union* (London and New York: Routledge, 2014), https://books.google.es/books/about/Malta_in_the_European_Union.html?id=sg8cBgAAQBAJ&redir_esc=y.

15 P. Ardizzone, *Studi maltesi-Lotte per l'egemonia culturale e politica a Malta: aspetti linguistici ed istituzionali* (2002), http://www.intratext.com/IXT/ITA2413.

16 R. Pace, "Malta's Foreign Policy in the 1990s," in *The Foreign Policies of the EU's Mediterranean States and Applicant Countries in the 1990s*, ed. S. Stavridis, T.

Couloumbis, T. Veremis, and N. Waites (London: Palgrave Macmillan, 1999), 195–249, http://www.palgrave.com/us/book/9780333751008#aboutBook.

17 R. Aliboni, "Italy and the Mediterranean in the 1990s," in Stavridis et al., eds., *The Foreign Policies*, 73–97.

18 M.G. Melchionni, "Accordo Italia - Malta 1981," *Rivista Di Studi Politici Internazionali* 48, no. 2 (1981): 288–301, http://www.jstor.org/stable/42735585.

19 In 2017 converted rates.

20 Aliboni, "Italy and the Mediterranean in the 1990s"; Governo Italiano, *Italia e Malta, 20 anni di cooperazione*, Dipartimento per l'Informazione e l'editoria, Presidenza del Consiglio dei Ministri Italiano (2001).

21 Harwood, *Malta in the European Union*; and Pace, "Malta's Foreign Policy in the 1990s."

22 The old "priority 1" mark stood for the most urgent cases in closing the structural gap with other European regions. For more information, visit https://ec.europa.eu/regional_policy/archive/policy/object/index_en.htm.

23 INTERREG Local Authorities, personal communication, May 2017.

24 Regione Sicilia, "Rapporto Finale di Esecuzione Programma di Cooperazione Transfrontaliera Interreg III A Italia-Malta 2004–2006" (Palermo, 2006), http://www.italiamalta.eu/component/option,com_docman/task,doc_view/gid,158/Itemid,29/lang,it; SiciliaInformazioni.com., "Cooperazione, spesi 7 milioni di euro per i 13 progetti tra Sicilia e Malta" (2008); https://italiamalta.eu, Programming Period 2007–13.

25 European Commission Authorities, Skype interview, March 2017.

26 Regione Sicilia, "Programma di Cooperazione Transfrontaliera: Italia-Malta 2007/2013" (Palermo, 2009), http://www.italiamalta.eu/component/option,com_docman/task,doc_download/gid,1/Itemid,29/lang,en; Regione Sicilia, "European Territorial Cooperation Cooperation Programme 'INTERREG V-A Italy-Malta,'" (Palermo, 2014).

27 T. Custro, *La Cooperazione Territoriale Europea: Analisi del Programma Operativo Italia-Malta 2007–2013* (Università di Palermo, 2013). This represents one of the very few academic studies (if not the only one) about the INTERREG Italy–Malta program before the doctoral research led by the author.

28 F. Camonita, "Una Euroregione per l'area transfrontaliera Sicilia-Malta?," *StrumentiRES-Rivista online della Fondazione RES Anno IX*, no. 1 (July 2017), https://www.researchgate.net/publication/319203933_Una_Euroregione_per_l'area_transfrontaliera_Sicilia-Malta_StrumentiRES-Rivista_online_della_Fondazione_RES_Anno_IX-n_1-Luglio_2017.

29 Neil Fligstein and Doug McAdam, *A Theory of Fields* (New York: Oxford University Press, 2012), http://doi.org/10.1007/s11186-014-9237-0.

30 Fligstein and McAdam, *A Theory of Fields.*

31 More specifically, in the 2007–13 funding period it was decided to remove an atypical separation between "ordinary" and pre-established "strategic" CB projects to make room for a more INTERREG-standard call in two phases.

32 INTERREG Local Authorities, Personal Communication, May 2017.

33 INTERREG Local Authorities, Personal Communication, May 2017.

34 R. Leonardi, "Perché la Sicilia non riesce a usare i fondi strutturali per decollare economicamente," in *Settant'anni di autonomia siciliana 1946–2016*, no. 1, ed. G. Armao and M. Saija (Palermo: Rubbettino Editore, 2016).

35 INTERREG Local Authorities, Personal Communication (May 2017).

36 See note 2.

37 INTERREG Local Authorities, Personal Communication (April 2017).

38 See note 2.

39 For a broader discussion on multisectoral CBC across European maritime and island territories, see Camonita, *A Methodology for the Design of Euroregional Cross-Border Organizations*.

10 A Bird's-Eye View of Cross-Border Governance Dynamics along the Pyrenees (France–Spain Border)

MATTEO BERZI

This chapter compares cross-border governance experiences along the French–Spanish border using the theory of fields analytical framework.[1] The theory has been previously applied to the San Diego–Tijuana case across the US–Mexico border.[2] But while other contributions in this book analyse a specific cross-border dynamic focusing on a geographical area of cooperation (e.g., the western Pyrenees in chapter 14, Cerdanya in chapter 13), this chapter offers a bird's-eye view of cooperation along the Pyrenean border. There have been empirical studies about cross-border governance in this region,[3] but comparative research that considers the entire borderland is largely absent.

According to Sanguin, the Pyrenees "represents the most expressive and condensed case study of confusion, redundancy, oversizing and entropy issues affecting the cross-border organizations in Europe."[4] Since the early 1980s, many local and regional cross-border agencies have been established in the region: Eurocities, Euromunicipalities, Eurodistricts, and Euroregions have steadily emerged from the Atlantic to the Mediterranean. These initiatives often overlap, providing different institutional and organizational capacities as well as different scopes and territorial strategies. Morata and Noferni argue that administrative, legal, and cultural impediments constantly challenge the stability of these French–Spanish cross-border agencies, resulting in a lack of stable networks among them.[5] Nonetheless, contrary to Sanguin, they argue that the high intensity of cross-border institutionalization promotes institutional learning, improves multi-level governance processes that increase cross-border consciousness, and provides socio-economic benefits such as new infrastructure, joint territorial strategies, and economic clusters. Indeed, empirical research[6] shows that cross-border organizations along the internal and external EU borders generate innovative sectoral policies in domains such as natural resource management,[7] local economic development,[8] transport and mobility,[9] and health care assistance.[10] Nonetheless, a fully cross-border regional innovation system is still a utopia.[11] Along with borders, the nation-state persists in many guises – culturally, ideologically, and symbolically.[12] In this sense, cross-border organizations comparable to Euroregions and similar structures should not be conceived as challenging the nation-state but rather as a strategic action field (SAF), promoted by regional and local players and aimed at coordinating territorial strategies. That is, cross-border organizations represent the most visible result of the synergy between top-down European policies and bottom-up initiatives, through which local and regional actors promote alternative territorial strategies (joint infrastructure and services, enhancement of shared economic, cultural, and natural resources, etc.), thus reinforcing the EU integration process.[13]

Based on this, we compare cross-border organizations active along and across the French–Spanish border through the theory of fields.[14] We argue that the theory of fields represents a suitable analytical framework for understanding cross-border cooperation processes as well as the role played by territorial agents in governing cross-border structures. According to the definition of an SAF, French–Spanish cross-border structures can be conceived as sub-national fields that emerge when regional and local stakeholders cooperate across the national boundary to address common challenges (e.g., rural and urban development, lack of transport, health care infrastructure deficiencies, environmental conservation, and the like). They craft a shared vision of the rules governing these fields, shape power relations, and establish the purposes of cooperation. These interactions are often facilitated by shared sociocultural and linguistic assets, such as the historical Basque and Catalan relations, located respectively at the Atlantic and Mediterranean ends of the Pyrenees. Fligstein and McAdam identify three main "states" to understand SAF's dynamics. First, the field emerges in a more or less documented process (it is often difficult to identify who moves the first steps of the field and how). Second, the field stabilizes through the constructive actions of the dominant players (incumbents), which establish the governance's structure and the boundaries of the field. Finally, the field reaches a moment of crisis, rupture, and resettlement promoted by internal and/or external challengers.[15]

The study of the evolution of cross-border fields begins with some pertinent key questions: What are "cornerstones" that trigger the emergence of the fields? And what are the specific factors that generate field change? After these questions are answered, the second section of this chapter focuses on the incumbents and the challengers involved in the cross-border fields and on how EU and state interventions (e.g., French administrative reforms) resettle the field. The players are identified and analysed in terms of three categories: scale (state, regional, local, or supra-local), nationality (French or Spanish), and their role in the field. After this, we examine how internal/external and direct/indirect crisis episodes shape the resettlement of the field. Lastly, we apply the concept of the broader field environment in two ways: we assess the existence of networks among SAFs to examine the hypothesis of Morata and Noferini,[16] and we consider a representative "broader field" of cooperation, asking whether and how the three potential European Transport corridors – Atlantic, Central, and Mediterranean – affect cross-border organizations. In our conclusion, we consider the application of field theory to compare the multiple and multi-scale experiences of cross-border cooperation (CBC) along the French–Spanish border.

The methodology is based on a qualitative comparative analysis among the cross-border structures across the Pyrenees. Three main sources of information have been consulted. First, six BORDERGOV interviews were conducted between 2012 and 2015 with active stakeholders in cross-border governance. Second, the COOP-RECOT II database provided accurate data regarding the partnership and governance structures for each case. Because new cross-border institutions have recently been established, it was necessary to collect up-to-date information (the third source) from the academic literature[17] regarding the institutional sources provided by the European Commission (EC) and the Euroregions. These include reports, Euroregional strategies, Web pages, and online press articles. As a result of that process, ten active cross-border structures were identified along the French–Spanish border (their institutional trajectory is synthesized in figure 10.1). The cross-border Hospital of Cerdanya is one of the most articulate and interesting fields of cooperation in the entire European scenario. It illustrates an ambitious experience of matching and harmonizing two very different national health care systems.

The Important Historical and Political Background

The French–Spanish borderland is an emblematic case study within the European Union.[18] The border between the two countries is one of the oldest and most stable in Europe.[19] Since 1659, it has separated the northern and southern sides of the Pyrenees. However, it took two centuries to establish the official international boundary with the Bayonne Treaties (signed between 1856 and 1868). The historical and geographical justification for the border was prompted by the French and Spanish emerging nation-states,[20] which imposed a new territorial paradigm on the pre-existing trans-Pyrenean dominions that did not recognize the mountain ranges as a political boundary (such as the Crown of Aragon to the east and the Kingdom of Navarre to the west). Franco's dictatorship (1939–1975) drastically reduced cross-border social and economic interactions and forbade public use of the Catalan and Basque languages in Spain. The border became highly militarized, and the national ideologies were strongly reinforced. However, the 1978 Constitution turned Spain into a democratic and decentralized state and established the Spanish Autonomous Communities (ACs).

Political stability, the new legal framework, and existing cultural and linguistic continuity across the Pyrenees were important catalysts inducing local

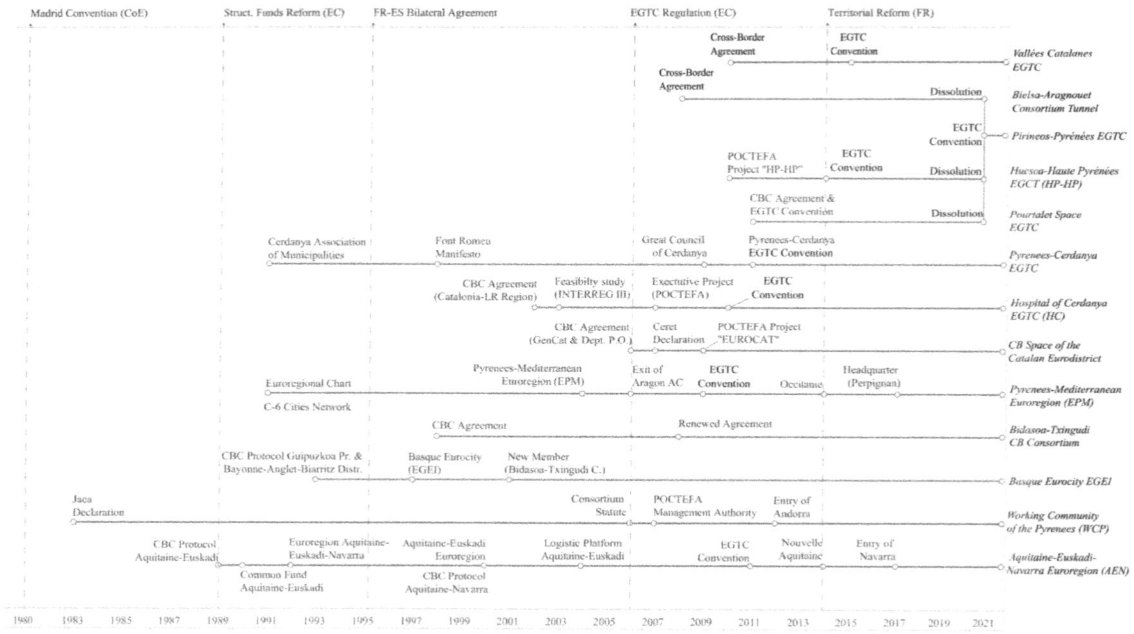

Figure 10.1. The institutionalization of cross-border cooperation across the Pyrenees

Source: Author's elaboration.

and regional CBC in the region, especially in the Basque-speaking and Catalan-speaking borderlands.[21] Currently, the entire French–Spanish border is covered by ten different but often overlapping cross-border structures. They represent great diversity in terms of geographical and chronological distribution. Figure 10.1 provides a comparative perspective on their institutionalization process, taking into account the main top-down initiatives that, since the 1980s, have directly encouraged many local and regional authorities.

The Top-Down Approach Inducing the Emergence of the Cross-Border Field

It is difficult to define the emergence of a process of cross-border institutionalization; however, one option could be the adoption of the Madrid Convention.[22] That was the first direct intervention by a European institution to promote local and regional cross-border initiatives. In 1982, the EC introduced an unprecedented juridical figure, the European Grouping of Economic Interest (EGEI), to give legal support to formal cross-border cooperation.[23] In 1983, the Working Community of the Pyrenees (WCP) emerged as a pioneering cross-border consortium (under Spanish law), and to this day it remains the only agency shared by all Pyrenean regional administrations. In 1986, Spain joined the European Economic Community, and since the 1989 reform of structural funds, its borderlands have received EU funds for regional development through the INTERREG programs. On the western side of the Pyrenees, the Aquitania–Euskadi–Navarra Euroregion (AEN) and the Basque Eurocity EGEI were established respectively in 1992 and 1993. Thus, Oliveras acknowledges myriad emerging local cross-border organizations across the Pyrenees.[24] Nonetheless, most of them have been abandoned due to a lack of economic and political support – for example, the Inter-Pyrenean Conference of Local Powers.[25] Conversely, other cases have followed a long and discontinuous process of consolidation: the C-6 City Network, for example, was promoted in 1989 by the Barcelona city council and involved Barcelona, Palma, Valencia, Zaragoza, Montpellier, and Toulouse. It was the prototype of the current Pyrenees-Mediterranean Euroregion (EPM).

The year 1995 represents a second important cornerstone, for two reasons. First, the French–Spanish Bilateral Agreement was signed to promote local and regional CBC. Second, the Schengen Agreement came into force, abolishing border controls between EU countries. The new legal framework increased the economic, social, and institutional permeability of the French–Spanish border, especially on the more urbanized Atlantic side. Within this new framework, the Bidasoa–Txingudi Cross-Border Consortium was created (1997) by the westernmost bordering municipalities of Irun (ES), Hondarribia (ES), and Hendaye (FR). By the end of the 1990s, the Atlantic side of the Pyrenees had three established cross-border institutions at various scales. However, across the central and eastern Pyrenees, the situation is quite different. In the former, cross-border interactions face constraints typical of peripheral mountain borderlands: a rural economic structure, low accessibility, high mountain ranges, and low population density. Local and regional actors are still not seriously considering CBC as an alternative and complementary field for overcoming their geographical and socio-economic disadvantages. On the eastern side, a more stable cross-border vision started to emerge at the end of the 1990s. At the regional scale, the EPM was established in 2004 among the regional governments of Catalonia, Aragon, the Balearic Islands, and the former Languedoc–Roussillon and Midi-Pyrénées. In this case, the Catalan players, particularly Pasqual Maragall (Barcelona's mayor in the 1990s and president of the Catalan government in the 2000s), promoted a cross-border vision for the central/eastern part of the Pyrenees.[26] On the local scale, the cross-border Valley of Cerdanya (a historical and geographical micro-region where the border splits the Upper Cerdanya, in France, from the Lower Cerdanya, in Spain) represents an emblematic case. The relative remoteness of the valley from the main centres of urban and economic growth, together with the presence of strong historical cross-border ties and the absence of physical impediments, generated many cross-border initiatives.[27] Local actors could consolidate CBC through INTERREG funds in fields such as natural resource management, cultural heritage, tourism, and health care assistance. This valley is also widely known in the field of border studies for hosting the first European cross-border hospital.[28] The emergence of CBC in health in Cerdanya has been analysed by Oliveras[29] and Berzi.[30] Historically, the valley's main hospital was in Puigcerdà (Lower Cerdanya), and for Upper Cerdanya's population the closest health care facility was 60 kilometres from the valley. Notwithstanding the geographical proximity, the French had "psychological barriers" toward the Spanish health care system, which was perceived to be worse than the French system, and cross-border flows to Puigcerdà's hospital were relatively scarce. However, in 1996 and 2001, adverse weather conditions cut off the Upper Cerdanya from the rest of the region. Those facts induced a change of perception. In 2001, local and regional authorities considered a shared health care facility. In 2003, the presidents of the former Languedoc–Roussillon Regional Council and the Government of Catalonia signed a cross-border agreement between the French Regional Hospitalization Agency (AR5H–LR) and the Catalan Health Service (CatSalut) as associated health partners. The feasibility study, funded in 2003 by INTERREG IIIA, led to the realization of the executive project, which later received €18 million from the European Regional Development Fund (ERDF) for the cross-border cooperation operational program France–Spain–Andorra 2007–13 (POCTEFA). The cross-border hospital is located in the border city of Puigcerdà, where it provides health care for the local population of 30,000 inhabitants and for seasonal tourists. From the beginning, the harmonization of French and Spanish legislation was the biggest challenge. The governance of the future

Table 10.1. Cross-border structures currently active (2022) along the French–Spanish border

Strategic action fields	Year	Geographical location
Working Community of the Pyrenees (WCP)	1983	Interpyrenean
New Aquitaine–Euskadi–Navarra Euroregion EGTC (AEN)	1992	Western Pyrenees
Basque Eurocity EGEI	1993	Western Pyrenees
Bidasoa–Txingudi Cross–Border Consortium	1998	Western Pyrenees
Pyrenees–Mediterranean Euroregion EGTC (EPM)	2004	Eastern Pyrenees
Cross-Border Space of the Catalan Eurodistrict (EUROCAT)	2007	Eastern Pyrenees
Hospital of Cerdanya (HC) EGTC	2010	Eastern Pyrenees
Pyrenees–Cerdanya EGTC	2011	Eastern Pyrenees
Vallées Catalanes du Tech et du Ter EGTC	2015	Eastern Pyrenees
Pirineos-Pyrénées EGTC	2020	Central Pyrenees

Source: Author's elaboration.

hospital was initially assigned to the Cross-Border Hospital of Cerdanya Foundation, though a more sophisticated legal tool was needed. In response, in 2006, the EC introduced the European Grouping of Territorial Cooperation (EGTC), an *ad hoc* juridical instrument for public authorities that responds to the frequent legal obstacles to effective cross-border governance. It has been widely implemented in the eastern and central Pyrenees (Table 10.1) and on the French–Spanish border. It is very important specifically for managing cross-border infrastructures such as the Col du Pourtalet (a mountain pass in the central Pyrenees) and the Hospital of Cerdanya, which adopted the EGTC statute in 2010.[31]

Who Are the Players? Overlapping Fields in a Fragmented Borderland

The ten cross-border governance structures involve forty-two different stakeholders – twenty-seven municipalities, five provincial administrations, seven regional councils, and three central authorities (French and Spanish states in the HC and Andorra in the WCP consortium). Almost two thirds of the partnerships are horizontal, involving the same territorial scale – that is, local consortiums, Eurodistricts (the Catalan Eurodistrict), and Euroregions. Cross-border fields at the local scale are generated in the eastern and western Pyrenees, and their strategy focuses on tackling practical and daily issues related to the local economy, especially tourism and urban development on the western side (Bidasoa–Txingudi and Basque Eurocity) and rural development on the eastern side (EGTC Vallés Catalanes du Tech et du Ter EGTC

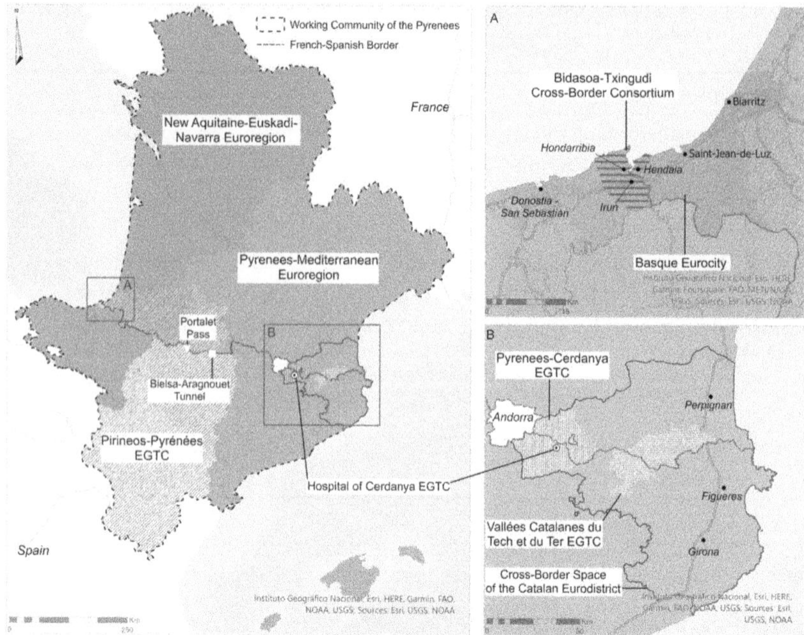

Map 10.1. Cross-border governance across the Pyrenees

Source: Author's elaboration.

and Pyrenees–Cerdanya EGTC). The French *départmentes* and the Spanish provinces are involved in two cross-border organizations (Pirineos-Pyrénées EGTC and the Catalan Eurodistrict), and their goal is to promote local economic development and stimulate local synergies to enhance cultural and natural heritage. Euroregional activity is more ambitious and has broader territorial strategies for transport integration (EAN, the Transfermuga project), economic competitiveness (EPM, the KISS ME and Links Up projects), environmental sustainability, joint R&D development, and so on.

The analysis also reveals three cases of multi-level partnerships based on two relationships. One is the Spanish provincial councils' cooperation with French local administrations in the Basque Eurocity, and the other is the Spanish AC's cooperation with French *départmentes* in the Catalan Eurodistrict and in the Pirineos-Pyrénées EGTC. The asymmetry is based on the fact that the Spanish partners possess the greater political and economic competences than the French partners with regard to mobilizing institutional, financial, and technical support.

The distribution of cross-border structures (map 10.1) reveals two characteristics of the French–Spanish borderland. First, it is highly fragmented because except for the WCP, it lacks transversal cross-border structures. This is a peculiarity of the French–Spanish border, which differs from other European borderlands, where shared networking, collaboration, and transversal joint actions exist. Along the Alpine region, for example, transversal networks of municipalities (Alliance in the Alps) and the network of natural protected areas (AlpParks) exchange information for joint action to implement the Alpine Convention – an international agreement signed in 1995 by the eight alpine countries to promote the sustainable development of the mountain area.[32] Similarly, the Spanish–Portuguese border acknowledges the Iberian Network of Cross-Border Entities (RIET), which promotes a common space of discussion for the development of the border regions. Among Central European borders, the six Czech–Polish Euroregions have developed a joint platform for collaboration, workshops, and information exchanges regarding governance and common awareness.[33]

Regional Incumbents versus State Challengers

Oliveras and colleagues (2010), define a CBC as a more or less institutionalized collaboration between contiguous sub-national authorities across national borders.[34] Its higher expression is reflected in the creation of cooperation-based organizations, which are in turn oriented toward the coordination of horizontal and vertical policies and joint actions. The local and regional players are therefore the main incumbents, which tend to stabilize their cross-border organization by improving the internal governance structure. With the exception of the Hospital of Cerdanya, which required an *ad hoc* multi-level governance body, the central states are not directly involved in the partnerships. The central government's primary role consists in promoting a favourable political environment by providing juridical and financial aid – for example, by crafting bilateral agreements and ensuring EU policy implementation. At times, though, it may also act like a challenger, impeding cross-border institutionalization and destabilizing the field. We provide two bits of empirical evidence. The first involves the Catalan Eurodistrict. Since its creation in 2007, the European Grouping of Territorial Cooperation (EGTC) has yet to be ratified by the French state. This has triggered a crisis (see next section) that has heavily destabilized the field and the cross-border partnership.[35] The second case involves administrative and legal complications in the governance of the Hospital of Cerdanya. That health care facility opened in September 2014 and achieved remarkable results in terms of medical treatment for residents on both sides of the border.[36] Nonetheless, three particular episodes underscore the challenges of central state intervention. First, in August 2014 the Spanish sub-delegation in Girona pointed out the "accidental" absence of Spanish translations on the hospital signage, which had been posted only in French and Catalan. In response, the state imposed the inclusion of Spanish; this was approved by the HC Advisory Board, with further costs. Second, the French administration raises legal obstacles for French users because the cross-border hospital is located on the Spanish side, in the city of Puigcerdà, and thus falls under Spanish law. Under French law, those who are born in the HC are automatically recognized as foreign-born French citizens, even though the hospital is just a few hundred metres from the border. Similar impediments apply to the repatriation of patients who have died, which requires complicated paperwork. François Calvet, the former French senator for northern Cerdanya, raised these legal difficulties with the French president. The issues were resolved in February 2017 during the French–Spanish summit in Málaga through a bilateral technical agreement that gives the HC stronger administrative authority. Third, an official public ceremony to inaugurate this ambitious and unique project of cross-border cooperation has still not been organized by state authorities.

European institutions, especially the European Commission (EC), influence local, regional, and national agendas through financial and legal initiatives to strengthen cross-border interaction. The impact of the EC has been noticeable. The INTERREG program has generated more than 700 cross-border projects along the French–Spanish border since the 1990s, involving a large number of local and regional actors.[37] Since 2007, the Working Community of the Pyrenees has been recognized as the management authority of the POCTEFA and has been placed in charge of its implementation and assessment. It is the only agency that gathers together *all* the Pyrenean regional administrations, and since 2012 it has also included the Andorran government. Currently, it is promoting joint environmental research projects through the Pyrenees Climate Change Observatory, created in 2010.

Also, the EC has reinforced European cross-border governance through the aforementioned legal instruments. Specifically, the EGTC regulation provides a flexible model of governance led by a director and an assembly; this can eventually be improved through other institutional bodies "with clearly defined powers,"[38] such as a presidency (implemented in all six EGTC structures), an executive committee, or a technical and scientific committee (just for the AEN, EPM, and the Vallées Catalanes du Tech et du Ter EGTC). Along the French–Spanish border, the EU's juridical instruments have been adopted in 70 per cent of the cases – that is, in one EGEI and six EGTCs. We can therefore argue that the EU institutions are succeeding in influencing local and regional cross-border governance in the Pyrenees.

The governance of the Hospital of Cerdanya EGTC requires a little more discussion here. There are no other instances, at least not in Europe, of a cross-border hospital shared by two countries. Thus, HC represents a pioneering experiment in cross-border multi-level governance. The Catalan and French authorities put up respectively 60 per cent and 40 per cent of the financial resources for the construction of the hospital. This division is reflected in the distribution of Spanish and French members on its governance units: the board of directors, the advisory board, the executive committee, and the management team. The EGTC is headed by a president and a vice-president, with biannual rotation between the Catalan and French governments. Local stakeholders are on the advisory board, but among the local administrators the municipality of Puigcerdà is the most influential because it hosts the health care facility and claims specific interests, such as urban development (the hospital represents a driving force for the future urbanization of the surrounding rural area and for the local real estate market). Regarding horizontal governance, the Hospital of Cerdanya aims to implement a cross-border health care district in Cerdanya in which the HC will have a clear leading role in promoting territorial synergies and networking public and private medical stakeholders (maternity, nephrology, dialysis, and geriatrics). Collaboration among the universities of Girona, Perpignan, Barcelona, and Toulouse is promoting research and specialization in mountain medicine (research, practice for medical students, seminars, etc.).

Internal versus External Episodes of Crisis

The evolution of the cross-border SAF along the French–Spanish border has been shaped by several crises. Two main types of crises can positively or negatively affect the evolution of cross-border organizations. The first type is internal and can result from partners' interactions that affect field governance. This can happen when there is a change in partnership, such as the entry or the exit of a player for largely political or financial reasons. The second type is external, an example being state intervention that directly or indirectly alters the stability of the field. Two examples for each type are provided here. In 2006, the government of the Aragon AC left the EPM as a consequence of an unsolved political dispute with the Catalan government regarding the ownership of artworks belonging to the Catalan-speaking area in Aragon bordering Catalonia (*La Franja*). Although both regional governments at the time were headed by socialists (PSOE-Aragón and PSC in Catalonia), the Aragon partner left the EPM and suspended relations with the Catalan government. This crisis generated another emerging field on the Atlantic side: in 2011, the Pourtalet Space EGTC was created between the Aragon government and the French *départmente* of the Atlantic Pyrenees to manage the Pourtalet mountain pass (reconverting France's customs building) and to enhance mountain economy and culture. In 2015, during a meeting in Barcelona, the Aragon and Catalan governments expressed their interest in reconciliation. The then president of the Aragon AC stated that it would join the EMP again once the conflict was solved. A similar dynamic arose in the Aquitania–Euskadi–Navarra Euroregion. In Navarre, the right-wing coalition espousing Spanish nationalism won the 2000 elections, defeating the former pro-Basque majority. As a consequence, the new government left the Euroregion and started a parallel CBC with the Aquitaine region by implementing a common fund for cross-border projects (see chapter 14). Then in the 2017 elections, the left-wing and pro-Basque political coalition came back into power as Navarre's government, and the region promptly rejoined the Euroregion.

The external crises have been created mainly by the Spanish and French states. The support of the central authorities is essential to cross-border cooperation. The analysis indicates that state intervention affects the stability of fields both directly and indirectly. An example of direct effects concerns the ratification of the cross-border partnership in the Catalan Eurodistrict. The implementation of the EGTC is being impeded by the French state, which has yet to ratify the agreement signed in 2008 by the local partners and the Spanish state. As a consequence, and due to an economic crisis, many local institutions such as the Catalan county councils (*consells comarcals*) have left the Eurodistrict's consortium. To this day, this cross-border field has yet to implement a proper governance unit, and its consolidation is far from complete. It is conceived as a political agreement between the Catalan government and the French *départmente* of the Eastern Pyrenees, which provides small-project funds for local initiatives. It seems that this episode has led directly to the non-evolution of the field and the stalling of the partnership. However, direct intervention by the central state can also generate positive effects when cross-border structures are being resettled. The French–Spanish Summit held in Málaga in March 2017 is an interesting example. On that occasion, the two national governments jointly announced a specific intervention to promote cross-border cooperation in the field of health care assistance regarding the functioning of the Hospital of Cerdanya (the technical agreement, under which the repatriation of the deceased falls – see above). Similarly, in the field of transportation, the decision was made to prioritize the construction of the Mediterranean and Atlantic railway corridors. This decision hampered the development of the central Pyrenean corridor, which generated a new conflict between the economic and institutional stakeholders of Aragon AC, on one hand, and the Catalan and Basque stakeholders, on the other. The trans-Pyrenean infrastructure is an ambitious project that requires a broader scale of analysis (see the following section). Indirect interventions occurred through a French territorial reform (*loi NOTRe du 7 août 2015*) that reduced the number of French regions from twenty-one to thirteen. As a consequence, there are now just two French regions bordering Spain: the New Aquitaine Region includes the former regions of Limousin and Poitou-Charentes, and the Occitanie Region has merged the former regions of Languedoc–Roussillon and Midi-Pyrénées. Even if the French reform represents a top-down intervention creating a recentralization process and thereby reducing regional competences,[39] it does not represent an impediment to regional cross-border cooperation.[40] Indeed, one could argue that the French state's indirect intervention in cross-border cooperation *strengthened* the role of the French stakeholders within the Euroregions. The EPM has moved its headquarters from Barcelona to Perpignan, in the Eastern Pyrenees *département*. According to the stakeholders we interviewed, this intervention can be viewed as a compromise with the Catalan partners toward a new Euroregional phase.

The European Transport Corridor as the Broader Field Environment

Within Fligstein and McAdam's theoretical framework, SAFs are embedded in a complex web of other fields.[41] This means there is a broader environment in which the fields interact with one another along two dimensions. The first one is the *approximate* distance, which is based on the intensity of the relations among fields. In the French–Spanish borderlands, a broader environment is created when two or more cross-border agencies participate in the same governance structure or in the implementation of a joint cross-border project. Within this framework, two overlapping areas have been identified. First, there is a broader Basque cooperation field, and specifically the cooperation between the Basque Eurocity and the Bidasoa–Txingudi Consortium, where the latter is a member of the former. Both of them are located within the wider space of the New Aquitaine–Euskadi–Navarra Euroregion, whose 2014–20 strategy claims to seek more effective, multi-level cross-border governance with two local cross-border structures.[42] Second, there is the Cerdanya Valley, within which a high level of interaction has been generated between the Hospital of Cerdanya EGTC and the Pyrenees–Cerdanya EGTC. Formally, HC's governance structure involves the Cerdanya local administration (which constitutes the Pyrenees–Cerdanya EGTC). This synergy is promoting the implementation of the cross-border health care district. It also generates local economic development.[43] In this scenario, the Catalan Eurodistrict plays an important role in financing small health-related projects. The EPM, despite specific research projects (eHealth Eurocampus), is not deeply involved in this CBC network – its strategies focus mainly on other sectoral policies on a wider geographical scale.

The second dimension of interaction is based on the direction of influence that characterizes the relationships between fields. Across the Pyrenees, the WCP's key role relates to the management of INTERREG funds. This creates a vertical "financial" dependence viv-à-vis the local actors for which the WCP acts as the incumbent. Again, few horizontal networks among the three cross-border sectors (western–central–eastern) have been found. Recent developments in the central Pyrenees led to the unification of three pre-existent fields (HP-HP EGTC, the Portalet EGTC, and the Bielsa–Aragnouet Consortium Tunnel) under the Pirineos-Pyrénées EGTC.[44] At the eastern end of the Pyrenees, EPM is still weakly networked with the other cross-border fields. As with the situation with proximate distance, important differences in aims of cooperation exist. The Hospital of Cerdanya serves as the core of the eastern Pyrenees cross-border network among the EPM health care initiatives, the Catalan Eurodistrict, and the Pirineus–Cerdanya EGTC.

Another consideration is the broader areas of cooperation that go beyond the local or regional scale, such as in the transportation sector.[45] The French–Spanish borderlands are viewed as crucial to the Trans-European Transport Network Policy (TEN-T). The EC has identified the Atlantic and Mediterranean sectors as priority corridors for the economic competitiveness of the entire EU.[46] The former connects the Atlantic ports of Portugal (Porto and Lisbon) and Spain (Algeciras and Bilbao) with the French port of Le Havre and the cities of Strasbourg and Mannheim (Germany). The international connection between Irun (ES) and Hendaye (FR) is still a railway bottleneck. The latter corridor links the western Mediterranean ports and urban nodes (mainly Algeciras, Cartagena, Valencia, Barcelona, and Marseille) with Italy and Eastern Europe (currently reaching the Hungarian–Ukrainian border). It has had better cross-border connections since the high-speed line Barcelona–Perpignan was inaugurated in 2013. In both cases, the AEN and the EPM Euroregions have folded the development of transportation into their priorities.[47] In fact, the EAN implements specific cross-border actions (such as the Transfermuga Project, financed by INTERREG). EPM simply mentions transportation as a primary issue, with no mention of specific projects. Nonetheless, there are still significant obstacles that slow the realization of these projects. On one hand, there are technical problems due to the difference between the Iberian gauge (1668 mm) and the international one (1435 mm).[48] On the other hand, geopolitical conflicts arise in the Spanish political arena. Indeed, a third corridor does exist, the Central Pyrenean Corridor, which would connect Madrid with Zaragoza and the French cities of Pau and Toulouse through the international train station of Canfranc, built in 1928. The line was active until 1970, when a train accident cut the cross-border connection. Since 2000, the Aragon government has wanted to reactivate the railway, and in 2003 it endorsed the Trans-Pyrenean Foundation, which involves the main economic, administrative, and political Aragon stakeholders. The aim was to promote the Central Corridor as a viable cross-border mode of transport between the Iberian Peninsula and the rest of Europe. Thanks to the support and lobbying activities of the right-wing Spanish government, the Central Corridor was included in the TEN-T Strategy and the coastal path of the Mediterranean Corridor was removed.[49] Lobbyists for the Atlantic and Mediterranean Corridors were not pleased about this. In the 2011 revision of the TEN-T Strategy, the Central Corridor option was excluded because of technical, financial, environmental, and organizational difficulties, and specifically because of the lack of cross-border-cooperation.[50] Instead, the Mediterranean corridor was restored. This decision was confirmed during the 2017 French–Spanish Summit, when both governments agreed to finance specific actions to speed up the implementation of both coastal corridors. Nonetheless, geopolitical instability in Catalonia brought Aragon's actors to propose the Central Corridor again as a feasible option in public opinion. A realistic long-term approach, shared by EU institutions,[51] would involve reactivating the Pau–Canfranc missing link, but only for local and tourist activities.[52]

Discussion and Conclusion

The application of the theory of fields to the French–Spanish border region uncovered the complexity and multifaceted dimension of increasing activity in cross-border governance in the region. Since the 1980s, local and regional agents have developed several forms of cross-border structures on different scales (Eurocities, Eurodistricts, Euroregions) and pursued different aims (from targeted objectives to wider territorial strategies). Their distribution follows three easily detectable north/south axes of cooperation: the western Pyrenees, which encapsulated several well-structured cross-border agencies; the central Pyrenees, a zone of cooperation that has been established fairly recently; and the eastern Pyrenees, where the most emblematic case of the European CBC is located, the Hospital of Cerdanya. The Working Community of the Pyrenees represents the only cross-border agency covering the entire borderlands, and it is involved in the management of the POCTEFA program. Cross-border governance results are highly fragmented, confirming the findings of Morata and Noferini.[53] Some CBC best practices from elsewhere in Europe that have been briefly highlighted, such as the Alpine region, the Spanish–Portuguese borderlands, and the Czech–Polish borderlands, could be implemented along the French–Spanish border to improve networking between the cross-border agencies. We slightly disagree with Sanguin, who defines local and regional cross-border governance structures along the French–Spanish border as redundant, chaotic, and "oversized."[54] The diversity and large number of players involved in local and regional cross-border partnerships reveal that cross-border governance represents a valid territorial strategy. Indeed, each agency provides a specific scope according to the geographical location and territorial scale.

The contribution of the theory of fields analytical framework has been twofold. First, its application has allowed us to systematically comprehend and compare the cross-border initiatives in the entire study area as well as to identify similar patterns of cross-border governance units (such as the EGTC), the common cornerstone and a characteristic of the broader field environment, with a specific focus on the transportation infrastructures. Second, the theory is a suitable instrument to understand a single SAF's internal logic through the analysis of incumbents and challengers. While the European institutions have succeeded in influencing local and regional territorial governance in the Pyrenees, the French and the Spanish states' actions are much more ambivalent.

Sometimes they challenge the existence of the field (as with the lack of French state support for the Catalan Eurodistrict), and other times they cooperate to facilitate local and regional CBC (as in the case of the 1995 bilateral agreement) and to resolve specific legal and technical impediments for cross-border integration (as in the 2017 French–Spanish Summit in Málaga). We argue that the French–Spanish border represents the complexity of current EU cross-border cooperation. But further research is needed to understand the perspective of cross-border regional governance in light of urgent political and socio-economic issues. The COVID-19 pandemic led to an unprecedented suspension of the Schengen regime in the EU's history. Border regions faced an unexpected situation of hard rebordering in which cross-border flows of people and goods were drastically truncated. The temporary closing of borders negatively affected the EU's CBC in the short and medium term. However, local and regional agents seem to be quite resilient thanks to the specific CBC know-how developed in recent decades: joint projects, *ad hoc* governance structures, and shared infrastructures, services, and facilities have all increased mutual trust to overcome border obstacles – and all are supported by the EU's legal and financial tools. In some cases, new shared cross-border human capital has emerged, as with the Hospital of Cerdanya.[55] In this theoretical context, the COVID-19 pandemic represents an unprecedented crisis that may in the end boost cross-border cooperation and even untangle pre-existing border obstacles in the long term. Even the recent trends toward rebordering, spurred by waves of nationalism and populism in Europe, have not interrupted these processes of bottom-up cross-border integration. In this sense, following the path already traced by other scholars,[56] the theory of fields represents a potential analytical framework for fostering comparative analysis with other European borderlands and between the EU and North American cross-border dynamics.

NOTES

1 Neil Fligstein and Doug McAdam, *A Theory of Fields* (New York: Oxford University Press, 2012), http://doi.org/10.1007/s11186-014-9237-0.

2 J.E. Mendoza and B. Dupeyron, "Economic Integration, Emerging Fields, and Cross-Border Governance: The Case of San Diego–Tijuana," *Journal of Borderlands Studies* 25, no. 5 (2017): 59–88.

3 F. Letamendia, A. Borja, and K. Sodupe Corcuera, *La construcción del espacio vasco-aquitano: [un estudio multidisciplinar]: Jornadas Euskadi-Aquitania, Bilbao, 13–15 de noviembre, 1997* (Bilbao: Universidad del País Vasco/Euskal Herriko Unibertsitatea, Servicio de Publicaciones, 1998); J. Häkli, "Governing the Mountains: Cross-Border Regionalization in Catalonia," in *Cross-Border Governance in the European Union*, ED. O. Kramsch and B. Hooper (London:

Routledge, 2004), 56–69, https://trepo.tuni.fi/bitstream/handle/10024/66149/governing_the_mountains_2004.pdf?sequence=1; A.-L. Sanguin, "Euroregions and Other EU's Cross-Border Organizations: The Risk of Confusion, Redundancy, Oversizing, and Entropy:. A Critical Assessment," *Annales, Series Historia et Sociologia* 23, no. 1 (2013), http://zdjp.si/wp-content/uploads/2016/05/sanguin.pdf; Francesc Morata and Andrea Noferini, "Gobernanza y capacidades institucionales en la frontera pirenaica," Institut de Ciències Polítiques i Socials (Barcelona, 2014), http://www.recercat.cat/handle/2072/243262; M. Berzi and A. Durà, "Le reti transfrontaliere locali nelle aree di confine montane. Analisi dei casi della Wipptal e della Cerdanya," *Archivio di Studi Urbani e Regionali* 121, no. 3 (2018): 73–95, https://doi.org/10.3280/ASUR2018-121004; A. Durà, M. Berzi, and A. Noferini, "Coopération transfrontalière dans l'aire du programme européen SUDOE: un bilan," in *Régions en tension, régions en recomposition. Sud-Ouest Européen*, ed. T. Perrin and F. Syes, no. 48 (2019): 85–98.

4 Sanguin, "Euroregions and Other EU's Cross-Border Organizations," 159.

5 Morata and Noferni, "Gobernanza y capacidades institucionales."

6 J.B. Harguindéguy and A. Sánchez Sánchez, "European Cross-Border Regions as Policy-Makers: A Comparative Approach," *Journal of Borderlands Studies* 32, no. 2 (2017): 249–65, http://doi.org/10.1080/08865655.2016.1195706; Michaela Trippl, "Developing Cross-Border Regional Innovation Systems: Key Factors and Challenges," *Tijdschrift voor Economische en Sociale Geografie* 101, no. 2 (2010): 150–60; M. Perkmann, "Cross-Border Regions in Europe," *European Urban and Regional Studies* 10, no. 2 (2003): 153–71, http://doi.org/10.1177/0969776403010002004.

7 J. Blatter, "From 'Spaces of Place' to 'Spaces of Flows'? Territorial and Functional Governance in Cross-Border Regions in Europe and North America," *International Journal of Regions in Europe and North America* 28, no. 3 (2004): 530–48, https://onlinelibrary.wiley.com/doi/10.1111/j.0309-1317.2004.00534.x.

8 M. Berzi, "The Cross-Border Reterritorialization Concept Revisited: The Territorialist Approach Applied to the Case of Cerdanya on the French–Spanish Border," *European Planning Studies* (2017): 1–22, http://doi.org/10.1080/09654313.2017.1321622.

9 O. Löfgren, "Regionauts: The Transformation of Cross-Border Regions in Scandinavia," *European Urban and Regional Studies* 15, no. 3 (2008): 195–209, http://doi.org/10.1177/0969776408090418; Nathalie Christmann, Martine Mostert, Pierre-François Wilmotte, Jean-Marc Lambotte, and Mario Cools, "Opportunities for Reinforcing Cross-Border Railway Connections: The Case of the Liège (Belgium)–Maastricht (the Netherlands) Connection," *European Planning Studies* 28, no. 1 (2020): 105–24, https://doi.org/10.1080/09654313.2019.1623976.

10 K. Footman, C. Knai, R. Baeten, K. Glonti, and M. Mckee, "Cross-Border Health Care in Europe" (2014), https://www.euro.who.int/__data/assets/pdf_file/0009/263538/Cross-border-health-care-in-Europe-Eng.pdf.

11 K.J. Lundquist and M. Trippl, "Distance, Proximity, and Types of Cross-Border Innovation Systems: A Conceptual Analysis," *Regional Studies* 47, no. 3 (2013): 450–60, http://doi.org/10.1080/00343404.2011.560933; F. Cappellano and T. Makkonen, "Cross-Border Regional Innovation Ecosystems: The Role of Non-Profit Organizations in Cross-Border Cooperation at the US–Mexico Border," *GeoJournal* (2019): 1–14.

12 A. Paasi and E.-K. Prokkola, "Territorial Dynamics, Cross-Border Work, and Everyday Life in the Finnish–Swedish Border Area," *Space and Polity* 12, no. 1 (2008): 13–29, http://doi.org/10.1080/13562570801969366.

13 Harguindéguy and Sánchez Sánchez, "European Cross-Border Regions as Policy-Maker"; Perkmann, "Cross-Border Regions in Europe"; J.W. Scott, "European Politics of Borders, Border Symbolism, and Cross-Border Cooperation," in *A Companion to Border Studies* (Chichester: John Wiley and Sons, 2012), 83–99, http://doi.org/10.1002/9781118255223.ch5.

14 Fligstein and McAdam, *A Theory of Fields.*

15 Fligstein and McAdam, *A Theory of Fields*, 165–7.

16 Morata and Noferini, "Gobernanza y capacidades institucionales."

17 M. Berzi and M. Castañer, "Los Pirineos entre las políticas europeas y las iniciativas locales de cooperación transfronteriza: El caso de la Cerdaña," *Documents d'Analisi Geografic* 64, no. 3 (2018): 529–50; Morata and Noferini, "Gobernanza y capacidades institucionales"; X. Oliveras, "La cooperación transfronteriza en la Cerdanya (frontera España-Francia)," *Boletín de La Asociación de Geógrafos Españoles* 62 (2013): 25–48; Durà, Berzi, and Noferini, "Coopération transfrontalière."

18 Morata and Noferini, "Gobernanza y capacidades institucionales"; Sanguin, "Euroregions and other EU's cross-border organizations."

19 P. Sahlins, *Boundaries: The making of France and Spain in the Pyrenees* (Berkeley: University of California Press, 1989).

20 Sahlins, *Boundaries.*

21 J.M. Beck, "Has the Basque Borderland Become More Basque after Opening the Franco-Spanish Border?," *National Identities* 10, no. 4 (2008): 373–88, http://doi.org/10.1080/14608940802518914; and Häkli, "Governing the Mountains."

22 Council of Europe (CoE), "European Outline Convention on Transfrontier Co-operation between Territorial Communities or Authorities," European Treaty Series no. 106 (Madrid, 1980), https://www.coe.int/en/web/conventions/full-list/-/conventions/rms/0900001680078b0c.

23 It goes beyond mere cross-border cooperation; it is used in the wider European public and private partnership. It acknowledges, among other things, the French–German television network ARTE.

24 X. Oliveras, *La Construcció metageogràfica de l'arc mediterrani* (Barcelona: Universitat Autònoma de Barcelona, 2009), https://ddd.uab.cat/record/63887.

25 J. Martín-Uceda, "Europa en l'horitzó: Barcelona i Catalunya en l'articulació i la construcció europea. Les relacions transfrontereres en el pensament i acció de

govern de Pasqual Maragall," working paper no. 5 (Fundació Catalunya Europa, 2018), https://www.catalunyaeuropa.net/ca/publicacions/65/europa-en-l-horitz%C3%B3-barcelona-i-catalunya-en-l-articulaci%C3%B3-i-la-construcci%C3%B3-europea.html.

26 Martín-Uceda, "Europa en l'horitzó."

27 Oliveras, "La cooperación transfronteriza en la Cerdanya"; Berzi, "The Cross-Border Reterritorialization Concept Revisited."

28 M. Berzi and A. Durà, "La coopération transfrontalière en matière sanitaire dans l'UE à travers le cas emblématique de l'Hôpital de Cerdagne (Pyrénées)," in *Maillages et interfaces, les enjeux territoriaux de la santé*, ed. F. Moullé and B. Reitel (Bordeaux: Presses Universitaires de Bordeaux, 2021), 79-96, http://dx.doi.org/10.46608/santencontextes1.9791030008067.7.

29 Oliveras, "La cooperación transfronteriza en la Cerdanya."

30 Berzi, "The Cross-Border Reterritorialization Concept Revisited."

31 Hôpital de Cerdagne, *Convention de coopération sanitaire transfrontalière et de constitution du Groupement Européen de Coopération Territoriale (GECT)* (Spain, 2010), http://sac.gencat.cat/sacgencat/AppJava/organisme_fitxa.jsp?codi=18905.

32 Berzi and Durà, "Le reti transfrontaliere locali. »

33 See www.euregions.org.

34 X. Oliveras, A. Durà, and M. Perkmann, "Las regiones transfronterizas: balance de la regionalización de la cooperación transfronteriza en Europa (1958–2007)," *Documents d'anàlisi geogràfica* 56, no. 1 (2010): 21–40.

35 M. Castañer and J. Feliu, "L'eurodistricte català transfronterer. Un espai emergent sense marc administratiu Margarida castañer," *Treballs de La Societat Catalana de Geografia* 74 (2012): 41–58, http://doi.org/10.2436/20.3002.01.12.

36 Berzi and Durà, "La coopération transfrontalière."

37 Jaume Feliu, Matteo Berzi, Javier Martín-Uceda, Roser Pastor Saberi, and Margarita Castañer i Vivas, "Cuatro fronteras europeas bajo la lupa. Una metodología para el análisis de los proyectos de cooperación transfronteriza (INTERREG)," *Documents d'Anàlisi Geogràfica* 64, no. 3 (2018).

38 European Grouping of Territorial Cooperation (EGTC), (Art. 10).

39 A. Brennetot, "A Step Further towards a Neoliberal Regionalism: Creating Larger Regions in Contemporary France," *European Urban and Regional Studies* (2017), http://doi.org/10.1177/0969776417693884.

40 J. Boudry, *Information. Nouvelles régions françaises et réforme territoriale: quels effet sur la coopération transfrontalière?* (Paris, 2017), http://www.espaces-transfrontaliers.org/fileadmin/user_upload/documents/Documents_MOT/Communiques_Presentations/Note_Nouvelles_regions_francaises_reforme_territoriale.pdf.

41 Fligstein and McAdam, *A Theory of Fields*, 18.

42 AECT Eurorregión Aquitania-Euskadi, *Plan Estratégico* (2014), http://www.naen.eu/wp-content/uploads/2016/05/plan_es.pdf.
43 Berzi, "The Cross-Border Reterritorialization Concept Revisited."
44 CoR - Pirineos Pyrénées EGTC (europa.eu).
45 E. Medeiros, R. Ferreira, R. Boijmans et al., "Boosting Cross-Border Regions through Better Cross-Border Transport Services: The European Case," *Case Studies on Transport Policy* 9, no. 1 (2021): 291–301, https://doi.org/10.1016/j.cstp.2021.01.006.
46 European Commission, *Atlantic Core Network Corridor Study* (Brussels, 2014), https://ec.europa.eu/transport/sites/transport/files/atlantic_study_0.pdf; EC, *Mediterranean Core Network Corridor Study* (Brussels, 2014), https://ec.europa.eu/transport/sites/transport/files/mediterranean_study_0.pdf.
47 AECT Eurorregión Aquitania-Euskadi, *Plan Estratégico* (2014); CoR, "L'Eurorégion Pyrénées-Méditerranée demande à Bruxelles de prioriser le Corridor méditerranéen" (2012), http://cor.europa.eu/en/news/highlights/Pages/Euroregion-pyrenees-mediterranee-demande-a-bruxelles-de-prioriser-le-corridor-mediterraneen.aspx.
48 J. Martí-Henneberg, "European Integration and National Models for Railway Networks (1840–2010)," *Journal of Transport Geography* 26 (2013): 126–38, http://doi.org/10.1016/j.jtrangeo.2012.09.004; M. Berzi, "Optimising Cross-Border Regions Impact of theTEN-T Corridors," presentation at the Conference "Boosting Cross-Border Regions through Better Transports!," organized by the EC (DG Regio, DG Move (November, 2019), https://eu.eventscloud.com/file_uploads/a110df9adfa05fe448ad2836a56d986c_1_Optimisingcross-borderregionsimpactoftheTEN-Tcorridors_MatteoBerzi.pdf.
49 Project 16 freight railway axis Sines/Algeciras–Madrid–Paris.
50 TEN-T Executive Agency, "Freight Railway Axis Sines–Madrid–Paris: New High-Capacity Line through the Pyrenees. 2007-EU-16010-S. Part of Priority Project 16" (2007), https://ec.europa.eu/inea/sites/inea/files/download/map_review/ppbundles/pp16.pdf.
51 Directorate-General for Mobility and Transport of the European Commission (DGMOVE, 2018).
52 European Commission, "Comprehensive Analysis of the Existing Cross-Border Rail Transport Connections and Missing Links on the Internal EU Borders: Final Report" (2018), https://ec.europa.eu/regional_policy/en/information/publications/reports/2018/comprehensive-analysis-of-the-existing-cross-border-rail-transport-connections-and-missing-links-on-the-internal-eu-borders.
53 Morata and Noferini, "Gobernanza y capacidades institucionales."
54 Sanguin, "Euroregions and Other EU's Cross-Border Organizations."
55 Berzi, "The Cross-Border Reterritorialization Concept Revisited."
56 J.W. Scott, "European and North American Contexts for Cross-Border Regionalism," *Regional Studies* 33, no. 7 (1999): 605–17, http://doi.org/10.1080/00343409950078657;

J. Blatter and N. Clement, "Cross-Border Cooperation in Europe: Historical Development, Institutionalization, and Contrasts with North America. II: Introduction to the Volume," *Journal of Borderlands Studies* 15, no. 1 (2000): 14–53, http://doi.org/10.1080/08865655.2000.9695541; J. Blatter, "Debordering the World of States: Towards a Multi-level System in Europe and a Multi-polity System in North America? Insights from Border Regions," *European Journal of International Relations* 7, no. 2 (2001): 175–209, http://doi.org/10.1177/1354066101007002002; Cappellano and Makkonen, "Cross-Border Regional Innovation Ecosystems."

11 Cultural Policy within Euroregions: Dynamics of a Cross-Border Sectoral Field

THOMAS PERRIN

Culture is a recurrent field of action among the European cross-border cooperative organizations commonly known as "Euroregions." Euroregions can have different proper names: Euregio, Europaregion, Grande Région, Regio, and so on.[1] Due to the intrinsic polysemy of the term "culture," the notion of cultural policy – and consequently of cross-border or Euroregional cultural policy – encompasses a wide range of actions and projects in various domains. It is nevertheless possible to circumscribe cultural policy to some of the most frequently recognized domains of intervention, from the core artistic fields to the whole chain of cultural and creative activities and industries, such as the arts, literature and linguistic projects, media and communications, and educational and socio-cultural projects. ESSnet-Culture, the European statistical system network on culture, identifies ten cultural domains: heritage, archives, libraries, books and press, visual arts, performing arts, audiovisual and multimedia, architecture, advertising, and arts and crafts.[2]

A study on cross-border cultural cooperation in France reports that cultural projects represented 17 per cent of the budget and 15 per cent of the projects within EU cross-border INTERREG programs between 2000 and 2006.[3] To put this in perspective, 1 per cent of a state's budget allotted to culture is generally considered to be a good share. On a broader scale, a study commissioned by the European Commission (EC) estimated that cultural projects represent €6 billion within the entire EU regional policy budget for 2007–13 and 1.7 per cent of the funds allocated to this policy.[4] Another study by the European Spatial Planning Observation Network[5] shows that culture and tourism rank first among the domains of territorial cooperation; those domains include all forms of cooperation between sub-state authorities, including cross-border and non-contiguous cooperation, such as networks of sister cities. Another indicator of culture's place in cross-border cooperation is the fact that, among the five task forces set up by the Association of European Border Regions to deal with specific cross-border issues and challenges, one is dedicated to culture.[6] Clearly, culture occupies a remarkable place in cross-border cooperation. Thus, a form of cross-border cultural policy has emerged paralleling the development of Euroregions, creating a Euroregional cultural policy.[7]

This chapter addresses Euroregional cultural policy as a strategic action field encompassing various stakeholders, structures, and phases of development, reflecting the concepts advanced by Fligstein and McAdam.[8] Documentary and bibliographic sources include the work of researchers and specialists in the subject. Field data were collected during PhD research from 2006 to 2010[9] and from various postdoctoral research projects from 2011 to 2018, all conducted at the Universitat Autònoma de Barcelona and the University of Lille.[10] The data include the following: some forty-five semi-structured interviews with cultural stakeholders and political and administrative bodies concerned with the implementation of Euroregional cultural policies, as well as with experts and academics; quantitative data from questionnaires sent to beneficiaries of support schemes for cultural and artistic initiatives in the Eurorégion Pyrénées-Méditerranée; active observation and follow-up of various Euroregional cultural events and projects, in a mid-term scale perspective (2006–2018); and ongoing collection and analysis of administrative documentation and literature related to the field being analysed.

This chapter's first section presents the field of action. It introduces the realm of Euroregional cultural policy and its place in the study of cross-border governance, presenting the cultural policies developed within the framework of two Euroregions in particular: the Eurorégion Pyrénées-Méditerranée and the Grande Région. The next section interprets the field of action. It approaches Euroregional cultural policy as a sub-SAF of cross-border governance and discusses the emergence and stabilization of this field, with its opportunities, limits, and perspectives. Each of these phases implies different stakeholders at different levels. It also provides a specific view of the analytical potential of the theory of fields when applied to cross-border structures and processes.

Presentation of the Field: Culture, Cross-Border Cooperation, and Euroregions

European cross-border cooperation and governance has been well-documented and analysed, due especially to the development of border studies,[11] complemented by additional approaches and works in different fields.[12] Cross-border cultural cooperation, however, has been less scrutinized as a proper and specific domain of cross-border cooperation, even though some works address it more specifically.[13] It is interesting to grasp the peculiarities of a single policy sector within the entire field of cross-border cooperation, and in this regard, cultural policy presents a particularly interesting case.

Cultural policies play an important role in the narrative and symbolic construction of any sociopolitical organization, *a fortiori* when it comes to emerging and "low capacity" institutions such as Euroregions and other cross-border institutions. Cultural policies, because of their symbolic and representational dimensions, can deliver "meta-geographical" references about territory(ies) coterminous with a specific formal authority and contribute to legitimating identity-building and institutional marketing in a specific polity, be it the nation-state, a region, or another territorially delineated institutional space.[14] In other words, "artistic work is strong enough not only to renew the perspectives of landscape perception but also imbue it with a strong capacity for political influence."[15] Also, Euroregional cultural policy constitutes a policy domain *per se*, with instruments, stakeholders, and procedures that vary from other sectors of cross-border cooperation. Cultural cooperation gives way to a specific form of cross-border cultural governance. Thus, cultural policy forms both a political representational instrument and a cross-border policy sector.

Given this, the aim here is to deliver an overview of the characteristics, designs, dynamics, and outlooks of Euroregional cultural policy. To that end, the focus will be on the use of the instruments and concepts advanced by Fligstein and McAdam[16] in their theory of strategic action fields (SAFs). Considering this proposition, we assume that Euroregional cultural policy is a sub-strategic action field that pertains to the general SAF of Euroregional cooperation. It is assumed that there are interactions and parallels between these different fields and that Euroregional cultural policy also has its own specific features. Moreover, dealing with cultural cooperation allows a certain "decentring" in the use of the theory of fields in a cross-border context, for it concentrates on a policy sector rather than on a cross-border organization or geographic area. Adopting such a sectoral approach can contribute to showing the plasticity and cross-cutting nature of the theory of fields to comprehend the different dimensions of cross-border cooperation and governance: the geoterritorial dimension (cross-border areas), the organizational dimension (cross-border structures and institutions), and the sectoral dimension (cross-border policies). To develop this, two examples of Euroregional cultural policy are examined: the Pyrénées-Méditerranée Eurorégion, at the eastern end of the French–Spanish border, and the Grande Région, between Luxembourg and the border regions of Belgium, France, and Germany. Other examples from other Euroregions complement these illustrations.

Cases of Euroregional Cultural Policy

The Eurorégion Pyrénées-Méditerranée was created in 2004. It gathers the French region of Occitanie[17] and the Spanish autonomous communities of Catalonia and Balears. The autonomous community of Aragon was part of the

Map 11.1. Euroregion Pyrénées-Méditerranée

Source: http://www.euroregio.eu

Euroregion at first, but it gave up the partnership soon after due to a conflict with Catalonia that invoked cultural and identity matters, demonstrating the limitations of the Euroregional cultural policy SAF. The conflict was about the property of some pieces of sacred art. The pieces come from churches in the autonomous community of Aragon but are currently in a sub-region, the Franja de Ponent, geohistorically part of the Catalan-speaking areas. This sacred art is kept in Catalan museums, but the AC of Aragon wants the property back. There are other political reasons influencing this fracture among incumbents of the Euroregion, but this episode confirms that cultural matters can influence their participation.

Today, the Grande Région is a Euroregion created between the Great Duchy of Luxembourg and the surrounding regions of Wallonia in Belgium, once part of the Grand Est region in France and the German *Länder* of Sarre and Rhine-Palatinate. This Euroregion comes from one of the oldest European cross-border organizations, Sar-Lor-Lux, formed in the early 1960s around the coal and mine industries. This Euroregion is linked to the history and *raison d'être* of European construction. It comprises various organs, which structure cooperation at different levels and in different sectors: summits and a rotating presidency, working groups, parliamentary council, inter-city cooperative networks, trade union councils, statistical observatory, the University of the Greater Région, the think tank Institut de la Grande Région, and others.

When it was created in 2004, the Euroregion Pyrénées-Méditerranée made culture a founding principle of Euroregional cooperation. In 2006, a cultural portal of the Euroregion was set up to display the cultural forces and assets of the region, provide cultural information and resources, and foster cultural life.[18] The Euroregion organized annual cultural meetings to encourage networking and synergies among stakeholders. Calls for artistic and cultural projects were launched annually to finance projects among actors from the different parts of the Euroregion. Gradually, a Euroregional cultural corpus emerged with projects in various cultural fields such as street art and circuses, contemporary dance, design, photography, museums, and art centres. Over ten years, from 2009 to 2019, the Euroregional cultural funds supported fifty projects involving 500 cultural professionals and representing a total amount of €1.5 million.[19]

The Euroregion achieved a new phase in 2010 when its members agreed to adopt the status of European Grouping of Territorial Cooperation (EGCT). This legal status in European law was created in 2006 to improve the structure and governance of cross-border organizations.[20] Since 2010, the EGCT Pyrénées-Méditerranée has been acting as the administrative agency of the Euroregion. Its technical team of eight members is in charge of managing calls for projects and other Euroregional policy programs. In effect, when it was first created, one of its tasks was cultural cooperation.

In the Grande Région in 2007, Luxembourg proposed to share Luxembourg City's title of European Capital of Culture (ECOC) with its partners and to extend the event to the whole Euroregion. Under the label "Luxplus 2007," Luxembourg became the first cross-border ECOC with one quarter of its programming occurring at a cross-border scale. Lille had included in its ECOC programming some cross-border projects and partnerships as early as 2004, but Luxplus 2007 was the first ECOC to make the Euroregional dimension its main

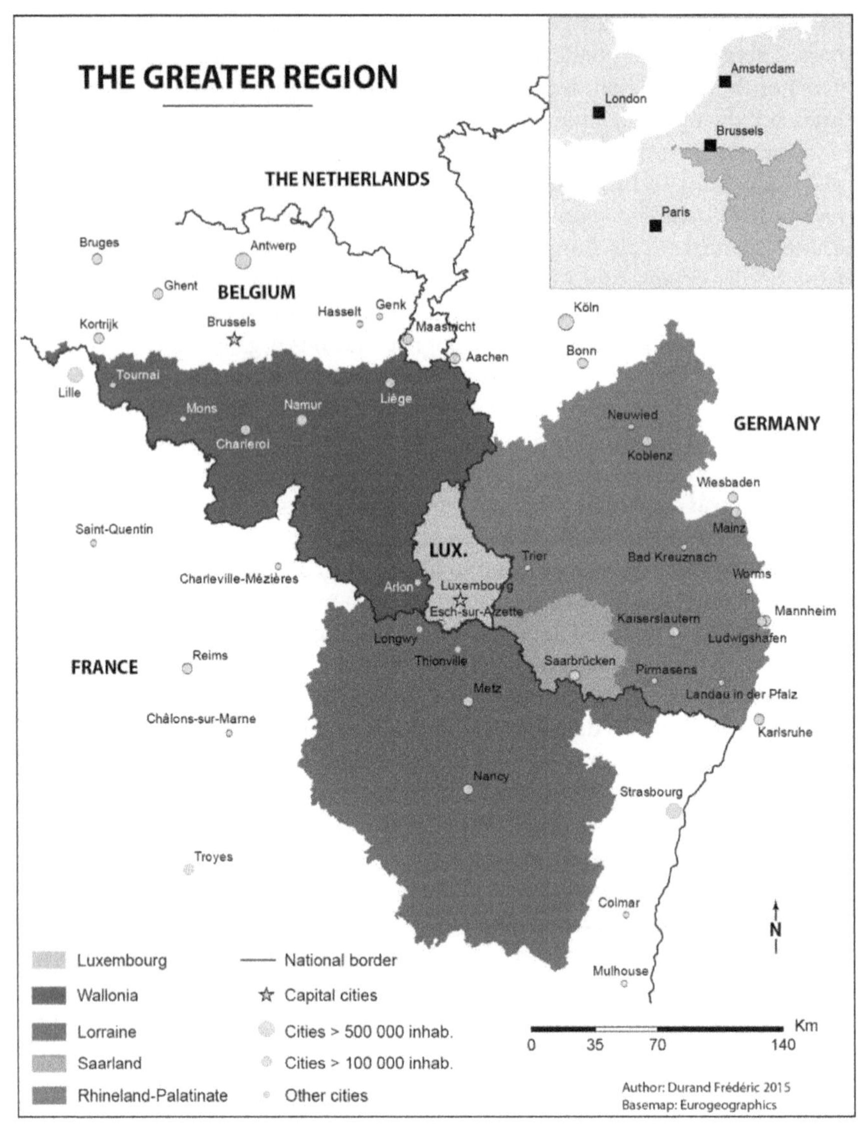

Map 11.2. Grande Région

Source: author Frédéric Durand, Luxembourg Institute of Socio-Economic Research (LISER)

Figure 11.1. Campus en ima[t]ges: photographers' residencies between different university campuses of the euroregion

Sources: https://www.librairieflammarion.fr and http://www.euroregio.eu/ca/espai-cultura; Illustration 3ter: ETAC, the Contemporary Art Space of Euroregion Pyrénées-Méditerranée; http://etac-eu.org.

action line. Moreover, following Luxplus 2007, a certain trend toward "cross-regionalization" of the ECOC was present, with an expanded mapping of the ECOC above the usual city or metropolitan limits: Essen with the Ruhr 2010, Marseille and Provence in 2013, Mons and the French–Belgian border area in 2015, San Sebastian and the cross-border Basque region in 2016, cooperation between the Romanian and Serbian cities of Timisoara and Novi Sad within the Euroregion of the Banat, for the ECOC 2021.[21]

After Luxplus 2007, members of the Grande Région agreed to create the Espace culturel Grande Région, a permanent cross-border cultural association based in Luxembourg. This "cultural space," financed in part by European funds, has the mission of maintaining the dynamics of Euroregional cultural policy past 2007. One of the mottoes of the Luxplus 2007 ECOC was "2007 starts in 2008."

The Espace culturel Grande Région is in charge of informing Euroregional cultural life[22] and operates various programs to assist and promote cross-border cultural projects, the mobility of stakeholders and the public, and the professionalization of the Grande Région cultural scene. It mainly acts as an

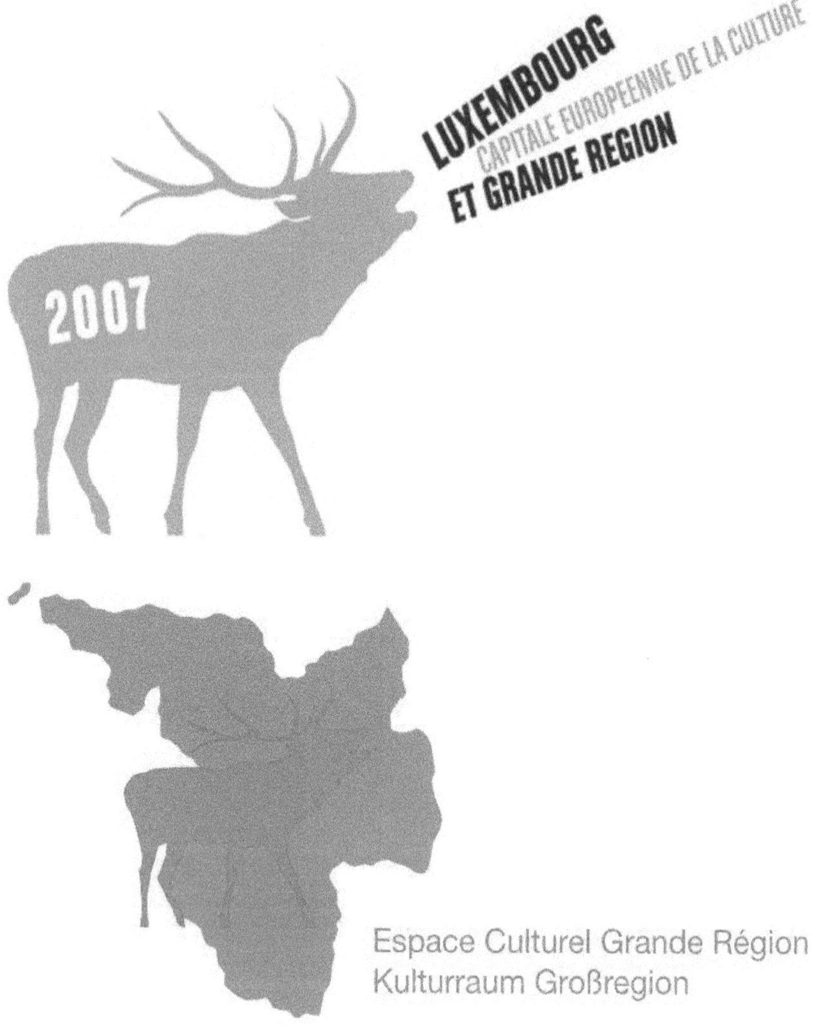

Figures 11.2 and 11.3. The blue stag, from Luxplus 2007 to the Espace culturel Grande Région. Continuity of the cultural "corporate image" of the Euroregion … and of the policy?

Source: http://www.mcesr.public.lu and http://www.espaceculturelgr.eu

information centre and a secretariat that coordinates the links and contacts between the (Euro)regional coordinators appointed by each authority of the Grande Région to deal with Euroregional affairs.

In these two Euroregions, identity-building is a salient issue of cultural cooperation. A principal incentive of Luxplus 2007 was to complement the high level of socio-economic interactions in the Euroregion, based on the daily flows of cross-border commuters. The objective was to promote a more "incarnated" approach to the Euroregion through cultural cooperation, exchanges, and cooperation; this would foster a sense of belonging to a common territory among the population. The ECOC was expected to be the departure point for this "identity transition" of the Grande Région.

In the Euroregion Pyrénées-Méditerranée, geohistorical identity has long been a salient element of the region's cultural policies. This Euroregion unites sociopolitical entities that present specific geohistorical cultural characteristics – not to say "peripheral," to refer to Stein Rokkan's works[23]– when considered within the state of which they are part. In the French part of the Euroregion, the promotion of Occitanie as a cultural ensemble faces objective limitations based on the early cultural and linguistic homogenization of the French Republic; the focus there remains on supporting Occitan language courses and literary heritage. The Catalan culture is much more assertive as a specific national element, one that garners recognition within the Spanish "State of the Autonomies." The autonomous communities of Spain are in charge of education and cultural policies within their own territories. Catalonia has, in fact, enjoyed constitutional status as a "historical nationality" since Spain resumed democracy at the end of the 1970s. There also exists a movement for independence that advocates for the creation of a Catalan Republic, distinct and separate from the Kingdom of Spain. This movement has long mobilized cultural elements to assert and distinguish Catalonia as a nation without a state. Moreover, the Pyrénées-Orientales, a district (*département*) of the French region Occitanie, was historically part of the Aragonese–Catalan confederation until the French–Spanish border was delineated in 1659. It is often referred to as Catalunya Nord (Northern Catalonia), in particular in the Catalan language. In this territory too, private and public cultural policies and initiatives advocate for the Catalan culture and language, though in practice, these identity elements remain "add-on" traits for a large part of the population, which was long ago integrated into the French nation-state's cultural system.

Yet in both cases, the supported projects and programs have begun to embrace more contemporary issues, such as cultural diversity, or the creative identity of a territory as an attractive feature that draws in economic resources. Such an orientation somewhat reflects the EU rhetoric on culture and cultural cooperation, suggesting a certain field interaction between Euroregion and EU cultural agendas.[24]

In terms of policy governance, the creation and implementation of operational cultural programs and structures at the Euroregional level introduces the question of cross-territoriality as a multi-level process of coordination and regulation of territorial complexity.[25] This issue refers not only to the cooperative articulation between the partners of the Euroregion but also to the interactions between the Euroregional organization itself and other territorial authorities that act within the same territory without taking part in the Euroregional framework – for instance, articulation between regions and metropolis or between state territorial prerogatives and the actions of sub-state authorities. Cross-territoriality also relates to the inclusion of Euroregions in the global territorial context. Indeed, participating in a Euroregion can be an instrument of paradiplomacy for a territorial authority, as well as a way for it to reinforce its position in the European and international political arenas. In any case, achieving a cross-border inter-territorial virtuous cycle can be a challenge, and cultural and identity matters are not the simplest ones to cope with, as the field analysis in the next section demonstrates.

The Field: Evolution, Governance, and Perspectives on Euroregional Cultural Policy

Applying the theory of fields to Euroregional cultural policy enables an analysis of the stakeholders, phases, and the evolution of a new form of cultural governance that is forming at the cross-border level.

Incumbents and Challengers: From One Position to Another and Vice Versa

The cases of Eurorégion Pyrénées-Méditerranée and Grande Région demonstrate the emergence of Euroregional cultural policy following an impulse from the main incumbents in the field – that is, a Euroregion's institutional and leading actors who decide to support cultural cooperation. In this situation, *incumbents* refers to the administrations in charge of cultural affairs tasked with developing Euroregional cultural programs. Euroregions are not "one-headed" systems of governance. Rather, they are cooperative organizations that can have several incumbents at different levels. These leaders set cultural policy as a priority of Euroregional cooperation and instruct their departments to inform and prepare cultural professionals about the options available for cooperation.

In Eurorégion Pyrénées-Méditerranée, the incumbents are located at the level of the regional authorities that form the Euroregion and are members of the EGCT created to manage the region. The EGCT remains a distinct body, but member-regions still determine its composition, functions, and resources. Regarding cultural cooperation, the main impulse came from Midi-Pyrénées[26] and Catalonia when the Euroregion was launched. The leaders of both regions had clear and ambitious cultural agendas. The governance of Grande Région is more complex, gathering not only the member-regions but also city governments (in particular the city of Luxembourg and the main regional capitals of the Grande Région). Representatives of the German federated states (*Länder*), the French districts (*départements*), and the French state bureaux (*préfectures*) are also involved in the governance of the Grande Région. For instance, in the Espace culturel Grande Région, nine coordinators represent the different incumbents. In this complex multi-level pattern, the state of Luxembourg occupies a leadership position vis-à-vis other incumbents due to its stronger capacity and greater resources as a sovereign state. Moreover, the Luxplus 2007 ECOC was an event essentially organized by and for Luxembourg. The secretariat of the Espace culturel Grande Région is located in Luxembourg at the Maison de la Grande Région, which is home to all the Euroregional offices and organs. We find in both cases similarities in terms of field emergence: they all foster the involvement of cultural actors – for example, by networking, organizing meetings, forums, working groups, and round tables, and encouraging a shared routine among cultural stakeholders.

In the Grande Région, the ECOC candidacy was prepared years before 2007 by authorities who chose to give it a Euroregional scope. Within a few years, the field had evolved from having a near absence of cross-border cultural cooperation to having more than 100 cross-border projects validated by the ECOC. In Pyrénées-Méditerranée, when launching the first calls for projects, the cultural administrations set out to generate a response from the "cultural milieu." They directly contacted various cultural stakeholders – those with a suitable profile or background in European and cross-border projects – to inform them about the new programs. In this sense, cultural stakeholders at first occupied the role of challengers in the field vis-à-vis the decisional institutions: they received information on the cooperation options and decided whether to develop projects within the lines drawn by the incumbents.

However, the developers of cultural projects, through their feedback or actions, can acquire influence over the direction and design of Euroregional cultural policy. For instance, in Pyrénées-Méditerranée, several projects in various disciplines benefited from a reallocation of financing that allowed their projects to continue. These multi-annual projects have determined certain priorities for the Euroregional cultural policy, in effect influencing that policy. In some supported projects, the same stakeholders are often encountered more than once; typically, they represent flagship or core domains of Euroregional cultural policy:[27] contemporary art institutions, music industry agencies, circuses and street art companies (for instance, artistic circuses are being promoted as a cultural sector of excellence in Occitanie and, to a certain degree, in Catalonia).[28] In this sense, some challengers in the field are gradually taking up the position of incumbents. Their growing experience in Euroregional projects has enabled them to form sectoral networks; also, they have learned how to formulate proposals that fit the Euroregional calls for projects; also, they are now seen as reliable stakeholders in which authorities can "invest." In the Grande Région, some events or projects initiated during the ECOC became regular events over the following years, such as the dance festival "Le Transfrontalier" and various projects targeting youth audiences.

Given that the incumbents' objective is to develop a "Euroregional cultural corpus" and to establish a Euroregional cultural scene, the cultural professionals, who might at first appear to be challengers or followers, can gain more influence by playing a crucial role in achieving the incumbents' objectives.

Another "challenger" in Euroregional cultural policy is the audience for that policy. Indeed, in both cases importance is assigned to the general public's reception of Euroregional cultural policy as a means to reinforce the attractiveness of the area and its competitiveness as a place of creativity and innovation. This is also the case with the objective of reinforcing a sense of belonging to the Euroregion among its inhabitants. So far, the audience remains a rather weak link in Euroregional cultural policy. Surveys conducted after the ECOC in the Grande Région found that it was a "cross-border event more for institutions than for [the] population."[29] In Pyrénées-Méditerranée, the fifty Euroregional projects developed over ten years have had only marginal effects on the cultural life of the region, and the budgetary figures reflect this. The €100,000–150,000 that is invested yearly in Euroregion Pyrénées-Méditerranée must be compared to the €35,000,000 budgeted for cultural and artistic activities in Occitanie in 2019 and the €11,253,428 the Catalan government planned to spend in 2020 just for its program "Internacionalització de la cultura" (which in itself was a marginal sum, given Catalonia's overall cultural budget). In Grande Région too, funding for Euroregional cultural policy is hardly a core part of that region's cultural budget. During Luxplus 2007, cross-border projects represented only 10 per cent of the overall budget of the ECOC for 24 per cent of the projects, even though they were expected to embody one of the core lines of the ECOC.

Moreover, the people of the regions seem barely aware that Euroregions exist, and the cultural programs and events have little influence on them. However, this point merits further inquiry, given that cross-border programs and institutions are recent, especially relative to past identity-building processes. The Madrid Convention on cross-border cooperation dates from 1981, and the first EU programs for territorial cooperation were launched in the early 1990s. Besides, Euroregions are still rather technocratic organs, and they are not conceived as replacements for existing national or regional institutions. They face the same challenges as the EU but on another scale. In terms of culture and identity, the challenge is not to replace or reproduce national, state, or other cultural frameworks, but to overcome the apparent contradiction between these and a sense of common destiny that has been much longer entrenched.

But "consciousness" of being part of a Euroregional community is evolving, and further data are necessary to assess it. The EC has recently surveyed cross-border populations,[30] and recent works have found that the representational and symbolic aspects of cross-border cooperation are growing in importance.[31] Building cross-border sociopolitical communities remains a work in progress.

Field Evolution

Other insights offered by the theory of fields shed light on the evolution of Euroregional cultural governance. After the emergence phase, led mainly by territorial authorities, a stabilization phase arises. Members of the Euroregion Pyrénées-Méditerranée applied for and obtained almost €1 million in EU funds to develop and install their cultural program, the project LabTechnoCulturS, which ran from 2007 to 2010. The creation of dedicated structures helps stabilize the field, including the EGCT in the Eurorégion Pyrénées-Méditerranée and the Espace culturel Grande Région. This structural evolution has enabled a certain stability of cultural governance in the Euroregion, with the launching of recurrent calls for projects and the installation of identified interlocutors. This points to a certain institutionalization of Euroregional cultural governance. Concomitantly, we observe some elements of field transformation, some adjustments that depend on relations to other fields. Obviously, the financial crisis had an impact on budget contributions in partner regions, showing the fragility of structures that are not entirely autonomous but rather are based on the priorities and cooperation policies of member authorities. Since 2015 in the Pyrénées-Méditerranée Région, authorities have focused their calls for cultural cooperation on projects that can find additional funding from European programs such as the Creative Europe program; this can be viewed as a way to "finance more for less." The Espace culturel Grande Région created a common and similar application form for the region's cultural stakeholders. This was a step toward the convergence of cultural governance in the Euroregion. Still, stakeholders must submit their applications to the administration to which they are applying, which means there is neither a common cultural fund nor integrated file processing for the Grande Région.

A Euroregion was established in 1991, encompassing the French *département* Nord-Pas-de-Calais, the English county of Kent, and the three Belgian regions of Flanders, Brussels-Capital, and Wallonia.[32] As a result of internal discrepancies and lack of interest, the partners dissolved this Euroregion in 2004. Yet that did not prevent cross-border cooperation, including in the cultural sector. For instance, there was the Next Festival, a network of contemporary art of the Euroregion, as well as an online portal Linked Euroregion Arts Development Network, which operated for several years even after the Euroregion disappeared.[33]

Clearly, then, Euroregional cultural policy can take root and grow with or without a Euroregional "central" structure. Moreover, since the French–Belgian–British Euroregion folded, other Euroregions have emerged in the area. The first EGCTs ever created, in 2008, were the Eurométropole Lille–Kortrijk–Tournai and the EGCT Dunkerque-Flandres-Côte d'Opale. Both cross-border organizations develop cultural initiatives.

Field Interactions and Limitations

An examination of Euroregional cultural policy sheds light not only on the flexible evolution of the field but also on the apparent limitations of cross-border governance. In all the situations analysed in this chapter, we have found that EU funds have played a crucial role in support of Euroregional cooperation, besides fostering links between EU and Euroregional frameworks. In Grande Région and Pyrénées-Méditerranée, the incumbents have been inclined to invest in culture and to label this policy a distinguishing feature and initiative of "their" Euroregion, yet many important policies were possible only because EU funds were made available, examples being LabTechnoCulturS (territorial cooperation program SUDOE) and the Espace culturel Grande Région (a territorial cooperation program called the Grande Région program). As we saw in Eurorégion Pyrénées-Méditerrannée, since 2015, applying to an EU program has even become a condition for receiving "additional" Euroregional support. In this case, the field's incumbents – mainly the Euroregion's decision-making authorities – can concurrently occupy the challenger, or rather "follower," position for their respective state and the EU, in the sense that they will orient Euroregion development according to the options and decisions of these "incumbents." Indeed, many Euroregions or equivalent structures have been created specifically to manage EU funds for territorial cooperation. We observe here how the negotiations and outputs of some incumbents, the member-states and the EC, condition the responses of the challengers (i.e., the authorities that decide to form a Euroregion).

In France, a state-initiated territorial reform shrank the number of French regions from twenty-two to thirteen through mergers, and this transformed Euroregional governance at France's borders. In Pyrénées-Méditerranée, the two French regions that had originally been part of that Euroregion are now one region, Occitanie, and this may improve the governance process by reducing the number of partners. On the Spanish side of the border, the movement for Catalan independence intensified in the 2010s following disputes with the Spanish government over the status of Catalonia in a context of a harsh economic and social crisis. After October 2017, these antagonisms brought about a serious sociopolitical crisis between the Spanish state and the Catalan government,[34] including the organization of an independence referendum, the imprisonment of several Catalan political leaders for sedition, and the flight of the Catalan president to Belgium. The Spanish state took control of the Catalan government institutions; the following regional elections resulted in a majority of seats in the Catalan Parliament for the pro-independence parties, though they had not earned a majority of the vote. New regional elections were announced for 2020. Here also, such developments, though external to the Euroregional partnership *stricto sensu*, can nevertheless impact Euroregional policies as they concern one of its main incumbents.

Regarding the Grande Région, Lorraine in France is now part of a much broader entity called Grand Est, which contains three previous regions and is also part of Euroregional organizations located on the French–German border, including the Franco–German–Swiss Conference of the Upper Rhine and the Eurodistrict Strasbourg–Ortenau. Additionally, the creation of EGCT depends on a decision by the states in which the ECGT's members are located. A state can also be part of an EGCT, as in the case of the Eurometropolis Lille–Kortrijk–Tournai. But once again, this is not a one-way process. Authorities involved in Euroregional cooperation can influence the decisions of the states and the EU in this domain via various channels of representation and consultation, such as the national representative bodies for cities and regions, the Committee of the Regions of the EU, which set up an EGCT platform, and the Association of European Border Regions.

The EU revised the EGCT regulations in 2013 following demands from the territorial authorities represented on the Committee of the Regions. Representatives of the Grande Région proposed that the EU program for territorial cooperation in their area be adjusted so as to correspond to the actual Grande Région mapping. This situation reflects the distinction between vertical and horizontal fields, and we can see that Euroregional cultural governance comprises both aspects. There can be relations of hierarchy, as well as of dependence, among different stakeholders with different responsibilities. One relation appears to be a key factor in the functioning of the field when it comes to Euroregional cultural governance, that being relations between members of the Euroregion, which we could call the horizontal sub-SAF of Euroregional politics. This sub-SAF can end up choking off the development of Euroregional cultural governance. Indeed, the involvement of the incumbents in cooperation can vary according to political lines and majorities, and partnerships can be more or less active despite having stable structures. Some Euroregions can simply disappear or fall dormant. For instance, the Eurorégion Alpes–Méditerranée had an ambitious cooperation program when it was created in 2007, including a cultural program. But the Euroregion faced difficulties in its implementation, largely due to political discrepancies between the members. Moreover, those members have recently engaged in a new scheme of European territorial cooperation at another scale: the EU Strategy for the Alpine

Region,[35] which could minimize their involvement in the Eurorégion Alpes–Méditerranée. Interestingly enough, Euroregional cooperation was revived by an initiative from the chambers of commerce and industry with the creation of the association AlpMed.[36] Regarding culture in particular, there is a kind of paradox between its status as a "low intensity," "low cost" domain of cooperation despite its strong symbolic dimensions and the related discourse attached to this form of cooperation. "Culture is what talks to people," noted an officer of Pyrénées-Méditerranée Eurorégion. Officials regularly declare that cultural cooperation is a marker of robust cooperation, but the budgets allocated for it, and the public attendance figures, reveal that Euroregional cultural policy is in fact fragile.

Two reflections can be made at this point. First, limitations arise from the nature of the field itself, derived from the nature of cultural policy. The strong identity dimension linked to cultural matters can sometimes make cooperation more difficult. Cultural policy can be an instrument of demarcation rather than cooperation, and some authorities and leaders can have difficulty "sharing" the symbolic attributes of culture beyond the consensual discourses. A professional in cultural affairs at the Council of Europe, the headquarters of which is in Luxembourg, notes: "At my level, I can see that it can be easier to have Georgia working with Spain than Belgium with France, or France with Germany … The wounds of borders, the scars of history can remain present."[37] This statement recalls the observation of Pierre Bourdieu that the frontier, resulting from an act of delimitation, *produces* cultural difference as much as it is the product of such difference. To some extent, recent developments in Catalonia exemplify this "cultural bordering ambivalence."[38] We already noted that the defenders of independence for Catalonia utilized cultural elements to push their agenda. Soon after the Spanish state took control of the Catalan region at the end of 2017, the sacred art that had been claimed by Aragon for years – and that was one of the reasons why it withdrew from the Euroregion – were returned to it. Defenders of Catalan independence viewed that as a polemical operation, as one more affront to Catalan sovereignty by the Spanish state.

Second, the cases analysed here show a certain evolution of the field in terms of the importance now being assigned to the non-identity and socio-economic aspects of cultural cooperation. Such cooperation is now viewed as a source of innovation and attractiveness that can be mutually beneficial. An evolution of the field is being linked to the evolution of the EU, where thirty years of programs for territorial cooperation have created a certain path dependency or at least a mainly agreed-upon recognition of the benefits of cooperating within a European framework, including cultural cooperation. As one stakeholder emphasized: "Culture is perhaps a little easier than other areas." When asked why, this person continued: "It's not like working in other areas … The objectives are clearer and I think that we can look more easily at the fallout, make sure that everyone gets something out of it. Yes, it's more human and there may also be fewer differences in practice … I think it's promising." Comparing this narrative to others on the "borders' limits" illustrates the ambivalent nature of cultural cooperation. In the Grande Région, it can hardly be said that a "Grande Regional identity" has emerged among the population since the cultural year Luxplus 2007; in that regard, it was hardly a complete success. Even so, the agenda shone a "spotlight" on that Euroregion. One stakeholder thinks that this "identity objective" was somehow "too much on culture's shoulders to support"; it was "like sending culture to the firing line … I do not believe that 2007 became a 'go-between' between the politico-economic summits and the daily life of citizens … We can hope it will have left in the minds the idea that, yes, [the Grande Région] exists, yes, we asserted to the rest of Europe that a Grande Région exists." According to a stakeholder in Eurorégion Pyrénées-Méditerranée, "culture is really something very strong because you realize that it's a real way of being closer to the people and it's the easiest thing to share … Culture can help to make the Euroregion more tangible. I do not know if it can help the development of other major projects and objectives but, in any case, it is a strong pillar now … This is really one of the major themes of the partnership." Clearly, perceptions, representations, and outlooks on cross-border dynamics have evolved as a consequence of European construction,[39] even though no approach is irreversible and much depends on geopolitical fluctuations (for instance, Brexit, wars close to the external EU borders, and migration and climate crises).

Finally, the field perspective on Euroregional cultural policy underscores the relevance of the seventh proposition of the theory of fields.[40] It shows how important it is for a sectoral sub-SAF of cross-border governance to be connected to other SAFs if it is to acquire resources and stability. The fluid and quite unstable positions of incumbents in Euroregional cultural policy reveal a certain dependence and relative fragility of the field. Indeed, there does not seem to be a major crisis that would drive changes in the field; rather, there have been small changes or minor adjustments in the maintenance and evolution of the field, reflecting that the field's evolution depends on neighbouring fields. The connection to the "politics field" appears here to be crucial to guarantee the functioning of cross-border frameworks, which depend heavily on the political will to invest in them. In this sense, viewing the Catalonia/Spain crisis as a "crisis in the field" would be an overinterpretation as far as Euroregional cultural policy is concerned. We can presume that this political crisis has consequences for Euroregional affairs, yet Euroregional activities continue. To some extent, this may confirm the relatively low intensity of the political profile of Euroregional organizations, or on the contrary, their relative resilience when faced with high-intensity political events. Only further research can validate such assumptions, or not.

There is also a strong interdependence between the cultural projects that are labelled and promoted at the Euroregional scale and the use of EU funds, in particular from the INTERREG program, to implement those schemes. Euroregional cultural policy seems to depend on the guidance and resources of EU programs, which are not solely designed and decided by the Euroregions' authorities, but imply other incumbents at other levels, in particular political negotiations among European states and the EC. Finally, cultural policy, with its modest costs and potentially strong imagery, can help attract political interest generally speaking. But interest among the people, and participation by them, remain crucial elements when it comes to political promotion and accountancy, and a change in the political priorities can easily undermine the available resources for Euroregional cultural policy.

Conclusion

This analysis of Euroregional cultural policy in the Eurorégion Pyrénées-Méditerranée and the Grande Région shows dynamics of emergence and stabilization of this sub-SAF of cross-border cooperation. It also reveals more general features of cross-border governance, be it the connections between some fields or the opportunities and limitations of these particular types of "cross-border" sociopolitical organization. Indeed, Euroregional cultural policies challenge the cultural and territorial dimensions of European construction, in which Euroregions appear to be "sociospatial" entities that emerge in a territorial, institutional, and even geopolitical "in-between" zone – between local and global, identity and diversity, convergence and differentiation. "Europe's euregions indeed offer the sites for a potential re-negotiation and re-working of basic categories of political life normally tied exclusively to the nation-state … In this respect, … border regions may be considered agents provocateurs par excellence of the early 21st century political imagination."[41] The analysis raises stimulating questions, and further comparative studies are required to confirm or invalidate the trends identified in these cases.

The theory of fields is especailly enlightening as a means to grasp the complex dynamics and interactions we find in cross-border governance and policy processes. Applying this approach to a sector of cross-border governance, rather than to an area or an organization, proves to be a relevant analytical choice that deserves further comparative developments. This may not be that novel an approach, for it recalls several existing concepts and instruments already used to analyse cross-border phenomena – path dependence, multi-level governance, and social capital, for instance. But it remains a critical insight in the sense that it groups and combines these conceptual tools in an overall and flexible rationale, one that is needed to better analyse, comprehend, and compare cross-border processes and organizations on a global stage.

NOTES

1 Francesc Morata, "Euroregions i integració europea," *Documents d'Anàlisi Geogràfica* 56, no. 1 (Universitat Autònoma de Barcelona/Universitat de Girona, 2010): 41–56.
2 Valérie Deroin, "European Statistical Works on Culture : ESSnet-Culture Final report, 2009–2011," *Culture Études* 8, no. 8 (2012), https://www.cairn-int.info/journal-culture-etudes-2011-8-page-1.htm.
3 M. Stange, *La coopération culturelle transfrontalière. Une étude sur les projets culturels transfrontaliers dans le programme Interreg III A* (Paris: Relais Culture Europe and Mission Opérationnelle Transfrontalière, 2005), http://www.espaces-transfrontaliers.org/document/semculture_etude.pdf.
4 Mike Coine (CSES) and Andreas Wiesand (ERICarts), "Study on the Contribution of Culture to Local and Regional Development. Evidence from the Structural Funds," Centre for Strategy and Evaluation Services (CSES) and ERICArts Institute (2010), http://ec.europa.eu/culture/key-documents/doc2942_en.htm and https://www.ericarts-institute.org/projects.php?aid=218&lid=en&al=&rid=330.
5 European Spatial Planning Observation Network (ESPON), "European Territorial Cooperation," Evidence Brief (May 2013), https://www.espon.eu/topics-policy/publications/evidence-briefs/european-territorial-cooperation#.
6 See http://www.aebr.eu/fr/activites/task_forces_detail.php?taskforce_id=10.
7 Thomas Perrin, *Culture et Eurorégions. La coopération culturelle entre régions européennes* (Brussels: Presses de l'Université de Bruxelles, 2013).
8 Neil Fligstein and Doug McAdam, "Toward a General Theory of Strategic Action Fields," *Sociological Theory* 29, no. 1 (2011): 1–26; Bruno Dupeyron, "'Secondary Foreign Policy' through the Prism of Crossborder Governance in the US–Canada Pacific Northwest Border Region," *Regional and Federal Studies* 27, no. 3 (2017): 321–40.
9 *Culture et eurorégions. Enjeux institutionnels de l'action culturelle eurorégionale*, under supervision of Pr. Guy Saez, Université de Grenoble Alpes, Science Po Grenoble.
10 In the framework of different programs and projects: Program Explora-Pro (région Rhône-Alpes), Program COOP-Recot (Spanish Ministry of Research), Program BQR Émergence (Université de Lille 1), Erasmus+ Program (European Union), Euborderscapes Project (7th Framework Program of the EU).
11 Gregory Hamez, Anne-Laure Amilhat Szary, Didier Paris, and Bernard Reitel, *Modelling and Benchmarking of Borders | Modèles de frontières, frontières modèles?* (Belgium, 2013). See for instance the papers available on the site of the European project Euborderscapes: http://www.euborderscapes.eu/index.php?id=working_papers.
12 Markus Perkmann and Ngai-Ling Sum, eds., *Globalization, Regionalization, and Crossborder Regions* (Basingstoke: Palgrave Macmillan, International Political

Economy Series, 2002); James Anderson, Liam O'Dowd, and Thomas Wilson, eds., "Culture and Cooperation in Europe's Borderland," *European Studies: A Journal of European Culture, History, and Politics* 19 (2003); Barbara Hooper and Olivier Kramsch, eds., *Cross-Border Governance in the European Union* (Abingdon: Routledge, 2004); Guy Lachapelle and Stéphane Paquin, eds., *Mondialisation, gouvernance et nouvelles stratégies subétatiques* (Quebec: Les Presses de l'Université Laval, 2004).

13 Anderson, O'Dowd, and Wilson, "Culture and Cooperation in Europe's Borderland"; A-L. Amilhat Szary, "Walls and Border Art: The Politics of Art Display," *Journal of Borderlands Studies* 27, no. 2 (2012): 213–28; Perrin, *Culture et Eurorégions*; Jordi Baltà Portolés, *Cross-Border Cooperation and Cultural Communities in Europe* (Brussels: Centre Maurice Coppieters, 2015), http://www.ideasforeurope.eu/paper/cross-border-cooperation-and-cultural-communities-in-europe; Fabienne Leloup and Thomas Perrin, "La culture objet de coopération: de la marge frontalière au talus transfrontalier," in *Frontières*, ed. F. Moullé (Bordeaux: Presses Universitaires de Bordeaux, 2017), 267–87.

14 A. Paasi, "The Resurgence of the 'Region' and 'Regional Identity': Theoretical Perspectives and Empirical Observations on Regional Dynamics in Europe," in R. Fawn, ed., *Globalising the Regional, Regionalising the Global: Review of International Studies* 35, special issue S1 (2009): 121–46; Thomas Perrin, "New Regionalism and Cultural Policies: Distinctive and Distinguishing Strategies," *Journal of Contemporary European Studies* 20, no. 4 (2012): 459–75.

15 Amilhat-Szary, "Walls and Border Art," 222.

16 Fligstein and McAdam, "Toward a General Theory of Strategic Action Fields"; Dupeyron, "'Secondary Foreign Policy.'"

17 In 2016, a territorial reform in France changed the regional division of the country from twenty-two to thirteen inland regions by merging some of the existing regions. The region Occitanie was born from the merging of two former regions: Midi-Pyrénées and Languedoc-Roussillon, both of which were previously part of the euroregion.

18 See http://www.euroregio.eu/fr/espace-culture.

19 See the Activity Report 2019 at https://www.euroregio.eu/consulteu-linforme-dactivitat-2019 and https://www.euroregio.eu/wp-content/uploads/informeactivitat19ca.pdf.

20 European Parliament, "Regulation (EC), no. 1082/2006, amended by the Regulation (EU), no. 1302/2013," *Official Journal of the European Union* (2006), https://eur-lex.europa.eu/legal-content/EN/TXT/PDF/?uri=CELEX:32006R1082. See the portal of the EGCT at https://portal.cor.europa.eu/egtc/Platform/Pages/welcome.aspx.

21 On this topic, see in particular the inputs and outcomes of the European project "European Capital of Culture and Cross-border Urban Cohesion (CECCUT)," http://www.ceccut.eu/en/home.

22 See https://www.granderegion.net.

23 Peter Flora, Stein Kuhnle, and Derek W. Urwin, eds., *State Formation, Nation-Building, and Mass Politics in Europe: The Theory of Stein Rokkan* (Oxford: Oxford University Press, 1999).

24 Perrin, *Culture et Eurorégions*.

25 P. Taylor, "Beyond Containers: Internationality, Interstateness, Interterritoriality," *Progress in Human Geography* 19, no. 1 (1995): 1–15; M. Vanier, "What Territories Do We Need in Europe, Today?," AAG Annual Meeting, Chicago, 2006, http://halshs.archives-ouvertes.fr/halshs-00177617.

26 See note 17.

27 See https://www.euroregio.eu/fr/?s=culture&Submit=Rechercher.

28 See, for instance, the annual event "Occitanie fait son cirque en Avignon," held during the International Festival of Avignon, https://www.polecirqueverrerie.com/occitanie-fait-son-cirque-en-avignon.

29 EC, "Report from the Commission to the European Parliament, the Council, the European. Economic and Social Committee and the Committee of the Regions" (Brussels, 2021), 19, https://eur-lex.europa.eu/legal-content/EN/TXT/PDF/?uri=CELEX:52021SC0232&rid=1.

30 EC, "Flash Eurobarometer 422: Cross Border Cooperation," Directorate-General for Communication Survey (2015), https://data.europa.eu/data/datasets/s1565_422_eng?locale=en.

31 Frédéric Durand and Thomas Perrin, "Eurometropolis Lille–Kortrijk–Tournai: Cross-Border Integration with or without the Border?," *European Urban and Regional Studies* 25, no. 3 (2018): 320–36; Sylvie Considère and Thomas Perrin, eds., *Frontières et représentations sociales. Questions et perspectives méthodologiques* (Louvain-la-Neuve: Academia, 2017).

32 Thomas Perrin, "La coopération culturelle dans l'eurorégion Nord-Transmanche: Une institutionnalisation sans institution?," *Fédéralisme Régionalisme* 12 (2012), http://popups.ulg.ac.be/1374-3864.

33 See "Linked Euroregion Arts Development," phase 2, https://keep.eu/projects/4993/Lead-Linked-Euroregion-Arts - EN.

34 M. Kölling, "The Catalan Secession Bid: Between Structural and Contemporary Tensions within the State of the Autonomies," in *Regional Governance in the EU: Regions and the Future of Europe*, ed. G. Abels and J. Battke (Cheltenham: Edward Elgar, 2019), 88–105.

35 See https://www.alpine-region.eu.

36 See https://cci-alpmed.eu.

37 A person in charge of of the cultural routes of the Council of Europe.

38 Pierre Bourdieu, "L'identité et la représentation. Éléments pour une réflexion critique sur l'idée de regíón," *Actes de la recherche en sciences sociales* 35, no. 1 (1980): 66.

39 Durand and Perrin, "Eurometropolis Lille-Kortrijk-Tournai."

40 Neil Fligstein and Doug McAdam, *A Theory of Fields* (New York: Oxford University Press, 2012), 189, http://doi.org/10.1007/s11186-014-9237-0.
41 O. Kramsch and V. Mamadouh, "Crossing Borders of Political Governance and Democracy," *Journal of Borderlands Studies* 18, no. 1 (2003): 45.

12 Galicia and the Norte Region of Portugal: An Experience of Cross-Border Cooperation on the Portugal–Spain Border

CELSO CANCELA OUTEDA

On the European continent, cross-border cooperation among sub-national bodies (local and/or regional) has been a long journey. This phenomenon is not exclusive to the European continent, but it is here that it has achieved its most remarkable development in quantitative and qualitative terms. There are more than 100 cases and experiences, as well as a vast heterogeneity derived from the longevity of the experience, the participating agents (local, regional, national), the level of institutionalization, the economic output, the socio-economic achievements, and so on. Cross-border cooperation, fostered by organizations such as the Council of Europe (CoE), which encourage the signing of treaties or conventions between states, and the European Union (EU) through various programs, has a heterogeneous profile.[1]

Evidence of this is found in the case of Galicia (Spain) and the Norte Region of Portugal (G-RNP, in Spanish). These neighbouring regions share much the same geography, and have cultural affinity and linguistic proximity, and all of this has contributed to a multitude of contacts and relations between the two. Relations between these border regions have been a historic constant. Around three decades ago, common needs and opportunities arose that favoured Galician–Portuguese cooperation at the formal and institutional levels. Note well that beyond specific and tangible accomplishments (e.g., the building of rail infrastructure), this cooperative experience has forged an intangible collective heritage – a mainly political-institutional and cultural environment that favours the development, intensification, and enhancement of cooperation and a (Euroregional) identity.

At the institutional level, two and a half decades ago (in 1991), the Galician and Portuguese authorities created the Galicia–Norte Region of Portugal Work Community (CT-GNP, in Spanish) as the main instrument for channelling cooperation among diverse political-administrative agents. In 2008, under the regulatory umbrella of the EU, the Galicia–Norte Portugal European Grouping for Territorial Cooperation (GNP-EGTC in English) was created to overcome various administrative obstacles that were affecting cooperation (lack of capacity and legal security, tardiness and rigidity in public procurement and common service provision, reduction of inefficiencies in cooperative initiatives, etc.). From a political point of view, this operation meant renewing the political commitment of two of the main actors in cooperation, the Xunta de Galicia (Galician regional government) and the *Comissão de Coordenação e Desenvolvimento Regional do Norte* (Commission of Coordination and Regional Development of the Norte) (CCDR-N, in Portuguese).

However, these were not the only institutional agents involved in cross-border cooperation, which has also involved, since the early 1990s, the *Eixo Atlántico do Noroeste Peninsular* (Atlantic Axis of the Northwest Peninsula). Today, this is an inter-regional entity of thirty-eight cities in Galicia and Norte Portugal. And three other Eurocities are involved in the cooperation: Chaves-Verín, Tui-Valença, and Monçao-Salvaterra de Miño. In contrast to the experience of the Atlantic Axis, these experiences have been developed with a local base in specific areas or spaces of the Galician–Portuguese border and are, in a strict sense, cross-border. In February 2018, the Minho River–European Grouping for Territorial Cooperation (MR-EGTC) was created. This new entity has brought together sixteen Galician municipalities and ten Portuguese *câmaras municipais* (also involved are supra-local authorities).

In terms of the theoretical framework provided by strategic action fields (SAFs),[2] the following pages will provide an account of cross-border cooperation on the Galician–Portuguese border. This constitutes an example of collective action insofar as diverse agents, mainly governmental, are framed in different levels of government (regional and local) in two border states and cooperate continually (creation of institutions) and rationally (definition of strategic objectives). The relatively detailed overview that is set out here should allow the use of the main elements (SAFs, units of governance, and strategic objectives) of the above-mentioned theory.

Since the 1980s, the EU (and the CoE) have encouraged initiatives and programs that stimulate cross-border cooperation. The purpose has been to create territorial cohesion within the single European market. In this specific case, a variety of collaborative or cooperative relationships have germinated among the involved governmental agents, which had developed several SAFs. The response of the agents has been relatively homogeneous and convergent (they have had similar objectives). The strategic objectives of the agents are, in some cases, specific (the management of programs and specific projects), and in others, broad and vague (positioning, visibility at state and European levels, influence within the respective decision-making processes). Besides generating financial resources, these agents have created pressure groups and think tanks in relation to state (Spanish and Portuguese) and European authorities with the aim of influencing diverse political agendas.

In order to delimit the strategic action fields, this chapter restricts itself to a discussion of agents that are legal entities, that have strategic action capacity (resources, symbolic mobilization potential, etc.), and that have generated new entities (collective agents): the CT-GNP, the GNP-EGTC, the Atlantic Axis, and the Eurocities (these entities are inter-related with economic and social agents, but due to space limitations, they will not be addressed). This contribution will focus on the stages of formation and stabilization in the SAF, covering aspects from the founding of the CT-GNP (1991) to the creation of the Eurocity Monção–Salvaterra de Miño (2015) (in these cases, there have rarely been critical or break episodes). A thorough understanding of the study case will require some context within the general framework of cross-border cooperation at the European level. That context is provided in the following section.

Cross-Border Cooperation in Europe (CBC-E): Understanding the Case of the Galicia–Norte Region of Portugal

In the introduction to this volume, the editors presented a historical overview of the formation and development of the phenomenon of cross-border cooperation in Europe. In this chapter, I help advance that understanding for the specific case of the G-NRP (Galicia–Norte Region of Portugal). As noted earlier, Europe has more than 100 cross-border cooperation (CBC) cases, under various labels (Euroregions, work communities, interest communities, etc.) and harbouring different realities and profiles (motivations, resources, dynamics and involved agents, degree of institutionalization, outputs, etc.).[3] The first experiences with CBC date from the 1950s; then in the 1990s, the number of cross-border regions began to rise.[4] From a general European perspective, the development of cross-border cooperation had five main stages, as observed in the changes affecting participating public authorities, institutionalization, and territorial areas.[5] For this specific case, I will be focusing on the stage 1981–90, which began when the Madrid Outline Convention came into force in December 1981.[6] That same year, the AEBR passed the European Charter for Border and Cross-Border Regions, the intent of which was to foster cross-border cooperation as an instrument for ameliorating the impact – of whatever kind – that the presence of borders might have on those in their vicinity. In 1985, at the request of the Conference of Peripheral Maritime Regions, the Assembly of European Regions (AER) was founded to defend regional interests, one of which was cross-border cooperation.[7] Around this time, cross-border cooperation took root along the borders of the Iberian Peninsula, specifically along the French–Spanish border, through two initiatives: the Working Community of the Pyrenees (1982) and the Association Midi-Pyrénées–Aragón (1990).

So far, I have barely mentioned the EU. That is because it has been in the background. Since 1988, around when regional policies were being reformed, the EC has been the main promoter of cross-border cooperation. More specifically, it has been the EC that allocates funds for cooperation in order to mitigate the anticipated negative effects of the single market (1992). After 1988, new cooperation entities were established on the initiative of regional authorities, with the EC taking the lead from the CoE.[8]

Regarding the next stage (1991–2006), we emphasize two elements. First, cross-border cooperation organizational structures were created under conventions and agreements signed by the states to complement the Madrid Outline Convention.[9] Then in 1995, the Treaty of Bayonne was signed between France and Spain, coming into force in 1997. Second, the EC contributed economic resources through the INTERREG initiative.[10] According to Domínguez, quoting Tambou, this initiative invited the "territorial agents (authorities or civil society) to redirect their policies, taking into account the existence of neighbour collectivities in order to establish partnerships and be able of participating of the community aids."[11] During this phase, the Work Community Galicia–Norte Portugal was constituted (1991).

A new stage in cross-border cooperation (fifth stage: 2006–16) began once Regulation 1082/2006 on European Grouping of Territorial Cooperation (EGTC)[12] was passed and came into force.[13] This was the beginning of what experts refer to as "second generation" or "proximity" cooperation, characterized by the provision of services, the recognition of rights, and the strategic positioning of the respective territories.[14] This regulation set out to provide a stable legal framework for cross-border cooperation. After an initial period of application, a number of dysfunctions were detected in the ECGs,[15] which tried to amend the 2013 reform.[16] By mid-2018, sixty-nine EGTCs had been created and twenty-two were being prepared.[17] As we have indicated, in 2008, the GNP-EGTC was created as the third EGTC.

We can state that notwithstanding the initial difficulties and the limited results of the phenomenon we are examining, cross-border cooperation helped break the mould, shift the dynamics, and expose the barrier effect as inherent to the border fact. The border was now shown to be a problem in itself and an obstacle to creating new opportunities so as to improve the welfare of affected populations. These same initiatives have also fed a new narrative that highlights the advantages and possibilities of cross-border cooperation (for instance, today we usually we talk about the "Euroregion"), and this has helped turn the traditional concept of "border separation" into a new concept: "border reunion" or "border zone," as a location where human communities and territories familiarize themselves with one another and renew their ties.[18] The Spanish–Portuguese border has not been an exception to all of this. Arguably, cross-border cooperation "is one of the fields with higher bilateral activity after the accession of both countries [Spain and Portugal] to the European Community. The boost given by both governments, within the community framework, to this cooperation done by border regions has allowed fostering many initiatives of major social impact that imply economic and shared services activities."[19] The following section describes a specific case, starting with a thumbnail account of the regions involved.

A Brief Presentation of the Euroregion Galicia and Norte Region of Portugal

As will be discussed later, cooperation among political institutions is no longer limited to cross-border issues; it has also acquired an inter-regional dimension within the framework of the Galicia–Norte Region of Portugal Euroregion, which is not a legal entity but rather a space for forging socio-economic relations.[20]

Galicia, in Spain's northwest, and northern Portugal enjoy a common historical and cultural-linguistic heritage. They are neighbours, divided in places by the Minho River. Until the 1980s, their formal relationship reflected a classic international pattern, which today has a lingering impact (scarce and insufficient communication routes, for example).

From a European perspective, the Galicia–Norte Portugal Euroregion is a peripheral territory on the southwestern Atlantic seaboard. It includes Galicia (NUTS 2),[21] A Coruña, Lugo, Ourense and Pontevedra (NUTS 3), and Norte Portugal (NUTS 2), Minho-Lima, Cávado, Alto-Trás-os-Montes, Grande Porto, Ave, Támega, Douro, Entre Douro and Vouga (NUTS 3). The region has a total area of 50,700 km^2.

The Euroregion has 6.4 million inhabitants, with 2.7 million living in Galicia and 3.6 in Norte Portugal. Galicia has an aging population; Norte Portugal has a younger population. The population density is 132.8 inhabitants per km^2. In both regions, the population is concentrated on the coast, to the clear detriment of inland areas (less populated means less developed). In both regions, there are a great many population centres, which makes it difficult and expensive to provide some public services (health, education, welfare)[22] or infrastructure, especially in the border areas. Note that the population density in Galicia and Norte Region of Portugal is very high compared to the rest of the Spanish–Portuguese border (which is practically uninhabited).[23]

From a European perspective, the Spanish–Portuguese borderland is not an especially significant economic axis. In economic terms, both sides of the border are Objective 1 regions (convergence objective regions with a per capita GDP less than 75% of the EU-25 average),[24] which means they receive EU funding. For 2014–20 programming, Galicia is considered a "more developed region" (GDP per capita over 90 per cent of the EU average), due to the "statistical effect" of EU expansion, while Norte Portugal is considered a "less-developed region" (GDP per capita less than 75 per cent of the EU average). They both

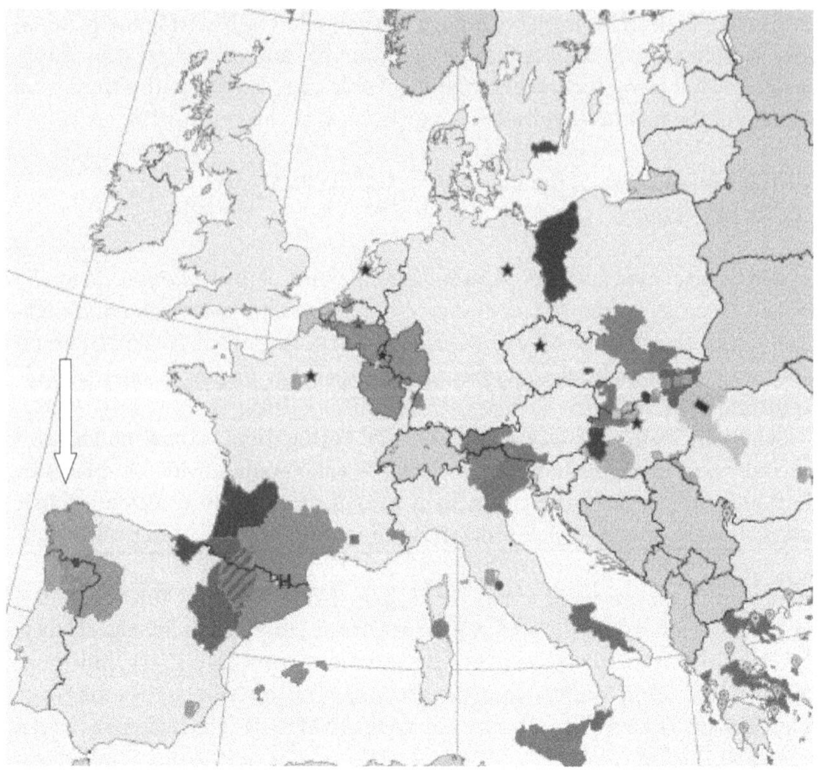

Map 12.1. Localization of the EGTC G-P

Source: Map of European Groupings of Territorial Cooperation, Committee of the Regions (2015)

have a low level of economic development. This is evident, for example, in the presence of structural-style debts that have conditioned cross-border cooperation, orienting them toward infrastructure, at least in the initial years. These investments are now shifting toward innovation and the development of sustainable technologies, as well as scientific research, in line with the Europe 2020 strategy.

The two regions' respective economic structures are generally complementary.[25] In Norte Portugal, production revolves around on textiles, machinery, and electrical equipment. In Galicia, the key sectors are the automotive industry, the agro-food industry, and the metals industry. This has facilitated important economic exchanges (Norte Portugal is the preferred destination for Galician exports) as well as social and cultural exchanges.[26] The strong economic interdependence in the region means that 40 per cent of trade traffic between Spain and Portugal is along the northern border, between the towns

Table 12.1. Basic data

	Galicia	Norte Region of Portugal
Surface (km²)	29,574.8	29,574.8
Population (millions)	2,317,439	3,666,234
Population density (inhabitants/km²)	93.9	171.7
Life expectancy at birth (years)	82.9 (2013)	81.3 (2013)
Employment rate (%; 15–64 years)	56.3 (2014)	60.5 (2014)
Unemployment rate (%; 15 or over)	22 (2014)	17.1 (2014)
Human resources in science and technology (% active population)	40.3 (2013)	24.7 (2013)
Employment in high-tech sectors (% total employment)	2.7 (2013)	2 (2013)
Gross domestic product at current market prices (€ PPS/inhabitant)	22,100 (2013)	16,900 (2013)
Gross domestic product at current market prices (€ PPS/inhabitant/EU)	83 (2013)	64 (2013)
Households that have internet access at home (%)	70 (2014)	63 (2014)
Households that have broadband access (%)	69 (2014)	61 (2014)

Source: Author's elaboration with data from *Eurostat*.

of Tui and Valença. The "weakening" of the border and the development of joint strategies have together generated economic and commercial benefits for the entire Euroregion of Galicia–Norte Portugal. Since 1986, trade between the two regions has multiplied twentyfold, and foreign direct investment has also increased significantly. In general terms, the growth of economic and business relations along the Spanish–Portuguese frontier has been especially strong between Galicia and Norte Portugal because of their greater population density and interdependence.[27] As a result, some joint business groups have been created: many Galician companies have established a presence in industrial parks in Norte Portugal; joint industrial land projects are being planned; and tourist flows have notably increased.[28]

All of this has given Euroregional bodies (the Working Community and the Atlantic Axis) good reason to defend certain strategic Euroregional initiatives, such as a high-speed rail link between the cities of Vigo and Oporto, in front of their respective state governments and the EC. In general, these agents have adopted a cooperative, non-competitive dynamic.

We must also consider this Euroregion's political-organizational diversity, which has a bearing on cross-border and Euroregional cooperation. The decentralization that has occurred within various European states has helped trigger cross-border cooperation,[29] and this case is not an exception. Since 1981, Galicia has been an Autonomous Community with political powers defined by its Statute of Autonomy. It has its own political institutions: the Galician Parliament (which has legislative powers), the Galician Regional Government and President (the Xunta de Galicia, which has executive power), and public authorities. Its territory is divided internally into provinces (A Coruña, Lugo, Ourense, and Pontevedra; the latter two provinces border Portugal), which are governed by provincial councils as well as by 313 municipal councils with their elected governing bodies. In the realm of cross-border cooperation, the players besides the state authorities (ministries) are the regional government, provincial councils, and municipal councils.

One of mainland Portugal's five administrative regions is Norte Portugal. Since 1979, it has had a Commission for Regional Coordination and Development–Norte (CCDR-N), with powers related to regional macroeconomic coordination and planning, the management of EU funds, and supervision and technical advice for local authorities. Nevertheless, it is a decentralized body and not a legal entity *per se*, for it lacks decision-making authority. At an infra-regional level, first we have the districts (there are eight in the region), the metropolitan areas, and associations of different councils. Next, there are eighty-six municipalities that have two elected bodies. Here, the political-administrative players involved are the central government, the regional government, and the supra-municipal and municipal authorities. The Portuguese municipalities are, in general, larger than the Galician councils. From all this, we can conclude that there exists an institutional and organizational asymmetry between the two regions that sometimes obstructs cooperation.

In addition to the diverging historical-political trajectories of Norte Portugal and Galicia, there are sociocultural affinities that continue to endure: religiosity; agricultural land tenure (smallholdings are typical); a subsistence-based and self-consumption economy; dispersion of the population; the parish as the basic relational centre (church-based organizational units); high population density; and emigration.[30] From a historical perspective, these affinities have their roots in pre-Roman times. Romanization, when it finally arrived, brought with it among other things the development of an urban network (Braga, Lugo, Astorga) as well as road communications. Also during that era, the Latin language, Christianity, and political-administrative divisions (*convents*) were all introduced. During the Low Roman Empire, the northwest of the Iberian Peninsula was carved into an administrative entity called Gallaecia with internal subdivisions (*convents*) called *bracarense, lucense, and asturiense* (the first two of these roughly coincide with today's Galicia and Norte Portugal).[31]

In the fifth century, barbarian invasions destroyed the Roman Empire. The Swabians settled in the northwest of the Iberian Peninsula, establishing a kingdom whose political-administrative, religious, and intellectual centre was the current Portuguese city of Braga. In the year 585, Visigoths invaded this kingdom. Still, the former Gallaecia maintained throughout the Middle Ages a certain degree of political autonomy as well as complete cultural and linguistic unity.[32]

From a territorial and political point of view, that unity was fractured at the end of the eleventh century with the creation of the country of Portugal to the south of the Minho River, which effectively broke with the territory to the north (today's Galicia).[33] After the twelfth century, a political border began to take form, coinciding with the transfer of political and cultural life to Lisbon as a result of the "Reconquest." Both territories were progressively separated into independent political entities with separate and rival political trajectories (Castile and Leon versus Portugal).[34] This distancing occurred as a result of the founding of the Castilian and Portuguese monarchies, which were military and political rivals with respective overseas empires and ultimately became separate nation-states. If we had to name a date that definitively marked this distancing process, it would be 1640, for that was the year that Portugal restored its own monarchy and recovered its independence. The historiography tells us that a negative image of Portugal took hold in Galicia as a result of ignorance, distrust, and mutual suspicion.[35] Later, Portuguese nationalism, characterized by a fierce anti-Spanish sentiment (Spain had many times tried to annex Portugal) and international alliances with England, as well as Spanish alliances with France, only reinforced the existing physical, political, and mental frontiers (as well as the reciprocal generation of negative stereotypes).

In 1864 the Spanish–Portuguese border (Portugal's only land border) was established quite definitively with the signing of the Treaty of Lisbon. There has been peace along it ever since. It is also worth noting the absence of irredentist political movements in Portugal, despite a common past and the linguistic and cultural links that exist with Galicia. Similarly, except for small political groups, Galicia has presented no demands for reinclusion in the Portuguese state (this is not the case in linguistic circles, however; there have been many advocates for bringing the Galician language closer into alignment with Portuguese, a movement referred to as reintegrationism). Pro-Iberian positions (Iberianism) have been voiced, with varying degrees of associated prestige, postulating some form of Iberian union, but with zero practical impact.

Later, we will show that the first formal contacts between the Galician and Portuguese authorities were a result of so-called cross-border cooperation, which was viewed as a means to correct these negative effects. The G-NP Working Community has been operational since 1991, as an outgrowth of those contacts. Later, other agreements and entities arose (the Eixo Atlántico [Atlantic Axis], the European Grouping for Territorial Cooperation Galicia–Norte Portugal, etc.), driven by different agents and at the shared initiative of European programs.

Institutionalization of Cooperation between Galicia and Norte Portugal

The previous section described the Euroregion of Galicia–Norte Portugal. Next I describe how this cross-border cooperation was fostered. After that, I will analyse in detail the steps toward the formal configuration of a new strategic action field (SAF) (stages of formation and stabilization).

Factors

The development of cross-border cooperation involved the erosion of political, social, and cultural dynamics established over time and marked by misunderstandings, distrust, and mutual suspicion. The 1980s brought a modification in the historical pattern of neighbour relations. What can this change be attributed to? Several factors played a part in the initiation and consolidation of cross-border cooperation along the banks of the Minho River and the fully fledged inter-regionality that later flowed from it.[36]

Political and legal factors related to the democratization of the two Iberian states were present from the start. This brought about a reorientation of their respective foreign policies toward a common space – Europe – and especially toward European communities striving for democratic consolidation and looking to take full advantage of opportunities for socio-economic development.[37] The bilateral relationships between the two states entered a new stage in 1977 with the signing of the Spanish–Portuguese Treaty for Amity and Cooperation. Generally speaking, this treaty laid the foundations for greater inter-state cooperation, including cross-border initiatives in several sectors (e.g., use of natural resources, improved communication routes). Since 1986, Iberian summits have been held between the two states, with the participation of the respective heads of government and other ministerial representatives (with the presidents of the border regions' Spanish Autonomous Communities also typically attending the summits).

In keeping with this vein of cooperation, in 1988 and 1990, Portugal and Spain respectively ratified the European Outline Convention on Transfrontier Cooperation between Territorial Communities or Authorities (1980), which manifested a different political approach in this area. But it was not until 2002 that Spain and Portugal signed a bilateral treaty on cross-border cooperation between territorial entities and authorities (which entered into force in 2004). That treaty helped clarify the legal framework and reaffirmed both countries' political commitment to cross-border cooperation between regional and local authorities.

Another key political-administrative factor that helped launch cross-border cooperation was the political decentralization of the Spanish state, which resulted in the establishment of the Autonomous Communities, concomitant with the local and regional administrative restructuring undertaken in Portugal, which resulted in the strengthening of these administrative levels. As a consequence, new political-institutional players came forward, who, notwithstanding the asymmetry of their relative authorities, were capable of forging coordinated initiatives and strategies. Specifically, in the case of Galicia, political leaders arose (the president of the Galician regional government) who backed and actively encouraged cooperation initiatives. Thus, for example, the leadership of Manuel Fraga Iribarne, president of the Galician regional government from 1989 to 2005, and Luis Braga da Cruz, president of the CCDR-N from 1985 to 2001, helps explain the advances made in cross-border cooperation in that period. Also notable was the influence of other players (e.g., the central governments in Madrid and Lisbon and local entities in both regions – local authorities were not, in this case, at the forefront of cooperation). The greatest impediment to cross-border cooperation is political-institutional asymmetry. Specifically in this regard, the lack of a true regional political power to the south of the Minho River was one of the most notable obstacles. The Commission of Coordination and Regional Development of the Norte is a decentralized body of the central government, and this slows down and hinders initiatives because consultations with and decisions made by Lisbon are unavoidable. Despite this political asymmetry with respect to the autonomous Galician institutions, the CCDR-N (Commission of Coordination and Regional Development of the Norte) has an excellent understanding of the regional reality and is able to mobilize local and supra-local players in its territory.

Lastly, as with other European experiences of cross-border cooperation, European integration has had both direct and indirect negative and positive influences on the commencement and evolution of cooperation between Galicia and Norte Portugal. Negative: elimination of state borders by the Schengen Agreement. Positive: EC initiatives, notably INTERREG, to establish the single market. Coletti explains:

> The practices of cross-border cooperation have become an important instrument in the field of economic development. From this point of view, the border areas are usually peripheral with regard to their national centres and sometimes are affected by the policies of their own States. In relation to this, in the European case, the cross-border cooperation practices have offered the territories the possibility of creating new centralities at a transnational level, supplementing many functions located in the centre of their respective countries. The cross-border areas become development centres at a supranational and global level, and not as periphery of the political-administrative division defined by the national states.[38]

This analysis is applicable to the cooperation between Galicia and Norte Portugal. Despite their relative youthfulness and beyond the specific, tangible operations (building bridges, improving roads, etc.), there is an intangible heritage associated with this initiative: the creation of a largely political and institutional context that encourages cooperation among the diverse political-administrative and socio-economic agents, thus surpassing what could be considered purely cross-border in the strictest sense of the term, and acquiring a Euroregional (or interregional) dimension. This evolution involves making the most of opportunities for – and facing challenges to – socio-economic development; improving the competitiveness created by European integration (the EU single market); and embracing economic globalization. In short, it is an attempt to create a socially and economically attractive territory, thus reducing its peripheral character and promoting social cohesion. The different agents that act in the Euroregion, CT-GNP (Galicia–Norte Portugal Work Community), AECT-GNP (Galicia–Norte Portugal European Grouping for Territorial Cooperation), Atlantic Axis, and Eurocities, have helped increase its visibility and political centrality at the Iberian and European levels. Along similar lines, the Atlantic Axis fostered the constitution (2009) of Red Ibérica de Entidades Transfronterizas (RIET; Iberian Network of Cross-Border Bodies)[39] as a pressure group.[40]

Formation Phase

Initial formal contacts between Galician and Portuguese authorities date back to the early 1980s, after a series of political and administrative transformations. In the early days, the meetings and encounters generated jointly drafted documents and preparatory studies for specific cross-border initiatives, which were presented to the respective state governments in Madrid and Lisbon.[41]

Later it was decided that these initiatives would have to be institutionalized in order to provide them with continuity and coherence and to increase the number of initiatives required to face the upcoming challenges presented by the European internal market. In 1991, the president of the Galician regional government and the chairman of the CCDR-N signed an agreement to set up the Galicia–Norte Portugal Working Community.[42] Unlike similar working communities, this initiative came from two regional entities (NUTS 2), not from local entities. This improved its functioning, for decisions were now made by consensus by two members alone; it also added political weight (with regard to higher-level players, such as central authorities) and made it possible for strategies to be designed and for inter-regional-level projects to be undertaken.

The Working Community is a forum, not a legal entity with its own staff and budget. It was created to assist the development of both regions within the framework of growing inter-regional interdependence and solidarity and to help improve the lives of both border populations. It addresses matters of common interest, promotes information exchange, coordinates initiatives, and generates agreed solutions to problems. It acts in sectors such as economic development, transportation and communications, agriculture, environment, natural resources and land planning, fishing, health and social affairs, local development, regional and local administration, education, training and employment, scientific research and universities, culture and heritage, and tourism.[43]

The Working Community has both political and technocratic dimensions. It is governed by a chairman (a position held for a two-year period), a vice-chairman, the board (a plenary body whose members are equal), and a coordination committee. There are also four sector committees (sustainable development and planning, economic development and tourism, innovation and energy efficiency, and citizenship), a specific committee for the Atlantic Axis (including cities from the Euroregion), and four territorial cooperation communities (with a local base, which allows local and provincial authorities to be involved in the management of initiatives and programs). Lastly, there is a cross-border observatory and a strategic analysis and reflection group.

The Working Community is a milestone in recent history: for the first time in centuries, the two banks of the Minho River have a common forum for debating shared business and promoting coordination. This allows shared problems to be addressed through combined short-, medium-, and long-term strategies. In 2007, for example, the community passed the 2007–13 Galicia–Norte Portugal Strategic Cooperation Plan; and in 2014, the Plan de Inversiones Conjuntas de la Eurorregión Galicia–Norte de Portugal (2014–20).[44]

Apart from these initiatives, the Working Community played a key role in relations between Galician and Portuguese authorities. Originally, this involved promoting cross-border cooperation, but the scope is now Euroregional. In practice, the Working Community has established itself as a territorial-based lobby that acts for the authorities in Madrid, Lisbon, and Brussels.

Stabilization Stage

In 2008, in Santiago de Compostela, the European Territorial Cooperation Agreement was signed between the Galician government and CCDR-N (Commission of Coordination and Regional Development of the Norte). The agreement led to the establishment of the GNP-AECT (Galicia–Norte Portugal European Grouping for Territorial Cooperation) (its articles of association were also passed). Its objective is to facilitate and encourage territorial cooperation (cross-border, transnational, or inter-regional) among members for the exclusive purpose of strengthening economic and social cohesion. It is a legal entity and has the legal power to act in both states. It has its own staff, a joint management team (with the chairperson originally being Portuguese and the secretary–assistant director being Galician). It also has its own budget, provided in equal shares by the Galician government and CCDR-N.[45]

The AECT-GNP helps overcome difficulties that have dogged cross-border cooperation (the lack of a legally established entity that can intervene in relationships with other players or clarify the legal framework). It also provides a joint, flexible vision of daily management. In the past, all common projects had to be validated by the respective central governments of each country and were carried out and managed in each territory independently. Today the programs can be defined, presented to Brussels, and directly managed by the GNP-AECT, for it is a legal entity with administrative authority to tender, contract, and perform public works, to expropriate land, to jointly manage facilities, and to run services of general interest.

The creation of the GNP-AECT cooperative instrument has brought about a "before" and "after" in the history of the relationship between Galicia and Norte

Portugal, which now have a common institution. The GNP-AECT created two entities that coexist in the field of cross-border cooperation: the Working Community, which acts as a political body, and the GNP-AECT, which functions as the effective executor of the cooperative projects financed with its own funds or funds awarded through funding calls. To achieve coordination between these two entities, the AECT-GNP has a superior council integrated by the general coordinators of the Working Community, representing the Galician regional government and the CCDR-N. It is, then, the organic link between the GNP-AECT and the regional heads of government. In addition, there is an assembly (formed by four representatives of the Galician regional government and four representatives of CCDR-N, designated by the respective presidents at their discretion); its powers consist of the annual approval of the program of activities and budget, the approval of tariffs, levies, taxes, or prices, the imposition of disciplinary sanctions, prior authorization for the signing of collaboration and cooperation agreements, prior authorization for loan and credit operations, and so on. The organization has a director (appointed by mutual agreement between the president of the Galician regional government and the chairperson of the CCDR-N for a two-year period, on the condition that s/he have a nationality different from that of the secretary–assistant director and that of the outgoing chairperson) and a secretary–assistant director. Decision-making and the composition of the bodies must observe the principles of consensus and equity in the case of bodies formed by multiple members. In the case of single-person entities, these must act in accordance with the responsible, individual criteria of the respective holders.[46]

Other Strategic Section Fields: Local Authorities as Cross-Border Agents

It is possible to detect other strategic action fields built around local authorities. Indeed, local authorities (NUTS 3) also intervene in territorial and cross-border cooperation. An example of this is the northwestern Peninsular Atlantic Axis (Eixo Atlántico).[47] It was established in 1992 as a private-law association on the initiative of a dozen cities in Galicia and Norte Portugal, without any link with the Working Community. In 2000, a protocol was signed between the two entities establishing an institutional link. In particular, a specific committee was created within the Working Community to accommodate the association, granting it full membership. This has allowed them to pursue their respective objectives for the consolidation of the Euroregional space, which on many occasions were complementary, while avoiding duplication. At present, two political-institutional players are operating with a Euroregional mandate: the Working Community and the Eixo Atlántico (Atlantic Axis). This entity has progressively increased its membership: the twelve founding cities have grown to thirty-eight (including two provincial councils: A Coruña and Lugo), which means that the number of initial members has almost tripled.

The Atlantic Axis maintains its own operations in a series of priority areas: infrastructure, transport, urban development, the environment, tourism, sport, and culture. Its main objective is to organize a common territory that allows advances to be made in internal cohesion, favouring inter-regional and cross-border cooperation at a local level and, more generally, contributing to the development of the European urban element and European integration. In practice, the Atlantic Axis acts as a cross-border lobby in relation to public (European, state, regional, etc.) and private agents and as a promoter of diverse projects and initiatives;[48] it also acts as a think tank (as seen in the elaboration of diverse strategic documents, studies, and reports). Its presence makes the cooperation more than cross-border in nature: it favours an interregional or Euroregional approach, while also involving urban public players in a more intense manner, making them more dynamic and closer to citizens' needs. This foregrounds its importance in demographic, political, and economic terms.

Other initiatives that are territorially limited and strictly cross-border in nature have arisen within the G-NP Euroregion and involve local authorities. The Unimiño project has been under way since 2005. It is a result of a collaboration agreement between two supra-municipal entities: the Inter-Municipal Community of Vale do Minho (integrating five municipalities) and the Provincial Council of Pontevedra (involving sixteen Galician municipalities). Its objectives are to promote cooperation and establish initiatives among the municipalities to carry out public works, manage common services, and elaborate projects for presentation in European and state calls for tenders. Currently, Unimiño is not especially prominent. In February 2018, it created the above-mentioned MR-EGTC, which brings together sixteen Galician municipalities and ten Portuguese *câmaras municipais* (also involved are supra-local authorities).

In the Euroregion G-NP (Galicia–Norte Portugal), other cooperative initiatives have flowed from the experiences of the preceding thirty years. One of these involved four Eurocities: Chaves-Verín, Tui-Valença, Monçao-Salvaterra de Miño, and Vilanova de Cerveira–Tomiño.[49] The Eurocities aim to share services and carry out common projects in sectors such as tourist promotion, health provision, education, transportation, culture, and the environment. These four Eurocities are located on the Galician–Portuguese border; they are cross-border in an actual sense and thus are inspired by the logic of the "proximity" or "second generation" cooperation. Their objectives are to provide public services, acknowledge citizens' rights, and position their respective territories strategically. Such projects are the result of the initiative, support, and advice of other pre-existing entities linked to cross-border cooperation; specifically, the Eurocity Chaves-Verín was created under the Atlantic Axis, and the Eurocity Tui-Valença was supported by the CT-GNP (Galicia–Norte Portugal Working Community).

The Verín-Chaves Eurocity was launched in 2007 and involves the Galician town of Verín (15,000 inhabitants) and the Portuguese town of Chaves (45,000 inhabitants). Since July 2003, it has been constituted as an EGTC. It is located in an inland part of the Euroregion, in the so-called *raia seca* zone, where economic activity and population density are both low. Like similar initiatives, it is an attempt to share services and carry out common projects in the tourism, health, education, transportation, environmental, and cultural sectors. More specifically, it aims to provide common resources through the joint management of services and facilities in both municipalities, thus avoiding unnecessary and expensive duplication. Its specific initiatives include the Eurocitizen Card, which allows the use of social, sporting, recreational, and cultural facilities and services under identical conditions for the residents of either of the two municipalities. It aims to promote exchanges between the populations of both municipalities, while increasing the number and diversity of services on offer.

A similar initiative, inspired by the one just described, involves Tui and Valença (2012), both located on the Minho River and the main communications route along the Spanish–Portuguese border. This is another excellent example of cross-border cooperation. The two cities are separated by the Minho River and linked by an international bridge. The Galician city, Tui, has 16,884 inhabitants, and the Portuguese city, Valença do Minho, has 14,129 (2011). An EGTC has not yet been created, but there is a willingness to do so. The two cities have already organized joint sport and cultural events.

The third initiative involves Monção and Salvaterra de Minho. They are taking their first steps, having signed an agreement in December 2014; both municipalities and the EGTC[50] participated in it. The main fields of common interest are the promotion and development of the Minho River area, local oenology and gastronomy, and the development of natural heritage tourism.

The fourth initiative, the most recent one, having been formally launched in October 2018, involves Vilanova de Cerveira and Tomiño (22,602 total inhabitants). In 2017, these two cities adopted the Strategic Agenda for Cooperation Amizade Cerveira–Tomiño, which included a variety of cultural and sporting activities financed by INTERREG V-A with almost €500,000. That agreement laid out an "Orzamento Participativo Transfronteirizo" (Cross-Border Participatory Budget), under whose terms the two entities would select their joint activities together. This included shared management of public services (a municipal swimming pool, a school of music) and the development of an Europarque (cross-border park) that would link the two banks of the river with a pedestrian/bicycle bridge (O Casteliño Park and the Fortress of Goián).

These four experiences, which could be referred to as "micro-cooperation," affirm that "the projects of cross-border regionalization within the EU framework are an experimental field due to its link to a change in the significance of the border. From a peripheral area for the states, they turn into receivers and transmitters of guidelines to invert the meanings that were historically and socially built, in spatial terms. … The [Eurocities] have been configuring themselves as agent[s] of daily spatial socialization in the municipalities of Chaves and Verín, however, with unequal incidence."[51] As stated on the website of the Eurocity Chaves–Verín, Eurocities are "truly laboratories of shared and built citizenship, of a shared living among equals."[52]

So far in this chapter we have focused on initiatives promoted by public entities, but we could also mention those that bring together civil society actors, such as business associations, trade unions, and non-governmental organizations. Examples here include CECOTRAN (Centro de Cooperación Transfronterizo–Cross-Border Cooperation Centre), the cross-border business association of the G-NP Euroregion; the Interregional Union Council Galicia–Norte Portugal (created in 1995 by Galician and Portuguese unions); the Asociación Cultural e Pedagóxica Ponte … nas ondas (Cultural and Pedagogical Association Ponte … nas ondas); and various public universities (Iacobus Program, International Campus of Excellence, Campus do Mar). And this list could be even longer further (so as to include, for instance, the Nortear Literary Award).

Some Final Considerations

The cooperation that has been developed in the Galicia–Norte Portugal Euroregion is a result of initiatives by public institutions. These started at the regional level. Later, local-level players with diverse objectives began to participate, which helped promote cooperation. In this way, both SAFs have been configured around the CT-GNP and the EGTC-GNP, the Atlantic Axis, and the Eurocities. Agents from civil society are also involved.

Improved cooperation among various agents has undoubtedly helped generate a discourse that views cooperation in a positive light, as an opportunity to overcome shared disadvantages. It presents the Euroregion as a territorial space capable of generating opportunities in the context of the competitiveness that has intensified as a result of globalization and European integration. The sense that there exist strategic, converging, or shared interests in sectors such as transportation, the environment, natural resources, research, and land planning – all of which require coordination – has progressively taken hold. So it is possible to distinguish between specific strategic short-term objectives (derived from initiatives and European projects), on the one hand, and general, medium- and long-term objectives (linked to changes in the Euroregional development model), on the other. This cooperation provides a competitive advantage to the border territories; it is also key to their socio-economic development (cooperation as a response to the barrier effect).[53] Furthermore, cooperation has provided political visibility to the Euroregion G-NP and given it a central place in development. Nowadays, the institutional agents acting within this framework are able to wield influence over the various other political agendas (state, interstate, European).

Note that Eurocities' new-found capacity to create new institutions and cross-border initiatives has sometimes generated a new EGTC, which helps increase institutional density. One result is that a certain rivalry among the main agents of the Euroregion – CT-GNP/EGTC-GNP and the Atlantic Axis – can now be detected.

Specific programs have been established and are, of course, of great importance, but we should not overlook what has been achieved in the terrain of perceptions, ideas, and discourses – that is, the intangible heritage of cooperation. Since the first years of cross-border cooperation between Galicia and Norte Portugal, a unique discourse among political leaders, socio-economic agents, and the mass media has been generated, and so has a Euroregional identity.[54] Quoting Coletti, "the stability of the cross-border cooperation initiatives is due to the metaphoric and imaginary value that goes beyond the specific results of these practices. The creation of cross-border cooperation areas is usually linked to the building of an identity. Linked to cultural and historical common routes of a territory or to the economic and social development opportunities that open for the new cross-border community."[55] From this perspective, cross-border cooperation helps reinforce the idea of a united Europe, one that has inspired and guided integration.[56] At the present time, cooperation within G-NP would do well to distance itself from initiatives related to physical infrastructure and instead address second-generation cooperation (public services, R&D&I), in keeping with EU guidelines (Europe 2020 Strategy).

Our examination of cross-border cooperation between Galicia and Norte Portugal from the perspective of SAF theory allows us to extract some findings. First, it is a cooperative (i.e., non-confrontational) experience that mainly involves public (state) actors engaging in cross-border cooperation. Remember, also, that G-NP is a new SAF and that it is possible to refer to its different phases (note here that no crisis episodes have been detected, even during the 2008 economic crisis). In our case, this theory evinces the phase of emergency within the field during which two or more actors, with linked interests, orient their actions toward one another but an agreement over the basic conditions of the SAF has yet to emerge. In such situations, they are gradually compelled to take one another into account in their mutual actions. Collective strategic action does have different dynamics in states and markets, as well as in non-state and non-market fields. So the modes of collective action are different in markets and states. The G-RNP also constitutes a stable field (i.e., hierarchical structures, agreement on means and ends) as well as a vertical one (i.e., hierarchical) in which unequal resource allocations (financial, social, knowledge-based) are visible.

This case also shows an increase in institutionalization: several governance units have been established (EU, Working Community, EGTCs, Atlantic Axis) that state organizations (with public resources) have promoted in a context characterized by high institutionalization (and efficiency). Thus, there are several SAFs that respond to the "Russian doll" structure comprising a number of other SAFs. Cross-border cooperation is seen as an opportunity (generated by CoE and EU; both organizations are exogenous forces because of their legal and financial resources). These actors help create a complex environment and promote the transformation of the various fields (and states). Consequently, actors oriented their actions to the benefits derived from European regional policy, thus generating a competitive logic among different SAFs (state, regional. and local).

Would cross-border cooperation continue without EU financial incentives? As it happened, the strategic actions of the various actors created and maintained stability in their respective fields. In connection with this, it is possible to detect an ability to mobilize other actors such as universities and civil society actors and the consequent generation of informal networks (companies, unions, associations).

Economic actors pursue their goals selfishly. By contrast, public actors (promoted by other political institutions and fed with public funding) tend to harmonize their actions in search of mutual understanding. There is no opposition to cross-border cooperation or to the actions of the governance units (WC and EGTCs, mainly). Those units have been able to cooperate and build formal or informal networks (for example, RIET). These governance units and the networks thereby created barely exercise political initiatives, yet they have managed to extend the strategic objectives (initially limited to the cross-border cooperation field) to broader interregional objectives (sustainability, innovation and research, quality of life, public services). The actors understand that there are dependent interests they should consider in their mutual actions. So to achieve strategic objectives, they use their political and administrative resources.

In our case, the configuration of a collective identity is an interesting element. Such an identity is based on "a collective set of meanings shared by other actors in which those actors' identities and interests are defined."[57] In other words, a collective identity has emerged as a result of the EU´s narrative (the CoE's as well) and the intervention of other actors (regional or local) that participate in narrower SAFs by disseminating ideas and values on cross-border cooperation (we see here a narrative based on Euroregional or Eurocity perspectives). Also remarkable is the impact of a set of shared understandings of the rules in the field. So actors understand what kinds of tactics are possible and legitimate in the field (i.e., they share an interpretative frame that individual and collective strategic actors use to make sense of what others are doing).

Related to this, according to Fligstein and McAdam, "the state is also a significant source of new strategic fields … State fields can also intentionally or unintentionally undermine stable SAFs through direct or even indirect actions."[58] So states' actions can produce intended and unintended consequences in relation to SAFs. In this sense, we can conceive of emerging new political spaces (with their own identities), which coexist with those defined by the states, as outcomes of the phenomenon of cross-border cooperation.[59] Finally, the theory of SAFs is a mid-range theory that provides a sophisticated and flexible theoretical framework allowing observation and explanation of strategic collective action (conflict or cooperation). It gives attention to the composition of the fields and the strategies of the actors. However, at the micro-level, the actors' identity is less important. So aspects related to ideology, identity (values, symbols, beliefs), or the context in which the SAF emerges and is consolidated are not well-examined. There is also an economic bias (utilitarian functional) in line with the logic promoted by European regional policy and territorial cooperation. Regarding cross-border cooperation, that logic emphasizes a technical-functional dimension (rationality and utility), while neglecting the political aspects (strengthening the position of certain actors in the intra-state framework, or generating territorial-based competition). It would be advisable to expand SAF theory or combine it with other theoretical frameworks capable of capturing the political, identity, and ideological elements. We must emphasize that cross-border cooperation has expanded toward new themes generating new strategic visions that exceed the cross-border scope.

To finish, SAF theory can be especially useful for understanding the phenomenon of cross-border cooperation in North America, where the role of non-state actors is remarkable. Perhaps it is not so useful in Europe if we take into account, on the one hand, the main role played by state actors (in contrast to the secondary role played by non-state actors) in cross-border cooperation and, on the other hand, the presence of conflicts between national minorities. In the EU context, European legal and financial support and the fact that the European internal market is already functioning must be taken into account. European cross-border cooperation shows a clear political-administrative dimension in contrast to the North American kind. This has broad implications for comparative studies.

NOTES

1 Raffaella Coletti, "Cooperación transfronteriza y trayectorias de desarrollo: aprendizajes de la experiencia europea," Centro Studi di Politica Internazionale (2009), https://www.cespi.it/en/ricerche/cooperacion-transfronteriza-y-trayectorias-de-desarrollo-aprendizajes-de-la-experiencia; J. Trillo and R. Lois, "La frontera como motivo de atracción: una breve mirada a las relaciones Galicia-Região Norte," *Geopolítica(s)* 2 (2011): 109–34.

2 Neil Fligstein and Doug McAdam, "Toward a General Theory of Strategic Action Fields," *Sociological Theory* 29, no. 1 (2011): 1–26; J. Pont, "Estrategia y movimientos sociales: la hidroeléctrica de la Amazonia brasileña," *Revista Mexicana de Sociología* 77 (2015): 243–73.

3 For general insight into the European situation, consult the websites of the Association of European Border Regions (AEBR) (http://www.aebr.eu/en/members/map_of_members.php) and the Mission Opérationnelle Transfrontalière (MOT) (http://www.espaces-transfrontaliers.org).

4 In practice, there is no regional or local authority that does not develop cross-border cooperation activities. So it is appropriate to differentiate between the experiences of cross-border cooperation and the cross-border regions that imply any type of institutional agreement or result.

5 L. Domínguez, "Cincuenta anos cooperando entre fronteiras na Europa (1950–2000)," in *Europa e a cooperação transfronteriça, Porto, Eixo Atlântico do Noroeste Peninsular*, ed. L. Domínguez (2006): 151–85.

6 However, its effectiveness was burdened because the signatory countries made the cooperation initiatives of the territorial authorities dependent on the signing of interstate bilateral agreements that were established some years after. The Outline Convention was the first step toward establishing cross-border cooperation structures based on public law. The proponents of this convention intended to avoid the obstacles arising from the excessive control exerted by the central state authorities through the border commissions. Nevertheless, few entities were constituted under this text. The Euroregions preferred to use alternative institutional formulas. The constitution scheme of the Euroregions is the following: first, on each side of the border, the local or supra-municipal entities had to create an association according to their respective state laws. Second, both associations agreed, on the basis of a cross-border agreement, to the establishment, under the private law, of the cross-border region. The CoE contributed to the creation of a favourable political environment for the border authorities to collaborate in a situation shadowed by the insecure legal presence of "soft" institutions.

7 Due to the persistence of the AER and other organizations, in 1988 the European Commission created the Consultative Council of Regional and Local Authorities.

8 Notably, the EU now supports cross-border cooperation through INTERREG. The allocation of funds has been placed under the control of the central or regional governments, which are accountable to the European Commission for the implementation of the policies. Generally, the EU has backed a more pragmatic and economic approach, unlike the CoE, which has backed a legal approach (the creation of political-administrative entities).

9 In 1995, the CoE passed a protocol to supplement the Madrid Outline Convention that came into force in 1998. Under this protocol, local and regional entities have the authority to establish cooperation agreements with entities from other states with a view to creating permanent cross-border cooperation structures under

public or private law. These structures will be compulsory for the signatory entities. In May 1998, a second protocol on "inter-territorial cooperation" was passed, and, finally, in November 2009, a third protocol regulated the Euroregional Cooperation Grouping (ECG).

10 In its first call, INTERREG allocated all the community funds for cross-border cooperation to funding projects in industries such as transport, communications, environment, tourism, and rural development. The INTERREG that followed incorporated other lines apart from cross-border cooperation. Since 1990, there have been the following periods of INTERREG programming: INTERREG I (1990–93), INTERREG II (1994–99), INTERREG III (2000–06), INTERREG IV (2007–13) and INTERREG V (2014–20).

11 Domínguez, "Cincuenta anos cooperando entre fronteiras na Europa."

12 Regulation (EC) no. 1082/2006 on a European Grouping of Territorial Cooperation (EGTC) regarding the clarification, simplification, and improvement of the establishment and functioning of such groupings.

13 X. Oliveras, A. Durà, and M. Perkmann, "Las regiones transfronterizas: balance de la regionalización de la cooperación transfronteriza en Europa (1958–2007)," *Documents d'Anàlisi Geogràfica* 56 (2010): 21–40.

14 L. Dominguez and E. Varela, "Construyendo 'Europolis' a partir de la cooperación local 'informal' en los espacios transfronterizos de Europa: el caso de la RIET," *Geopolítica(s)* 6, no. 2 (2015): 225–46, https://doi.org/10.5209/rev_GEOP.2015.v6.n2.48428.

15 Regarding this, Draft Opinion CDR 308/2007 on the "European Grouping of Territorial Cooperation: New Impetus for Territorial Cooperation in Europe" (Rapporteur: Mercedes Bresso) can be consulted, as well as the Draft Opinion on "New Perspectives for the Revision of the ECTC Regulation" (2011/C 104/02) (Rapporteur: Alberto Núñez Feijóo) and the EC's report from the 29 July 2011, aimed at the European Parliament and the Council of Europe regarding the application of the Regulation 1082/2006.

16 Regulation (EU) 1302/2013 of the European Parliament and the European Council on 17 December 2013, amending Regulation (EC) 1082/2006 on European Grouping of Territorial Cooperation (EGTC) regarding the clarification, simplification, and improvement of the establishment and functioning of such groupings.

17 Visit the website of the Committee of the Regions (https://portal.cor.europa.eu/egtc/CoRActivities/Pages/egtc-list.aspx) or the EGTC monitoring report 2014, "Implementing the Strategy Europe 2020" (https://cor.europa.eu/en/engage/studies/Documents/EGTC_MonitoringReport_2014.pdf).

18 A. Rojo and R. Ricoy, "La cooperación transfronteriza: de la separación al reencuentro… ¿y a la integración?," Ponencia XII Congreso AECPA (Universidad del País Vasco/San Sebastián, 2015), https://aecpa.es/es-es/la-cooperacion-transfronteriza-de-la-separacion-al-reencuentro-y-a/congress-papers/1546.

19 R. García, "La cooperación transfronteriza hispano-portuguesa: retos y oportunidades," *Cuadernos de Yuste* 7 (2013): 463–87.

20 The use of the expression "Euroregion Galicia–Norte Portugal" commonly refers to the territorial area of the autonomous community of Galicia and the Portuguese area between the Minho and Duero Rivers. In our view, this is important, for it contributes to the appearance of a certain and symbolic Euroregional identity.

21 Regarding the NUTS system, see "Common Classification of Territorial Units for Statistical Purposes" (NUTS) at https://eur-lex.europa.eu/legal-content/EN/TXT/HTML/?uri=URISERV:g24218&from=ES.

22 The following case exemplifies this situation. In 2010, five Portuguese municipalities close to the border demanded that their citizens be treated in the Hospital Meixoeiro in Vigo because it was nearer than the equivalent centres in Portugal. See "Cinco pueblos de Portugal piden usar un hospital de Vigo," *El País*, 8 April 2010, https://elpais.com/internacional/2010/04/08/actualidad/1270677609_850215.html.

23 This section of the Spanish–Portuguese border accounts for 49 per cent of all heavy goods and car traffic along the entire frontier and sees high daily cross-border traffic in individuals and goods. This is due to factors such as geographical proximity, easily navigated terrain (the absence of significant landforms hindering communications), and cultural and linguistic affinities. These exchanges cause problems of different types (health, occupational, crime, labour, etc.), which have brought the need for coordinated operations with the involvement of public (at different administrative levels) and private players – for example, in situations where Portuguese trucks were doing irregular transportation in the province of Ourense (See M. Rodríguez, "Frenan el paso de camiones lusos que hacían cargas ilegales de arena," *La Voz de Galicia*, 30 June 2015, https://www.lavozdegalicia.es/noticia/ourense/verin/2015/06/30/frenan-paso-camiones-lusos-cargas-ilegales-arena/0003_201507O1C3991.htm); or the daily traffic of Portuguese workers to Galicia (See M. Sío Dopeso, "Portugal reconoce el paso a diario de obreros a Galicia en furgones ilegales," *La Voz de Galicia*, 18 March 2018, https://www.lavozdegalicia.es/noticia/galicia/2008/03/18/portugal-reconoce-paso-diario-obreros-galicia-furgones-ilegales/0003_6661763.htm). See also Trillo and Lois, "La frontera como motivo de atracción." In 2010, the Portuguese authorities established a toll system on the highways that negatively affected border vehicle traffic, which was reduced by an average of 10 per cent. This provoked the mobilization of diverse socioeconomic agents and public entities against this measure. See the Report "Impact of the Toll System of the Portuguese Highways on the Commercial Relationships Galicia-Norte Portugal," GNP-AECT, 2010.

24 The main goal of the Convergence objective is to foster growth-enhancing conditions and factors leading to real convergence for the least-developed territories.

25 Trillo and Lois, "La frontera como motivo de atracción."

26 A. Vaquero, "Galicia-Norte de Portugal: una suma de oportunidades", *La Región*, 22 June 2015, http://goo.gl/ga351D.

27 In 2021, there was intense competition between Galicia and the Norte Region in the field of industrial land to attract companies.

28 Trillo and Lois, "La frontera como motivo de atracción."

29 Coletti, "Cooperación transfronteriza y trayectorias de desarrollo."

30 L. Domínguez, "Europa e a fronteira luso-galaica: historia e reencontro," in Domínguez and N. Venade, *As eurorrexións e o futuro de Europa: o modelo da eurorrexión Galicia-Norte de Portugal* (Porto : Eixo Atlântico do Noroeste Peninsular, 2004), 3–51; Trillo and Lois, "La frontera como motivo de atracción."

31 R. Villares, "Minho River: A History in Common," in Ernesto Sánchez Pombo, *The Euroregion Between Two Centuries* (Vigo/Porto: Eixo Atlântico do Noroeste Peninsular, 2011), 23–35.

32 Álvaro X. López Mira, *A Galicia irredenta* (Xerais De Galicia Edicions, 1998).

33 Villares, "Minho River," 2011.

34 C. Barros, "La frontera medieval entre Galicia y Portugal," *Mediavalismo* 4 (1994): 27–39.

35 A. Rojo, "Percepciones mutuas e imágenes recíprocas: España y Portugal ante el espejo," in *España y Portugal. Veinte años de integración europea*, ed. R. García and L. Lobo-Fernandes (Santiago de Compostela: Tórculo, 2007), 235–52.

36 C. Cancela, "Panorama de la cooperación territorial en la Eurorregión Galicia-Región Norte de Portugal," *Documents d'Anàlisi Geogràfica* 56 (2010): 149–65; C. Cancela, "Galicia and North Portugal: From Cross-Border Suspicion to Euroregional Cooperation," *Journal of Cross Border Studies in Ireland* 8 (2013): 89–102.

37 J. Palmeira, "Geopolítica de Portugal: Atlântico é arma estratégica para combater periferia na Europa," *Revista de Pensamento do Eixo Atlántico* 6 (2004): 105–12.

38 R. Coletti, "Cooperación transfronteriza y trayectorias de desarrollo: aprendizajes de la experiencia europea," *Revista de Estudios Transfronterizos* 10, no. 1 (2010): 161–80.

39 The RIET was created with the specific objective of lobbying, influencing the creation of the public agendas of the respective national governments (Spain and Portugal), specifically the agenda of the Iberian Summits. Domínguez and Varela, "Construyendo *Europolis*."

40 Domínguez and Varela, "Construyendo *Europolis*."

41 In this regard, for example, in April 1986 the working document "Eligible Projects of Joint Consideration by Galicia and the Norte Region of Portugal" was signed.

42 See http://galicia-nortept.xunta.es. In this way, the resistance from the governments of Madrid and Lisbon, which favoured the creation of a single working community for the entire Portuguese–Spanish border, was overcome. In February 2007, it was decided that a Joint Technical Secretariat would be responsible for managing and channelling the community funds for the cross-border cooperation programs on

the border. Due to the specific weight of the Euroregion Galicia–North Portugal, both governments set the Secretariat's office in Badajoz (Extremadura), though this decision was criticized in the G-NP.

43 The approved projects from 2007 to 2013 and 2014 to 2020 are available at http://www.poctep.eu/es.

44 This Joint Investment Plan can be consulted at https://iacobus.gnpaect.eu/sites/default/files/docs/descarga/pic_eurorrexion_gnp_13.pdf.

45 C. Cancela, "Una nueva fase en la cooperación transfronteriza Galicia-Norte de Portugal. Las Agrupaciones Europeas de Cooperación Territorial," in *Cooperación transfronteriza: comparando las experiencias ibéricas*, ed. C. Cancela (Santiago de Compostela : Tórculo, 2008), 155–84; C. Cancela, "Galicia and North Portugal."

46 Note that Portuguese, Galician, and Spanish are the working languages. All of the documents generated by the GNP-AECT have full legal validity in any of these languages, without the need for translation.

47 See http://www.eixoatlantico.com/index.php/es.

48 For example, in 2010 the Atlantic Axis developed a series of initiatives against the establishment of payment tolls on the Portuguese highways of the Euroregion Galicia–North Portugal.

49 C. Cancela, "Atlantic Lessons: Cross-Border Cooperation between Galicia and the Region of North Portugal," *Eastern European Journal for Regional Studies* 5 (2019): 40–61.

50 In relation to the three mentioned Eurocities, considering its demographics and its reduced territorial dimensions, it is interesting that some experts consider it a threat or drawback. Thus, Monção has a population of 19,179 (2011) and a territory of 211.5 km^2, and Salvaterra de Miño has a population of 9,619 (2014) and a territory of 62.5 km^2.

51 M. Lois, "Re-significando la frontera: el caso de la Eurociudad Chaves-Verín," *Boletín de la Asociación de Geógrafos Españoles* 61 (2013): 317.

52 See the Eurociudade Chaves Verin official website at https://portal.cor.europa.eu/egtc/CoRActivities/Pages/Eurociudade-Chaves-Verin.aspx.

53 E. Varela, C. Cancela, and C. Cordal, "The Consolidation of the Euro-Regional Territory and Its Consequences: The Case of the Galicia–North of Portugal Euro-region," *Journal of Territorial and Maritime Studies* 2 (2015): 77–95.

54 J. García-Álvarez and J.M. Trillo-Santamaría, "Between Regional Spaces and Spaces of Regionalism: Cross-Border Region Building in the Spanish 'State of the Autonomies,'" *Regional Studies* 47 (2013): 104–15.

55 Coletti, "Cooperación transfronteriza y trayectorias de desarrollo."

56 Coletti, "Cooperación transfronteriza y trayectorias de desarrollo."

57 Fligstein and McAdam, "Toward a General Theory."

58 Fligstein and McAdam, "Toward a General Theory."

59 During the closure of the border between Spain and Portugal caused by the COVID-19 crisis, there were protests due to the negative impact on economic

and social activities, particularly on the border between Galicia and the Northern Region of Portugal. Several associations and entities (municipalities, businessmen, and some NGOs) requested the reopening of the border, specifically, more border bridges. In particular, the EGTC Río Minho presented a socioeconomic report on the impact of the pandemic on its territory, which had a strong impact in the media. See the report by Francisco Xavier Martínez Cobas and Carlos María Fernández-Jardón, "Impacto socioeconómico da pandemia da COVID-19 no territorio do Río Miño Transfronteirizo. Análise de urxencia" (Spain, 2020).

13 Cooperation and Cross-Border Conflicts in Cerdanya (Spanish–French Border) in Early Twenty-First-Century Environmental and Economic Crises

XAVIER OLIVERAS GONZÁLEZ

Researcher and Professor at El Colegio de la Frontera Norte
Member of the Department of Urban and Environmental Studies

This chapter examines the strategic action field (SAF) of cross-border governance in Cerdanya, a valley between Spain and France (map 13.1). Cross-border cooperation in this region has a long history that began even before European institutions supported and stimulated it; but at the same time, there have been several conflicts that have antagonized local actors on both sides of the border.[1] Thus, the cross-border governance field in Cerdanya can be understood as a continuous process of contention and settlement. This chapter focuses on the field's most recent resettlement in the wake of two chronologically consecutive exogenous shocks: an environmental crisis (2006–8) and an economic one (2008–15). Those two crises led to two conflicts, one over transboundary waters and the other over cross-border business competition and labour (particularly in the construction and real estate development sectors), which then impacted other fields of action, such as tourism.[2] The subsequent containment and resettlement resulted in the reconfiguration and expansion of the cross-border governance field, including the creation of two new cross-border organizations, one by public actors and the other by private ones, in 2012 and 2018, whose aims and structures have largely been responses to the impacts produced by those two conflicts. Hence, this case study allows us to compare and evaluate the effects produced by two exogenous shocks in the SAF. The particular temporalities and local actors largely explain their similarities and differences.

As will be shown, during contention and settlement several resources were mobilized, including the Spain–France border and multiple identities. The border, more symbolic and legal than physical, has long been used, reproduced, or denied according to the local actors' circumstantial interests. In Cerdanya the

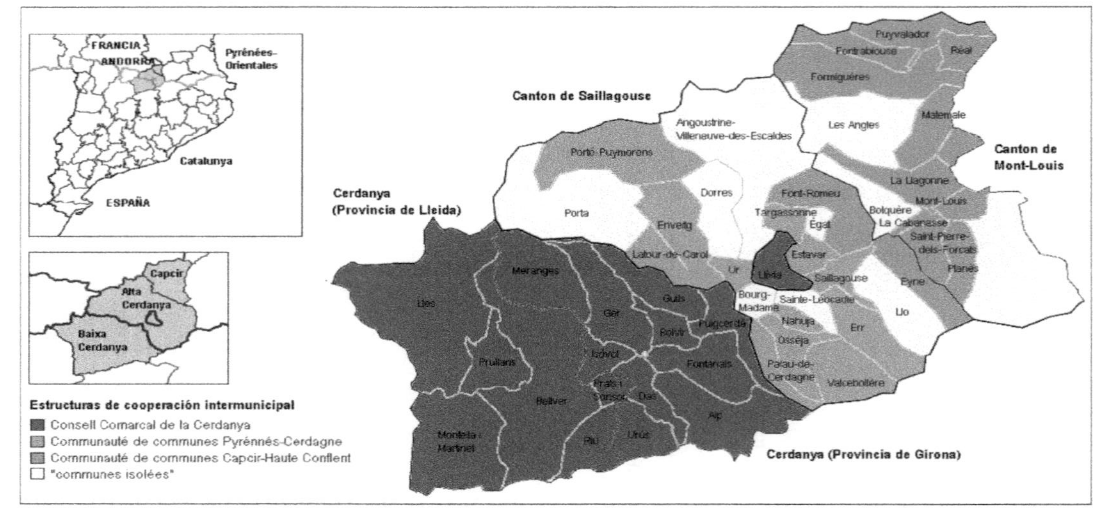

Map 13.1. Political-administrative division of the Cerdanya

Source: Author's elaboration.

border is, as Mancebo describes it, an "à la carte border."[3] Likewise, territorial and cultural identities come into play – at times a cross-border unity identity (Cerdanyan and Catalan), but also, when appropriate, opposed national identities (Spanish or French).[4] Thus, in the two conflicts, cross-border interests were put aside; instead, local actors in Spanish and French Cerdanya mobilized national identities and reclaimed the intervention of their respective national governments. Common interests were not put into play again until the contentions were contained and resettled. In that sense, this case study shows how exogenous shocks become nationalized and how rebordering weakens cross-border unity. Moreover, the case highlights the vulnerability of even well-established cross-border governance to a reassertion of nationalized mindsets.

The data, from two kinds of sources, were collected through a qualitative methodology. First, information about cross-border cooperation and conflicts in Cerdanya was gathered into a database. Information from local and regional digital media on both sides of the border (*Regió 7* and *El Punt*, from Spain; and *La Clau*, *L'Indépendant*, *La Semaine du Roussillon*, and *Midi Libre*, from France) was also complied. The resort to different media guaranteed wider coverage as well as a diversity of perspectives. Second, in 2011–12 and in 2017, fieldwork in Spanish and French Cerdanya was conducted: semi-structured interviews of key informants (mayors) as well as non-participant observation at the meetings that led to the creation of one of the new cross-border organizations (which were held alternatively in two border towns: Puigcerdà, Spain, and Saillagouse, France). Data were then subjected to a qualitative content analysis to identify actors, places, events, resources, and discourses. Throughout, the complexities of the empirical evidence were simplified in order to facilitate analysis and representation.

The structure of this chapter follows the theory of fields and several of its key components. First, I briefly analyse the SAF of cross-border governance, which is grounded in a cross-border unity narrative and in cross-border cooperation projects and organizations. The analysis entails identifying four historical stages of settlement, as well as the incumbents (the Spanish local actors) and challengers (the French ones). This is followed by a characterization of nearby fields (the transboundary waters and the construction and real estate development sectors) and their shocks (the environmental and economic crises). I then describe the main episodes of contention and the processes of resettlement of cross-border governance. The chapter wraps up with a few brief thoughts and conclusions.

The Field of Cross-Border Governance and Its Local Actors

Local actors have developed a cross-border governance field, which has been legitimized through a narrative of "cross-border unity" built upon historical, natural, cultural, and economic circumstances. A prominent historical fact, which has been somewhat romanticized, is that the region was a single polity until the Treaty of the Pyrenees of 1659, by which Spain and France split the region. According to this narrative, this new boundary divided natural (the upper Segre River valley) and cultural (family ties, Catalan language and identity) entities. Based on this understanding, local actors conceive cross-border cooperation as a means to restore their earlier unity and to counteract the (negative) impact of bordering processes (border controls and regulations, the Spanish and French political-administrative divisions and cultural systems, etc.). Taking cross-border cooperation as a variable for defining this field of action, cross-border governance can be traced back to the end of the nineteenth century. Four stages can be identified based on their different degrees of intensity and consolidation.

The first stage started at the end of the nineteenth century and lasted until the 1930s, when mayors (*alcaldes* and *maires*) from both sides of the boundary gathered ocassionally in informal assemblies. Among other things, these assemblies led to the creation of a number of cross-border commissions. These governance units addressed issues of common interest, such as improvements in trans-Pyrenean transportation (a Barcelona-to-Paris railway) and the desire to protect natural resources, especially water, from appropriation by forces beyond Cerdanya (for example, hydroelectric development). This cross-border governance was halted by an exogenous shock, the Franco dictatorship in Spain (1939–78), which prevented any formal cooperation.

The second stage corresponds to the emergence of cross-border cooperation in the late 1970s and early 1980s, just before Spain entered the EU (1985). In those years, cultural associations played a decisive role in setting the field (notably the Cerdanya Studies Institute / Institut d'Estudis Ceretans, IEC); their activities served as meeting points for several local actors from both sides of the border. There was a willingness to think about the region as a single unit based on natural, cultural, and historical realities that justified such unity. This period was characterized by a number of thriving cross-border projects in different fields (urbanism, industrial development, tourism, culture, environmental management), but these, in general, were not in the end carried out due to several obstacles: the lack of coordination between the diverse local actors and between projects, disputes between actors on both sides, and an inability to establish common aims. One of the few successful initiatives was the organization of "Cerdanya Day" by the IEC, which with several exceptions (see below), has been held annually since 1981 in several towns, alternating between France and Spain. Local governments and associations, as well as the populace, participate in this festival. Like other border festivals,[4] Cerdanya Day seeks to erase the international boundary and to build and reinforce a narrative of cross-border unity.

In the third stage, in the 1990s, the leadership and legitimacy of cross-border governance shifted from civil society to local governments. This resettlement was influenced by an endogenous factor (the gradual erosion of cultural associations) and by an exogenous one: the increasing regulation of cross-border cooperation by national and European institutions, which privileged governmental actors. With the launch of the EU's INTERREG programme in 1989, *alcaldes* and *maires* (Spanish and French mayors) grew keenly interested in cross-border cooperation, and Cerdanya Day became the time of the annual Trobada d'alcaldes (cross-border mayors meeting). As the years passed, several cooperation projects were proposed and discussed in various fields of action: environmental management, health, transportation, tourism, water management, culture, education, and so on. Some of them were achieved thanks to successful cross-border cooperation and EU funding. In spatial terms, cross-border cooperation was implemented at two different scales: sometimes between neighbouring border *municipios* and *communes*, with greater urban and functional integration (Puigcerdà and Bourg-Madame, and Llívia and Estavar); and other times covering (almost) all of Cerdanya. Regarding the latter, in 1991, the Cerdanya Municipalities Association (Asociació de Municipis de la Cerdanya, AMC) was created, whose aims were to manage common challenges and to promote cross-border economic development. But expectations were set too high and EU funding was too low, so that growing frustration led to its dissolution in 1998.

The fourth stage, the current one, initially emerged in 2006 within the legal framework of the European Grouping of Territorial Cooperation (EGTC), which offered the opportunity to create cross-border organizations with greater authority and financial autonomy. In this context, in 2012 the EGTC Pirineus–Cerdanya was established, whose goals focused on transportation, territorial planning, the Catalan language and culture, and the economy and tourism. As will be seen later, since its inception that organization has been promoting a cross-border business cluster in which small and medium-sized companies from both sides participate. In addition to the EGTC, other cross-border projects have been developed: cross-border facilities, a hospital in Puigcerdà on the Spanish side (opened in 2014), a slaughterhouse on the French side (in operation since 2017),[5] and even a cross-border landscape master plan.[6]

Two main objections have arisen to the "cross-border unity" narrative, particularly from French local actors. First, the territorial differentiation between the two Cerdanyas has deepened since the mid-twentieth century as a result of strengthened bordering and nationalization processes. A sociolinguistic fact will suffice here to explain this: the Catalan language has been subordinated to Spanish and French in a diglossia situation, and while it continues to have a strong presence in Spanish Cerdanya, it has almost vanished from French Cerdanya. Additionally, since the 1980s, the tertiarization of the local economy has contributed to territorial differentiation. According to Pujadas and Moncusí, the shift to tourism, services, and real estate development has altered the regional unity of earlier times, which had been based on agriculture as well as long-standing family and community interests.[7] Related to that issue, a power asymmetry between the two sides has developed: since the 1980s, Spanish Cerdanya has acquired greater economic and political dominance. Note that a similar asymmetry has taken hold at the upper administrative level, in that Catalonia is now one of the wealthiest regions in Spain and Pyrénées-Orientales is one of the poorest *départements* in France. Again, the change in the distribution of territorial power is associated with the process of tertiarization, which within a few decades has transformed the patterns of behaviour and collective identity between the two sides. As a result of this recent unequal distribution of power, French local actors have developed a certain amount of resentment toward the Spanish side, often perceiving the narrative of cross-border unity as Spanish Cerdanya's mechanism for strengthening its dominance of the French side.[8] Thus, French local actors usually perceive, suspect, and fear that efforts at cross-border cooperation are beholden to Spanish local actors' interests. The French actors perceive Spanish Cerdanya as attempting to capitalize on territorial dynamics and European financing (particularly in its capital city, Puigcerdà) – that is, to accumulate greater power at the expense of French Cerdanya. Especially in times of crisis and border conflict, French actors mobilize these arguments, as will be shown later.

Nearby Cross-Border Fields

Cross-border governance is linked to other fields of action, two of which are of interest for our study: transboundary waters and the cross-border construction and real estate development sectors. As noted earlier, these fields have long been linked. Thus, water resources led to the emergence of cross-border governance in the late nineteenth and early twentieth centuries; likewise, economic development has been one of the principal cooperation goals since the 1980s.

Transboundary Waters

The relevance of this field arises from the misalignment between the international boundary and the actual watershed. Most of the Spain–France boundary coincides with the region's river basins, but in a few places, it does not. For example, the Segre River (and some of its tributaries, including the Querol/Carol River) flows from the French side to the Spanish side. Under the terms of the 1866 boundary treaty, the two countries together regulated the use of shared waters, as well as a set of transboundary water rights largely dating back to mediaeval times.[9] Regarding those rights, the ownership and use of the so-called Puigcerdà Canal is a prominent concern. That transboundary canal was dug in the fourteenth century to divert Querol River water from Latour de

Carol, France, to Puigcerdà, Spain. The 1866 treaty recognized and confirmed Puigcerdà's ownership of and rights to the canal; it also established the amount of water that could be diverted and its fair distribution between Spanish and French users. Finally, based on the treaty, a joint international commission was created to administer the canal and resolve possible disputes.

Despite the provisions of the 1866 treaty, several conflicts have arisen since the mid-twentieth century due to various factors whose characteristics and consequences were difficult or impossible to foresee in the mid-nineteenth century. Among those worth mentioning are new water uses (such as hydroelectric power production), changes in territorial and economic structure (from a predominantly rural economy to a tertiary one), increasing water demand (especially for domestic, urban, and tourist uses), the increase in wastewater, and, more recently, the effects of climate change. Faced with this situation, local actors on both sides have repeatedly requested that Spain and France update or renegotiate the 1866 boundary treaty. In general, neither state has responded, except in a few cases and belatedly. An example is the conflict over the hydroelectric use of the waters of Lake Lanoux on the French side, which arose in 1917 but was not resolved until 1958 with a new agreement (modified in 1970).[10] The national actors' slow and weak response has often meant that conflicts have been left for local actors to resolve.

Another factor that hinders the management of transboundary water is that the distribution of authority over it is highly fragmented among the various administrative levels and watershed management bodies, both within each country (the Ebro Hydrographic Confederation, the Catalan Water Agency, the Rhône-Mediterranean-Corsica Water Agency, etc.)[11] and at the local, regional, state, and EU levels. Occasionally, a third border state, Andorra, must be added to the mix.[12]

The Cross-Border Construction and Real Estate Development Sectors

Since the 1980s, with improvements in transportation toward the international boundary, Cerdanya has been progressively integrated into the metropolitan regions of Barcelona, Spain, and Toulouse and Perpignan, France. Metropolization strengthened in the 2000s with the Spanish real estate boom, due to the urban population's residential mobility and the development of winter tourism and second homes. Around those economic sectors, several service businesses developed: construction, interior design, gardening, leisure, restaurants, and so on. The importance of tourism and services is evident in the number of people that sector now employed – around 70 per cent of locals as of 2008; the construction and real estate development sectors accounted for another 21 per cent that same year. In addition to metropolization, there is also increasing cross-border residential mobility because of the comparative advantages each side holds.[13] French Cerdanya has developed a cross-border real estate market, derived from three phenomena: cheaper land and house prices than on the Spanish side, the saturation of second-home subdivisions in Spanish Cerdanya, and EU monetary unification.[14] Thus, in the mid-2000s, 61.5 per cent of the new houses built in French Cerdanya were in the second-home market, and, in some locales, up to two thirds were owned by Spaniards. According to French local actors, this has led to a "Barcelonaization" or "Spanishization" of the economy and residential landscape in French Cerdanya. Some actors in French Cerdanya were opposed to this process; even so, local governments generally set out to boost urban and tourist development (through zoning rules, building permits, etc.) because it represented an important source of tax income and jobs: it was manna from heaven.[15] Local governments argued that tax income allowed them to strengthen their limited financial autonomy.

In addition to this, small and medium-sized Spanish companies were active in urban and real estate development in French Cerdanya.[16] Their headquarters were mostly in Barcelona and Girona provinces, although some established secondary headquarters in French Cerdanya and in Perpignan. Their expansion into the French market was facilitated by geographical proximity and by the origins of many of their customers, as well as by the EU's service directive (2006) (better known as the Bolkestein Directive), which guarantees the freedom of establishment and free movement of services among the member-states. At the same time, though, these companies prefer to employ workers residing in Spain, to the detriment of French workers.

Consequently, cross-border labour mobility has increased, although the Franco-Spanish border is characterized by less labour mobility than in border regions in the European megalopolis.[17] Since the 1980s, there has been slight but steady growth in cross-border labour mobility as a result of European integration and the growth of specific economic sectors (construction, tourism, commerce). In the 2000s, coinciding with the real estate boom and the introduction of the euro, the volume of cross-border commuters along the entire border increased to around 4,500.[18] In areas such as Cerdanya, most cross-border commuters reside on the French side, although about 70 per cent of them are Spanish citizens;[19] this is explained by residential mobility. However, informal work was not calculated, especially in the construction and tourism sectors, so the total number of cross-border commuters is probably higher, as well as inverse (i.e., a majority of employees in France live in Spain).[20]

Exogenous Shocks: Two Crises

The first years of the twenty-first century saw two exogenous shocks that directly affected those two nearby fields: the first of these was environmental (the drought of 2006–8), the second economic (2008–15). These shocks led to cross-border conflicts in which several local actors were involved.

The Drought of 2006–2008

From autumn 2006 to autumn 2008, Catalonia and Pyrénées-Orientales suffered a severe drought that, due to its long duration, caused a significant decrease in water reserves and thus a water supply crisis from April 2007 until January 2009.[21] In the upper river basins, including the Segre, there was no rainfall for fifteen consecutive months. Additionally, in Cerdanya the crisis reduced snow cover, which had a direct impact on ski resorts and winter tourism.[22]

As a result of the water scarcity, the diversion of water from the Querol River by Spanish *municipios* became a source of conflict with the French. Despite the drought, Puigcerdà and other border *municipios* with transboundary rights continued to divert the maximum water allowed by the 1866 treaty, which does not take the minimum flow of the river into account. In response to the drought, the government of Puigcerdà built a second tank to store water from the transboundary canal. The diversion and the scarce rainfall left several French towns, mainly Latour de Carol and Enveig, practically without a water supply. From the end of 2006 to the beginning of 2008, the French representatives on the canal's international commission of the canal, as well as the affected local governments, repeatedly asked the Spanish representatives to reduce the amount of water they were diverting, citing ethical, ecological, and equity reasons, but the Spanish local governments consistently refused to do so. By the beginning of 2008, tensions were running very high and several acts of sabotage were perpetrated on the French side both at the intake and in the canal itself; for example, in mid-2008, the intake valves were blocked, preventing the diversion of water into the canal. The Spanish *alcaldes* accused the French *maires* of being directly involved in those actions, and as a response to them, the Puigcerdà government installed a fence and security cameras around the intake. Those works were carried out without the corresponding administrative permits; the French actors understood them as illegal actions committed by a foreign actor on French territory.

Rain finally fell in the autumn of 2008, but the conflict continued for several more months. Between December 2008 and January 2009, local governments in France and Spain complained to their respective national governments, each accusing the other of having broken the 1866 treaty. France and Spain sought a peaceful resolution within the framework of the International Commission of the Pyrenees. The issue was not resolved satisfactorily until 2012, when Spain and France refused to modify the treaty but agreed to increase the monitoring and verification of the volume of water being diverted.

The same drought affected the water supply of metropolitan Barcelona.[23] As a solution, in the spring of 2008 the government of Catalonia planned a provisional transfer of water from the Segre River, in Spanish Cerdanya, to the Llobregat River, which supplies the metropolitan region. This proposal was rejected unanimously by local actors in Spanish Cerdanya. That rejection was based on fears that rights to use (e.g., for agriculture and domestic consumption) would be violated. It was argued that the river did not have enough water to supply metropolitan Barcelona and that the transfer would have deleterious social, economic, and environmental impacts on the Segre River basin; also, local actors doubted that it would be a provisional transfer and feared that it would become a permanent one, as had happened already in other basins.[24] Every *municipio* in Spanish Cerdanya, one after the next, approved a motion against the transfer and asked the *communes* of French Cerdanya for their support. On the French side, that proposal was viewed as a provocation, and local actors showed utter indifference to that issue, arguing that they were not affected because they were upstream. However, their refusal to support Spanish Cerdanya heightened the conflict over the Querol waters. The French local governments viewed the position of the Spanish ones as particularly contradictory: on the one hand, they rejected the transfer to Barcelona because they wished to ensure the support of the French local governments based on a cross-border logic; on the other hand, they did not waive their water diversion in French territory, thus using the 1866 border treaty to their advantage. Before Spanish Cerdanya could do anything more about this matter, the Catalan government aborted the Segre transfer project when a political backlash to it developed both in Catalonia and in Spain (in fact, the Spanish government vetoed the project). It opted for other projects (the transfer of water from the Ebro River and even from the Rhône, which implied a negotiation with France).[25]

The Economic Crisis of 2008–2015

The global economic crisis of 2008 directly impacted the construction and real estate development sectors. The real estate market collapsed, and in 2008, Spain saw a 40–50 per cent reduction in construction projects. This drove up unemployment, especially in Spain (where it peaked in 2013 at 26.9 per cent) and in the French border regions (10–14 per cent in the same year). In French Cerdanya, buildings were abandoned half finished and many firms related to the sector disappeared (real estate agencies, construction companies, garden centres, furniture companies, etc.). Similarly, in the entire *département* of Pyrénées-Orientales, 3,200 construction jobs were lost between 2008 and 2013. Both phenomena were perceived by some French local actors as direct consequences of the "Spanish invasion."[26]

The economic crisis led Spanish construction companies to show more interest in expanding into southern France, and by 2011 they were responsible for about 35 per cent of construction work in the *département* of Pyrénées-Orientales.[27] Business groups from Girona organized training courses for entrepreneurs interested in moving to France. In Pyrénées-Orientales, where there had also been a slowdown in the construction sector, the arrival of Spanish companies led to growing competition for a shrinking number of projects. Awareness of Spanish companies' presence heightened as unemployment surged; also, there was growing suspicion that these companies were engaging in irregularities in order to reduce costs (especially labour costs) as they duelled with French companies. In particular, a form of cross-border dumping was suspected – that is, workers residing in Spain were being employed in France but being paid the Spanish wage (the so-called country of origin principle, which in the end was not included in the Bolkestein Directive). This led to Spanish companies being accused of violating French labour regulations as they applied to foreign employees, in addition to breaking the French–Spanish agreement regarding the tax regime for cross-border workers.

By 2012, the authorities in Pyrénées-Orientales had detected several Spanish companies practising this form of cross-border dumping, and several French media, employers, unions, political parties, and local and regional public officials immediately launched a campaign against that practice. Protests were supported especially by the construction employers' organization and union; these lasted until the end of 2013. The campaign focused on two controversial themes: xenophobia, and Eurosceptism and protectionism. Regarding the first of these, Spanish workers found themselves stigmatized, as symbolized by the figures of the *maçon espagnol* and the *peintre espagnol* (the Spaniard bricklayer and painter); regarding the second, protectionism raised its head, with calls for France to recover its right to "close the borders." Employers' and employees' organizations demanded several measures of their national, regional, and local governments: a reduction in the number of Spanish workers allowed; a hardening of the criteria applied to foreign companies to compete in France; and an outright ban on Spanish companies. In addition to all this, unfair competition that involved non-compliance with tax and labour regulations was criticized, and calls went out for regulations and wages in both countries to again be made uniform to prevent cross-border dumping. Most protest actions were carried out in Perpignan, where the construction sector maintained sufficient activity thanks to public works and where the departmental administration is located. By contrast, French Cerdanya saw only a few such protests, partly due to its distance from the decision-making centres and partly because the construction sector had been virtually dismantled. Protests there had little effect on the populace or on local governments; on the contrary, they seemed to be aimed at regional, national, and European actors and media. Thus, a blockade – including the building of a brick wall – was carried out by the construction union at the border crossing between Bourg-Madame and Puigcerdà. With the blockade and the border wall, the union expressed its opposition to competition from Spanish companies and workers, notwithstanding the free circulation guaranteed by the EU. The blockade and the border wall symbolized the reification of the border, in a manner never before seen in French Cerdanya.[28]

In a broader context, that campaign was part of what Bourgeois calls "cross-border outrages,"[29] and in that sense, it was directly related to protests against the Bolkestein Directive in 2004–6. In France, this rejection was symbolized by the *plombier polonais* (the Polish plumber), a figure who represented the fear of lower-paid migrant workers from Eastern Europe, as well as a trope for unfair labour competition more generally.[30] Fear was directed not only at unfair competition but also at the competition between "domestic workers" and "foreign workers" for scarce jobs. Thus, the *chômeur d'Europe du sud* (the unemployed from southern Europe) were viewed more as a threat than as a victim of the reforms and austerity imposed in Spain, Portugal, and Greece. In addition, these cross-border outrages revealed the structural problem of the lack of competitiveness of French companies, especially in economic sectors such as construction, were there had been little innovation.

Contention and Settlement: From Conflicts to Greater Cross-Border Integration

Both crises, the environmental (2006–8) and the economic (2008–15), impacted the field of cross-border governance, although with different repercussions due to differences in timing and in the actors involved. Their settlement led to stronger cross-border integration (the fourth of the stages previously identified) so as to minimize the consequences of disputes and resolve future conflicts more efficiently.

The conflict over transboundary waters directly altered several cross-border cooperation projects led by *local* actors; projects that depended on *regional* and *state-level* actors, such as the cross-border hospital, were not affected.[31] This was immediately visible on "Cerdanya Day" in 2006. The yearly meeting of *alcaldes* and *maires* was scheduled to be held in a Spanish town, but the French *maires* announced that, in protest, they would not attend, so it was suspended. The same happened in the following two years: in 2007, it was scheduled to be celebrated in a French town, but it was not even organized; and in 2008, it was celebrated in Spain, but only a handful of *maires* attended (i.e., only those whose *communes* had been less affected by the conflict or those who were willing to seek a solution). The same shock wave reached the field of regional and cross-border transportation infrastructure, which Spanish *alcaldes* wanted to address at the mayors' meetings. They especially wished for a better road connecting the metropolitan areas of Barcelona and Toulouse, for the benefit of tourism. In 2005 and 2006, when France and Catalonia approved new transportation master plans, neither prioritized improvements to the roads leading to the border. In response, several local governments on both sides of the border claimed greater attention; among them were those of Barcelona and Toulouse and those of Spanish Cerdanya. However, French Cerdanya and the entire Pyrénées-Orientales département refused to join them, in protest against the transboundary waters issue. Similar ruptures occurred within other cross-border cooperation projects. For instance, since the early 2000s, several *municipios* and *communes* have cooperated to treat the wastewater discharged into the Querol River. A treatment plant was planned on the French side, next to the river just before it flowed across the boundary, for which INTERREG funding was used. Its construction began shortly before the drought began, but in 2008, the government of Puigcerdà withdrew as a response to the conflict over transboundary waters.

After the drought ended, during the 2008 meeting of *alcaldes* and *maires*, it was agreed to find ways to minimize conflicts such as the one that had occurred, recognizing that local cross-border cooperation in water management would be better solved at the national level – local authorities did not have sufficient clout to address it. Undoubtedly, the end of the drought helped resettle this field one year later, and thus, "Cerdanya Day" of 2009 was celebrated as usual in a French town and with the assistance of the majority of *maires* and *alcaldes*. Moreover, at the end of 2009, the wastewater treatment plant on the Querol River was officially opened with an event that was attended by the *alcalde* of Puigcerdà and other mayors from Spanish Cerdanya. In this act of public reconciliation, the *alcaldes* and *maires* expressed their willingness to re-establish friendly dialogue and maintain and intensify cross-border cooperation. Thus, the conflict over transboundary waters was left to be solved by the national governments through bilateral frameworks, such as the one offered by the International Commission of the Pyrenees. As of 2019, Spain and France were in talks but an agreement had yet to be reached.[32]

At the same time, at the meeting of *alcaldes* and *maires* in 2008, it was agreed to create a new cross-border organization, similar to that of the 1990s but more powerful. The first steps were taken in 2009, when Spanish Cerdanya attempted to establish a special legal regime that would recognize its cross-border nature and endow it with greater authority and financial autonomy.[33] However, the proposal was rejected by the government of Catalonia and did not come before the Spanish and French governments. Finally, it was decided to take advantage of the EU's new EGTC regulation, and what would end up being the EGTC Pirineus–Cerdanya was finally created in 2012. The process was long and complex, given the outstanding disputes between the two main *communautés de communes* (interlocal associations) in French Cerdanya. During the period 2009–11, those disputes led to a crisis within the Communauté de Communes Pyrénées-Cerdagne, which ended with the departure of Font-Romeu, the commune that contributed most to its financing, and its subsequent integration in 2012 into the Communauté de Communes Capcir-Haute Conflent. As a consequence, the EGTC was constituted under a great territorial imbalance. On the one side, it included all the Spanish Cerdanya *municipios*, gathered in one interlocal association (Consell comarcal de la Cerdanya); on the other, only the *communes* of Pyrénées-Cerdagne. This imbalance meant that French Cerdanya was in an inferior position in demographic, political, and financial terms. However, the conflict over transboundary waters gave French local governments advantages, in that it was easy for them to accuse Spanish Cerdanya of intending to subordinate French Cerdanya. Thus, the EGTC Pirineus–Cerdanya ended up having a structure more similar to a French *communauté de communes* than to a Spanish *consell comarcal*. And instead of proportional territorial representation (as in a *consell comarcal*), it was granted an equal one (as in a *communauté de communes*), with a governing body made up of ten members, five per side. Its structure did not depend on population and financing, which would have given greater political weight to Spanish Cerdanya. Likewise, the denomination proposed by French Cerdanya was imposed (it is the same as that of the Communauté de Communes Pyrénées-Cerdagne) against the preferences of Spanish local actors (simply "Cerdanya"). And finally, the headquarters was established in the French town of Saillagouse, instead of in Puigcerdà, which for Spanish actors was the "natural" and historical capital for both sides.

The creation of the EGTC Pirineus–Cerdanya was carried out in the context of the economic crisis, although, unlike with the environmental crisis, the shock in the real estate and construction sectors did not imply a significant resettlement for cross-border governance. This is partly because the local governments of French Cerdanya did not perceive the economy of the second home as a threat or a "Spanish invasion," but rather as a source of local development.[34] At the same time, the actors on both sides of the border shared the vision that the economic crisis and its causes affected both sides equally and that overcoming it was a common challenge. In this sense, given that the construction and real estate sectors were perceived as having caused the crisis, the cross-border recovery strategy should not go through those sectors. However, there was a significant change: local governments perceived that the participation of private economic actors was needed. Thus, local governments, through the EGTC, committed themselves to cooperating with private actors to promote economic development and, in the short term, counteract the economic crisis. The EGTC Pirineus–Cerdanya and business associations from both sides began in 2012 to lobby for a cross-border business cluster, "El Sol dels Pirineus–Le soleil des Pyrénées" (the Sun of the Pyrenees), which gathered some forty small and medium-sized companies (twenty-five from Spanish Cerdanya, fifteen from French Cerdanya). It was formally created in 2018, and even though a cross-border organization, it had to be legalized both in Spain and France according to their respective laws. So it has two headquarters, in Llívia, Spain, and Osséja, France. This strategy sought to gather local companies from five strategic economic sectors – tourism, food, sports, health, and sustainable development – in order to promote innovation and improve competitiveness. Its first action was a health tourism plan. The construction and real estate sectors were absent, for the reasons already mentioned.

Final Reflections

In this chapter, I have analysed the shocks produced in two fields (transboundary waters, and the cross-border construction and real estate development sector) and their impacts on the cross-border governance field. The contention and settlement were impacted by multiple interactions with other fields, which for reasons of space could not be given the attention they deserved here (e.g., the presence of subnational, national, and supranational fields [Catalonia, Spain, France, and the EU], tourism, local governments' authority and financial autonomy, territorial fragmentation, local governments' inefficiency, competition, personal and political disputes between parties, and interlocal cooperation). Nevertheless, they need to be pointed out, and a more thorough analysis than the one I have conducted here would have to factor them in. This chapter, then, has provided only a partial account.

Regarding the main objective of the research, I have shown that the drought of 2006–8 and the economic crisis of 2008–15 led to two cross-border conflicts that altered the field of cross-border governance, albeit with different repercussions (qualitatively larger with the environmental crisis than with the economic one). This difference also reflects a different degree of impact on local governments, but also on the containment and resettlement of the field. The environmental shock eventually reconfigured the governance unit; the economic shock a few years later served to expand the field based on that new unit. More importantly, the results show that even well-established cross-border governance, such as in Cerdanya, is vulnerable to exogenous shocks and to a reassertion of nations and borders. In this case, the cross-border governance field was structured around a "cross-border unity" narrative, which was then challenged as the two crises' causes, consequences, and solutions were nationalized. This seems to be what typically happens in cross-border conflicts – there is a "nationalization of interest[s]," in the words of Sahlins, to the detriment of common cross-border interests.[35]

Thus, during the conflict over transboundary waters, the local governments on either side tried to ensure they received the greatest possible quantity of water, basing their arguments on the rights guaranteed by Spain and France in the 1866 boundary treaty. Each side resorted to its respective state as champion in the dispute; the paradox is that once the national governments were constituted as arbitrators, they entrusted the local governments to solve the problem amicably. Likewise, with respect to the conflict over unfair cross-border business competition and dumping, the French actors produced a discourse based on the nationalization of "us" against the "others," whether those others were people, companies, or territories: France for French workers and companies, and Spain for Spanish workers (painters, bricklayers) and companies. In this way, they nationalized the causes of the crisis, as reflected in labels such as the "Spaniardization" of the landscape and economy of French Cerdanya. The consequences of that nationalization were a push for rebordering – for a closed border and a closed national territory (the brick wall on the border crossing, the fence around the water intake) – and a rejection of debordering as guaranteed and represented by the EU and its programs and directives.

By contrast, the resettlement of the field involved the reverse of this process: local actors sought to restore the "cross-border unity" narrative as a mechanism for overcoming crises. The search for this unity was evident in the founding of new organizations for cross-border cooperation, such as the EGTC Pirineus–Cerdanya and the business cluster "El Sol dels Pirineus–Le soleil des Pyrénées." This coincides with the conclusions reached by Berzi, who views the formation of the business cluster as confirmation that the economic crisis was an external stimulus for public *and* private local actors to respond in creative and innovative ways to conflict, competition, and cooperation from a cross-border perspective. In fact, during the resettlement process, the French local governments (the challengers) mobilized both positions (cross-border unity and border division), and this gave them a decisive advantage over the Spanish local governments (the incumbents), who wished to mobilize only the unity narrative.[36] Thus, as has been stated, the EGTC Pirineus–Cerdanya was built mirroring French interlocal associations despite French actors' lesser political, financial, and territorial weight.

To summarize: this case study shows that the theory of fields is a useful analytical tool. It demonstrates that fields of action are transformed through exogenous shocks and contention between incumbents and challengers, and then settled. Remember, however, that the theory of fields is only a *framework* within which conflicts and cooperation can be interpreted and described; it offers no explanation for their causes and consequences. As Fligstein and McAdam themselves warn us, it is not truly a "theory"; rather, "it is principally a methodological technique for modeling various aspects of the relationships between actors within a field."[37] Again taking this case study as an example, it can be acknowledged that the two crises were settled, but I cannot give a clear answer as to *why* they were, and it cannot be known why the two crises did not instead weaken the cross-border governance field. Another question arises: To what extent can an analysis as simplified and fragmentary as this one allow us to draw *any* conclusions? Given how complex such fields are and the (infinite?) multitude of actions at play, identifying explanatory relationships within a particular case poses a challenge. Finally, in our case study, social skills were not as relevant as symbolic resources (narratives, meanings, and identities). A common criticism of Fligstein and McAdam's theory of fields is that it places too much emphasis on individual actors' social skills.[38] In this sense, more than the social skills of any individual, collective actors (in this case, one for each side of the border: the "Spanish Cerdanya," the incumbent, and the "French Cerdanya," the challenger) mobilized symbolic resources, both national and cross-border. Those resources do not constitute a unified system, but as this case shows, they can serve as tools for conflict and cooperation.

NOTES

1 P. Sahlins, *Boundaries: The Making of France and Spain in the Pyrenees* (Berkeley: University of California Press, 1989); F. Mancebo, *La Cerdagne et ses frontières: conflits et identités transfrontalières* (Perpignan: El Trabucaire, 1999); Mancebo, "En Cerdagne, des clivages qui relient, des unions qui divisent: réorganisations spatiales et actions transfrontalières en Cerdagne après l'ouverture des frontières," *Revue de l'économie méridionale* 48, no. 192 (2000): 441–60; A. Moncusí, *Fronteres, identitats nacionals i integració europea: el cas de la Cerdanya* (Valencia: Afers/Universitat de València, 2005); X. Oliveras, "La cooperación transfronteriza en la Cerdanya (frontera España-Francia)," *Boletín de la Asociación de Geógrafos Españoles (AGE)* 62 (2013): 25–48; M. Berzi, "The Cross-Border Reterritorialization Concept Revisited: The Territorialist Approach Applied to the Case of Cerdanya on the French-Spanish Border," *European Planning Studies* 25, no. 9 (2017): 1575–96; M. Berzi and M. Castañer, "Los Pirineos, entre las políticas europeas y las iniciativas locales de cooperación transfronteriza: El caso de la Cerdaña," *Documents d'Anàlisi Geogràfica* 64, no. 3 (2018): 529–50; J. Pujadas and A. Moncusí, "Cerdanya, territorio fronterizo y lugar en sí mismo. Los vaivenes del borderland franco-español en un enclave catalán," *Studi Emigrazione* 55, no. 211 (2018): 351–72.

2 P. Bachimon, P. Dérioz, and M. Marc, "Développement touristique et durabilité en Cerdagne française," *Revue de Géographie Alpine* 97, no. 3 (2009), https://rga.revues.org/1056.

3 Mancebo, *La Cerdagne et ses frontières*, 1999.

4 X. Oliveras, "Fiestas transfronterizas y representaciones espaciales en la frontera México-Texas," *Economía, Sociedad y Territorio* 16, no. 50 (2016): 133–69.

5 Berzi, "The Cross-Border Reterritorialization Concept Revisited," 2017; Oliveras, "La cooperación transfronteriza en la Cerdanya," 2013; X. Oliveras and J.M. Trillo, "Fronteras en el contexto español: ¿Barreras o puentes para la cooperación sanitaria?," *Documents d'Anàlisi Geogràfica* 60, no. 1 (2014): 135–59.

6 J. Nogué and P. Sala, "La planificació i la gestió d'un paisatge transfronterer. El Pla de Paisatge de la Cerdanya," *Documents d'Anàlisi Geogràfica* 64, no. 3 (2018): 567–86.

7 Pujadas and Moncusí, "Cerdanya, territorio fronterizo y lugar en sí mismo," 2018.

8 Mancebo, *La Cerdagne et ses frontières*, 1999; Mancebo, "En Cerdagne, des clivages qui relient," 2000; J.-B. Harguindéguy, *La frontière en Europe, un territoire? coopération transfrontalière franco-espagnole* (Paris, France: L'Harmattan, 2007).

9 J. Capdevila, *Historia del deslinde de la frontera hispano-francesa. Del tratado de los Pirineos (1659) a los tratados de Bayona (1856–1868)* (Madrid: Centro Nacional de Información Geográfica, 2009); X. Oliveras, "La cooperació transfronterera en la gestió de conques fluvials a la frontera franco-andorrano-espanyola," *Estudis d'Història Agrària* 24 (2012): 233–49.

10 Oliveras, "La cooperación transfronteriza en la Cerdanya," 2013.

11 C. Maury and S. Richard, "La difficile gestion de l'eau en contexte transfrontalier: Un exemple franco-espagnol," *Journal of Urban Research* 6 (2011), https://articulo.revues.org/1736; I. Aldomà, "Del conflicte d'usuaris a la confrontació política passant per l'autoafirmació regional. A propòsit de la crisi de la sequera del 2008 a Barcelona i els transvasaments," *Treballs de la Societat Catalana de Geografia* 74 (2012): 11–39.

12 Oliveras, "La cooperació transfronterera," 2012.

13 A. Decoville, F. Durand, C. Sohn, and O. Walther, "Comparing Cross-Border Metropolitan Integration in Europe: Towards a Functional Typology," *Journal of Borderlands Studies* 28, no. 2 (2013): 221–37.

14 Mancebo, "En Cerdagne, des clivages qui relient," 2000; N. Ahn and M. Blazquez, *Residential Mobility and Labor Market Transitions: Relative Effects of Housing Tenure and Other Variables* (Madrid: Fundación de Estudios de Economía Aplicada, 2007); P. Bachimon, P. Dérioz, and V. Vlès, "Les phénomènes de dédoublement résidentiel dans les trajectoires de plusieurs systèmes touristiques pyrénéens: Cerdagne (P.O.), Vicdessos (Ariège) et haute vallée d'Ossau (P.A.)," *Sud-Ouest européen. Revue géographique des Pyrénées et du Sud-Ouest* 39 (2015): 81–95; G. Nerb, ed., *Scientific Report on the Mobility of Cross-Border Workers witihn the EU-27/EEA/EFTA Countries* (Brussels: European Comission, DG Employment and Social Affairs, 2009); Bachimon, Dérioz, and Vlès, "Les phénomènes de dédoublement résidentiel," 2015; J.M. Prat and G. Cànoves, "Las actividades organizadas para los turistas como elemento de cohesión en los destinos residenciales de montaña: el caso de la Cerdanya," *Documents d'Anàlisi Geogràfica* 65, no. 2 (2019): 345–69.

15 M. Lefèvre, "Périphérie et transfrontalier comme catégories d'action politique. Sud-Ouest européen," *Revue Géographique des Pyrénées et du Sud-Ouest* 28 (2009): 31–43.

16 Mission Operationnelle Transfrontaliere (MOT) and Universitat de Girona (UdG), *Libre blanc de l'Eurodistricte, per a un futur transfronterer* (Barcelona, and Perpignan: Generalitat de Catalunya / Conseil Régional des Pyrénées-Orientales, 2008); Bachimon, Dérioz, and Marc, "Développement touristique et durabilité en Cerdagne française," 2009; Bachimon, Dérioz, and Vlès, "Les phénomènes de dédoublement résidentiel," 2015.

17 V. Soutif, *L'intégration européenne et les travailleurs frontaliers de l'Europe occidentale* (Paris, France: L'Harmattan, 1999).

18 A. Luengo, *Gent de frontera. Un peu a cada banda. Presència, 1684* (2004): 2–8; Mission Opérationelle Transfrontalière (MOT), *Atlas de la coopération transfrontalière. Dynamique transfrontalière et projets de territoires* (Paris: Mission Opérationelle Transfrontalière, 2007); MOT and UdG, *Libre blanc de l'Eurodistricte.*

19 Ahn and Bázques, *Residential Mobility and Labor Market Transitions*, 2007.

20 MOT and UdG, *Libre blanc de l'Eurodistricte*; F. Sol, ed., *Rapport d'étude de faisabilité de l'EURES-Transfrontalier Pyrénées-Méditerranéennes* (Montpellier: Observatoire régional de l'emploi et de la formation, 1996).

21 A. Urgell, "Abastament d'aigua a l'àrea metropolitana de Barcelona. Sequera," *Territori. Observatori de Projectes I Debats Territorials de Catalunya* (2008), http://territori.scot.cat/cat/notices/2008/12/abastament_d_aigua_a_l_Area_metropolitana_de_barcelona_sequera_029.php; A. Ribas and D. Saurí, *2008, l'any de la sequera. Territori. Observatori de projectes i debats territorials de Catalunya* (2010), http://territori.scot.cat/cat/notices/2010/10/2008_l_rsquo_any_de_la_sequera_2729.php; H. March and D. Saurí, "La Sequera del 2007–2008 a la Ciutat de Barcelona: Gènesi, gestió i visions discordants," *Treballs de la Societat Catalana de Geografia* 76 (2013): 289–306.

22 Bachimon, Dérioz, and Marc, "Développement touristique et durabilité en Cerdagne française"; V. Vlès, "Stations de ski en crise et construction territoriale en Catalogne française," *Revue de Géographie Alpine* 100, no. 2 (2012), https://rga.revues.org/1815.

23 Urgell, "Abastament d'aigua a l'àrea metropolitana de Barcelona"; Aldomà, "Del conflicte d'usuaris"; March and Saurí, "La Sequera del 2007–2008."

24 Aldomà, "Del conflicte d'usuaris."

25 Urgell, "Abastament d'aigua a l'àrea metropolitana de Barcelona"; March and Saurí, "La sequera del 2007–2008"; S. Gorostiza, H. March, and D. Saurí, "Flows from beyond the Pyrenees. The Rhône River and Catalonia's Search for Water Independence," *Political Geography* 60 (2017): 132–42; S. Gorostiza, H. March, and D. Saurí, "Piercing the Pyrenees, Connecting Catalonia to Europe: The Ascendancy and Dismissal of the Rhône Water Transfer Project (1994–2016)," in *Water, Technology and the Nation-State*, ed. F. Menga and E. Swyngedouw (London: Routledge, 2018), 34–48.

26 Bachimon, Dérioz, and Marc, "Développement touristique et durabilité"; J. Gómez, *Coopération transfrontalière et fabrique identitaire. Le cas catalan*, Phd diss., Université Panthéon-Assas, Paris, 2015.

27 J. Caubet, *BTP: le peintre espagnol joue au plombier polonais! La République des Pyrénées* (2011), http://www.larepubliquedespyrenees.fr/2011/06/17/btp-le-peintre-espagnol-joue-au-plombier-polonais,199332.php.

28 Gómez, *Coopération transfrontalière.*

29 I. Bourgeois, "'Affaire Amazon': de l'art du campaigning," *Regards sur l'Économie Allemande* 108 (2013): 37–9.

30 D. Duez, "Libre circulation, contrôles aux frontières et citoyenneté," *Belgeo. Revue belge de géographie* 16, no. 2 (2015), https://belgeo.revues.org/16701; M. Unger, "La défense égalitarienne de la liberté de circulation à l'épreuve du cas européen," *Éthique Publique* 17, no. 1 (2015), https://ethiquepublique.revues.org/1726.
31 Oliveras and Trillo, "Fronteras en el contexto español"; Berzi, "The Cross-Border Reterritorialization Concept Revisited."
32 M. Spa, "Espanya i França obren negociacions sobre l'ús de l'aigua a la Cerdanya," *Regió 7* (2019), https://www.regio7.cat/cerdanya-alt-urgell/2019/10/15/espanya-franca-obren-negociacions-sobre/573701.html.
33 X. Crehuet, "Llei sobre el règim especial de la Cerdanya," *Territori. Observatori de projectes i debats territorials de Catalunya* (2010), http://territori.scot.cat/cat/notices/2010/02/llei_sobre_el_rEgim_especial_de_la_cerdanya_2102.php.
34 Bachimon, Dérioz, and Marc, "Développement touristique et durabilité," 2009.
35 Sahlins, *Boundaries: The Making of France and Spain in the Pyrenees*, 1989.
36 Berzi, "The Cross-Border Reterritorialization Concept Revisited."
37 Neil Fligstein and Doug McAdam, *A Theory of Fields* (New York: Oxford University Press, 2012), 29, http://doi.org/10.1007/s11186-014-9237-0.
38 J. Jasper, "Book Review: A Theory of Fields," *Cultural Sociology* 8, no. 2 (2014): 212–13.

14 The Evolving Cross-Border Cooperation of Nouvelle Aquitaine–Euskadi–Navarre (Western Pyrenees Boundary): Multiple Actors and Aims of Cooperation

ANTONI DURÀ-GUIMERÀ

Along the border that separates the Spanish and French states along the Pyrenees, institutionalized cooperation between the territories on both sides is relatively recent when compared to other parts of the European continent. This can be attributed to Spain's late integration into the European Community in 1986. Indeed, the first initiatives along the border were recorded during that decade. An analysis of these early collaborative proposals reveals an intention to develop cross-border cooperation (CBC), particularly at the eastern and western ends of the border, with fewer and weaker proposals in the central zone. This emphasis on the outer ends of the borderlands can be explained by geography: the Pyrenees are higher at the centre, decreasing in altitude toward the eastern and western ends, where settlement, economic activity, and connectivity are all more easily facilitated. Also important is how ties between the populations in the outward areas have evolved over the centuries. To the east there is Catalonia with Roussillon, or Northern Catalonia, in what today is the region of Occitanie; and to the West, there is the Basque Country and Navarre with the Northern Basque Country, or Iparralde, in what is now Nouvelle Aquitaine. These historical cross-border links have mattered over time: ethnic groups straddle the mountains – that is, the Basques in the west and the Catalans in the east – each having its own linguistic and cultural identity as well as prior political structures. Both France and Spain have in the past had an interest in erasing these regions' unique characteristics, which challenge their broader nationalist designs; despite this, today both groups are rebuilding their capacities for self-governance, especially in Spain. It is also noteworthy that in some European territories, the EU is now encouraging cross-border cooperation. Unlike in other regions, where ethnic cross-border communities do not exist, CBC in the western and eastern Pyrenees has arisen not only from functional necessity (communications, economic and social relations, etc.) but also from the desire to renew historical ties. This, even though the rigidity of borders

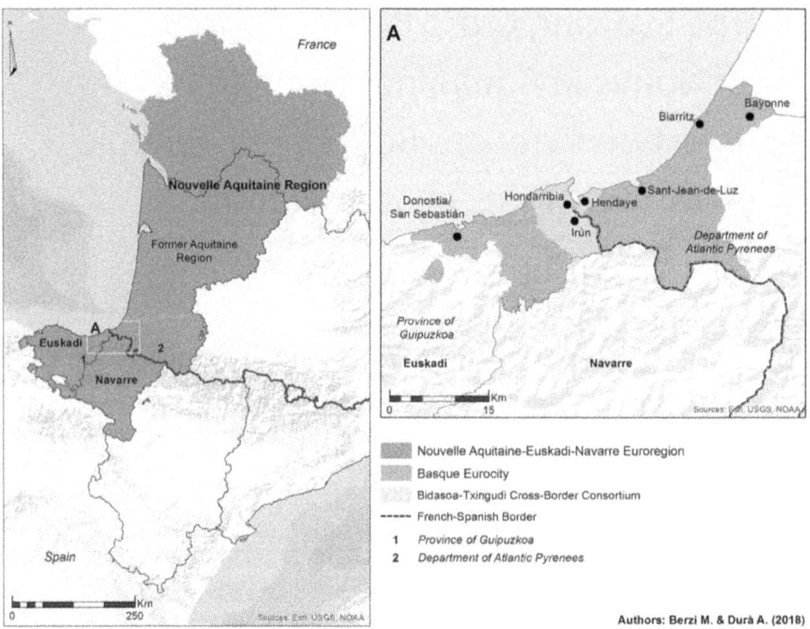

Map 14.1. CBC territories in the Nouvelle Aquitanie–Euskadi–Navarre Euroregion

Source: M. Berzi and A. Durà, 2018.

established by modern nation-states weakened cross-border ties considerably over two centuries.

This chapter examines the construction of CBC in the Basque Country – specifically, the autonomous communities of the Basque Country and Navarre on the Spanish side and those in the region of Nouvelle Aquitaine (known also as "Aquitaine" until 2015) on the French side. The period examined runs from the first initiatives in the 1980s until today. That is an ideal time frame to examine, because over the past thirty-five years a considerable number of CBC proposals have been consolidated. Those proposals have involved different territorial levels, depending on the actors and, more broadly, on their political perspectives and the issues they want to address. The Nouvelle Aquitaine–Euskadi–Navarre Euroregion on a regional scale, and the Basque Eurocity and the Bidasoa–Txingudi Cross-Border Consortium at a local level, should be noted for their greater degree of development (map 14.1).

The development of cross-border institutions went through different stages, during which many difficulties were encountered in terms of organizational challenges and issues specific to the political arena. The departure and return of the community of Navarre to the Euroregion should be of particular interest. The reasons for this disruption were largely political and ultimately stemmed from the same ethnically diverse configuration of these territories. In the case of other institutions, such as the Basque Eurocity and Bidasoa–Txingudi Consortium, less conflict is evident, but there are still signs of potential organizational conflicts of interest, such as those stemming from relations between different administrations. In any case, the current condition of this region should be considered positive, for in general, most of the initiatives studied here evidence a high degree of consolidation as well as a dynamic that seems to ensure continuity in the medium term. To understand how the obstacles have been overcome, it is worth noting the crucial role played by the European Territorial Cooperation Policy (ETCP).

This chapter analyses CBC in terms of the creation and development of various institutions, reflecting on their strengths and weaknesses as well as the opportunities they present, with a focus on the roles played by the different actors. The methodology of strategic action fields (SAFs) proposed by Fligstein and McAdam has proven to be useful for analysing the interrelations of institutions in the Spanish and French states as well as the links between their respective administrations concerning cross-border cooperation.[1]

Interpreting CBC in Nouvelle Aquitaine–Euskadi–Navarre Region Using SAF

To use the terms applied under the SAF approach, CBC initiatives promoted at the regional and local levels of government (the *challengers*) represent a clear challenge – multi-level governance – that the national states (the *incumbents*) must address. CBC compels states to rethink their structures and operating mechanisms at the local level. Each nation-state sees itself as a watertight compartment in relation to its neighbours. When structures and operating mechanisms for CBC are designed, each nation-state is obliged to cede part of its authority in the arena of international relations. At the local level that is ever more difficult to maintain. Fundamentally, the challenge comes from sub-state actors and institutions; but it also comes from the EU, due to the policies it promotes, which have been agreed upon by the nation-states themselves. Thus, the EU is a challenger, given that it works in favour of the Europeanization of policy at all levels. The result is that central governments find themselves in constant tension between their willingness to promote European integration and their desire to maximize control of the "action field" – that is, between nation-state jurisdiction and CBC. Recent European history has evidenced the desire for harmonious European integration, albeit with variations over time and by state. Meanwhile, the opening of Europe's internal borders has led to continuous pressure for local actors to address a multitude of specific issues, and central governments often view this as detrimental to themselves. So in this action field, it can be said that decentralization and Europeanization feed into and affect each other.

At another level of analysis, consider the interactions among institutions participating in CBC at different overlapping territorial levels. In this relationship sphere, an SAF-subject exhibits multiple dynamics in terms of administrative powers, political relations, diverse strategic visions, and so on. This means that concrete actions can be derived in each of the institutions involved. In our case study, the ways in which the actors are positioned around the conflict of identities within a territory (Basque, Spanish, French, and, albeit to a much lesser degree, Occitan) should also be taken into account. This conflict, which has permeated the social and political realities of this space for centuries, not only is fraught with violence – which perhaps has been effectively resolved – but also interacts with institutional CBC strategies. Thus, actors must overcome deeply rooted sensitivities when striving to establish the climate of trust required to facilitate the participation of all involved.

On the basis of the existing bibliography on CBC in relation to the territories of our study based on the SAF analytical framework, we can say that challenges come from two different directions. This observation is underscored by fieldwork that includes interviews with four actors involved in CBC on both sides of the border, contacts with border areas, and visits to various institutions linked to cooperation: Diputación de Gipuzkoa, Agency of the Basque Eurocity, and the Bahia de Txingudi Cross-Border Consortium. These visits were made at different times between 2013 and 2015. Useful also were the constant exchanges of opinions with colleagues from the University of the Basque Country, with whom our university's research team has been sharing a research network on CBC in Europe (RECOT Network) since 2007.[2] All coincide in this finding.

For an analysis of Euroregions, Perkmann's seminal study provides an adequate framework for any case study on CBC.[3] One of Perkmann's key contributions is his observation that CBC requires one essential element – willingness among the adjoining territories to cooperate. The rest is mechanics. This assertion seems empirically true, for it flows from comparative analyses of more than 100 European CBC experiences. An examination of other factors only reinforces that a willingness to cooperate is paramount. These other factors include ethnic and linguistic links, highly connected territorial spaces (e.g., urban spaces divided by a border), economic ties, and geographic conditions (valleys, plains, etc.) that facilitate proximity or alignment). And often, many of these factors overlap and feed into one another. They are also present in varying degrees, as with the case of Nouvelle Aquitaine–Euskadi–Navarre relations, and as such, they clearly condition the attitudes and strategies of the various actors involved in this active field.

Today, there is a broad spectrum of literature dealing with CBC in Europe. Among the researchers who have contributed to the contextualizing of our case study are Scott and Liikanen, who, in their twenty-five-year analysis of INTERREG programs, highlight the link between sub-state actors developing CBC and the Europeanization policies of the EU, focusing on the growth of CBC.[4] At the same time, an institutional report of the Committee of the Regions from 2017 warned about possible involution triggered by restrictions enforced by the EC concerning the movement of persons within the Schengen Area.[5] Also, there has been in recent decades considerable international academic literature dealing with the phenomenon of regionalisms or emerging nationalisms in Europe, some of this relating specifically to CBC. The most interesting texts on the Basque case include Keating,[6] Letamendia,[7] Keating and Bray,[8] Filibi,[9] and Gillespie.[10] In all of these, relations between the Basque Country and Navarre, as well as cross-border external actions, are seen as manifestations of emerging national processes. Contributions referring to CBC at the French–Spanish border are also useful, generally and in comparison to different experiences, particularly with the noted Catalan and Basque cases. The references cited include Harguindeguy,[11] Harguindeguy and Bray, De Castro, Letamendía, and Morata,[12] Feliu, Berzi, Vicente, Castañer, and Llussà,[13] Durà and Oliveras,[14] Morata and Noferini,[15] Noferini, Camonita, and Durà, Oliveras, Colomb, and Durà,[16] Colomb, Morata, Durà, and Oliveras,[17] and Durà, Berzi, and Noferini.[18] Most of these arose from cooperation projects within the RECOT network. Among the academic publications referring to CBC in the Nouvelle Aquitaine–Euskadi–Navarre region, worth noting are the contributions of researchers at Euskal Herriko Unibertsitatea (University of the Basque Country) – for example, Borja, de Castro, and Letamendía,[19] Letamendía, Gómez, and Etxebarría,[20] Letamendía,[21] and Alberdi,[22] while Fourny and Vélasco-Graciet offer an Aquitaine perspective,[23] and Bray and Keating offer an external vision.[24]

The Sociopolitical Context of Constructing CBC in the Basque Country, Navarre, and Nouvelle Aquitaine

As in most border areas, human relations (economic, social, family, etc.) between the territories on the two sides of the western Pyrenees have been maintained over time, but while they may have overcome the vicissitudes of history, they are not exempt from conflict. Institutionalization in terms of agreements and cooperative bodies is a recent phenomenon, given that few such precedents could be found in Spain during Franco's dictatorship. It was not until the arrival of democracy in Spain in 1978 that the first solid steps were taken in this direction. And those steps came more quickly after Spain joined the EC in 1986; that development signalled progressive participation in European policies on territorial cooperation, which underwent notable expansion throughout the 1990s as a means of supporting European expansion and integration. During this phase, devolution processes of varying intensity took place within both countries (in Spain, autonomous communities with legislative power and authority; in France, weak regional decentralization). For the most part, the nationalist debate is present in all areas of the Southern Basque Country (hereafter Euskadi), Navarre, and, notably, in the Northern Basque Country (hereafter Iparralde).

Thus, despite the ongoing nationalist debate, various CBC initiatives prevailed. These were consolidated throughout the first years of the twenty-first century, driven by steps taken by the EU in matters of territorial cooperation. The economic crisis and Euroscepticism seem to have affected them in their approaches and actions but not in their intentions. Instead, from the very beginning, the ongoing interaction imbued with the objectives of Basque nationalism clearly acted as an additional engine of CBC – something that should be highlighted. And later, the most significant change, after a period of disengagement, was the reincorporation of Navarre into the Euroregion. This move reflected the solid political connection that by then existed between the Navarrese and Basque nationalist leaders, even though they represented different political parties. Meanwhile, in Iparralde, the long-pressed demand for an autonomous administrative department led to the creation in 2017 of the Basque Country Agglomeration Community, a local governance structure that developed out of the voluntary association of the municipalities comprising it and that recognizes it as a public entity. These very recent changes provide insight into the extent to which the SAF of CBC in these territories presents a constantly evolving setting.

Announcing an Emerging Field: CBC Precedents along the Pyrenean Border

In the case of Nouvelle Aquitaine, Euskadi, and Navarre, the beginnings of modern CBC, understood as an institutional policy based on cooperation among sub-state administrations, can be traced back to 1986, the year that Spain joined the EC. However, a number of elements in the Basque Spanish and French situations need to be considered to understand the developments thereafter.

The first of these has to do with the politics of modern Basque nationalism since the late nineteenth century as it relates to the relations between the territories of Euskadi, Navarre, and Iparralde. In 1931, a statute of shared autonomy was proposed in Euskadi and Navarre. However, it did not see the light of day. Only Euskadi eventually benefited from the provisions of the proposed statute until its derogation by the Franco regime. In Iparralde, the petition for a smaller *département* comprising only the Basque territory was a historically pivotal moment. (France had been divided into administrative *départements* since the French Revolution.) It also constituted an important push in the 1970s in the context of the recurring debate over decentralization in France. By then, Iparralde had become an important refuge for many Basque exiles from Spain, including those who ended up in the ranks of the Euskadi Ta Askatasuna (ETA), the armed leftist Basque nationalist and separatist organization (founded on 31 July 1959, dissolved on 2 May 2018), which for decades had conducted terrorist activities. Thus, cultural factors and their political expression have remained an important driver of the willingness to cooperate between territories. Spain's isolation and the political and cultural repression there during the four decades of the Franco regime prevented the development of any type of CBC. However, the progressive opening in the 1960s and 1970s did give way to international agreements between Spain and France, which allowed for partial health coverage for cross-border workers throughout the Pyrenees. In France, there were only timid attempts at decentralization, which were always met with strong resistance from a nation-state with a resolutely unitary "Jacobin" spirit. To this day, France has yet to ratify the European Charter of Languages, which poses a serious obstacle to the development of the Basque language in Iparralde.[25]

The Emerging Field: The First Nouvelle Aquitaine–Euskadi–Navarre Cross-Border Institutionalization

The arrival of democracy in Spain was accompanied by negotiations for that nation's entry into the EC, under a more liberal and economically open regime. By this time, European policies favouring CBC had undergone significant development; in fact, cooperation had existed at the borders of the nine member-states since the late 1950s. The first impulse toward this came from the Council of Europe (CoE), a body that operated beyond the scope of the EC. In 1981, in Madrid, the Framework Agreement on Cross-Border Cooperation was signed, consolidating this process; thereafter, member-states accepted the participation of sub-state entities in areas previously with their sole authority.

In 1983 the CoE, acting as a bridge between the EC and its neighbouring countries, provided legal coverage for the creation of the the Pyrenees Working Community (CTP). Autonomous communities (ACs) were by then emerging in Spain as paths toward political devolution. The ACs began developing bodies for their external activities, especially in the field of CBC, and they quickly familiarized themselves with European programs. The ACs of Euskadi and Navarre soon discovered that their political and financial capacity was superior to that of their French counterpart, the Aquitaine region (both ACs enjoyed the right to collect their own taxes, remitting an agreed portion to the central government). The provincial border province of Gipuzkoa made the same observation in relation to the French *département* of the Atlantic Pyrenees. In addition, there was evidence that the French regions played only a minor role in relation to the *départements*, with the latter considered the "real" agents deploying policies transmitted from Paris. Overall, this meant that the weight of CBC initiatives would soon be felt mainly to the south of the border, especially in the Basque Country. Conversely, the French government would strive to strictly control any form of cross-border institutionalization, which had been systematically developed under the various modalities offered by the French legal regime. Thus, the relations between the actors at different levels of power in the field of CBC have been essentially defined by the different political-territorial structures existing on the two sides of the border. Finally, at this stage, the crystallization of tensions between Euskadi and Navarre is worth pointing out: the latter's attitude toward Euskadi is sharply divided between supporters and opponents, due to identity factors. Recall here that the Spanish Constitution of 1978 incorporated a so-called Transitory Provision, which contemplated the possible incorporation of Navarre into Euskadi in the event that the population and institutions of Navarre chose to incorporate as such. With this, the interactions among all parties greatly increased in complexity.

In the course of all these developments, the first cooperation initiative was born around 1989, when the CBC Protocol between Euskadi and Aquitaine was signed. This was reinforced the following year by the creation of the Common Fund for Cooperation, which provided funding for the first shared projects. This fund was important for several reasons, above all for its continuity up to the present day, which has ensured the fund's longevity due to its independence from mainstream European funding. This is relevant if one takes into account that many initiatives in Europe are often fleeting, because of their dependence on external aid, which can itself be fleeting. It is crucial to reflect on this initial period because, on the one hand, the protocol did not include Navarre; on the other, special mention was made of the Northern Basque territories as a CBC objective. Thus, the concrete formation of such an initiative can be viewed as the first successful result of the movements among the actors in play.

The 1990s: A Rapid Stabilization of the CBC Field

The 1990s saw the deployment of new cooperation initiatives at the local level. The European context greatly facilitated this. With the Single European Act of 1991, the willingness to advance toward integration was reinforced; the Territorial Cooperation Policy would be highly instrumental in this. The financing was channelled through the first INTERREG programs (1991–93 and 1994–99), which grew substantially over time and which during these years included newly incorporated Mediterranean countries (particularly Spain) as funding recipients. In addition, in 1995 the Spanish–French Treaty of Cross-Border Cooperation (or Bayonne Treaty) was signed, in which the two states declared their acceptance of the Madrid Framework Agreement in relation to their common border.

At the regional level, this favourable framework was accompanied by a certain relaxation of relations between Euskadi and Navarre, which led to a second CBC protocol in 1992 signed by the ACs together with Aquitaine. Significantly, among other action fields the protocol maintained support for the Basque language. Moreover, since 1998 the Basque government has invested additional funds for interregional cooperation, which involves more territories than the border regions covered by the Common Fund. This space was eventually recognized as the Euskadi–Aquitaine–Navarre Euroregion, but it became necessary to wait somewhat longer for this reality to be constituted as such in the form of the EGTC. Aquitaine also appreciated the adoption of a broader perspective of cooperation with other surrounding regions. In 1989 the creation of the Atlantic Arc Commission within the framework of the Conference of Peripheral and Maritime Regions included Aquitaine, Euskadi, and Navarre. These three regions assumed the role of a space for raising other issues, such as road and maritime communications and environmental and economic aspects that required a broader vision.

Soon, opportunities for cooperation were identified at the local level, particularly in the coastal zone, where a dense urban network has fostered international transportation flows and greater ease of passage. The Bayonne–San Sebastian Conurbation was created as the first association of border municipalities. This entity, which received the support of the Council of Gipuzkoa and the Biarritz–Anglet–Bayonne District, was part of the 1992 Regional Protocol. Sometime later, within the framework of the Bayonne Treaty, it would adopt the legal form of the European Economic Interest Association, an instrument that was driving, to a remarkable degree, territorial cooperation throughout Europe due to its flexibility and its potential for overcoming barriers put in place by international law. The area later adopted the name "Basque Eurocity." Among its priorities are transportation infrastructure and preservation of the environment.

In the early 1990s, local cooperation among the municipalities closest to the border was proposed. Concern for the effects of enforcing the Single European Act led to the first Irun–Hondarribia–Hendaye Agenda, which would be concretized in 1995 as the Bahía de Txingudi Consortium, taking advantage of the framework of the Treaty of Bayonne. Today, the consortium focuses on four areas of action – culture and Euskera, sports and youth, mobility and the environment, and cross-border tourism. INTERREG funds, the Common Fund (once again decisive for the continuity of this agency), and resources made available by the Council of Gipuzkoa have provided indispensable support. The consortium is also part of the Basque Eurocity, and as such, the two deal with many topics together.

By the end of the decade, three areas of cooperation had materialized. Territorially speaking, like Matryoshka dolls, they were formed in a nested fashion.

It is worth asking here why other local initiatives, inland from the border, did not emerge in Navarre and Iparralde. Geographic factors and low population density do not seem sufficient, given that Fourny and Velasco-Graciet have pointed out the existence of consolidated cooperation initiatives in Alpine areas experiencing greater communication difficulties.[26] So it is necessary to cast a light on less interested local actors, who had probably paid little heed to the possible benefits of reinforcing border ties.

Conflicts and New Opportunities in the Early 2000s: A Not-So-Stable Consolidated Field

The twenty-first century heralded a new phase in European enlargement and integration, which in turn affected CBC in the Euskadi–Aquitaine–Navarre Euroregion. Concerning integration, significant steps were taken once the euro currency and the Schengen Treaty came into force, for these facilitated the circulation of capital, goods, and people within the EU. Moreover, ETCP was economically strengthened,[27] in anticipation of the entry of new members from Eastern Europe. European institutions would divert substantial funds to those new member countries, to the detriment of CBC in the Mediterranean. The EU gave way to a new legal instrument, the European Grouping for Territorial Cooperation (EGTC), which aimed to strengthen legal coverage for European territorial cooperation in its various modalities (inter-regional, transnational, and cross-border).

At the internal level, the governments of the Basque Country and Navarre have been dealing with tensions. In Spain, the conservative People's Party, radically opposed to the nationalists, and determined to reduce the power of the ACs, won an absolute majority in 2000 for the first time. The government of Navarre, which represented the opposite of Basque nationalism, established greater cooperation with the central government and reinforced its distance from Euskadi, which for its part prepared a much more advanced proposal for autonomy (i.e., the Ibarretxe Plan, rejected by the Spanish Parliament in 2005). In 2000, Navarre decided to abandon the Euroregion entirely and signed a separate cooperation protocol with Aquitaine. During these years, the pressure on ETA to halt its violent activities increased extraordinarily even within the Basque Country itself, but it would take another decade for the violence to end. All of these considerable tensions during these years had a strong impact on the political climate in the two Pyrenean territories. Yet this did not significantly affect relations in the northern territories. Aquitaine saw the start of a period of stability, which its Socialist government, led by the president of the Regional Council, Alain Rousset, would maintain for a long time. Rousset advocated for improved cross-border relations, including a high-speed rail connection between Madrid and Paris via Bordeaux and Bilbao. Ongoing initiatives like these reflect a perspective that closely mirrors the one also taken by the Atlantic Arc, in that they do not pertain solely to the border areas. As for CBC, it is now consolidating bodies created earlier at the regional and local levels, and meanwhile, complementary initiatives are emerging to address new issues or reinforce the lines of cooperation around earlier ones.

Despite Navarre's withdrawal, activities within the Euroregion have stabilized at the regional level. With the help of the Common Fund and the European funds of INTERREG, the Euroregion has promoted hundreds of bilateral projects in various fields (economy, environment, society, culture, and sports, among others). In addition, in 2004 regional governments promoted the Aquitaine–Euskadi logistics platform, in the legal form of the EEIG, to improve transportation infrastructure, confirming that this issue was strategic for both. Navarre and Aquitaine established similar dynamics, albeit with less intensity. At the cultural level, interest in protecting the Basque language took a prominent place: the Basque government and the Public Office of the Basque Language signed a CBC agreement in 2017 (holding until 2022) concerning linguistic matters, whereby the latter could subsidize private bodies promoting the Basque language in Iparralde. A second agreement was negotiated in 2009 between the Basque government's Department of Culture and the Navarre government's Institute of the Basque Language.

A key step was taken toward the end of the decade, in 2009, when an agreement was reached to convert the Aquitaine–Euskadi Euroregion into an EGTC. This new institution was established in 2011, with headquarters in Hendaye. This consolidated the Euroregion through a legal device recognized by the EU; it also stimulated a new optimism among the participating territories regarding the willingness to continue cooperation. Also significant for the border area was the change in structure of the Working Community of the Pyrenees (WCP). Formerly a pioneer actor for CBC in the area, in 2006 it transformed itself into a consortium, which enabled it to assume the role of managing authority of the EU Operational Program of Territorial Cooperation Spain–France–Andorra (POCTEFA). This meant the WCP could now channel the cross-border resources coming from Europe. Indeed, given its key position in the distribution of INTERREG funds, all the Pyrenean territories participate in this body.

In addition, at the local level both the Basque Eurocity Bayonne–San Sebastian and the Bidasoa–Txingudi Cross-Border Consortium have deployed strategic projects in their different spaces, giving rise to initiatives of notable continuity. Thus, the Eurocity places particular emphasis on issues related to transportation and waste management, while the consortium is dedicated to environmental concerns affecting the Bay of Txingudi, particularly its shared natural spaces and waters, but also its historical and cultural heritage.

Finally, worth noting is the creation of the Interregional Conference in 2007, which continues to bring together regional and local leaders to address problems of a local cross-border nature. The conference does not create its own projects but rather acts as a necessary space for coordination. This initiative was yet another proposal of the Basque government, an indication that it is Euskadi actors who are the strongest advocates for CBC development, due to their national objectives and their stronger capacity to make decisions and manage the day-to-day problems. Today, different actors perceive effective coordination among the various areas of cooperation as necessary, with the main action fields being health, transportation, drug prevention and treatment, local development, and the environment.

It is worth noting that the conference's scope of action makes special reference to the culturally Basque territories of the north, which have been recognized as "Pays Basque Française" (French Basque Country or "Northern Basque Country"). These entities, approved in France in 1995 (the Pasqua Law), are voluntary associations of municipalities and are therefore outside the territorial administrative structure. The Pays Basque Française was a kind of response to the central government's repeated refusal to create a proper Basque *département*. Its purpose was to share developmental strategies and lead projects through the Council of Elected Representatives and the Development Council.

Recent Changes in a Stable Yet Constantly Transforming Field

Recent developments are a consolidation of dynamics generated during previous stages, although some significant changes need to be pointed out. Regarding the European and international contexts, the most significant issue to arise was the global economic crisis, which affected the budgets of public administrations. Also, more recently, the EU has faced a rising tide of Euroscepticism. Relevant manifestations of this include Brexit, new border controls on immigration, the emergence of xenophobic and anti-European parties, and the impact of the COVID-19 pandemic. However, these factors do not seem to have significantly altered the strategy of the actors involved in CBC in the Nouvelle Aquitaine–Euskadi–Navarre Euroregion. On the southern side of the border, two factors may provide some insights into why this is so: strongly pro-European sentiments, and the favourable tax system enjoyed by the two autonomous communities. Also, various internal changes have had a strong impact on relations between the distinct territories. In 2014, France redrew the map of its regions so as to reduce their number. This also, of course, increased their size. Thus, in 2015, Aquitaine absorbed the *départements* of Limousin and Poitou-Charentes and was renamed Nouvelle Aquitaine. These added *départements* are farther from the Pyrenean border, so there is a risk that the region's interest in CBC will weaken. However, the consolidation of relations and the greater capacity of the new region allow us to envision a more optimistic future. Recently, a nationalist party's takeover of the government of Navarre has revamped its relations with the Basque Country and Nouvelle Aquitaine. In 2017 this led to the return of Navarre to the Euroregion (now the EGTC) and its rapid incorporation into the 2014–20 Strategic Plan. Other actors in Navarre society, such as the chambers of commerce and other social and cultural organizations, can now conduct their cross-border activities under the umbrella of the Euroregion.

And at the local level, there has been another qualitative leap toward the future. New life was breathed into Iparralde's association of municipalities of the "Pays Basque" when the municipalities forming it voted in favour of turning it into the "Communauté d'Agglomeration du Pays Basque." It could now be recognized as a "Public Organization for Interdepartmental Cooperation." In 2013, the French government had again denied the Pays Basque the right to form its own *département*. As a response, a process for working toward a more voluntary association was launched in 2014, culminating in January 2017 in the current association, which consists of 158 municipalities. This new actor is not an obstacle to maintaining relations between the Diputación of Gipuzkoa and the *département* of the Atlantic Pyrenees, which in 2016 signed its third Transboundary Cooperation Agreement (2016–20).

All of this has led to the development of new projects in a more optimistic environment in line with the objectives of the main actors that drive CBC. These proposals cover more and more strategic sectors (the Strategic Plan of the Euroregion establishes four main areas: Euroregional citizenship, knowledge economy, sustainable territory, and open governance). I mention here the signing in July 2017 of the first agreement for the promotion of the Basque language among the territories of Euskadi, Navarre, and Iparralde. That agreement partly addresses the aspiration of designing a shared management space for all Basque cultural territories. Only time will tell how strong this agreement actually is.

Conclusions

The results, presented here as a chronological account of CBC construction, show that it has been possible to consolidate a network of organizations capable of guaranteeing the continuity of CBC within the territorial scope of Nouvelle Aquitaine–Euskadi–Navarre. Verifying this would open up a series of considerations regarding the roles played by the various actors in the establishment of an SAF to finally arrive at a global vision of the current situation and its near-term evolution. From this case study, a number of general conclusions can be extrapolated to other border relations (at least in Europe) and to SAF methodology as a means to understand actors' roles and interactions in cross-border cooperation.

Local and regional actors, central governments, and the EU. It is evident, according to the SAF analysis scheme, that the local and regional actors, since emerging in a first stage, have taken advantage of the opportunities offered in the European and global contexts to carve out a space for their own foreign relations. Conversely, central governments, which have long held exclusive authority in this action field, have been giving up space by passing laws that have opened the gates to multi-level governance. This has been a cyclical process: as a consequence of the steady pressure exerted by local and regional actors, new European directives and various inter-state agreements were approved, and power was progressively decentralized. True, this devolution of powers is circumscribed, and the states continue to play a decisive role in that they have the authority to cancel the agreements should they consider it necessary. A final point: the EU has been strengthened to the extent that member-states have accepted that CBC policy acquires greater capacity over time. It can be argued that this kind of equilibrium among regional, state, and supra-state actors wobbles to some degree with the federal or centralized characteristics of each EU country. Nonetheless, the SAF framework is a reminder that these are accepted dynamics necessarily derived from the respective actors' roles.

The role of suprastate actors: The EU in the consolidation process. A general conclusion is that, during the decades of significant advances in European integration (ca. 1980–2000), nation-states agreed to devolve powers to CBC, starting with the Framework Agreement of 1980 and, in the French–Spanish case, the Bilateral Treaty of 1995. These were subsequently reinforced by minor agreements. However, in recent years, the economic crisis, the surge in migration to EU territiories, threats of terrorism, and the COVID-19 pandemic have brought about some retreat from the commitment to open borders. This is more so where the pandemic's consequences have imposed strong restrictions. So, though European institutions have established strong positions as actors guiding CBC policies, it will be crucial (no matter how difficult) to review these roles in the coming years in the context of a relaunching of the European project.

Nature of relations between actors on both sides of the border. These relations are characterized by the diversity of objectives each of the regional and local actors pursues as well as by their respective institutional capacities. Thus, Nouvelle Aquitaine tends to be committed to broader objectives linked to economic development and infrastructure. And it accepts the interest of its southern neighbour in a closer relationship with the territory of Iparralde (now evident in the new association of municipalities), for cultural and political reasons as well as functional ones, since most everyday cross-border problems are located in that area. Today, the greater political and economic capacity of Euskadi and Navarre has found a counterpart in the monitoring role of the central state in France; accordingly, all initiatives must ensure the greatest possible consensus between the two sides of the border. In this sense, asymmetries among border territories tend to be less an exception than a general rule – one that can be applied all over the planet in CBC. SAF theory can help identify how these asymmetries are shaped at a specific border.

Interactions among actors on the same side of the border (Basque Country and Navarre). A weakness of CBC that we noted in our case study relates to the relationship between the governments of the two ACs of Euskadi and Navarre. The evolving political context has conditioned approaches at different stages up until now. Still, the disappearance of terrorist violence may facilitate the continuation of the current phase of greater cooperation. It cannot be ruled out that a change of government in Navarre could affect this scenario; that said, respectful collaboration between the different sensibilities that benefits both parties is slowly gaining ground. The SAF framework can help identify fluctuations in the intensity of cooperation as an important locus of CBC fragility. This holds true in terms of evolving political will as it relates to cooperation, even among actors on the same side of the border.

Interaction between levels. Finally, CBC development at local and "regional" levels poses different challenges among actors, though there do not seem to be conflicts among them. They often work at different levels of action, based on the fields of management that correspond to each. Nevertheless, there are also common areas where cooperation is convenient. In our case study, problems generated by a lack of dialogue led to the establishment of a Euroregional Conference to at least partly resolve possible conflicts, though over time that body has become somewhat redundant. Moreover, local agencies have strong decision-making capacity in many fields. Ultimately, actions at the different levels have reinforced perceptions that CBC is becoming increasingly powerful. In this regard, SAF theory has helped shape an understanding of these sometimes overlapping relationships (which are very typical in border territories) while highlighting a need to address this factor in order to improve the efficiency of CBC.

The evaluation of these five areas of interaction in the field of CBC allows for several final and general assessments to be extracted from the specific SAF analysis of the Euskadi–Navarre–Nouvelle Aquitaine case. First of all, CBC has not yet been consolidated, so there is considerable room for actors with capacity, initiative, and a clear strategy to occupy an important place in the context of existing relations. Political changes in each government can jeopardize the continuity of existing projects and may even lead to very different lines of action – something that could paralyse cooperation. However, after twenty years of continuous development, a strengthening of cross-border links is apparent, encouraged by the desire of the Basque culture to strengthen the bonds that unite its members and by a common desire to promote economic development throughout Euskadi, Navarre, and Nouvelle Aquitaine. Thus, the

SAF analysis for CBC in this area points to the development of a remarkable stability. Even so, major crises are still possible, arising from different areas of interaction that could change future contexts in a meaningful way. In efforts to provide a broader perspective on EU and North American CBC through SAF methodology, it is quite possible to assume that some dynamics (e.g., asymmetries among border actors, political conflicts between or within border sides, and the ability to conceal roles in different levels of governance) are visible in all CBC relationships. However, others are more likely to be shaped by specific actions of the EU as a supra-state actor, as it increasingly embeds CBC in processes of European integration.

NOTES

1 Neil Fligstein and Doug McAdam, *A Theory of Fields* (New York: Oxford University Press, 2012), http://doi.org/10.1007/s11186-014-9237-0.

2 A special mention goes to Professors Francisco Letamendia, José Luis de Castro, and Igor Filibi for their kind readiness in providing support in this investigation.

3 Markus Perkmann, "Cross-Border Regions in Europe: Significance and Drivers of Regional Cross-Border Cooperation," *European Urban and Regional Studies* 10, no. 2 (2003): 153–71.

4 J.W. Scott and I. Liikanen, "Civil Society and the 'Neighborhood' – Europeanization through Cross-Border Cooperation?," *Journal of European Integration* 32, no. 5 (2010): 423–38; B. Wassenberg, B. Reitel, J. Peyrony, and J. Rubió, *Territorial Cooperation in Europe – a Historical Perspective* (Brussels: European Union, 2015).

5 Institutional Report of the Committee of the Regions, *EGTC Monitoring Report 2016 and Impacts of Schengen Area Crisis on the Work of EGTCs* (Brussels: EU, 2017).

6 M. Keating, "The Minority Nations of Spain and European Integration: A New Framework for Autonomy?", *Journal of Spanish Cultural Studies* 1, no. 1 (2000): 29–42.

7 F. Letamendia, "Multiple Identities and Self-Government in the Basque Country," in *Mastering Globalization: New Sub-States' Governance and Strategies*, ed. G. Lachapelle and S. Paquin (London and New York: Routledge, 2005): 167–87.

8 M. Keating and Z. Bray, "Basque Nationalism, European Integration, and the Ibarretxe Plan," *Journal of Ethnopolitics* 5, no. 4 (2006): 347–64.

9 Igor Filibi, "The Autonomous Community of the Basque Country in European Institutional Architecture", in *Basque Political Systems*, ed. P. Ibarra and X. Irujo (Reno: Center for Basque Studies, University of Nevada, 2011): 87–98; Igor Filibi, "Fractal Federalism for Complex Societies: The Basque Case," in *The Ways of Federalism in Western Countries and the Horizons of Territorial Autonomy in Spain,*

ed. A. López-Basaguren and L. Escajedo San Epifanio (Heidelberg: Springer, 2013), 825–43.

10 R. Gillespie, "Between Accommodation and Contestation: The Political Evolution of Basque and Catalan Nationalism," *Nationalism and Ethnic Politics* 21, no. 1 (2015): 3–23.

11 J.-B. Harguindeguy, *La frontière en Europe: un territoire? Coopération transfrontalière franco-espagnole* (Paris: L'Harmattan, 2007).

12 J.L. De Castro, F. Letamendia, and F. Morata, eds., *Cooperación Transfronteriza Comparada: Cataluña, Galicia, País Vasco* (Barcelona: Institut Universitari d´Estudis Europeus / Universitat Autònoma de Barcelona, 2010).

13 J. Feliu, M. Berzi, J. Vicente, M. Castañer, and R. Llussà, "Analysis of Cross-Border projects between France and Spain 2007–2013 – Stakeholders and Territorial Impact," *European Journal of Geography* 4, no. 4 (2013): 33–46.

14 A. Durà and X. Oliveras, "A Typology of Agents and Subjects of Regional Cooperation: The Experience of the Mediterranean Arch," in *Europe's Changing Economic Geography. The Impact of Inter-Regional Networks*, ed. N. Bellini and U. Hilpert (London: Routledge, 2013): 101–23.

15 F. Morata and A. Noferini, "The Pyrenees-Mediterranean Euroregion: Policy Networks and Institutional Capacities," in *Europe's Changing Geography as a Result of Trans-Regional Cooperation*, ed. N. Bellini and U. Hilpert (London: Routledge, 2013), 171–90.

16 A. Noferini, F. Camonita, and A. Durà, "Comparando fronteras entre Europa y EE.UU.: el proyecto internacional BORDERGOV La presentación de los casos europeos," in *Las fronteras ante sus espejos. Relatos transfronterizos sobre Europa, América, Asia y el Magreb*, ed. E.J. Varela and C. Cancela (Santiago de Compostela: Andavira, 2016), 173–84; X. Oliveras-González, C. Colomb, and A. Durà-Guimerà, "La cooperación transfronteriza en el contexto pirenaico: Retos de la multiplicidad," in *Fronteras en la Investigación Peninsular: Temáticas y Enfoques Contemporáneos/Fronteiras Na Investigação Peninsular: Temáticas e Abordagems Contemporáneas*, ed. J.M. Trillo and I. Pires (Santiago de Compostela: Universidade de Santiago de Compostela, 2016): 29–48.

17 C. Colomb, F. Morata Tierra, A. Durà Guimerà, and X. Oliveras González, "The Multi-Level Geographies of Trans-Boundary Cooperation, Territorial Development, and Europeanisation in South-West Europe: The case of Catalonia," in *Territorial Policy and Governance: Alternative Paths*, ed. I. Deas and S. Hincks (London: Routledge, 2017), 92–123.

18 A. Durà, M. Berzi, and A. Noferini, "Coopération transfrontalière dans l'aire du programme européen SUDOE: Un bilan," in T. Perrin and F. Syes, eds., *Régions en tension, régions en recomposition. Sud-Ouest Européen* 48 (2019): 85–98.

19 Jesús Antonio Borja Álvarez, José Luis de Castro Ruano, and Francisco Letamendia Belzunce, eds., *La Cooperación transfronteriza Euskadi-Aquitania: (aspectos económicos, políticos y de relaciones internacionales)* (Bilbao: Universidad del País Vasco, 1994).

20 F. Letamendia, M. Gómez Uranga, and G. Etxebarria, "Astride Two States: Cross-Border Cooperation in the Basque Country," in *Borders, Nations, and States: Frontiers of Sovereignty in the New Europe*, ed. L. O'Dowd and Th-M. Wilson (Aldershot: Avebury, 1996): 91–116.

21 F. Letamendia, "Régime institutionnel et coopération transfrontalière. La comparaison entre le Nord et le Sud est-elle possible?," in *L'Europe aux frontières. La coopération transfrontalière entre régions d'Espagne et de France*, ed. J. Palard (Paris: PUF, 1997), 51–69; F. Letamendia, "Basque Nationalisms and Cross-Border Cooperation between the Southern and Northern Basque Countries," *Regional and Federal Studies* 7, no. 2 (1997): 25–41; F. Letamendia, "La lógica nacional y regional en la cooperación transfronteriza: el caso de Euskadi-Aquitania", in *La construcción del espacio vasco-aquitano: Un estudio multidisciplinar*, ed. A. Borja, F. Letamendia, and K. Sodupe (Leioa: Universidad del País Vasco, 1998), 311–38.

22 J.C. Alberdi, "Éxitos y fracasos de la cooperación transfronteriza: El ejemplo del Bidasoa," *Estudios Fronterizos* (2019): 20, http://ref.uabc.mx/ojs/index.php/ref/article/view/828.

23 M-Ch. Fourny and H. Vélasco-Graciet, "L'eurorégion Aquitaine Euskadi Navarre, un espace transfrontalier émergent?," *Sud-Ouest Européen* 19 (2005): 71–84.

24 Z. Bray and M. Keating, "European Integration and the Basque Country in France and Spain," in *Divided Nations and European Integration*, ed. T. Mabry, J. McGarry, M. Moore, and B. O'Leary (Philadelphia: University of Pennsylvania Press, 2013), 127–56.

25 It was only in April 2021 that the French National Assembly recognized the need to provide some support to regional languages. This has probably come too late to have a real effect, since the number of speakers has diminished dramatically in the last decades.

26 Fourny and Velasco-Graciet, "L'eurorégion Aquitaine Euskadi Navarre. »

27 Interreg-III, 2000–06; Interreg-IV, 2007–13.

Conclusion

15 Comparing Cross-Border Governance in North America and Europe: Conclusions

BRUNO DUPEYRON, ANDREA NOFERINI, AND TONY PAYAN

Given the complexity of governance in the modern world, whether territorial or policy issue–oriented, identifying and articulating theoretical building blocks that allow for an understanding of how governance emerges, develops, and functions is a critical undertaking. Such a project is doubly complicated in cross-border spaces and transboundary policy areas where two nation-states must coordinate their actions for the sake of effective problem-solving. Given this requirement, it is no wonder that attempts to achieve effective cross-border governance have befuddled not only policy-makers but also border scholars, many of whom have made significant albeit unsystematic contributions to its study. Case studies of cross-border governance in the literature reveal a broad variety of approaches to the problem but few universalizable patterns. The result is that no single theoretical framework has emerged in border studies to explain the emergence, the development, and the functioning of cross-border governance. To address this has been the central goal of this volume.

The contributors to this volume are aware of the problem of cross-border governance in border studies – including the difficulty of developing a grand theory for the field. So, to address the issue of cross-border governance, we decided to make a more modest appeal to a meso-level theory, the theory of fields, out of sociology, in order to take a fresh look at the problem. We adopted, adjusted, and applied the building blocks of the theory of fields to cross-border governance cases in Europe and North America. In the theory of fields, we saw the potential to craft a coherent set of conceptual elements of governance as well as opportunity to lay these elements over our object of interest, cross-border governance. Our decision turned out to be wise: the theory offered a disciplined and practicable way to examine cross-border governance, although it had to be adjusted to the peculiarities of cross-border issues, which are unique by virtue of the adjacency of two nation-states with exclusive exercise of sovereignty at the edges of bounded national territories but with policy issues that straddle the border. To be sure, the theory had some limitations, and these challenged the authors to supplement it by combining the weaker parts of the theory with various external concepts. This too proved valuable. With this lesson in tow, we now outline what we have learned from the theory's application to cases in Europe and North America. We also explain how the theory itself, with small refinements, has increased its explanatory power in contexts its authors did not consider. We are more convinced than ever that the theory of fields is a valuable tool for explaining governance in many cross-border contexts around the world, regardless of location, stage of evolution, or level of conflict.

Moreover, the North American and European cases presented in this volume illustrate substantive concerns regarding contemporary cross-border governance, including politics, practices, and representations. They depict the struggles among actors for control of the principles, norms, and rules of governance. This is true regarding both territorial and policy issues. Some, for example, favour strong control of the territory and law enforcement policies (e.g., advocating border walls); others more flexible and integrative policies (e.g., greater trade and human mobility). Our cases also exemplify how struggles for dominance over the shape and nature of the border evolve and show which events enable one vision of the border to prevail over another. They also show that struggles remain even in contexts of deeper integration and in efforts to create border-centred identities. The contributors to this volume, guided by the theory, have focused on the emergence, reproduction, and change of cross-border governance frames, as well as on dynamics that involve agents (collective and individual) and structures (principles, laws, norms, regulations, and material power relations). Together they reveal that such studies require deep analytical perspectives on how cross-border governance should be scrutinized. And here the theory of fields is useful, for it speaks directly to the dynamics among agents and structures – how they interact or fail to interact – to determine cross-border governance, despite the sovereign lines dividing spaces that both join and divide two nation-states, but where coordination is required if good governance is to be achieved. As for the theory of fields itself, our case studies have exposed some of its weaknesses. For instance, certain actors do not fit neatly into the categories proposed by Fligstein and McAdam, and others are simply invisible. Moreover, some scales of cross-border governance elude the theory of fields – for example, binational contexts. Similarly, the delimitation of fields is a tricky task – one that seems too subjective when complex cross-border governance cases are examined. Finally, using the theory of fields in cross-border governance contexts may oversimplify certain complexities that are unique to borders.

Adding Another Ingredient: Comparison

To double-check the theory's utility, we divided the cases into two blocks, North America and Europe, which are different in their internal logics and framed by distinct regional practices. This division offers comparative insights into North American and European cross-border governance. The first group of cases has shifted from a multi-polar to a monocentric form of governance, due to strong federalisms. It is heavily influenced by security matters (which are dominated by US concerns). The second group of cases, in Europe, has favoured cross-border integration. These cases are also multi-level in scope, notwithstanding proclivities to reborder and local chauvinistic practices that weaken some regions and clash with the possibility of joint cross-border governance. So the theory, if truly powerful in its explanatory value, should be able to explain both distinct blocks of case studies, one with strong national(istic) and intergovernmental logics, and the other with strong supra-national frameworks favouring border region integration. In our view, this comparative component should serve as a check on the theory itself.

The organization of case studies into two blocks also proved useful because it spoke to three elements of social science research. First, what can be learned from case studies when comparative methods are conducted within a disciplined and structured framework? Second, what can be gained from subjecting a theory to a new context – an exercise that can make it stronger, lead to its rejection, or force modifications to it? Finally, what are the lessons learned, be they theoretical or empirical, that allow us to formulate new research hypotheses and theory-building for other contexts in the future, such as Asia, Africa, and Latin America, and even in internal border contexts? This was also possible because the case studies were strung together by the subject of cross-border governance. Indeed, this was a disciplined, structured comparative study, within regions and across regions, with implications for the object of study but also for an inspiring sociological theory. The lesson that cannot be lost is that comparing in a focused way, which only a solid theory can help do, can turn out to be a meaningful approach to understanding not just one set of case studies but an entire empirical reality. One more word is merited regarding the value of focused, structured comparison for both empirical knowledge and theoretical development. It is not enough to ask: What are the salient cross-border-governance building blocks relevant to the comparative analysis of our North American and European case studies? What do we ultimately *learn* when comparing border governance building blocks in North America and Europe? When comparing, as George and colleagues write, "it should be noted that a merely formalistic adherence to the format of structured, focused comparison, will not yield good results. The important device of formulating a set of standardized, general questions to ask of each case will be of value only if those questions are grounded in, and adequately reflect, the theoretical perspective and research objectives of the study."[1]

George and colleagues contend that structured, focused comparisons are most productive when all the case studies are done by a single author. However, the same goal can be achieved in collaborative studies through a carefully planned process to impress upon all contributors the importance of sticking to the requirement of structure and focus. And we did just that.

To complement our structured, focused approach, we chose our cases based on deliberate methodological criteria for extracting the lessons on cross-border governance from the studies, when compared to one another within a block of cases, and when compared to the case studies in the other block of cases. To that end, we applied several comparative approaches when selecting the cases: (1) a most similar system design, (2) a most different systems design, and (3) a binary, paired comparison. Each method of case selection, although admittedly intuitive (but not uncritically) in the beginning, magnified this project's comparative potential.

Regarding the most similar systems design, we picked North American and European cases on the understanding that, while the borders of the US with Canada and Mexico are characterized by a strong sense of sovereignty, they also share many of the same characteristics in terms of integration processes, population trends, cross-border flows, and so on. In Europe, the cases share these characteristics, but in a broader context of pooled sovereignty. The big difference was the regional context – one dominated by a powerful nation bent on strong bordering, the other by a supra-national entity bent on debordering. The assumption is that this should have made a difference when comparing one block of cases with the other. Moreover, in North America, despite differences between the US–Mexico and US–Canada border regions, the two have similar border governance arrangements, in which border security dominates. The US federal government imposes similar border security policy priorities (terrorism, immigration, etc.), and this affects border governance frameworks in similar ways. And in Europe, despite different border governance structures and dynamics, the material and symbolic influence of the EC – and its European Regional Policy, in place since the 1980s – tends to homogenize and downplay those differences.

Regarding the most different systems design, the choice of case studies also had to vary sufficiently that we could seek out key lessons from subtle local variations. Thus, we instructed the contributors to pay particular attention to how local variation might affect the emergence and development of governance in unexpected ways. When comparing one local context to another, we found enough differences to understand that grand theories often miss this along the way and are sometimes knocked sideways by the outcomes of governance. At the same time, keeping in mind the so-called binary or paired comparison approach discussed by Tarrow[2] allowed us to compare the two blocks as a whole and to extract the universal findings from the two main parts of the book. This helped us discern the main differences and similarities between cross-border governance on the two continents. For instance, we found that the role of the nation-state in cross-border governance is still predominant in border governance schemes on both continents. Similarly, internal divisions often undermine, fragment, or shape border governance frameworks (with one or two exceptions) and states can use this to establish their power.

Balancing several levels of comparison in case choice (most similar and most different) was not easy. It seemed paradoxical. This was a strongly debated point among us. In the end, when a theory is used in a study, it is important to make sure that similarities and differences can be detected at the macro-, meso-, and micro-levels, when appropriate, in the cases chosen. That way, in contemplating the case studies, it can become evident that there are macro- or continental dynamics, there are meso- or border-specific dynamics, and there are also local dynamics. Thus, our approach, which mixed a disciplining meso-theory with a carefully designed comparative approach, helped ensure that the broader elements and the smaller differences in cross-border governance were not missed.

Lessons Learned: Linking Empirical Findings and the Theory's Building Blocks

In this section, we outline some of the major empirical findings from an in-depth reading of the case studies. The summaries illustrate the findings of each case through the lens of the theory. Some cases emphasized the field environment, others the challengers and incumbents in the field, still others the internal units of governance (IGUs), still others the struggles for control in the face of change, and so on (see the explanation of the theory in the introduction). All showed how the theory's core concepts played out in the case narratives. The theory of fields was valuable in providing the building blocks for interpreting the evidence; it also helped make sense of the detailed local knowledge the contributors brought to bear on their studies and on the comparative approaches used in each of the cases in this volume. These key findings will be organized around five main questions: (1) Do politics in general and national populist politics in particular affect cross-border governance (CBG), and if so, how? (2) What have we learned about the possibilities and limitations of shared regional cultures developing in the various cross-border regions (CBRs), and how do these shared cultures relate to CBG? (3) Considering that CBG is generally structured vertically in North America, and horizontally or transversely in Europe, what is the impact of the field structure on challengers' power dynamics? (4) What is the role of adjacent state fields in CBG? And (5) how have external shocks impacted and reshaped CBG? The following paragraphs address these questions generally.

When comparing CBG in North America and Europe, politics at the national level matter the most in North America, whereas in Europe politics at both the national and sub-national levels often have a more limited impact on CBG. In

North America, following 9/11, security and border policy reforms escalated the securitization of CBRs, with national security placed at the top of the CBG agenda. This contributed to undermining subnational CBG and CBC initiatives, not only on the US–Mexico border but also on the Canada–US border. Since 2017, there has also been a "Trump effect," in the sense that national populist politics have dramatically impacted CBG. President Trump used the US–Mexico border politically and symbolically to disparage Latin American immigrants and to push for a reassertion of state sovereignty at the border. Also, the COVID-19 pandemic has disrupted cross-border flows within all CBRs. Yet despite the considerable influence of national politics in North American CBG over the past two decades, borders are constantly negotiated by challengers (e.g., business organizations) or adjacent fields (e.g., organized criminal groups); simultaneously, other segments of the population are denied access to the borders.[3]

In Europe, CBG is less affected by national politics. The EU's integration process has served to limit and attenuate the impact of such politics on CBG. Regarding the EU's external borders, the international climate and the various crises of recent years (financial, migratory, Brexit, and COVID-19, for example) drew the EU and its member-states toward a more cautious and inward-looking approach aimed at the securitization of borders. But regarding the EU's internal borders, the institutional umbrella provided by the EC and its Cohesion Policy contributed to shoring up existing CBG structures and practices. In this context, domestic politics at the level of the member-states lacked the power to dismantle or radically modify the structure of CBG. Still, changes in national and regional political majorities may affect the speed or the understanding of cross-border cooperation (CBC). It follows that the continuity of political actors is crucial for current CBG frameworks. But so far, when political actors have changed, they have not interrupted or paralysed CBG arrangements, largely because of the role played by EU funding, the ongoing strength of European norms that anchor CBG, the stability of CBG institutions, the roles played by experienced leaders to train and support neophyte leaders in the field of CBG, and the continuity provided by CBG public servants. Nevertheless, CBG is under stress and may yet succumb to national and international political pressures.

In addition, CBRs are especially dynamic spaces since they are at the intersection of globalization and regional integration. To respond to this, CBG frameworks bridge the two forces of globalization (centrifugal force) and regional integration (centripetal force). Here culture can be useful, but it is not sufficient to structure and stabilize CBG fields. The US–Mexico borderlands offer a vivid illustration of a shared border culture that barely translates into institutional initiatives. The same comment can be made regarding the US–Canada border, where shared border cultures do not generate CBG schemes. Thus, a shared culture can facilitate CBG, but political will and CB institutions seem to be much more important. In Europe, cross-border cooperation is characterized by singularity, diversity, and complexity.[4] That is, each CBR is unique in terms of its history and ethnic/linguistic links, with highly connected territorial spaces (e.g., urban spaces divided by the border), pre-existing economic, cultural, and social ties, and/or particular geographic conditions that facilitate proximity or alignment. All of these have usually determined the nature, the structure, and the dynamics of CBG. The pioneering experiences of cross-border cooperation among local actors along the Dutch–German and Franco–German–Swiss borders in the late 1950s were pragmatic, oriented toward solving problems. More than "overcoming national frontiers to heal the scars of history," local administrations were seeking practical solutions to border problems that arose when national frontiers were crossed in daily life. As Europe's integration process began scoring wins – with the establishment of the common market, for example – EU institutions and the member-states began to consider the negative effects of integration, especially those that materialized along national borders. By the 1990s, the increasing flows of people and goods that had irrigated cross-border spaces did require a more cohesive approach, and this generated a Cohesion Policy that contributed to the development of a more cooperative attitude toward cross-border needs and problems. National or regional identities were at times misaligned; even so, the process of integration succeeded in promoting a functional-oriented and cooperative understanding of the advantages and potentials of a more coordinated and collective management of cross-border spaces. Internal mobility, sustainability and the environment, tourism, local economic development, and health care were some of the policy areas in which novel approaches of cross-border governance were initiated. Over time, hundreds of cross-border projects have helped foster regional integration in peripheral and often underdeveloped spaces. Thus, in Europe, three conditions need to be met in order for a stable CBG to emerge: flows of people, goods, and services (including cultural flows); active regional and local governments; and funds from the EC. CBG bridges cultures, allows scars to heal, and helps CBRs resist external shocks. CBG constitutes a virtuous circle that has no equivalent in North America.

In continuing to address our questions, it is important to note that the structure of CBG fields tends to affect the shape and role of challengers. In North America, CBG fields are dominated by security and border agencies – the incumbents. Along the US–Mexico border, the actors that could potentially be challengers seem too weak to mount a coalition (e.g., human rights organizations), or they calculate that they can defend their interests without becoming challengers (e.g., business actors). An important question relates to criminal organizations whose activities have an impact on incumbents. Should criminal organizations be viewed as challengers, or, because of their illegal status, should they be perceived as belonging to an adjacent field? Payan suggests that the latter makes more sense, for criminal organizations do not directly challenge incumbents for power in the CBG field. On the US–Canada border, timid challengers include provinces and states, whereas business actors remain absent from the CBG field, since they turn to provincial and state leaders to defend their interests.[5] In Europe, integration has introduced a more cooperative culture for addressing common challenges at the borders. Incumbents and challengers have had to learn how to mutually gain from cooperation and coordination and how to establish win–win solutions at the border. The financial, legal, and normative support provided by EU institutions and their cross-border programs have provided incentives sufficient to foster this more collective approach. Member-states and central governments have maintained a privileged position as gatekeepers by taking a tolerant attitude toward those more active regional and local governments – and in many cases, challengers – that took the first steps toward joint cross-border action. At the same time, challengers have learned how to play their role in a dense network of strategic fields in which mutual understanding and cooperation have provided more gains and returns than conflict and going-it-alone strategies. As a global result, internal and external shocks have been mitigated. Even when CBG fields find themselves stressed by challengers, CBRs remain only marginally affected. At worst, they are paralysed, but they do not disappear, given the robustness and the perceived utility of CBG institutions (see Noferini).

Advantages and Limitations of the Theory of Fields

Any study must speak back to the theory and improve on it. We have examined how the chapters dialogue with the theory through the latter's conceptual elements; now, in order to explain the empirical evidence, it is important to analyse what the case studies have to say about the theory. Put another way, we must determine the theory's value for cross-border governance cases. The major challenge, of course, is that the theory was not designed for cross-border governance cases. The cases that Fligstein and McAdam explored were related to the governance of policy fields within a sovereign nation-state. Fitting the theory to a *binational* or *cross-border* governance context, characterized by the jarring presence of a border, required that it be adjusted. To address this crucial challenge to the theory, the authors adjusted its concepts – for example, they sought ways to gain control of the IGUs not only *within* their side of the border but also often *across* the border. As it happened, we came to see the theory as still useful and able to explain the emergence and evolution of CBG. Thus, the theory gained from being applied in a new context – a cross-border context. Let us examine how.

ProblematizingField Actors: Incumbents, Challengers, and IGUs

Regarding the actors in the Paso del Norte borderlands, Staudt and Cruz discuss incumbents, challengers, and IGUs. The incumbents exploit a national security agenda, which has two characteristics: (a) it is defined in Washington, DC, and to a certain extent in Mexico City; and (b) it is supported at the Texas state level by politicians who exploit fears of terrorism, drug smuggling, and immigrants. IGUs enforce this agenda in the Paso del Norte region through "the vertically structured government agencies whose task it is to implement the security agenda and policy, from cabinet-level political appointees in the executive branch and national-level politicians in Congress, to local enforcement arms of the US Department of Homeland Security, the Drug Enforcement Agency in the Department of Justice, and the Department of Defense military units in the fragmented border security complex." But Staudt and Cruz also expand the group of challengers from local business organizations to local government officials – for example, El Paso City Council representatives and some state elected officials, such as former Congressman Beto O'Rourke, who, while he served (2013–19), deployed a challenger-like advocacy for the region in Washington. Interestingly, Staudt and Cruz find that not all *governmental* and *political* actors are incumbents simply because they hold power. Thus, even on one side of the border, the categories of actors are much more complex than the theory would suggest. Moreover, they find that actors on the Mexican side of the border are often much more submissive toward the IGUs prevailing north of the border, precisely because they can easily be broken if they do not bend. This demonstrates the long arm of incumbent power, which reaches well into the other side even when there is no legal framework for it to do so. Of enormous importance in Staudt and Cruz's contribution is, therefore, the fact that actors and IGUs require more nuanced definitions in cross-border contexts. Some who might appear to be incumbents – local politicians – turn out to be challengers to a much broader hegemonic incumbent – the federal government. And actors on the weaker side of the border often pose no challenge at all, precisely because they have little choice but to submit. Staudt and Cruz's contribution unpacks the complexity of actors and the ways they relate to IGUs.

Payan points out that the theory divides a given field into incumbents and challengers but does not account for other actors. The voiceless, the working poor, the excluded are one such set of actors. There are also organized criminals, who do not play the game but are still integral to it. These latter actors work for their own interests, with no desire for systemic change. Payan also points out that incumbency is represented by state agencies. Some of these dominate the narrative (security agencies, DHS) and "impose their mandate over the border security industrial complex," while others play a vital role in specific border sector governance (e.g., the US–Mexico Border Health Commission, the International Boundary and Water Commission [IBWC], the Commission for Environmental Cooperation [CEC], and the North American Development Bank [NADBANK]), but without being dominant. In that sense, there may be two types of incumbents, with some (security) wielding much more power than others (weaker government agencies, backed by legal and budgetary mandates). Challengers also include, most prominently, the business community, whose members are loosely organized into networks that protect and promote their economic and social interests and that enjoy a high degree of cross-border mobility; border security does not impede their prosperity. They may be unhappy with the status quo, the violence in some parts of the border area, and the lack of understanding of their needs as displayed by Washington and Mexico City, but they skilfully navigate both those power centres and, when possible, "educate" them about the need to ease their iron fist. And challengers are not restricted to the business community: the voiceless, the middle class, and the working poor also have some cross-border mobility, but they are not organized and are targeted by policies that encourage them to be invisible. The cross-border area allows the working poor and the middle class to get some sources of income, for instance in the service sector, but at the cost of being subjected to an oppressive border security apparatus that they hate but cannot resist. They must silently obey the dominant incumbents if they want to keep crossing the border to survive and prosper. Organized crime is another branch of "challengers": this one confronts incumbents with drug smuggling and human trafficking, which in turn legitimizes the incumbents' role in "securing" the border. In a perverse game, criminals do not hesitate to bribe federal agents on both sides of the border, intimidate and threaten them, and co-opt other actors to carry on with their criminal enterprises.

Mendoza Cota examined cross-border governance in the San Diego–Tijuana border region. Interestingly, he found that the incumbents there are not security agencies but rather business executives who have socio-economic and political interests on both sides. These incumbents have the support of local and regional officials. Other actors have emerged, such as academic institutions, and they, like security actors, aid in the development of the cross-border economy. All of this constitutes the "internal logic" of the IGUs. Nearly all policy, including policy change, allows for an increase in the flow of goods, people, and capital across the border region, with the result that border industries have been transformed from primarily *maquiladoras* into second- and third-generation manufacturing plants. These industries have power, and they push back against restrictive policies. Mendoza Cota finds that other social, cultural, and environmental actors are underfunded and have developed only limited cross-border initiatives. Meanwhile, the federal government, which others argue is the most powerful incumbent, is distant and does not respond to any of those initiatives. The real challengers may thus be the migrant organizations that have emerged without strong public support. They are a response to the increasing flow of Mexican migrants deported by US authorities, some of them due to criminal activity. Mexican border cities are facing an influx of Mexican migrants from the rest of Mexico and Central America who want to cross the border, whose presence generates health, crime, and labour problems. Migrant organizations provide programs for returning migrants, offering them temporary housing and medical care. Local and regional authorities may be on the boards of these organizations, but three factors limit their development: limited financial support from the Mexican government, the negative attitude held by border security agencies, and lack of collaboration with the private sector. In response to the impact of US immigration policy on the Latino population in the border area, these organizations have fostered a form of collective consciousness among the Latino population. This chapter speaks to the need to refine the concept of field actors. The incumbent/challenger division may be too simple.

The chapter by Correa-Cabrera notes that policy change on one side of the border may immediately create opportunities for established and emerging actors on the other – such as energy companies or criminal organizations. However, these emerging actors may not be interested in challenging the status quo; they may simply want to find new spaces to push their material interests, as both such emerging actors are, in the end, businesses. That is, they may not be interested in overturning any system, though they will be alert to changes in the field that provide new opportunities for profit. In that sense, they do not seek to capture the IGUs; they simply want to profit from changes as they occur. Thus, not all changes in the field lead to challenges to the system.

Konrad writes that on the Canadian side, there were no clear incumbents or challengers during the emergence of the field, which meant that cooperative governance was possible and bottom-up initiatives were not impeded in the 1990s. The original field was akin to a coalition. However, after 2001, a crisis of the field ensued, and US federal agencies in charge of national security, such as the DHS, along with their counterparts in Canada, clearly became incumbents in the field, thus relegating sub-national actors to the role of challengers. Those challengers now negotiate with the incumbents regarding ways to balance security with cross-border priorities, and in this sense, the Canadian government can be viewed as a subaltern incumbent that must negotiate with the US government. In the 2000s, sub-national cross-border actors remobilized and were able to negotiate adjustments to border security measures – for example, the Western Hemisphere Travel Initiative (WHTI), signed in 2007 for airports and in 2009 for land and sea ports, which was soon followed by the BC/Washington-led "enhanced driver's licence" to facilitate border crossing without passports for both Americans and Canadians. The IMTC, a binational coalition of government and business entities, proposed policy solutions in the Cascade Gateway, mostly in transportation and infrastructure – for example, prior to 2010, the Vancouver Olympic Games presented a window of opportunity to address existing and future traffic issues. Also, PNWER helps propose solutions and voice stakeholders' views on border issues.

Over to the east, Dupeyron shows that a significant facet of Quebec's paradiplomatic efforts relates to the Quebec–US borderlands. Quebec's commitment in the cross-border governance field must be seen as a sub-field of its paradiplomacy, aimed at acquiring material and symbolic resources. The presence of Quebec in governance structures serving as IGUs is visible in a dozen organizations, five of which focus on cross-border governance; these include the Council of Great Lakes Governors and the Conference of New England Governors and Eastern Canadian Premiers. Those cross-border governance organizations cover various policy sectors, such as the environment, water management, trade, transportation and infrastructure, and education. Quebec has also established relations with several levels of government in the US. Although Quebec has been increasingly recognized by neighbouring US states as an equal partner or incumbent, "la belle province" has also positioned itself as a challenger, during two *souverainiste* periods. Outside of these two momentary internal tremors, we have not identified any challenger in the field. However, external shocks arising from US administrations tend to destabilize the field, for instance, through the policy responses to 9/11 and the protectionist policies of the Trump administration.

In his chapter on the Pyrenean border, Noferini contends that the Euroregion Pyrenees Mediterranean constitutes a formal attempt to build up some model of shared cross-border governance that goes beyond more traditional state-centric models. In this respect, the EPM may be conceptualized as a strategic action field in which subnational actors SNAs (the challengers) interact with one another based on a shared understanding (not always consensual) of the field's purpose, which is to promote a cross-border space in the European and national arenas where central governments and EU institutions are the leading actors (the incumbents). Since the EPM involves SNAs from two sovereign states with different administrative, political, and institutional cultures, the analysis of the field addresses the impact of the above-mentioned asymmetries in the development of cross-border joint initiatives, which are usually settled at the minimum common denominator. The common understanding of the field's main dynamic and a shared common past have together mitigated the negative impact of the political border between Spain and France. Finally, Noferini injects some political perspective into the analysis by underscoring how the EPM has been, from the start, a highly politicized project. Surprisingly, this has not prevented the cross-border structure from surviving some dramatic shocks and internal and external crises, such as the premature withdrawal of a partner (Aragon left the EPM in 2006), a change in the legal structure in 2009–10, the Catalan secessionist movement since

2012, a territorial reform in France in 2016, and, finally, the suspension of the Catalan autonomy in 2017.

As this volume has shown, the European context aligns with the theoretical concepts presented by Fligstein and McAdam regarding the existence of multiple nested fields and a common broader field environment. Focusing on the Italo-Maltese borderland, Camonita maps the existence of various webs of cross-border SAFs, which to some extent are interdependent and/or dependent on the decisions generated in other SAFs, such as those at the EU level. In the Italo-Maltese field, however, CBG structures stand out because of the relative ease in identifying key players. In the straightforward political agreement presented by the INTERREG Italy–Malta program – the main driver of cross-border dynamics in the area – it is the Maltese government and the Sicilian regional government (overseen by the Italian government) that represent the incumbents in the cross-border field. Both have exploited the organizational structures provided by the INTERREG program, and IGUs have been established around the elaboration of the program. In line with the purpose of this volume – which is to test the theory in new contexts – Camonita's chapter stands out for its analytical ambition in reviewing and adapting some classical instruments of SAF theory, including the field's functionality, its effectiveness, and its participants. Because projects are executed by networks of stakeholders on both sides of the border, Camonita defines these networks of executing agents as field participants by stretching SAF terminology further. In his view, the participants are all those public and private actors who, though not directly involved in power relationships in the field, willingly contribute toward its strategy by securing funding for its activities. These actors are necessary in order to fulfil general strategies that enable the field to function.

In his bird's-eye view of the Pyrenean borderland, Berzi shows that the local and regional governments are the main incumbents and that they tend to stabilize cross-border dynamics by strengthening the cross-border governance structure. A privileged position is reserved for the Working Community of the Pyrenees (a "special" incumbent), which manages INTERREG funds; in doing so, it produces a sort of dependency, in that other entities rely on WCP funds to create and manage projects. Except for the Hospital of Cerdanya (which required an *ad hoc* multi-level governance body), the central states are not directly involved in the various CBG agreements; their primary role consists in promoting and enabling the environment by providing juridical and financial aid. Berzi reminds us how central governments may also act as challengers, impeding cross-border institutionalization and destabilizing the field. Above the state level, European institutions, especially the EC, influence cross-border agendas through financial and legal initiatives (e.g., the EGTC), which serve as strong incentives for action. In the complex set of adjacent fields surrounding the Pyrenean borderland, since the 1990s, and thanks to the INTERREG program, the EC has co-financed more than 700 cross-border projects along the French–Spanish border.

Perrin shows that Euroregions are animals not easily tamed because they are cooperative organizations. Euroregions "can have several incumbents at different levels." In the EPM, Midi-Pyrénées and Catalonia were the incumbents in the cultural policy sector. But in the Grande Région, nine coordinators representing the various incumbents (sub-national and national) influence cultural policy, though the state of Luxembourg is a dominant incumbent, owing to its resources as an EU member-state. Challengers can include the cultural stakeholders who propose and implement cultural projects, and perhaps also the audience of cross-border cultural policy – an audience that seems to be barely aware of the existence of such initiatives. As cultural cross-border fields emerge and stabilize, cultural stakeholders gain experience and expertise, grow their influence, and move from the position of challenger to that of incumbent. Moreover, Perrin indicates that relations among members of the Euroregion (which he labels "the horizontal sub-SAF of Euroregional politics") are fundamental and can impede or support not only specific cultural initiatives but also the existence of the cross-border governance entity: cooperation or isolation along political lines seems to play a decisive role in the cultural area. Finally, Perrin shows that cultural, political, and administrative stakeholders have a positive perception of cultural projects: they view culture, independently of its tangible effects, as an essential symbolic pillar in cross-border cooperation.

From an actor-centred perspective, Cancela Outeda notes that CBG in Galicia–North Portugal (G-NP) has been cooperative, with incumbents from the public sector of each country sharing a common understanding of the characteristics and potentials of the field. Despite the presence of institutional asymmetries among the actors from the two countries (Spain and Portugal), regional organizations have succeeded in orienting their mutual actions toward one another, even when an agreement on the basic conditions of the cross-border field has yet to emerge. This has contributed to the emergence of some degree of institutionalization with the establishment of formal organizations such as the Working Community, the Euroregions, the EGTCs, the Atlantic Axis, and four Eurocities. Once again, thanks to the benevolence of the central governments and the EC, the Galician–Portuguese borderland is today home to several SAFs, in a Russian doll configuration in which each SAF contains several other SAFs. In this scenario, CBC is viewed as an opportunity from the local perspective. Network governance presented opportunities for local governments and municipalities, as in the cases of the Atlantic Axis and the Eurocities that today complement CBG at the regional level. In his conclusions, Cancela Outeda does not state explicitly whether those local actors that represent most G-NP urban areas are incumbents or challengers. But in any case, the distinction between incumbents and challengers does not seem relevant in the G-NP borderland, for at a certain level cooperation among all these actors has prevented serious internal shocks and the emergence of crises.

Oliveras examines the main groups of actors in the Cerdanya (France–Spain) cross-border governance field and contends that the Spanish local actors are the incumbents and the French ones the challengers. A narrative of "cross-border unity" has been mobilized to refer to a period predating the Treaty of the Pyrenees (1659); that narrative idealizes a territory that was divided despite its shared natural environment and Catalan culture. Yet this narrative has been eroded due to three factors. First, there has been a divergence of economic growth on either side of the border, with the Spanish side becoming more diversified and dominating the French side. Second, a growing power asymmetry has been observed in favour of the Spanish side. Finally, French actors have been reading the narrative of "cross-border unity" as a Catalan discursive instrument to reinforce their material and symbolic dominance over the cross-border governance field.

In his chapter on CBG on the northern side of the Pyrenees, Durá Guimerá devotes great attention to cultural factors, and their political expression, that have justified and prompted cooperation across territories. In this cross-border area, the nationalist debate is present in all social areas of the southern Basque Country (hereafter Euskadi) and Navarre, in Spain, and in the northern Basque Country, Iparralde, in France. Durà-Guimerà maintains that local and regional actors have exploited the opportunities offered in the European and global contexts to carve out a space for cross-border issues. In terms of the SAF approach, these actors are the incumbents. Nevertheless, even though central governments have been backing away from their gatekeeper position, they continue to play a decisive role in the provision (or not) of some institutional and legal support for cross-border initiatives. Still, in a relatively consensual understanding of the cross-border area, regional and local actors have bargained their way to stronger positions so as to maximize their benefits from the establishment of cross-border joint initiatives. Thus, in the north, the Nouvelle Aquitaine region has preferred to commit itself to broader objectives linked to economic development and infrastructure. Meanwhile in the south, the Basque Country, largely for cultural and political reasons, nationalist and more ideological questions have attracted more interest, especially with regard to establishing a closer relationship with Iparralde. As others do in their own chapters, Durá Guimera explores the emergence of CBG at the local level by expanding the field to municipalities and cities as legitimate actors. The result has been an updated map of a dense set of cross-border fields that, like Matryoshka dolls, are formed in a concentric way: from the local to the regional to the national scale. The local and "regional" levels pose different challenges for emerging actors, yet there seems to be no conflict among them. They often work at different levels of action, based on the fields of management that correspond to each. In this sense, the founding of a Euroregional Conference is a promising example of institutional innovation, one that represents an effort to strengthen collective decision-making at the cross-border level.

Problematizing Change: Governance Emergence, Stability, and Crisis

Another building block in the theory of fields refers to change. This is one of the virtues of the theory, and the chapters in this volume collectively speak to it. Staudt and Cruz's chapter suggests that the border is a "rarely stable field." When the field *is* settled, it is because of foreign perils and iron fist responses from the US and Mexican governments. The Paso del Norte borderlands have seen this in several ways. In the 1990s, the growth of the "border security industrial complex" was justified by narratives surrounding immigration and drug wars. In the 2000s it was about the threat of terrorism, in that after 2001, new security measures were created that impeded the flow of people and goods. In the 2010s, criminal organizations also affected trade and people's cross-border mobility. In this context in which multiple crises have shaken the border, the sense of normalcy is very fragile and tends to legitimize the violence of security agencies and criminal organizations. For instance, research participants tell Staudt and Cruz: "I hope that security and commerce can balance out." More recently, we would add, the flows of asylum-seekers and migration caravans have demonstrated that the border field is never settled, constantly in flux. The theory will need to make sense of this in future studies.

Payan's chapter also shows the relative instability of the field. He demonstrates that the Mexican–US borderlands governance framework is constantly ebbing and flowing, easily losing stability, then resettling, only to become unstable again. Cross-border governance emerged, then became unstable/stable as a result of external shocks, large and small, notably the end of the Cold War; this was followed by a brief process of "debordering." NAFTA was viewed as an opportunity to remake CBG through processes of globalization. Then 9/11 – a massive external shock – presented an opportunity for the border security complex to completely dominate the field. The migration flows are a constant source of instability, because migrants are challengers. And criminal actors too are always pushing against the system. Finally, the domestic political landscape affects the borderlands; in this we include the border-focused toxic rhetoric resorted to by the Trump administration. So we can say that the stable field observed over the past thirty years has been accompanied by an underlying instability. Even so, two major categories of actors dominate the field: the security industrial complex (hegemonic) and the internationalized business and entrepreneurial community (privileged challengers). The first of these almost always dominates the second, justifying that domination by citing the need to combat criminal organizations, immigration, and so on. The ones who suffer are the working poor and the working class, who inhabit the bottom depths of the field.

Mendoza Cota maintains that economic interests are the incumbents in the San Diego–Tijuana borderlands, where governance is always in flux – emerging, stabilizing, and being challenged. It is permanently framed by business interests and governmental organizations at the regional and local levels, with little room for other actors to gain traction so as to realize their interests. Interestingly, it seems that the federal governments and their border security apparatuses have not deeply disrupted those regional and local incumbents – which sets it apart strongly from the Paso del Norte Region. What has happened instead is that federal border security agencies have destabilized the challengers, such as human rights organizations that defend migrants, while businesses are able to keep going as usual. This indicates that the theory's categories of emergence, stability, and crisis may be too general. Sub-categories need to be developed that specify better how each actor behaves over the course of emergence, stabilization, and destabilization, as well as who accommodates them within each of these stages.

The Correa-Cabrera chapter reinforces this point, as well as the need for refinement. Some actors view change not as an opportunity to capture the IGUs, but rather as an opportunity to improve their own positions in an already settled environment – the border field. The energy reform in Mexico encouraged specific actors, in both the business and criminal sectors, to expand their activities without confronting the incumbent security agencies. Thus, not all actors, when they observe an opportunity in a changing field, will opt to mount a challenge. Perhaps they seek to gradually advance their interests rather than capture the IGU.

Konrad contends that, setting aside earlier initiatives, the field emerged essentially in the 1980s as the BC provincial government responded to a newly favourable context: NAFTA, as well as the emerging notion of a cross-border region known as "Cascadia," partly propped up by shared interests (environmental and business-oriented), all leading to a shared vision in the late 1980s and early 1990s. This fostered the creation of two layers in this field: the "outer field," with the founding of PNWER in 1989, and the "inner field," with the creation of the BC/Washington State Environmental Cooperation Council (ECC) in 1992. Other initiatives complemented these in several sectors, including the environment, infrastructure, and trade, without the emergence of notable challengers. PNWER stabilized the field by championing several issues on its agenda, such as economic, environmental, and social themes, which were discussed in nine working groups. Other institutions populate the field, though they work at micro-regional and sectoral levels with limited resources (e.g., the BC–Washington State Environmental Cooperation Council). The federal governments have been "distant, meddlesome, and unhelpful": they have not opposed the creation of border organizations, but they also show no interest in being part of them. In the 1990s, the federal border security role was limited to combating drug smuggling, and this did not interfere with the local and regional actors populating the border governance field, where federal intrusion was limited to the fisheries and the forest industry. This was a balanced field, with no clear incumbents and challengers until 2001. In the wake of 9/11, the field became destabilized, and state, provincial, and local politicians in both countries became the challengers. As on the border with Mexico, the incumbents became the federal governments in national security and border policy. After incremental improvements in the transportation and infrastructure sectors in the 2000s, the field was resettled in 2011 with the Beyond the Border Accord, signed by both federal governments, which established four pillars of cross-border governance in an effort to balance security and trade priorities.

Dupeyron shows that a CBG field can take several decades to emerge. Quebec's paradiplomatic efforts have been especially visible since the 1960s and have focused on the Quebec–US border states. Much as what Konrad observed in the Pacific Northwest, episodes of crisis have been limited to the 9/11 terrorist attacks, which shook the field, which now had to incorporate Washington's national security agenda, supported by Ottawa. Since then, the field has been resettled, but Quebec remains concerned about the disproportionate power of Washington, which could jeopardize Quebec's interests. With the COVID-19 pandemic, the Canada–US border has been restricted, and this has affected cross-border spaces, especially in the tourism and culture industries.

Noferini reminds us that border areas in France and Spain suffered from the centralist construction of each state and that, historically, the development of territories around the Pyrenees was neglected by national governments. In the 1980s, after democracy returned to Spain, there was a renewed emphasis on decentralization; meanwhile, the EU developed its own regional policy. In recent decades, the French–Spanish cross-border area has slowly gelled. Initially, a cross-border field emerged with two competing perspectives: a choice between a Europe of Regions and a Europe of Cities. At this initial stage, regional governments (especially the Catalan one) committed themselves to exploring the potential for a cross-border entity that would include the corresponding regional levels in the Western Mediterranean; meanwhile, cities were orienting their strategies toward the formation of international networks that could improve their visibility and role at the international level. The smoothing of cross-border political relations at the regional level, the relative success of the C6 network, and the converging interests of all the actors paved the way for the launch of the EPM, officially created in 2004. Nevertheless, this did not happen without political tensions – for example, the project encountered hostility from the conservative leader of the Spanish government, José María

Aznar, and Aragon, a founding member, withdrew prematurely. Even so, by the second half of the 2010s, after more than a decade of activities, the field was considered stable. An important turning point occurred in 2009, when the EPM adopted the EGTC instrument, the European legal tool and framework that endowed the Euroregion with legal standing; this empowered the EPM to lead ambitious projects (e.g., CREAMED, EUROCAMPUS) and to strengthen its governance structure. However, since the early 2010s, crises have affected the cross-border scenario, as the Spanish government has intervened in Catalan self-governing political institutions. Yet these external shocks have not substantially arrested the development of EPM activities. In the case of the EPM, functional logics and a shared understanding of the goals of the cross-border organizations have allowed CBG to survive and to overcome internal and external threats that in other territories have led to the failure of many cross-border projects.

In his chapter on the cooperation between Malta and Sicily, Camonita explores CBG in a southern Mediterranean space, usually depicted as one in which sociopolitical institutions are weak and not conducive to the implementation and enforcement of effective public policies (even less cross-border joint policies). Camonita mixes the SAF approach with the multi-level governance approach. His resulting findings highlight an overall lack of political vision and identity-building for a cross-border region that is rarely referred to as such. According to Camonita, Sicily–Malta border governance emerged at the intersection of various external phenomena such as the accession of Malta to the EU in 2004, the proactive role of the EC, and the deployment of an INTERREG program in the region. When the INTERREG IIIA program was launched in 2004, some enabling conditions supported the establishment of the field. Maltese political and technocratic elites were able to strengthen their capacity-building in terms of cooperation processes; at the same time, Sicilian administrators were able to understand how to interface with a new member-state. Camonita concludes that there seems not to have been space here to alter the balance between incumbents and challengers. Indeed, among the four crisis episodes (two exogenous and two endogenous), no episode was strong enough to even modify the essential features and dynamics of the field. However, after identifying these shocks and the few challenges Camonita then seems to suggest that the status quo may not be the only possible scenario for CBC between the two Mediterranean islands. In the theory's terminology, the strongest barrier to a shift in the power dynamics is the exclusion of individual challengers and the lack of organizational support for them. The analysis carried out by Camonita implicitly assumes that the concept of an INTERREG Italy–Malta overlaps with the broader Sicily–Malta CBR. Extending the field's dimension beyond the operational area of the INTERREG could open new spaces for cross-border action. Under this new scenario – Camonita suggests – challengers would be provided with a new political arena in the quest for further acknowledgment and for new allies interested in moving beyond the current cross-border governance structure.

Berzi shows that CBG entities along the Pyrenees emerged after 1980, when Spain and France signed the Madrid Convention. In Berzi's understanding, cross-border organizations like the Euroregions (and similar structures) should be viewed not as challengers to the nation-state but rather as strategic action fields promoted by regional and local players aimed at coordinating territorial strategies. The cross-border SAF on the French–Spanish border has been shaped by a series of crises. Berzi identified two dimensions of these crises that have positively or negatively affected the evolution of the cross-border organizations. The internal dimensions of these crises are evident when frictions and misunderstandings arise from partners' interactions and directly affect the governance of the field. This happens, for example, when there is a change in the partnership, such as the entry or the exit of a player, be it for political or financial reasons. The second dimension of a crisis has an external dimension, being the product of central state intervention that directly or indirectly alters the field's stability. These sorts of crises are created largely by the Spanish and the French central governments. Berzi concludes that European institutions influence local and regional territorial governance in the Pyrenees, whereas the French and the Spanish states' actions are much more ambivalent. Sometimes they challenge the very existence of a field (as with the French state's lack of support for the Catalan Eurodistrict), and other times they cooperate to facilitate local and regional CBC (as with the 1995 bilateral agreement) and to solve specific legal and technical impediments to cross-border integration (the 2017 French–Spanish Summit in Málaga). Berzi suggests that in the end, the French–Spanish border perfectly mirrors the complexity of current EU CBC frameworks. Further research is needed to better understand the perspective of cross-border regional governance when it comes to urgent political issues like the COVID-19 pandemic, which led to an unprecedented rebordering of internal EU borders, and the recent Catalan secessionist attempt, which had long-term impacts on cross-border governance.

According to Perrin, the emergence of cross-border cultural fields is possible when the various actors demonstrate a visible commitment to attendance at meetings, forums, and so on, and to the development of social skills, networks, and the like. The availability of EU funds and EGCT legal instruments enables a field to form and stabilize. Indeed, many Euroregions and CBG entities are created in order to attract and manage EU funds. In this regard, exogenous shocks such as the economic crisis of 2008–9 have an impact on cross-border project funding, because they force governance entities to explore additional sources of funding. Also, Perrin shows that Euroregional cultural policy can happen with or without the support of CBG entities. Several cultural projects survived the disappearance of Euroregions; other cultural initiatives developed without the support of Euroregions. Perrin demonstrates that new Euroregions can emerge and support cultural initiatives.

In his chapter on the Galicia–North Portugal (G-NP) borderland, Cancela Outeda critically examines how cross-border governance emerged formally in 1991, with the creation of the G-NP Working Community, on the initiative of two regional entities. But it was in the late 1970s, when Spain and Portugal returned to democracy and were integrated into the EC, that bilateral relations were renewed so as to include CBC opportunities. The creation of the GNP-AECT cooperative instrument in 2008 was a turning point for cross-border governance in this area, for it provided the already existing Working Community with an effective executor of the cooperative projects, financing it with its own funds. As Cancela Outeda argues, cooperation developed in the G-NP Euroregion as the result of initiatives by public institutions, initially at a regional level. After this, local-level players began to participate with diverse objectives and initiatives, which helped promote cooperation. Although these governance units and the networks thereby created barely exercised political initiative, they managed to extend strategic objectives (initially limited to the CBC field) to broader (sustainability, innovation and research, quality of life, public services, etc.) inter-regional objectives. Differently from what happens on the southeastern side of the Franco-Spanish border, in the Galician–Portuguese borderland, internal governance structures and a more cohesive understanding of the field guarantee coordination among the AECT-GNP, the Working Community, and the regional heads of government. Despite some friction, there is no opposition to CBC or to the actions of the governance units (WC, EGTCs, mainly), which cooperate in building formal and informal horizontal networks (e.g., RIET). The principal hurdle faced by CBC in the region is asymmetry among political institutions. In the Portuguese institutional setting, the Commission of Coordination and Regional Development of the North (CCDR-N) is a decentralized body of the central government. Despite this political asymmetry with respect to the autonomous Galician institutions, the CCDR-N has an excellent understanding of the region's realities and has the capacity to mobilize local and supra-local players in its territory. This sometimes hinders initiatives because consultations and decisions from Lisbon are unavoidable.

Oliveras shows that over the past twenty years, two main crises have shaken Cerdanya's CBG. The first was environmental, specifically a drought that impacted transboundary water sharing (2006–8); the other was the economic crisis of 2008–15, which affected cross-border business competition and labour. These two crises had a common denominator: they were generated by adjacent fields, not by actors located within the field. The resolution of those consecutive crises led to the creation of an EGTC in 2012. Oliveras focuses on the mobilization of identities during episodes of contention and resettlement and finds that national symbols were mobilized during the phase of contention, whereas cross-border symbols were used during the phase of resettlement. In the resettlement phase, the EGTC Pirineus-Cerdanya helped mobilize business associations on both sides, specifically in the sectors of tourism, food, health care, and sustainable development, translating some effects of the economic crisis into creative and innovative efforts at a cross-border scale.

In his chapter on CBG in the Basque Country, Navarre, and Nouvelle Aquitaine, Durá Guimerá delineates the elements that help disentangle the complex political history of the cross-border area, which has been strongly influenced by the development of modern Basque nationalism associated with increased self-governance. Durà-Guimerà argues that the emergence of CBG in Nouvelle Aquitaine–Euskadi–Navarre was possible after Spanish democratization and integration into the EC. In the 1990s, the INTERREG program aided cross-border initiatives in the western Pyrenees, stabilizing the field. The 1995 Bayonne Treaty between France and Spain clarified the role of each state in the support and control of cross-border cooperation. This favoured CBC at the regional and local levels. Nonetheless, tensions persisted between the Basque Country and Navarre, with the government of Navarre aligning itself with Madrid regarding the Basque question. Navarre left the Euroregion in 2000, but Aquitaine maintained cooperation with both the Basque Country and Navarre, and this allowed the field to stabilize. Examples of governance stabilization include the transformation of the Euroregion Aquitaine–Euskadi into a European Grouping of Territorial Cooperation (EGTC) in 2009 and a number of agreements between the Basque Country and Navarre in the second half of the 2000s. Developments in the 2010s reinforced this stability, when administrative reform in France in 2014–15 extended to Aquitaine and Navarre returned to the Euroregion in 2017.

The Theory's Limitations

Staudt and Cruz contend that cross-border governance models pay too much attention to government and private organizations that influence policy-makers, thus leaving working people out of the analysis. They add that working people at the border pay through their local property taxes for the infrastructure that benefits both countries yet at the same time pay a heavy price in terms of the socio-racial control they suffer every day at the border. Similarly, Payan argues that border fields are not ordinary fields: they are complex and multi-layered, and they interact with adjacent fields demarcated by a sovereign logic, which complicates interactions. Moreover, the voiceless and often hidden actors are not part of the equation. These actors often find that privileges within the field (e.g., the SENTRI lane) have been put in place by incumbents (security agencies) as a reserved space for business and corporate communities to expedite travel and trade. Yet the poor must wait, under the scrutiny of security agencies. Also, criminals do not fit in this space; and, more importantly, should they be considered challengers, despite their illegal status? The Correa-Cabrera chapter also highlights the presence of other actors who may appear passive or even hidden, but who spring into action at the first opportunity. These include opportunistic business and criminal interests, which may not be interested in systemic change. They view change only as an added opportunity to make more money.

Konrad finds that it is generally useful to test the theory of fields and apply it to a specific case, the Pacific Northwest, and this road map offers a compelling account of the field's evolution. Yet Konrad also notes that "conceptualizing scale in globalization remains elusive in border theory, and although strategic action fields offer flexible situations in time and space to address this problem, the challenge remains to articulate the manifestations of these fields." Similarly, Dupeyron views some actors – for instance, business actors – as not formally incumbents, but as not challengers either. Thus, the relations between the province of Quebec in its paradiplomatic efforts and those actors resemble more a loose coalition with some differences among stakeholders, some having more power than others. This raises the question of the true role of adjacent fields, and under which circumstances actors positioned in an adjacent field have sufficient material or symbolic resources to influence incumbents and challengers in another field.

Noferini notes that delimiting the field is a frauht exercise. In a given case study, a researcher can define and justify a wide number of fields, surrounded by various adjacent and dependent fields. This is not to say that definitions of fields are arbitrary or undeterminable. Rather, it is to say that the difficulty of defining fields is a function of the analytical perspective a given author adopts. Evidently, at the macro-level the definition of a field is less ambiguous and more precise, for the number of actors is usually smaller. But when the analytical lens hopes to approximate the local scale and capture the variety of actors involved at the territorial level, the number of fields can sharply increase with the author's willingness to address the complexity of cross-border local dynamics. It can then be difficult to determine who the actors are. For example, in Camonita's Sicily–Malta border region, the incumbents are the two national governments and the Sicilian regional government. But how are we to account for the EC, which can also be seen as an incumbent, though it is not fully present in the CBG field? Here, Camonita posits that the EC is an external incumbent, for it belongs to an adjacent field and exerts considerable material and symbolic influence over neighbouring fields. Regarding to the Sicily–Malta border region, Camonita maintains that the theory of fields has "strong analytical potential in identifying both the power relations and the collective roles of all the actors involved in the CBC governance processes." Yet he also considers that the theory of fields has three main limitations and proposes to resolve them by creating three notions that offer a finer analysis. The first is functionality ("the specific operational processes and their significative evolution and changes through time enclosed in the daily actions of the governance units by the will of the incumbents"); the second is effectiveness ("a theoretical concept that can be applied when considering the daily obstacles compromising the functionality of the field itself"); and the third is field participants ("the [field] participants are all those public and private actors which, although not directly involved in the power relationships of the field"). According to Perrin, the theory of fields is useful for us to understand the complex dynamics in CBG. That theory recycles existing concepts that have been used in the European cross-border literature, such as path dependence, social capital, and multi-level governance, and the synthesis of those theoretical tools contributes to an improved analytical lens. Also, although Cancela Outeda does not explicitly criticize the theory of fields, his analysis of the G-NP borderland shows that the opposition between incumbents and challengers may not be pertinent. He concludes that there are no challengers in the field under scrutiny. Finally, Oliveras asks whether, given the great complexity of crises and resettlement efforts, it is possible to trust a theoretical framework that tends to simplify the analysis.

Final Remarks

It is important to reiterate that the building blocks of the theory of fields were useful when comparing salient CBG issues in North America and Europe. After workshops, discussions, and field research, the contributors agreed that the theory of fields can provide relevant conceptual pieces, with adjustments, to understand the emergence and development of CBG. The structural features of cross-border fields demanded, however, that an additional layer be considered: the existence of a sovereign border that complicates governance. Yet, the theory held, thanks to its own structure as a road map, and it captured the basic elements: actors and strategies; social skills, abilities, and resources; the broader contexts or environment in which all action is couched; opportunities for exerting change in the system; and periods of heightened or reduced conflict. That was true in all cases. Each author succeeded in using the theory, which permitted a disciplined and focused comparative process to trace the same core elements of the theory to make what Bengtsson and Ruonavaara call structured and focused sociohistorical comparisons.[6] The road map can be updated in future for research on other cases, as the general conceptual elements provided by the theory of fields are the same everywhere. Moreover, the comparative design component strengthened the discoveries made, resulting in a better understanding of CBG.

Even so, most of the authors who have put the theory of fields to the test recognize that it has limitations, especially in cross-border contexts. The force of sovereign division muddles the analysis. For instance, each author struggled to delimit each field (especially when it was crossed by a sovereign border) and to define the incumbents, challengers, and IGUs. Still, the analytical flexibility of the theory allowed us to stick to data and facts, filling in the boxes to offer a thick analysis of each case. At the same time, our comparative design contributed to stretching each concept of the theory of fields. For instance, in the US–Mexico border governance cases, the contributors agreed that the theory of fields does not include "the voiceless" or subversive criminal actors. The question, then, is how to create a model of fields that includes not only incumbents, challengers, and IGUs but also actors that are not represented in the theory and often remain invisible in the field structure itself. After all, they too inhabit the field. Similarly, social skills are not enough. Mobilizing resources in times of contention also counts, especially when interests are powerful.

Despite all these and other questions, the theory of fields did what it was supposed to do – provide the building blocks to enable a disciplined, focused comparison, which helped us understand CBG better and move a step further on the key question that all border scholars often ask: In our neck of the world of borders, who governs?

NOTES

1 Alexander George, Andrew Bennett, Graham H. Stuart, Sean M. Lynn-Jones, and Steven E. Miller, *Case Studies and Theory Development in the Social Sciences* (Boston, MA: MIT Press, 2005): 73.

2 Sidney Tarrow, "The Strategy of Paired Comparison: Toward a Theory of Practice," *Comparative Political Studies* 43, no. 2 (2010): 230–59.

3 Chris Rumford, *Cosmopolitan Borders* (Basingstoke: Palgrave Macmillan, 2014); see also Staudt and Cruz's chapter in this volume.

4 Birte Wassenberg, Bernard Reitel, Jean Peyrony, and Jean Rubió, *Territorial Cooperation in Europe – A Historical Perspective* (Luxembourg: Publications Office of the EU, 2015).

5 See Konrad's and Dupeyron's chapters in this volume.

6 Bo Bengtsson and Hanny Ruonovaara, "Comparative Process Tracing: Making Historical Comparison Structured and Focused," *Philosophy of the Social Sciences* 47, no. 1 (July 2016): 44–66.

Contributors

Matteo Berzi, GIS Specialist and Cross-Border Cooperation Expert, Commissioner's Office for the Mediterranean Corridor (Trans-European Transport Network)

Francesco Camonita, Barcelona Center for European Studies (BACES), Universitat Pompeu Fabra

Guadalupe Correa-Cabrera, Schar School of Policy and Government, George Mason University

Pamela L. Cruz, Research Analyst for the Baker Institute Center for the United States and Mexico

Bruno Dupeyron, Professor, Johnson Shoyama Graduate School of Public Policy

Antoni Durà-Guimerà, Department of Geography, Autonomous University of Barcelona, Inclusive Governance and Territorial and Coastal-Marine Sustainability (INTERFASE), European Network on Territorial Cooperation (RECOT)

Xavier Oliveras González, Researcher and Professor at El Colegio de la Frontera Norte, Member of the Department of Urban Studies and Environment

Victor Konrad, Adjunct Research Professor of Geography and Environmental Studies, Carleton University

Jorge Eduardo Mendoza Cota, Researcher and Professor in the Economics Department, El Colegio de la Frontera Norte

Andrea Noferini, Professor at CEI, International Affairs (Universitat de Barcelona) and at Universitat Pompeu Fabra

Celso Cancela Outeda, Professor of Political Science and Administration, Faculty of Political Science and Communication, University of Vigo

Tony Payan, Director, Center for the United States and Mexico, Rice University's Baker Institute for Public Policy, Universidad Autónoma de Ciudad Juárez

Thomas Perrin, Associate Professor in regional planning and social sciences, School of Architecture of Montpellier, University of Lille

Kathleen Staudt, former Professor of Political Science at the University of Texas at El Paso

Index

Milton Keynes UK
Ingram Content Group UK Ltd.
UKHW022050190724
445700UK00003B/34/J

9 781487 502881